PERSPECTIVES ON ADDICTION

For all who "care about their own destructiveness,
care enough to struggle with it"

Mike Eigen

MARGARET FETTING
University of Southern California

PERSPECTIVES ON ADDICTION

AN INTEGRATIVE TREATMENT MODEL WITH CLINICAL CASE STUDIES

Los Angeles | London | New Delhi
Singapore | Washington DC

Los Angeles | London | New Delhi
Singapore | Washington DC

FOR INFORMATION

SAGE Publications, Inc.
2455 Teller Road
Thousand Oaks, California 91320
E-mail: order@sagepub.com

SAGE Publications Ltd.
1 Oliver's Yard
55 City Road
London, EC1Y 1SP
United Kingdom

SAGE Publications India Pvt. Ltd.
B 1/I 1 Mohan Cooperative Industrial Area
Mathura Road, New Delhi 110 044
India

SAGE Publications Asia-Pacific Pte. Ltd.
33 Pekin Street #02-01
Far East Square
Singapore 048763

Acquisitions Editor: Kassie Graves
Editorial Assistant: Courtney Munz
Production Editor: Brittany Bauhaus
Copy Editor: Janine Stanley-Dunham
Typesetter: Hurix Systems Pvt. Ltd.
Proofreader: Sarah J. Duffy
Indexer: Rick Hurd
Cover Designer: Anupama Krishnan
Marketing Manager: Katie Winter
Permissions Editor: Adele Hutchinson

Printed in the United States of America

Library of Congress Cataloging-in-Publication Data

Fetting, Margaret.
Perspectives on addiction: an integrative treatment model with clinical case studies/Margaret Fetting.

p. cm.
Includes bibliographical references and index.

ISBN 978-1-4129-9099-8 (pbk. : acid-free paper)
1. Substance abuse. 2. Addicts–Family relationships.
3. Ethnopsychology. I. Title.

HV4998.F48 2012

616.86'06–dc23

2011036145

This book is printed on acid-free paper.

11 12 13 14 15 10 9 8 7 6 5 4 3 2 1

Brief Contents

Detailed Contents

List of Figures

List of Tables

Preface

My personal and familial experiences with addiction drew me into this field. America's responses and my clinical curiosities kept me in it.

I was a child of the 1950s and 1960s when drugs and alcohol were everywhere. Adults drank a lot around dinnertime and at cocktail parties. Young people in high school and on college campuses injected or inhaled drugs for recreation and with recklessness. Activists used drugs while protesting the political environment. Still others in the cities and farmlands, in the suburbs, or on the streets drank or drugged regardless of the times. Alcohol and other drugs (AOD) were socially sanctioned, defiantly used, or secretly savored.

During the mid-1970s and the early 1980s, I went to graduate school and somehow managed to get through. I earned an MSW and a PhD and then a license to practice clinical social work in California. As I began my psychotherapeutic and academic careers, my fascination with addiction perked up again. By this time, the revenge on the 1960s John Cheever cocktail parties in chic suburbs was in full force. There was more flagrant using and dangerous behavior in private homes and in public arenas. Whether on Wall Street or clubbing on the coast, white lines on glass tables were everywhere. The famous and the outcast celebrated the use of alcohol, amyl nitrite (poppers), cocaine, heroin, marijuana, and speed. AOD use and abuse scared parents and the nation. Wars on drugs and didactic education campaigns began.

During these times, I started teaching. I noticed something then, and I still notice it today. It's the peculiar and ineffective way we talk about addiction. We tend to whisper about whether someone's actively addicted or getting over it, anxiously judge what's going right or what's going wrong, or gossip about whether someone is in a good place or a bad place with his using. We don't talk about this—what does all this drug and alcohol use mean to us, our families, our nation, and other cultures? We don't seem to have meaningful conversations about what's behind this experience of desire and pleasure, this human need to "get high."

It starts when we are young and continues throughout our lives. When we are kids, we hold our breaths until dizzy and then faint. We actively seek out merry-go-rounds, teacups, tire swings, and roller coasters that make us spacey and giddy with delight (Siegel, 2005). Later, we "repeat and repeat" extreme sports for the thrills that they promise and deliver. Many adults become less interested in action highs and seem more willing to passively ingest a liquid, pill, or powder and wait for the desired effect (Fields, 2010, p. 28).

Throughout our lives, we seem hardwired to seek experiences that create an alteration of consciousness, alterations in feelings and moods, alterations in reality. We seek these over and over again, but rarely talk about why. We seem unable and unwilling to engage in truthful conversations with each other about where these desires come from, and under what circumstances they become increasingly interesting. We don't talk about the meanings behind our explorations. We don't talk about how our behaviors fit or don't fit into the rest of our lives. We don't explore why we continue, even though it may not be a good idea. We don't hear our worries or face our disturbing patterns. There is not much talking and even less listening.

In this vacuum, presidents started wars on drugs, public service announcements splattered the airwaves, and campaigns of "Just Say No" saturated the schools. In this vacuum, drugs or alcohol increasingly maimed and killed, while treatment industries expanded.

Without the talking, we decided to confront. It was called "tough love." Parents cornered kids, and some fought back—they lied or complied. Teachers and guidance counselors cornered adolescents, and most fought back—they lied or complied. Interventionists cornered addicted adults, and many fought back—they lied or complied.

We have done this for decades. Some cornering has worked. Some tough love has made a difference. We've seen people get better, and we've seen people get worse. We've seen people revisit disaster periodically, and we've seen some plateau into a disturbing pattern. We've seen people avoid it altogether. We've seen some people who manage their pleasures well. But all this really hasn't advanced our ability to talk to each other—to have meaningful conversations about this human experience of desire, oftentimes pleasurable, sometimes destructive.

We don't really talk about what's behind a sizable number of people salivating at 5 p.m. each day knowing that the day is over and that a beer, a glass of wine, a martini, or more will soon follow. Why do we start earlier than 5 p.m. on vacations and often continue drinking throughout the rest of these supposed stress-free days and evenings? What's behind our teenagers' furtive and focused plans to sneak out of their parents' houses most nights and get high with a group of friends? Why are most social occasions and holiday celebrations organized around drinking/drug use? Why do people feel ashamed if the family bar isn't fully restocked during an event? Why do we search for that bar as soon as we arrive at a party? Why do we look for seconds, and hope that we don't have to ask? Why are Super Bowl parties, charity and sporting events saturated with booze? Why do we notice nondrinkers? Why are some of us uncomfortable around them? Why are children's birthday parties filled with drunken parents? Why does drinking and drug use begin during lunch on many Saturdays and continue with brunch on Sundays? What's up with so much excess? Why is so much of our time filled with the help of alcohol and drugs? Why are we not more curious about our individual, cultural, and national preoccupation with AOD?

Shouldn't these questions be answered, these tendencies and preferences explored and not just intervened upon when they have crossed over to excess? Again, let's not just focus on whether we are in a good place or bad place with our use of alcohol and other drugs; rather, let's focus on what is the place of getting high in each of us, our families, and societies. This requires intimate explorations, as well as valuing the importance of these continued and ongoing conversations. We seem to nervously rush past these "talks" because we are either ashamed of our desires or dismissive of our troubles with these pleasures. Since we are an alcohol- and drug-saturated nation, it helps to understand why.

The questions continue. Why have we, all over the world, since humankind began, looked for a way to escape and expand consciousness? How do each of our cultures sanction or punish these urges and impulses? Why do some cultural practices protect this desire and others contribute to its abuse? Is it a hedonistic, dangerous, or rightful pleasure? How often should we do it? What makes it a good and healthy experience? What makes it a destructive or dangerous one? Who decides?

How does each and every one of us respond to this "drive"? Why do some love it instantaneously and need it repeatedly? Why do some start out fascinated and grow less interested over time? Why does it come and go in some people's lives? What's going on with people who are not interested in drinking at all? Why are nondrinkers considered a drag, and why do they call themselves nerds? Why does someone feel pressure to drink and feel awkward saying no? Why do nondrinkers view drunks as forms of amusement rather than people? What's up with people who can take it or leave it? Why do some have a nonexistent relationship with AOD, some an indifferent one, some a destructive one, and some an amicable one?

Our society has hastened to educate, eradicate, and treat but not meaningfully converse. If we don't grapple with answers to these questions, we will never fully embrace this human drive, we will never have satisfactory conversations with our loved ones, we will never deeply understand what we are treating when pleasure turns into excess, and we will never be able to reverse the relapse epidemic that arguably makes a mockery of the treatment industry today.

Our national discourse sometimes feels wearisome. This book is designed to jostle a nation that went to sleep after the recovery explosion of the 1980s and the 1990s. We don't have this one "handled." The complexities of this ancient desire deserve more ongoing consideration.

SOME THOUGHTS ON THE STATE OF THE FIELD

Still, I've noticed some wonderful changes and advances in the past 30 years. Some of these will be talked about in the following pages. Science has advanced, theory and treatment have developed, medications are more targeted, and rapid detox and intuitive healing offer alternatives to more traditional approaches.

Nonetheless, this has been and still is a field that is filled with a palpable tension. On the one hand, there is a vociferous determinacy behind preferred clinical approaches, shared dogma and rhetoric, and new scientific discoveries. Right knowledge and right treatment are preached. Righteous attitudes intimidate, and people passively enlist into a point of view. A treatment industry espousing Alcoholics Anonymous (AA) and the disease model of addiction dominates the land like a tsunami. While these approaches and programs have helped countless individuals and advanced the field tremendously, they have also littered it with a certainty that belies what we really know.

On the other hand, there is a noticeable lack of consensus about this rapidly expanding body of knowledge. There has been an abundant amount of research in the areas of genetics, neurobiology, and pharmacology. We've made tremendous strides in understanding how drugs work in the brain. While scientific advances have added impressive understanding in the field, they have also revealed how much we still do not understand or know.

We now know conclusively that there is no single gene for alcoholism, and we are still not sure how this runs in families (Dodes, 2002, p. 81). The field of addiction has yet to achieve consensus on several major concepts, including the notion of the "disease" of addiction, the definitions of an alcoholic or addict, as well as agreed-upon treatment approaches (Roskow, 2005, pp. 61–104).

Our enthusiastic scientific search for certainty seduces and unfortunately contributes to our sleepy national discourse. We fail to talk about the deeper meanings behind one of our national pastimes when we defer to scientific authority and assume science has a stronger hold than it does.

TEACHER AND STUDENT

Technically, I define my job as educating students about a controversial and rapidly expanding body of knowledge that is embedded in a highly charged, personal and political context. My teaching is structured to explore the human desire for intoxication, to convey both the determined rhetoric and the indeterminate body of knowledge that make up the field and study of chemical dependency, to present and explore new ideas, imaginative considerations, newer treatment formulations, and finally to converse about it all so that we become more fluent in something that impacts each of us so deeply.

Emotionally, my goal is to encourage students to become passionate about a subject matter that touches each of us, and often in very confusing and destructive ways. My final question at the end of the semester is, "Do you like this field more on the last day of class than you did on the first day?" If I generated both a personal and professional investment in the field and a healthy respect for what we know and what we don't know, as well as enthusiasm for what we are learning, I have done my job.

Here are a few student responses:

> "The integrative model of treatment is most interesting to me. I liked Brown's model with the psychoanalytic contributions of many of the self-medication theories. I liked how it breaks down the tasks of each stage of recovery. I think they are challenging tasks, but ones that truly seem to lay down the foundation for rebuilding a very broken addicted self with, as Khantzian and Steiner put it, a chaotic affect and difficulty connecting."

> "There are many aspects of the course that have had a positive impact on my learning experience. First, the suggestion that all theories should be applied first to oneself; second to one's family, friends and colleagues; and lastly to one's client shifted my conceptualization of the therapeutic process. All individuals can benefit from understanding themselves within the framework of the theories presented. Doing so brings about a deeper self-knowledge and an enhanced understanding of the theory itself. Secondly, the profiles of addiction satisfy my innate belief (and also curtail my frustration) that the *Diagnostic and Statistical Manual* cannot fully capture the human experience in regards to suffering. I used to think the world was divided into two types of people—those who are alcoholic and those who are not. The profiles of addiction were realistic in that both the pain and the method of treating one's suffering are individualized. Although many of the behaviors associated with addiction are similar, each individual's experience with addiction is highly personal. Additionally, Dr. Fetting's repeated reminder that the field of study is indeterminate is particularly impactful. Personally, I view this statement as an invitation and a professional responsibility to never conclude the search for understanding. As an avid learner, this reminder is incredibly appealing in its openness to possibility and in the professional challenge it offers to continue to evolve, grow, and learn. Finally, all of the theories discussed during the semester enhanced my awareness of the breadth

of knowledge in the field and the multitude of ways in which addiction can be understood, viewed, and analyzed."

"My experience in general with this class has been outstanding. The way the material was presented was very useful. I very much enjoyed the experiential process of teaching. Your lectures tease out meaning from theory and thought processes. I gained professional know-how and treatment skill through a better understanding of psychoanalysis and use of a psychoanalytic attitude. Use of many terms, including *registering impacts, interests of the self, natural history, fate, destiny, and idiom development, discounting, reverie, totalization of identity, psychic retreats,* and many more, enhanced my thinking about treatment. I enjoyed the mix of personal disclosure, asking questions, movement and use of space, eye contact and little repeated phrases such as 'pockets of meaning,' 'don't rush out into the street,' 'tinkering on the edges,' and 'trust your gut, do what you think is right, and see what happens.' I felt like real knowledge was given to me in this class."

"Overall, I feel that I am more of a comprehensive therapist after going through this course. I feel like I knew less than I thought I did in the beginning. I knew the basics and was not aware of how complex this subject matter really is. In general, the class allowed me to better understand the meanings behind addiction and see that the pain and suffering we all experience makes us vulnerable to becoming an addict or alcoholic."

"As I attended every class session, I felt saturated with information but confident that I was gaining a firm understanding of the subject. I think the most powerful aspect was that I was able to relate to almost every concept, either by applying it to myself or others close to me. On the professional level, I understand the importance of being flexible in the way addiction is understood and treated. The integrative psychoanalytic model provides a powerful guideline."

"Upon taking the class, my preconceived notion of addicts was that they were in a hopeless situation and that they were weak and had little willpower. I was very judgmental and clearly with no grounds for justification. Throughout the class my interpretation and analysis of drug addiction transformed from something negative to something productive. It changed from assuming that addicts were weak and hopeless to them being capable of having resilience and strength. This course has provided us with an understanding that addiction is not a flaw in someone's character."

"Substance abuse is a very sensitive and controversial issue. Throughout this course, I have shared with others the concepts that I have learned. For example, the profiles of addiction were useful in sparking conversations about our relationship with drugs and alcohol. I found myself beginning to question the level of my friends' alcohol or drug consumption. I worried they might be following a dangerous path to abuse. I have more confidence discussing these models and profiles with others because I have the knowledge and am able to share this information with co-workers, the court, supervisors, and managers. Surprisingly, all are very receptive to the information that I have shared with them, and it has created interesting conversations regarding beliefs of various treatment models and drinking profiles."

"I love the openness of the profiles. The fact that we can create our own and are encouraged to do so by you is one of the most valuable lessons I learned from this course. We are encouraged to think, innovate, and create. We are not bound by the existing theories and profiles. There is so much variation in substance use with *no cure,* so multiple profiles that shift and flow can only aid in the exploration and research in this field. One concern, however, is that this freedom can be taken to an unhealthy and unhelpful extreme, if proper thought and care have not been put into the thinking behind the profiles."

Acknowledgments

The solitary nature of writing is dependent on the support of many. Mike Eigen, a psychoanalyst and inspiration, imagines this support as the background presence of an unknown boundless other. Many thanks to these others. What follows are some supporters I know.

I am grateful to Vice Dean Paul Maiden and the School of Social Work at USC, who encouraged and supported this project from its inception.

Dreaming, sensitivity, boldness, and ongoing support flowed from Mike Eigen. His prolific works continue to have a profound influence on me. Ed Khantzian and his body of work have also profoundly guided me and so many in the field of addiction. His wisdom and dedication to the field as well as his generosity and encouragement fueled my devotion. Special appreciation for the work, experience, contribution, vibrancy, and support of Stephanie Brown, a leader in the addiction field as well. More appreciation for our developing relationship. Gratitude for the many levels of help from psychoanalyst and writer Bob Stolorow. Respect and heartfelt thanks to psychoanalyst and writer John Steiner.

Tom Gilmore and Larry Hirschhorn of the University of Pennsylvania introduced me to the love of learning. Ron Sager, psychoanalyst, introduced me to the thrill of dreaming. Linda Sobleman, psychoanalyst, reminded me of the power of compassion and grace. I am forever indebted to them.

I have profound appreciation for my USC colleague and friend Doni Whitsett, who reviewed chapters and provided generous and invaluable critiques. Dominique Robertson, a dear friend, offered insightful comments and suggestions as well. Our walks in Santa Monica, California, are full of love for each other, and love for psychoanalytic thinking and its application to addiction treatment.

My mother, brothers, sisters, and family on the East Coast provided steady encouragement; my community of living on the West Coast pitched in during times of need. Special thanks to Jo Ann Press, Ludger and Nicky Thole, and Phyllis Holdman for their ongoing support. I thank Neil Hofstetter for suggesting Ian Boys, and I thank Ian for introducing me to his employer, Sage Publications. I am indebted to the efficient editorial contributions of Dori Olsen. Melida Novoa, my research and reference assistant, came on board with steadfastness, humor, and invaluable coaching, particularly in the final hours.

I am eternally grateful to the wise tone and touch of Kassie Graves, Sage Publications, Senior Acquisitions Editor, Human Services.

Especially to Nicholas Ritsonis, we began again on a 10,000-mile whim and now live in our whimsical love story with more to come.

Deep thanks to Angela Harwood, my manuscript assistant and oftentimes editor. We began in the beginning and ended at the end. She is a dream come true. Her intelligence, work ethic, spirit, and commitment to this work have made all the difference. We had fun together.

The most profound gratitude is felt for all my patients who agreed to share their life stories, pains and struggles, growth and spirit with each of us. We are the lucky recipients of their faith and courage.

The thinking behind this book would not be possible without the outstanding contributions of so many in the field. The passion behind this book would not be possible without my patients and my students. The hope behind this book would not be possible without the belief that human beings always strive toward health. The excitement behind this book would not be possible without the evidence that the chemical dependency field is open to exploration.

Introduction

Many of us like the experience of being intoxicated, and that desire creates troubles for some of us. *Perspectives on Addiction* explores this desire and proposes a treatment path for these troubles.

Perspectives also covers the key content necessary for developing a comprehensive grasp of a complex body of knowledge that is filled with certainties and uncertainties, science and speculation, dogma and theory, as well as opinion and silence. *Perspectives* provides students and clinicians, addicts and their families with a reflective understanding of a confusing body of knowledge. *Perspectives* provides some passionate perspectives for you to consider.

Chemical dependency touches us all. *Perspectives on Addiction* is written and designed to have a personal, professional, educational, and treatment impact. Serious content is delivered with discipline and rigor, creativity and imagination, brevity as well as elaboration. Hopefully the reader will develop a novel appreciation for a human desire that pleasures, confounds, and destroys.

OUTLINE OF THE BOOK

This book is divided into four progressive parts composed of 12 chapters that were developed from 20 years of teaching semester-long graduate courses in Substance Dependence and Abuse in the School of Social Work at the University of Southern California. These chapters build on each other and are designed to become the building blocks of your own knowledge base. The content area covered, moving from bottom to top, is diagramed in Figure 1.1 on the next page.

The Preface and this introduction and the chapters in Part I invite the reader on a journey of individual, cultural, and social learning. Substance dependence or abuse is likely to touch us all. We have more experience than we think, more experience than we use. The personal and professional knowledge base developed in Part I becomes the anchor for future learning, not only in this course but also for future professional development in this field.

Some general special population statistics are presented, and the reader is invited to consider the influences of his own culture. Social forces that shape our

Figure I.1 Progressive Knowledge Base

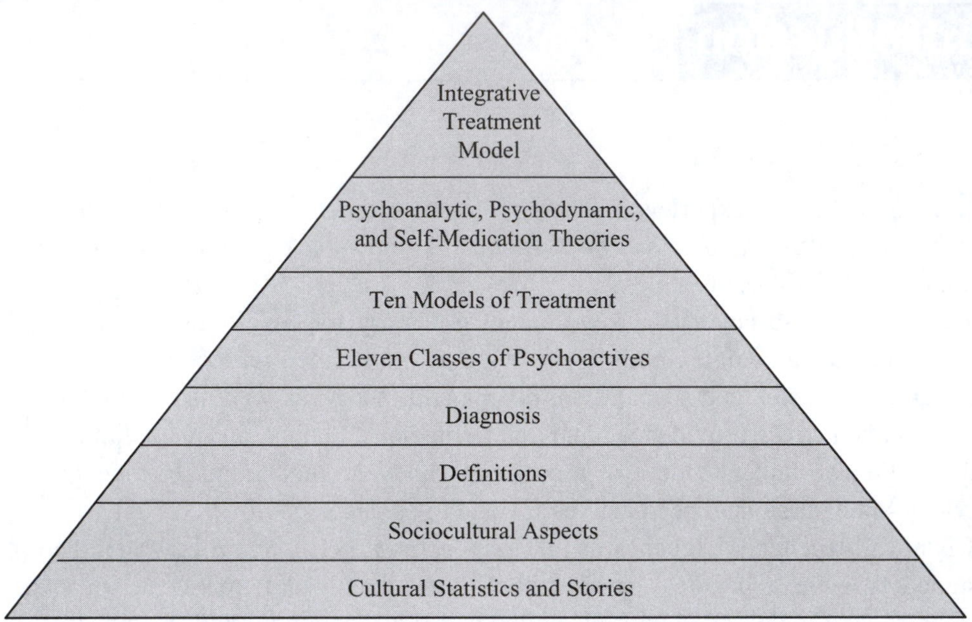

addictive thinking and behavior are explored. Definitions of key concepts and ideas are also presented. A reflective investment seems the necessary prerequisite for mastery of a complex, contradictory, and complicated field. A personally involved reader grasps and retains knowledge from a deep and meaningful perspective. Self-reflection grounds the learning journey.

Part II and Part III present a comprehensive overview of the essential elements of the chemical dependency field. Perspectives on diagnosis, psychoactive substances, models of treatment, and psychoanalytic and self-medication theories are shared.

Part IV provides a unique perspective on the world of treatment. The reader is now asked to digest more advanced theory and critically observe its application during therapeutic action moments in clinical case studies. An integrative model of treatment that infuses Stephanie Brown's stage-driven approach to recovery with a psychoanalytic sensibility is introduced. Addiction treatment is deepened when a nondirective, reflective, analytic perspective and attitude are coupled with the more traditional and sometimes confrontational approaches of recovery treatment. *Perspectives on Addiction* suggests that the combination of these clinical styles promotes more engaging treatment (McLellan, cited in White, 2010) and prevents relapse (Gorski and Miller, 1986; Marlatt, 1996).

CHAPTERS

Los Angeles is a city rich in cultural diversity. People come from all over the world. Chapter 1 looks at the relationship between culture, ethnicity, and addiction. Each semester begins with a discussion of our individual ethnocultural histories. Our African, Asian, European, Latin American, or Middle Eastern backgrounds influence our thinking about drugs and alcohol.

Not everyone in the world sees addiction as Americans do. Not everyone sees it as a disease. Not everyone values treatment. My students and I have engaged in wonderful and sometimes politically incorrect conversations and discussions over the years about what drugs and alcohol mean in their different cultures.

We talk about the using habits and patterns among the men and the women, the elders and the young, the powerful and the poor, and the mothers and the fathers. We share the prohibitions and tolerances of different people. We examine diverse ideas about drinking, drugging, and treatment. We try to understand a universal phenomenon from a universal perspective.

This chapter includes cultural stories about these ideas, as well as statistics of using among different cultures. Selected statistics provide a general contextual perspective. Stories flush out the nuances behind these numbers. Student reflections richly demonstrate the influence of our ethnoheritage on our individual understanding of drug and alcohol use. I always broaden and deepen my thinking about addiction when I hear these varied worldviews. It may help you as well.

Chapter 2 examines selected parts of two books that identify sociocultural influences on widespread addiction in Western culture. One integrative theory looks at some of the scaffolding of our culture—the societal structures, patterns, and forces that shape the ways we are compelled to live and also shape our responses to what is lacking. The expectations imposed on us by contemporary culture are not always simpatico with the way we are psychobiologically wired. These demands are too much for us. Drugs and alcohol relieve the pressures of trying to fit in or soothe the agonies of being excluded. These forms of relief seem to "work," but not without subtle and serious costs. The second integrative theory proposes that the loss of initiation rituals in contemporary culture has a profound impact on our psyche. We search and settle for more disturbing rituals, including alcohol and drug addiction.

Students, often for the first time, consider influences other than biology, family environment, and genetics in the development of addiction. It is illuminating, as well as sobering, to consider the plethora of social forces driving people into drugs, alcohol, and other compulsive behaviors. It is also somewhat discouraging to see that "society" doesn't seem to fully grasp its structural contributions to addiction, nor does it want to consider healthier ways to reorganize itself. But at least we can start having conversations. I encourage individuals to take these reflections to their everyday worlds—jobs, schools, hospitals, and families. While "society" itself may be baffled by this problem, individuals can make daily adjustments in their communities of living that may reduce the need for destructive use of the desire to experience an alternate reality.

Chapter 3 follows these ethno- and sociocultural discussions with definitions of addiction. These definitions represent a wide spectrum of thinking. Classroom discussions explore the biological, psychological, societal, and spiritual underpinnings of addiction and debate different points of view. Conversations generate reflective thinking on chemical dependency in general. How you think about addiction determines your own relationship with drugs and alcohol and also influences the way you respond to someone who has a problem. Students begin to identify and grasp the repetitive vocabulary, the political nuances, the preferences of the field, as well as the theoretical prejudices. As ignorances are explored, anxieties begin to diminish. Feelings previously avoided or ideas kept secret are slowly shared in a classroom setting. Students like the open-ended nature of these discussions and the opportunity to begin to more deeply examine their thinking about addiction.

Chapter 4 discusses the diagnosis of substance use disorders—a most thoughtful undertaking. Treatment providers are challenged with severe and life-threatening problems. Alcoholic and addicted families are filled with anxieties, avoidances, as well as wishes for control. In both contexts, there is a tendency to overdiagnose and prematurely label, or underdiagnose and look the other way. Both approaches miss the big picture as well as the nuances. The *Diagnostic and Statistical Manual of Mental Disorders* (American Psychiatric Association [DSM-IV-TR], 2000) uses two diagnostic terms: dependence and abuse. This limited selection belies the complexities and subtleties of our problems with alcohol and other drugs (AOD). The current "discipline of diagnosis" is filled with shortcomings, limitations, and intimidations.

This chapter considers these confusions and proposes 12 descriptive profiles of using and addiction that I have observed over 20 years of providing treatment. I started with 2; the possibilities of additions and deletions are ongoing. My goal has been to grasp the idiosyncratic story of the person sitting across from me and to develop a treatment response that is most suited to each unique expression.

While we might not have a shared consensus or scientific agreement in many areas of this field, we do long for a shared vocabulary of what we see and see often. This is affirmed by the way students respond to the profiles. It is a "get" for them. This chapter opens up their thinking and encourages creative responses to the diagnostic complexities of addiction. I challenge students to keep their eyes and ears open, and ask them to consider developing their own profiles in their future work. Furthermore, the progressive continuum profiles presented prepare the student for some of the revisions in DSM-V, scheduled for release in 2013. This chapter of clinical descriptors breathes spirit into *Perspectives on Addiction*.

Chapter 5 is an overview of the 11 classes of psychoactive drugs that people use, misuse, ignore, or abuse. The scientific findings and advances in our understanding of the relationship between psychoactives and our brain are overwhelming to comprehend. This chapter is designed to be blessedly brief and clinically practical. It provides readers with some neuroscience, as well as some comparisons between the natural mind and the one adulterated with alcohol and drugs. Salient features are included in 11 easy-to-read charts that serve as a ready reference guide for clinical work or emergency situations. This chapter includes a recommended reading list for further study. These books provide additional information about each drug, more in-depth clinical applications, and current research focus and findings. Readers are strongly encouraged to buy updated editions each year.

Chapter 6 provides a comprehensive and reflective overview of 10 models of treatment that currently populate or predominate the American recovery industry. These single- or multi-focused models reflect a point of view about the causality of chemical dependency, and accordingly propose different treatment alternatives. I encourage students to consider which ones seem to best capture how they think about chemical dependency, and also feel most simpatico with their own clinical intuition and style. Which ones would they be most likely to use and in what clinical, family, or treatment situations?

Over the years, I have observed that addicts or alcoholics arrive at my office with an intuitive sense of their "treatment of choice." Your partner, your husband, your wife, your child have a very specific sense of how they want to be treated. It may not be the best approach, but addicts often have strong ideas about which one of these models they want to start with. "You're not going to make me stop using" usually means that the person is not interested in the disease model and its insistence on abstinence but would rather be treated from a social, learning, self-medication, or harm reduction treatment approach. All of the models have some kind of value and utility. Unless the addict is in danger to himself or to others, I start with his "model of choice."

Year after year, students have favored one model of treatment. They are drawn to the self-medication theory of addiction founded by Dr. Ed Khantzian. I watch their countenance become alive with clinical interest as well as with feelings of personal relatability. Consequently, I have developed an entire lecture on this treatment approach. Chapter 7 provides concise overviews and brief clinical applications of selected aspects of the work of addiction specialists and psychoanalysts. These nine unique, yet overlapping theories propose that untreated human psychological suffering drives some people to self-medicate their pain with alcohol and other drugs. Each theory presented provides the reader with an insightful and useful perspective on what might cause this suffering. Classroom lectures enrich clinical understanding and invite more personal student participation. These include poignant, tragic, and victorious stories about the suffering and self-medication of siblings and friends, uncles and aunts, patients and parents. Most students begin to explore their own personal relationship with AOD either privately or publicly. These sensitive and courageous discussions have always enhanced personal growth and encouraged professional development. This chapter is the heart of this book.

Chapters 8 through 12 are the culmination of the semester, and the meat of this book. The contents of each chapter reflect 20 years of learning from my patients and their families, my students and addiction specialists, writers, and psychoanalysts. These are all assimilated into one integrated model of treatment. Stephanie Brown's well-regarded stage-driven model of recovery serves as its structural foundation.

Chapter 8 provides a cogent summary of selected parts of Brown's model of recovery. Her treatment approach is understood in one sentence: Recovery is about an identity reconstruction, nurtured over four stages of development. The stages begin while one is actively using, and progress through transition, early recovery, and ongoing recovery.

Brown's primary focus on an identity shift is the key to long-term recovery for the addict, and it is imperative for the treatment provider to keep as a focus. The addict is challenged to migrate from his known world of self-destruction and loneliness and to venture into an unknown one. This journey requires a leap of faith and needs so much support. The integrative model presented suggests a practical clinical roadmap for this identity reorganization and its journey. Relapse can be avoided if an "interest" in this difficult, wearisome, and wonderful path is vigilantly nurtured and always sustained and maintained (Phillips, 1998). Rainer Marie Rilke (1993), the German poet, advises us to "hold to the difficult" (p. 53). Recovery requires this, and for many, the life that follows is filled with previously unfelt experiences and unexplored passions.

Chapters 9 through 12 identify some of the challenges and opportunities that the recovering individual and the treatment provider face during each stage. A mix of treatment concepts and ideas as well as applications of psychoanalytic and other clinical theories are introduced to enliven, deepen, and broaden existing approaches to recovery. Therapeutic action moments are demonstrated in clinical case studies presented in each chapter.

The old and new and the traditional and innovative are joined together to invigorate well-worn treatment approaches. Successes and missteps are explored. Therapeutic action moments provide meaningful support and memorable interventions for those courageous souls on this journey of awakening and healing. Professional self-reflection is always encouraged in the fatigue-filled and also exuberant world of addiction treatment.

Chapter 9 highlights the importance of the therapeutic attitude in the development of the treatment relationship. A psychoanalytic style of receptivity, prior to interventions of activity, is encouraged. A mix of analytic ideas and clinical interventions, as well as Aaron Beck's cognitive treatments, is introduced. These encourage and support the addict's desire for a therapeutic connection, recovery, and growth. Clinical cases reflect the fear, anxiety, and hope residing in both therapist and addict during this frightening stage.

The addict's identity continues to evolve during the transition stage, as discussed in Chapter 10. Again, clinical concepts are introduced that support the work of this pivotal stage. The theories of psychoanalyst Adam Phillips suggest that maintaining the addict's interest in his evolving identity and newly discovered sense of self promotes sobriety and prevents relapse. This turbulent stage fatigues both patient and therapist. Moving through it requires patience and persistence. Clinical cases demonstrate these hearty treatment realities.

The fit of the environment is examined, and the state of the addict's mind is explored during early recovery. Chapter 11 asks the reader to consider a complex aspect of the mind that is camouflaged while under the influence, and makes itself known during early recovery. This unfolding puts a strain on the treatment relationship, as demonstrated in two clinical cases.

It is proposed that a clear understanding of the functions and facets of a psychic retreat, developed by psychoanalyst John Steiner, is needed to truly grasp the struggle and suffering of the patient during this stage. This adds a much-needed dimension to the work of recovery, and its introduction into the world of addiction treatment is extremely useful for identifying the mental and emotional antecedents of relapse.

Ongoing recovery is the last formal stage in addiction treatment. The migration of a recovering identity is nearly complete. Many in this stage of treatment begin to question what they thought they would never question and consider doing things that they thought they would never consider. Psychotherapy conversations turn to future possibilities. Chapter 12 provides therapists and readers with clinical theories and interventions that exquisitely complement the addict's identity evolution during this stage. Psychoanalyst Christopher Bollas's work on fate, destiny, and idiom development is introduced. Mike Eigen, psychoanalyst, elaborates on D. W. Winnicott's notions of the true self and false self, and these are also explored. Three case studies suggest uses of these concepts during this last stage of treatment.

TERMS TO CONSIDER WHILE READING

- The words *addiction* and *alcoholism*, *drinking* and *drugging, chemical dependency* and *substance dependency*, *substance use disorders*, and *addict* and *alcoholic* are each used interchangeably to describe a disturbed or pathological relationship with AOD.
- *AOD* stands for alcohol and other drugs.
- Readers and students are referred to as "he."
- A patient, addict, or alcoholic is referred to as "he."
- Treatment providers, clinicians, and sponsors are referred to as "she."
- An italicized word in the text emphasizes the importance of the content.
- An unconscious phantasy, an element of the evolving structure of the mind, is distinguished from conscious and preconscious fantasies or daydreams.

Part I

A Perspective on the World of Addiction

Chapter 1

Cultural Statistics and Stories

INTRODUCTION

This chapter encourages exploration of the influences of our individual ethnocultural histories on the seemingly universal human desire to escape and expand consciousness with the help of drugs and alcohol. Our cultural backgrounds shape our feelings, behaviors, and viewpoints. Our thinking about the uses and misuses of these substances, as well as our values and entitlements, denials and judgments about them, runs deeper than we think. It is important to identify the historical and generational forces that drive our current drinking and drugging behaviors. It is personally helpful and clinically useful to recognize these covert and overt influences. This chapter provides selected statistics that broadly contextualize alcohol and other drugs (AOD), as well as treatment admissions among diverse populations. It also invites the student to read the short stories of many other students, as he begins to reflect into the influences of his own history.

My teaching style and the sequence of my content coverage have evolved over time. It took me years to realize that cultivating students' investment in exploring their own ethnocultural history and current social context is the best prerequisite for the development of a meaningful knowledge base in the chemical dependency field. Students endowed with a sense of personal curiosity about the historical antecedents of their own relationship with AOD and with the courage to examine their own familial/cultural taboos and sanctions have the mental and emotional fitness needed for a deeper internalization of the complex content of addictive suffering and its treatment.

The School of Social Work at USC embraces the diversity in our culture and makes sure it exists in our classrooms. These rooms are populated with whites and blacks and people from both Americas, Europe, the Middle East, and other faraway lands. I teach students of all sexual orientations, many ethnicities, and varied cultural styles.

Our initial classroom conversations continue to consider many of the core questions posed in the Preface and begin to explore more culturally specific ones as well. How do you identify yourself ethnoculturally? In what ways does this identity shape your thinking about AOD? What are the meanings of AOD in your culture? How have you internalized these—how have these shaped your own relationship with AOD? Has an individualistic or collectivist environment been influential here? Who partakes in the pleasures of AOD? In what ways? Who does not, and why? What if problems develop? How are they defined? How do people address them? How do your cultural prejudices and biases shape your notions about treatment?

Over the semester, students ponder the relationship between their outlook on AOD and cultural forces, including degrees of acculturation, experiences of oppression and discrimination, language and communication skills and patterns, education, socioeconomic class, religion, age, and family structure.

Students tentatively open up and begin to share how their identified backgrounds shape their attitudes and values, as well as their prejudices and biases. They eventually seem to relish understanding how these are expressed in AOD individual and cultural habits, norms, and expectations. We hear how their cultures define addiction or problem using, as well as the ways they sanction or discourage getting help or treatment. A rich and mutually informative class discussion begins here and continues throughout the semester.

Below are selected statistics on special populations and composite ethnocultural stories shared by students during classroom conversations. Statistics on minority use provide hard, and oftentimes useful, facts. They provide patterns and suggest trends. They help contextualize. The stories presented capture many cultural complexities with a character and depth not often revealed by an overreliance on numbers and percentage points. These stories, while richly unique, seem to repeatedly organize themselves around universal cultural trends that reflect approvals, disapprovals, and avoidances. These themes are italicized.

SPECIAL POPULATION STATISTICS

The three bar graphs presented below provide a very general sense of the comparative usage of AOD among diverse population groups. Comparative treatment uses among groups is also displayed. These are presented to give the reader a general perspective on AOD usage among groups, as well as their treatment preferences. This will help contextualize the reading of the ethnocultural stories in this chapter and also help frame the students' developing understanding of the influences of their own cultural history and background. Do the numbers match your own sense of the diversity of usage and treatment among special populations? Do the numbers seem to match your sense of ethnocultural trends in general?

A more detailed statistical presentation is beyond the scope or design of this book.

Table 1.1 Alcohol Use in Past Month by Ethnic Group in the United States, 2005

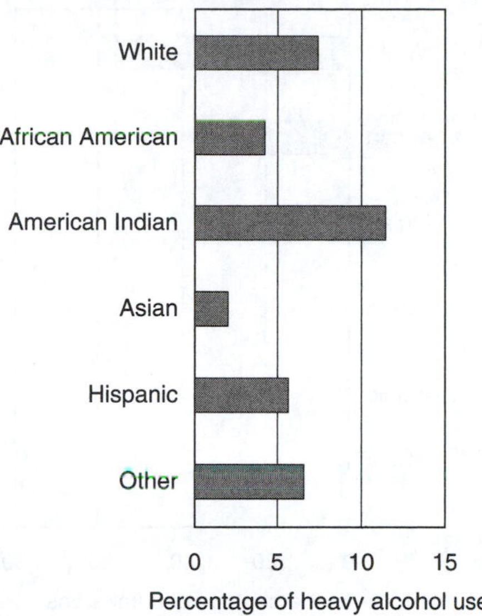

Source: Inaba and Cohen, 2007, p. 244.

Table 1.2 Estimated Prevalence of Recent Illegal Drug Use by Race/Ethnicity, 1999–2000

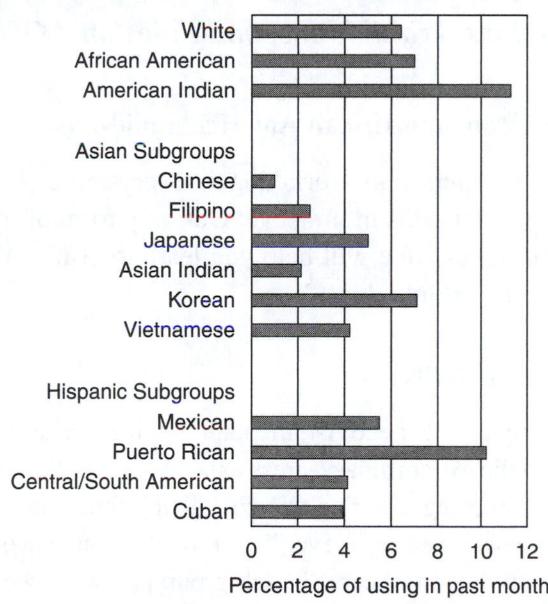

Source: National Household Survey on Drug Abuse, Substance Abuse and Mental Health Services Administration, Office of Applied Studies, 2001b.

Table 1.3 Admissions to Publicly Funded Substance Abuse Treatment Programs by Race, 2008

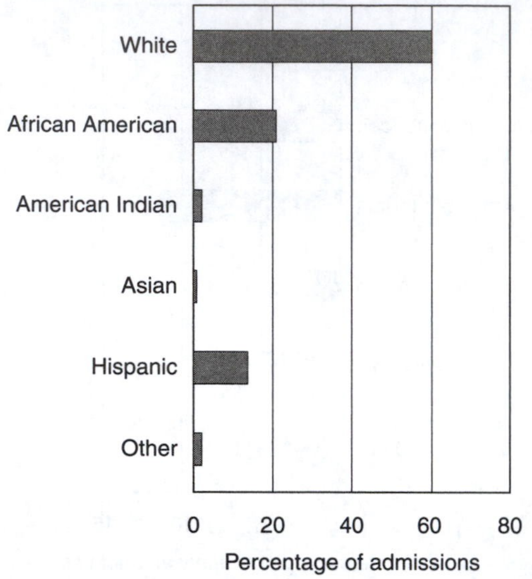

White
African American
American Indian
Asian
Hispanic
Other

0 20 40 60 80
Percentage of admissions

Source: National Institute on Drug Abuse.

ETHNOCULTURAL STORIES

Cultural Sanctions, Prohibitions, and Rules on AOD Use and Treatment

Armenian American and African American, mid-20s

Both women mentioned that drinking is everywhere. It starts with shots of cognac for colicky stomachs in infancy. "Our only form of treatment comes from elders. They counsel us, 'We will help you learn to drink. Watch us and the way we drink. If you can't drink, don't.'"

Korean Women, mid-20s

"It seems there is a collectivist mentality going on around drinking." These women described the extraordinary stress experienced in the workplace. The country seems to sanction evening drinking and socializing four times a week. "It's okay to get drunk. It's a social stress reliever." One of the young women described being forced to learn how to drink beer. She felt group pressure. "People gave me a drink and stared me down; I had no choice." A very popular beer for both men and women is a shot of tequila added to beer. "Still, it's a stigma for girls to get too drunk."

Armenian American

First generation. "There is a lot of drinking. The worst thing you can do is not handle your alcohol. It is a public embarrassment. Alcohol flows freely in all occasions. It is insulting not to abundantly replenish alcohol at a wedding." Her father had pancreatitis twice due to alcohol and almost died. He did not get treatment; he just stopped. People think he just doesn't drink. "I wonder if he does today and always look for signs."

Homosexual American Secular Jew

He never saw his parents drink or smoke. The message was, "Don't do either, especially in the house." "As a gay man, I live in a culture with a big alcohol and drug presence. It would really take a lot to get anybody into treatment. The biggest addiction in my community is cruising for sex, which includes use of methamphetamines."

Italian Irish

"My mom drank wine at dinner. My dad smoked weed every night. My grandmother needed her medicine, which was white zinfandel wine, with a shot of Dewar's [scotch]. Our family is relatively open about this drug and alcohol use." It helped her come to the decision to drink and smoke marijuana in moderation.

Mexican American, early 20s

Both parents were born in Mexico. "There is more alcohol than kids at birthday parties." Drinking is connected with gender. If girls drink, they get in trouble with their dad. The best decision for girls is to avoid "the situation completely."

Military, Conservative, Catholic

Raised to fear drinking. Preached to about danger of alcohol. Did not drink until junior year abroad—"learned about drinking from being in Rome. Don't drink in front of family."

Irish Italian

"Grew up with the joke of the seven-course meal—a six-pack and a baked potato." People who have problems with hard alcohol are stigmatized. Most won't get treatment.

Asian Woman, mid-20s

"I think there's a stigma attached to people who are addicts, a very negative stigma. The complexity of addiction is not taken into consideration, and instead people are judged for being weak and the issues of why they are using are overlooked or ignored. I've changed—if someone important in my life becomes addicted, I don't think I would be able to stand and watch them destroy their lives. I'd ultimately have to confront or find ways to help them."

Christian Caucasian

"I grew up in a strict, rigid, and conservative Christian home. My father is a pastor, and we were taught that drinking is a sin. I was taught that addicts or users are sinners. Sin is bad; therefore, they were bad and deserved to go to hell. When I got to college, I went through a partying phase where I abused alcohol. Believe me, I was quite aware I was sinning, and if God came, I'd go to hell."

African American

She grew up in the South. There was no alcohol in her family house. The family looked at drinking problems as deviant. Her brother-in-law had a drinking problem, including multiple relapses. He is in a nursing home at age 48 as a result of his alcoholism. Our family said, "Just let him go. It was progress that our family moved from viewing it as deviancy to viewing it as a disease."

Iranian Italian

First generation. Parents born in Italy and Iran. Prior to the revolution in Iran there was a lot of drinking, drugs, and prostitution. In her family, the men drink and do drugs freely in America. It is a rite of passage for cultural approval. "If you drink too much, it is not a problem. You get help only if mandated as a result of a DUI or assault charge." Women should not be seen drinking. Women have eating disorders.

Mexican American, mid-20s

First-generation female. Learning to drink is a male thing. Women aren't supposed to, although her mother hid a bottle in the closet and drank throughout the day. Her brother has a drinking problem and has been in AA (Alcoholics Anonymous). He relapses and the men humorously call him "poor little drunky."

Korean American

Parties are in different rooms in a house. The boys are with the men. The men teach the boys to drink so their face does not get red. They are taught to first have a beer, then take an antacid, then move to hard liquor. The boys are told to pace their drinking. "You whisper if there is a problem." Women don't drink.

Affluent Second-, Third-, Fourth-Generation Americans

"I grew up in an affluent community with the means to buy drugs and alcohol, and large unsupervised homes to abuse them in." She describes many Ecstasy and cocaine parties. Pill parties were stocked from parents' medicine cabinets. "Throw pills in a bowl and ingest them. Most of the kids have been in multiple rehabs. Young adults are successful, yet still party. Some died or some are seriously psychologically disabled."

White American

"My family's thoughts about addiction were distorted. Looking back, I see that much of the alcohol use was in the misuse and abuse range, but that was what was normal. I began drinking at an early age. It became normal to binge drink on the weekends. Today, our culture approves of binge drinking, and seems to say that to enjoy alcohol we must be drunk and totally wasted to consider it a good time. Basically, I think the culture that I am a part of sends a message that alcohol problems follow the disease model and I think they don't pay attention to the in-between problems. These also tremendously impact our lives."

Homosexual Jewish Male, mid-20s

"My culture has transmitted to me the following idea—it's okay if you use or become a drug addict as long as you are successful. Or, you're not really an alcoholic or drug addict if you're successful. Or, maybe you're an alcoholic or drug addict, but success makes it okay. In other words, we can treat your alcohol or drug addiction (like rehab), but there is no treatment for not being successful in the way we deem success (doctor, lawyer, money . . .)."

Caucasian Female

"American culture is one of overindulgence, which reinforces a gluttony that encourages people to shamelessly consume or pursue excessive pleasures/highs. This imprint lends itself to a level of use where many feel okay or even quite great about overindulgence. In Europe it's different. Many see a glass of wine at dinner as a ritual, whereas in the U.S. it is an event in and of itself."

Persian Armenian

"Both cultures, in my experience, do not tolerate drug use and shun friends and family members who become addicts or users. Referrals to support groups or treatment programs are usually after the individual has been kicked out of the house or shunned by the community. Oftentimes, the person is labeled as an addict, even after sobriety. It's unacceptable for women to develop addictions."

Christian Korean

"I grew up in a very strict Christian family background where my parents never drank except on occasion. In church, I learned not to get drunk, because it was not a 'holy' thing to do. My religious view of not getting drunk still holds. It is still a struggle and dilemma that I haven't figured out."

African American Woman, 20s

"It's okay to drink with other people." She described a family that viewed drinking as social and relaxing but never acceptable when alone. Someone will ask at a party, "Can you take Mike home if he drinks too much?" No one will bring up a serious conversation about his excessive drinking. "Drinking is everywhere; even if you are sick, the family will prepare a hot toddy."

Catholic/White Anglo Saxon Protestant

A woman in her 20s lost her brother to suicide. He had problems with drugs and alcohol. He committed suicide while sober. The family was devastated and has still not recovered. She got different messages from each generation of her family. Her grandparents drank martinis—it was okay to be tipsy after putting in a hard day's work. Her parents preached, "It's something to be afraid of, particularly after the loss of your brother." She's been in therapy and watches with alarm as her friends work hard and then get obliterated on weekends. She's cautious and scared.

Korean Woman

"In Korean culture, addiction is defined as mental illness. I used to perceive addicts as 'such a pity; sick people who cannot be cured or saved.' My church views addiction as a terrible sin that violates God's will. When I began to drink, I was terrified that my parents would blame and judge me, not love me or leave me."

Chicano Latino

She lives between the second and third generation. "Drinking is different at different levels of immigration." She shares that drinking is part of people coming together. It's accepted by both generations, but there's a big gender difference. Girls have to hide their drinks, while men can get drunk. Her dad did a lot of drugs, and it was kept quiet for years. When she returned from college, he was sober.

"Somehow, he got clean; it was never talked about. I think losing his job forced my mom and dad to deal with it." She describes parents who now actually enjoy a sober life together.

Mexican American Couple

"We like beer, all kinds of beer. We started drinking at around age 13. Our elders said to 'watch it, and shame on you if you can't drink.' We listened. We're getting married in a brewery garden."

African American Woman, mid-20s

"My family and extended family is cool with using drugs and alcohol. We celebrate holidays and birthday parties together. Each home or apartment has what is called 'the room.' That's where the drugs are used. When I'm ready to smoke pot, I just ask, 'Where is the room?'"

Privileged Upbringing

"I would define my culture as white, Jewish, and very, very privileged. Alcohol is a part of our Jewish traditions, and unlike the stereotype, we drink a lot. It's a bonding thing and it's the norm. Excess is viewed as irresponsibility."

Jewish American

"My family tends to use wine for many rituals, so drinking has always been an accepted part of the culture. On some occasions, you only need to take a sip of wine. On others, you are required to drink several cups of wine. And on some celebratory holidays, we are commanded to get completely drunk. On one particular holiday, the teaching is to become so drunk that 'you cannot tell the difference between good and evil.'"

Mexican American, mid-20s

Parents born in Mexico. Alcohol is normalized in the family. "I grew up seeing men, women, and children drinking. Most people do not see overdrinking as a problem. It's what people do."

Eastern European

A mid-30s woman grew up watching everyone drink straight vodka. There was no age restriction for the purchase of alcohol. Since age 5, she recalls daily walking to the grocery store to pick up her grandfather's vodka. She grew up believing drinking makes you more social. "Everyone does it, all the time." She believes, as a future clinician, she might normalize all drinking, even if it is a problem.

Avoidance of Communication on the Topic of AOD and Their Problems

Salvador an American, Mother of Two

Young children start doing inhalants at age 7 or 8, and teenagers start drinking at 14 or 15. "Drinking is ingrained in everybody. We drink to avoid feelings and sharing emotions. I know my husband has a problem with alcohol. He drinks every night. He never talks or expresses emotions. I just let him be."

Jewish

Addiction, if it exists, is downplayed and is considered dangerous. "There are nice Jewish boys, and girls will raise babies." If a problem is observed in a family, it is minimized or overlooked. It is even overlooked during the Jewish holiday of Purim. "If someone gets repeatedly intoxicated, it is best not to bring attention and disgrace to the family. Hopefully, it will quietly work itself out."

Latino

Drinking occurred every weekend. "I grew up in a family where you couldn't get enough Coors and Bud Light through the back door. We never talked about all the drinking in our family, even the serious problems." Her grandpa spent a month sweating it out in the back house, and her uncle moved to Atlanta and got sober. The family considers these two "cautionary tales."

Brazilian Woman

"I believe my culture discounts and ignores the use of alcohol and drugs. The problem is left untouched and unspoken about. This may be done to maintain the dignity of the family's name. On the first day of class, I was surprised when classmates disclosed their family history and past use and abuse. It has been modeled to me to never air out your dirty laundry, especially to strangers."

Vietnamese Woman

Parents were refugees. There was no alcohol in the household. The focus was on food. "You drink when you are of age. It's a rite of passage. If there's a problem, my culture says, 'Don't let anyone know. If others have a problem, that's their private family business.'"

Hispanic, Third Generation

A 26-year-old woman is the youngest of six children. Her father and all her siblings are either alcoholic or addicted to drugs. Her mother has tended to them all, quietly and alone. "She approached me when I was young and said, 'I want you to go to church.' Church is what saved me from addiction."

Salvador an American

A first-generation woman with parents born in San Salvador. The message—alcohol is wrong and just don't do it. There was a grandfather who was alcoholic and a "funny uncle." Drinking brings with it a negative stigma. The whole issue of drinking is burdensome to her. "Should I drink?" "Is it negative?" "How much is too much?" "Who can I talk to, as nobody is talking about this?"

African American/Belizean American

"I drank with my mom at age 12." Her mom did crack, alcohol, and prescription drugs. There was no talk of treatment. "This is what she was doing with her life." Her dad is homeless, an alcoholic, and a drug addict. She says he is not interested in treatment.

Mexican Guatemalan Catholic

"Being Catholic and from a Latino culture, I was told that drugs were evil. Only bad people like criminals use drugs. However, alcohol was not spoken about. My non-immediate family members drank heavily during the holidays, and my parents would remind me of their irresponsibility. I believed what I was told and was embarrassed by my drinking family members."

Traditional Mexican Family

"My personal experience with my culture has led me to believe that alcohol is normal and a part of life. It is always looked forward to in social gatherings because it means we are going to have a good time. When it comes to addictions, I realize that no one talks about it openly. We see it as 'Oh, your uncle, he is just an old drunk.' There is no emphasis on helping the individual with an addiction—you have to fix your own problems."

White Male, "Vaguely Jewish"

"I grew up in a house with an enormous amount of substance abuse coupled with an enormous amount of psychotherapy. It's all so spoken about, but the secrets are insidious."

Biracial, Ivy League Student

"As a woman of color, I felt shameful and secretive about my father's drug use. I connected this to the racism and classism in society's attitudes—people of color are deviant and dangerous and should be locked up. So the lesson I learned was to keep using a secret. When I went away to college and interacted with the elite upper class, I was floored to hear many of them laugh or even boast about their parents' drug use. It is clear [that] culture forms our beliefs and behaviors about drugs and addiction."

CHAPTER SUMMARY AND REFLECTIONS

Summary

Special population statistics provide a general perspective on some usage patterns and treatment preference among diverse population groups. Ethnocultural stories reflect the contradictions and commandments, tolerances and biases about the meaning and place of AOD in cultural, family, and individual life. Class discussions are a challenge. It takes time for students to feel safe enough to participate. Students hear themselves articulate the thinking and directives of their cultural elders. They slowly develop their own worries and preoccupations.

The courageous sharing of these stories over many years has repeatedly demonstrated a very disturbing universal pattern—our families, our cultures, and our nations too readily encourage us to remain distant and disengaged about our desire to get high as well as our wonders and our worries. They too readily provide "acceptable" sanctions and permissions and instill us with prohibitions and moralistic thinking. Tragically, this too often leads us to look the other way when a loved one or cultural comrade is in trouble with AOD. We notice, but don't intervene to help each other.

Many students leave these classes profoundly enriched and moved by our discussions. They take with them the understanding that treatment should always involve a deep exploration of the ethnocultural idiosyncratic meanings behind drug and alcohol use and misuse. These influences uniquely shape one's problems and perceptions, and they most certainly determine how one approaches getting help. I encourage all students to continue these conversations with their families, friends, and patients.

I look forward to these classroom conversations each semester. I receive ongoing positive feedback about our class discussions and their long-lasting impact on personal and professional development.

Reflections

Before leaving this chapter, make sure you consider:

- Your cultural identity and its influences on your relationship with AOD
- The role of culture in defining addiction, problems with drugs and alcohol, and recovery and treatment
- Any biases or prejudices you may bring to your approach to treatment
- The value of keeping up with current statistics on special populations and trends

Chapter 2

Sociocultural Aspects

INTRODUCTION

The individual addict is not solely responsible for his addictive behavior. He lives in a context, a society that in many ways invites and encourages widespread addiction. This chapter invites students and readers to continue their personal learning journey as they move from consideration of ethnocultural influences and in addition consider the influence of contemporary societal forces on our individual comprehension of alcohol and drug use and their disorders. Addiction, particularly in the United States, is not just the result of an increasing number of biological predispositions being passed on from generation to generation. Rather, widespread addiction, both with substances and other compulsive behaviors, also reflects the pained and self-destructive responses of human beings as they attempt to accommodate the demands and pressures of living in America.

Over the years, I have read and been influenced by the works of many writers who link an understanding of drinking and drugging behaviors to the social idiosyncrasies of a particular historical era. David Hanson's (1995) concise renderings of the history of alcohol and drinking around the world from ancient times to early modernity are extremely valuable. Herbert Bloch's (1949) writings about the peculiar American ideology concerning recreations are equally instructive. Susanna Barrows and Robin Room (1991) gathered a wonderful collection of essays on the place and meaning of alcohol in social history and the responses of family, social movements, institutions, political parties, professions, and states to drink. These are just a few.

I have chosen to lecture from two books that identify Western societal and capitalistic forces that keep this contemporary addiction alive. The first book, *When Society Becomes an Addict,* is written by writer, lecturer, and organizational consultant Anne Wilson Schaeff (1987). Dr. Schaeff trains health-care professionals around the world on the influences of context and processes in daily living. The second book, *Drugs, Addiction and Initiation: The Modern Search for Ritual*, is written by an internationally respected writer and teacher. Dr. Luigi Zoja (2000) is a Jungian analyst who now practices in New York City. He has long traveled the globe and written on violence, mythology, psychology, and addiction.

The following sections reflect my interpretation, assimilation, and expansion of both Dr. Schaeff's and Dr. Zoja's thinking on the contribution of societal forces to contemporary addiction (Schaeff, 1987; Zoja, 2000). Their works have inspired my imagination. As always, the reader's personal engagement and student discussions are encouraged.

When Society Becomes an Addict

Anne Wilson Schaeff (1987) suggests that we live in an addictive system (p. 12). The addictive context is composed of societal institutions; laws and policies; and political, cultural, and economic forces that shape each of us. During this shaping we internalize American values and expectations. This societal map influences how we each think and behave. More recently, the contemporary addictive context has been traumatically disrupted by an ongoing series of world crises—from 9/11 to the wars in Iraq and Afghanistan and, more recently, to the failing world economy. We live within and between these imminent threats, as well as with the internalized historical American values of survival and resilience.

Schaeff (1987) suggests that each of us is susceptible to becoming attached to substances and compulsive processes in unhealthy ways in order to survive the pressures, demands, and exclusions of this contemporary societal context (p. 19). The societal system calls forth these addictive behaviors, and the prevalence of addiction is often directly related to socio-environmental influences. Our universal need to get high is shaped by a historical and societal setting. Contextual forces greatly influence how we use alcohol and other drugs (AOD), make sense of our addictions, and address these problems. Again, I invite students and readers to apply this societal theory of addiction to their own lives.

Addiction of Inclusion and Exclusion

All of us can be attached to objects, events, and activities on a daily basis for the purposes of pleasure, relief of boredom, and frustration tolerance. These healthy attachments are embedded in our routines. They help get us through. Some of us overdo these experiences and they no longer are about helping us get through, but rather they become the focus of our living. These unhealthy attachments become symptoms, and symptoms serve functions. Schaeff (1987) says the function of addiction is to keep us out of touch with what is really going on (p. 13). A late-night talk show host in the 1980s used to begin his show with, "Let's get busy."

These destructive attachments to everyday objects and activities keep us busy and disconnected from our troubles, distresses, and emotional pains. Individuals blindly struggle, and families muddle through. American life drifts on, saturated in destructive, addictive habits.

The substances (objects) that we may become addicted to include alcohol, caffeine, drugs, food, nicotine, and sugar. The processes (events and activities) we can become addicted to include gambling, sex, work, religion, worry, power, entertainment, exercise, relationships, criminal activity, cleaning, prostitution, business, shopping, talking, gossiping, pornography, beautyism, self-mutilation, urgency, and caretaking. This list is incomplete.

I have identified two addictive system profiles. The first is addiction of inclusion. This addiction occurs among persons who are socioeconomically able to participate in the opportunities of our culture. This participation is increasingly coupled with much more pressure and stress. People self-medicate with AOD to relieve the tensions and anxieties they feel as they try to make it, fit in, or advance in this addictive context. The second addictive system profile is addiction of exclusion. This addiction occurs among persons who are marginalized from the playing field as a result of discrimination or high unemployment rates, poverty, or limited education. People self-medicate to numb feelings of inadequacy and rejection, isolation and alienation.

Addiction of inclusion suggests that we are not wired to live the lives this addictive context calls forth—the full catastrophe of pressured parenting, nights of little sleep, long electronic workdays, multiple jobs, and limited time for meaningful connections. Our psychological and biochemical makeup cannot tolerate this intense pace, with its repeated stressful impacts and unrelenting demands. We attempt to endure and then drink, drug, eat, gamble, sex, and shop. While we may be successfully thriving in the addictive system, our personal world is on a road to addictive shambles. We are seemingly well adjusted to everyday tasks, yet we live with these very painful and often closeted costs—reverberations felt by the individual, the family, and our society.

Those suffering from addiction of exclusion are persons rejected from participation in societal opportunities. They are probably not reading this book. They are born into misfortune, ravaged by abuse and neglect, and violently relegated to the sidelines of American life. They struggle to survive and endure by drinking, drugging, criminal activity, and other forms of destructive aggression. Sadly, all this ends up reinforcing more dismissal and rejection. More recently, an increasingly large number of Americans are being excluded from the workforce. This ominously portends that more will self-medicate as they accommodate to a shifting, shrinking, and turbulent economy. It is unknown what this addiction will look like, but it is sure to reflect the violent uncertainty of our times.

Clearly, it is not just genetic vulnerability and family influences that produce addiction. It also results from our attempts to self-medicate for the pain and pressures of living either within or on the outskirts of what American society has to offer.

Addiction of inclusion costs are increasingly destructive. Please consider your own individual addictive responses to everyday pressures and threats and their contributions to addictive living in America. We deaden ourselves through these numbing rituals, all to accommodate the irrational demands of the addictive context and its perversion of the American dream. We destroy ourselves, our creativity, our connections with others, and our lives—all to fit in. Our quality of life depends on facing our destructive tendencies and becoming more conscious of our ability to make choices. We don't have to participate in this pace and become its collateral damage. Mental well-being, creative experiences and expressions, the tranquility of peace of mind, and social cohesion are sacrificed.

Addiction of exclusion costs are increasingly destructive as well. The homeless and weary wander our streets and rural roads. They often live an aimless life of suffering and addiction. Many give up. Others trudge on and connect with each other. Some of these hear about recovery programs in their local neighborhoods or cities. The staff of these local programs attempt much, make some good headway, work hard, and passionately provide recovery opportunities for addicts living on the street.

Employees of Los Angeles programs were interviewed for this book. A director of a Salvation Army recovery treatment program was both hard-nosed and hopeful. "The responsibility is theirs. Even addicts on the street can feel entitled. We pray that they become willing and stay grateful. There are all kinds of programs in Los Angeles. Street people are smart. They will find them if they want them; the choice is theirs, but we are here" (Dan Petersen, Personal Communication, 2010).

This analysis of widespread addiction suggests that society and its forces abuse us either way, whether we are in the game or excluded from participating. The two profiles attempt to demonstrate that more and more people endure the suffering of their inclusion or exclusion with addictions.

Drugs, Addiction, and Initiation: The Modern Search for Ritual

Luigi Zoja (2000) is a depth psychologist and a student of Carl Jung. He compares premodern and modern society. His focus is on the absence of meaningful initiation rituals in our contemporary culture. His initiatory model proposes that widespread drug addiction reflects an unconscious search for what is missing (pp. 8–9).

Initiatory rituals honor developmental rites of passage that occur when we outgrow one stage of development and embark on a new phase of growth and renewed purpose (Zoja, 2000, pp. 2, 6). These honoring celebrations include weddings and funerals, bar and bat mitzvahs, graduations, and confirmations. We can also embrace and pay tribute to a host of daily beginnings and endings that are found in sharing family breakfasts and dinners, starting and completing a project, resolving an impasse, or working through a conflict.

Zoja (2000) describes a Western society in which rituals and initiation rites are profaned either by their nonexistence or by their hollow meaninglessness: "The profanity of cultural circumstances does not allow the need for renewal to develop in a calm and solemn process" (p. 62). We power through; there is no time to acknowledge or celebrate these ongoing passages of growth, development, and change. This results in a life bereft of meaning and vitality. This loss comes at a cost, according to Zoja.

These rites of passage satisfy the archetypal or innate desire for personal regeneration, as well as the universal need to die and be reborn again throughout one's lifetime (Zoja, 2000, pp. 2, 13, 18). Again, these death/rebirth moments occur on birthdays and graduations, during weddings or christenings, after vacations, when finishing a competitive season or finishing a semester. Rituals celebrate and honor both an end or a death of one phase or aspect of living and a beginning or birth of the next. They help to contain the anxieties of letting go of an outdated identity and moving into a new one.

Zoja proposes that these formalized good-byes (deaths) and hellos (rebirths) are very important. They recognize and cherish the individual courage needed to die or let go of what is developmentally and psychologically outdated. They also honor entry onto a new path. These rituals encourage and celebrate the daring involved in the search for more meaning in one's life. These communal experiences "hold" our developmental truths. They provide both vitality and containment. Zoja strongly suggests that they sustain and maintain cultural stability and civility as well.

Something is missing without them. What is absent causes suffering and sends us on an unconscious, uncontrolled, and irrational search to satisfy this death-rebirth experience, wherever we can find it.

Without healthy developmental rites of passage, we create unhealthy ones (Zoja 2000, p. 24). For example, we often hastily end or say good-bye to the tensions of a day with cocktails or drugs, affairs or bulimia. These addictive substances and processes provide an immediate sense of relief from daily pressures and ongoing agonies. This easy euphoria overlooks our need to share the emotional shifts of daily living, face what needs to be faced, or adjust what needs to be adjusted. These might include unworkable daily living patterns and routines, unhealthy parenting styles, unsatisfying jobs, and difficult or unloving relationships. These modern rituals of pleasure produce temporary satisfaction and provide a distorted sense of rebirth. They actually reverse a true death-rebirth experience. Dying to what is outdated or unworkable is delayed; a drug or alcohol fix provides a premature sense of rejuvenation. The pain of facing the need for a real change (death) is temporarily avoided; the pleasures of excess (false rebirth) are immediately satisfying but ultimately shallow (p. 63).

With further reflection, we also see that many contemporary cultural celebrations of death and rebirth are sadly saturated with drugs and alcohol. Widespread intoxication during birthdays, weddings, and christenings pollute the opportunity to meaningfully share the joys and struggles of developmental growth and change. Lubricated conviviality is a poor substitute for connections of meaning.

According to Zoja (2000), this ritualized world of intoxication is a perverted attempt to satisfy the loss of these death-rebirth moments, normally provided in initiatory rituals. The drug addict/alcoholic is a "negative hero or heroine" in search of transcendence, death, and rebirth in a culture that provides little or no meaningful opportunities for these (p. 15). While heroic in their seeming search for ways to honor comings and goings, beginnings and endings, their intoxicated choices are ultimately negative ones. The inverted death-rebirth rituals provide relief before it is developmentally earned. They are empty of true growth and development, satisfaction and meaning.

The addict returns to these rituals again and again, in a disguised search for transcendence and rebirth. Zoja (2000) calls these "downward initiations, initiations moving toward a lower form of life, towards non-life or darkness" (p. 61). Destructive use of alcohol and drugs too often provides a disguised sense of euphoria. These feelings of pleasure too often take precedence over the difficult and meaningful rituals of death and regeneration that individuals seem to long for throughout their lifetimes.

Alcoholics Anonymous—A World of Ritual and Death/Rebirth Moments

If one is lucky enough to make it to the other side, one does indeed surrender to the drug world and its empty rituals. The often desperate, but finally willing addict is ready to face a true death moment and a real rebirth moment when he enters the world of recovery. This initiates an ongoing search for regeneration and new meaning through sober developmental rituals of passage.

It is noteworthy that the path of recovery often includes participation in the world of Alcoholics Anonymous (AA). This is a world filled with rituals and death-rebirth moments in many forms. There are ongoing celebrations honoring sober anniversaries. Birthday chips are given for 30, 60, 90 days, and every year thereafter. These public celebrations honor both death and rebirth as honorees are requested to share "where you were, where you are, and where you are going."

There is developmental progression of step work with a sponsor, which includes dying to the work of step one, as one rebirths to the requirements of step two. After completing the steps, AA members are encouraged to die to the sponsee role and agree instead to sponsor newcomers through the same step progression. One is the recipient of others' service and is expected to be of service to others. These death-rebirth rituals create a wonderful sense of belonging, significance, and meaning.

Most AA members report that the world of ritual and community creates a sense of finally feeling at home in a world where they have previously felt emotionally, physically, and spiritually homeless. Dr. Zoja (2000) crafted my longtime favorite conceptualization of an addict: "True addicts don't use to escape life; rather true addicts use to find a place in life" (p. 15).

Zoja's work strongly suggests that these meaningful AA ceremonies satisfy archetypal needs to leave one phase of recovery, enter another, and share it with others in the form of ritual. They create a sense of growth, meaning, and purpose that one previously sought elsewhere in the world of drugs and alcohol. Coincidentally, most long-standing members of AA often share that attending meetings, doing step work and participating in the program keep them sober. Zoja's emphasis on the importance of death-rebirth moments shared with others in the form of rituals may explain why.

CHAPTER SUMMARY AND REFLECTIONS

Summary

This chapter looks at the relationship between social context and addiction. The reader is asked to consider societal forces and pressures, exclusions, and absences that contribute to widespread contemporary addiction. Anne Wilson Schaeff's work on the addictive context was developed, and the costs of inclusion and exclusion while living in the addictive system were considered. The stresses of participating call forth self-medicating behaviors with AOD. The humiliation and alienation of being excluded drive people to get relief for their suffering through AOD as well.

Luigi Zoja suggests that the loss of rituals honoring developmental rites of passage contribute to widespread addiction. Without these culturally sanctioned death-rebirth moments, we perversely look for them in the ritualized world of intoxication.

Students and clinicians are asked to consider the influences of societal forces in their own relationship with AOD and certainly consider them when assessing the social context of future patients.

Reflections

Before leaving this chapter, make sure you grasp the role of societal influences in addiction and understand:

- The nature of the addictive context and its contribution to widespread addiction
- Why addiction of inclusion exists
- Why addiction of exclusion exists
- How the loss of initiation rituals contributes to widespread addiction
- The importance and function of death and rebirth experiences in one's lifetime
- The place of death and rebirth moments in Alcoholics Anonymous

Chapter 3

Definitions

INTRODUCTION

By now readers have started to develop a more grounded sense of how their own cultural history and social context has influenced the direction of their relationship with alcohol and other drugs (AOD), as well as their thinking about substance use and its disorders and treatment in general. Reflective readers are now ready to consider and contemplate various definitions of *addiction* and *alcoholism*.

Everyone has ideas about what addiction and alcoholism mean to them. They have developed these from their own experiences and observations, their families, their friends, the streets, and the movies. These experiences leave impressions, and most of the time they are not neutral. Addictions evoke conflicting emotions that cloud our thinking. People develop judgments and values, fears and blind spots, expectations and entitlements.

We tend to hold on to these original notions and keep them at bay until we are forced to reconsider. A crisis situation disturbs our thinking about addiction and alcoholism, an addict and a co-addict. In its aftermath, we are challenged to confront old ideas. Hopefully, we take the time to ask new questions. How did my thinking about addiction influence the evolution of a crisis? Is the addict self-destructive and self-willed, or is he psychologically suffering and surviving in the best way he can? What motivates the co-addict? How, then, do I define an addict, an alcoholic, a co-addict? Is addiction a disease, and if so, what does that mean? How do I make sense of the impact of the environment, genetics, the brain, society, culture, and psychological suffering? Additional questions surface. Why are so many of us interested in getting high? Why do we pass so much time with alcohol? Is it one of our national pastimes? Why does a pleasure turn into excess? Finally, and most importantly, how do I define my own relationship with AOD?

This chapter introduces students to various definitions of *alcoholism* and *addiction,* as well as the *addict* or *alcoholic*. These come from a variety of reference points, including the medical model, science and biology, psychological suffering, psychoanalytic thinking, attachment, spirituality, choices, family, recovery and treatment, and Alcoholics Anonymous. The reader might be confused or frustrated by the lack of definitional consensus in the field. Hopefully, you will learn to embrace the uncertainty and value the diversity of thinking.

The following pages are designed to encourage students and readers to reflect into their own thinking about addiction and the suffering behind it, to explore the unexamined, and to consider new ideas. Class discussions invite students to open up their minds and hearts to new ways of conceptualizing the baffling phenomena of AOD use, disordered use, or dependence.

A chapter on selected definitions is unusual in an addiction text. It's good preparation for deeper retention of what is to follow and ultimately good preparation for flexibility during treatment. Take the time to develop your thoughts and reactions in the spaces provided beside each definition. You might want to return to this chapter as your thinking evolves with new learning. I do.

How we think about addiction influences the way we respond; how we think about addicts or alcoholics influences the way we treat them. We live in a society that is hesitant to talk about what's behind the drive to get high, how it sometimes gets us into trouble and distresses those around us. Again, we keep our thoughts and feelings at bay. Here is a chance for each of you to clarify what is confusing and address what you are avoiding.

These definitions are designed for thinking and conversations among students and clinicians, families and friends. Some are direct quotes; many are modified or further developed from the original source.

DEFINITIONS

Addiction:

- Is a dramatic conflict that avoids real conflict. ______________________
- Is a pathological love and trust relationship with an object that couldn't care less about you as a person (Sager, Personal Communication, 2008). ______________________ ______________________ ______________________
- "Is a substitute employed by those who cannot wait for time's unfolding" (Bion, 1992, p. 299). ______________________ ______________________
- "Exists when a person's attachment to a sensational object is exclusive and the person is increasingly dependent on this experience as the only source of gratification" (Peele and Brodsky, 1991, p. 43). ______________________ ______________________ ______________________ ______________________

- Is a brain injury rather than a brain disease as a result of repeated exposure to self-administered toxins. An addict's brain is different from a nonaddict's brain as a result of neurochemical changes due to prolonged substance misuse. As with other injuries, healing can occur when the source of the injury has been eliminated (Thombs, 2006).
- "Always represents an effort to bring about an internal change" (Director, 2005, p. 567).
- Is characterized by a person's marked impairment in his ability to control his alcohol or drug use (Hyman, 1995).
- "Is a passive activity. Individuals take pills, powders, or liquids and wait for the desired effect—an alteration of their consciousness. The individual passively changes what he or she feels by using alcohol/drugs instead of facing and working through feelings of boredom, sadness, stress, and loneliness. Changing your mood by more active approaches involves more effort and motivation" (Fields, 2010, p. 28).
- Is a syndrome with multiple opportunistic expressions. Development and maintenance of addiction suggest . . . neurobiological (dopamine) reward activity, learning and memory in the hippocampus, and emotional regulation in the amygdala. Regardless of the object of addiction, the neurobiological circuitry of the central nervous system is the ultimate common pathway for addictive behaviors (Shaffer et al., 2004, p. 367).
- "Involves conditions in which problems with regulating emotions, self-love, relationships and self-care interact in varying degrees with each other and also with genetic vulnerability and the environment" (Khantzian and Albanese, 2008, p. 19).
- To chemicals is an end-stage disease or a common end point, derived from different biological, social, and psychological paths (Doweiko, 2009, p. 53).
- Is not just defined by symptomatic using, but also defined by who is watching the user (Vaillant, 1983).
- "Is a radical escape from freedom" (Levin, 2001, p. 3).
- "Is the individual's behavioral and cognitive preoccupation with a substance, and an overwhelming compulsion to have the substance" (Brown, 1985, p. 71).
- Is a predictable response to social conditions that destroy self-esteem, hope, solidarity, stability, and a sense of purpose (qtd. in *Rolling Stone Magazine*).
- Functions to put a buffer between ourselves and our awareness or feelings. An addiction serves to numb us so that we are out of touch with what we know and feel (Schaeff, 1987, pp. 18–19).

Alcoholic/Addict:

- "Over the course of nearly a half-century of clinical work with addicted individuals, I have yet to meet a person who became or remained addicted to drugs because of the pleasurable aspect of their use, or whose motives in initiating and using drugs was suicidal in nature" (Khantzian, 2011, p. 3).
- One whose drinking creates problems (Alcoholics Anonymous member).
- "The addict's attachment to chemicals serves both as an obstacle to, and a substitute for, interpersonal relationships" (Flores, 2001, p. 64).
- Addicts crave being high. Being high is the opposite of being deep. Being high is a substitute for being spiritually deep. Being high prevents one from going to the deeper places where the human heart resides (Zoja, 2000).
- Drugs can give people a sense of magical oneness with the world. The problem is that the drugs wear off; the feeling is only temporary. Addicts are driven to search for more. This hyperfocus severely disturbs one's sense of self, as well as intimate relationships with others. Sexual relationships are not needed anymore. The ego tragically surrenders itself to all that the drug world promises (Loose, 2002, p. 105).

Alcoholism:

- "Perversion of social drinking into solitary excess" (Rotskoff, 2002, p. 74).
- "The peculiar charm of alcohol lies in the sense of careless well-being and bodily comfort which it creates. It unburdens the individual of his cares and fears. Under such conditions, it is easy to laugh or to weep, to love or to hate, not wisely but too well" (Emerson, 1932, p. 263).
- "The baffling feature of alcoholism is the utter inability to leave it alone" (Alcoholics Anonymous, 2001, p. 34).
- Is defined as a primary, chronic disease with genetic, psychosocial, and environmental factors influencing its development and manifestations. The disease is often progressive and fatal. It is characterized by periodic or continuous impaired control over drinking, preoccupation with the drug alcohol, use of alcohol despite adverse consequences and distortions of thinking, most notably denial. Each of these symptoms may be continuous or periodic (American Society of Addiction Medicine, www.asam.org).

- Saturates the lives of those it touches—their families, friends, and work associates; their decisions and plans; their aspirations and dreams; their identities and self-concepts; their very assumptions about what is real and possible (Denzin, 1987).
- An emptiness and spiritual void that requires spiritual healing (Vaillant, 1983).
- Once an individual has lost control in a grand way, continued use of alcohol can be a cause of a syndrome labeled alcoholism.
- Is a chronic, progressive, and potentially fatal disease characterized by tolerance and psychological and/or physical dependency.
- Is better defined as alcoholisms with varying signs, symptoms, and developments (Franklin, 1987, p. 214).
- Is a disorder of intimacy. The alcoholic is extremely anxious over matters of interpersonal closeness, involvement, and intimacy. He wants closeness, but it is safest to keep others at a distance. Pre-consciously and unconsciously the addicted individual equates interpersonal intimacy and closeness with annihilation, rejection and potential destruction of one's self. By drinking alcohol, and through the medium of intoxication, the alcoholic achieves a distorted or neurotic ability to be intimate (student).
- Is consistent use despite negative consequences (Alcoholics Anonymous member).
- Has *nothing* to do with alcohol and *everything* to do with alcohol.
- Alcoholism is a disease that I have. But it was also a symptom of a far more destructive, hidden disease. The disease was a broken heart from childhood. Alcohol was what I used to try to cure and hide it from myself and the world. It was so hidden away behind my emotional fortress that I did not even know it was there. It took a lot of time to poke enough holes in that dark wall to let the light in (student).

DIAGNOSTIC AND DESCRIPTIVE TERMS

- **Tolerance** occurs when a dependent or disordered user requires increasing or decreasing doses to achieve the original/desired effect. A change in the amount of the substance.
- **Physical Dependency** occurs when the body has been exposed to AOD continuously for days/weeks and the addict has to maintain the dose/amount in order for the body to stay "physically balanced."

- **Psychological Dependency** occurs when the psyche has been exposed to AOD continuously for days/weeks and the addict has to maintain the dose/amount in order for the body to stay "psychologically balanced."
- **Withdrawal** occurs when a dependent or disordered user stops using. The physical and psychological symptoms that occur when someone abruptly stops drinking or drugging.

CHAPTER SUMMARY AND REFLECTIONS

Summary

This chapter has encouraged the reader to develop a more personal and thoughtful perspective on the meanings behind substance use and addiction, as well as the alcoholic and addict. Carefully selected definitions from multiple sources were presented. Personal reflection and class discussions were encouraged. Students were asked to consider the application of these in their personal and professional worlds. The reader was exposed to the field's tolerance for different viewpoints and also its lack of consensus. Return to this chapter as your learning evolves.

Reflections

Before leaving this chapter, make sure you have:

- Reflected "into" each definition and participated in class discussions
- Recorded your differences, additions or deletions, and reflections in the spaces provided to the right of each definition

Part II

A Perspective on Diagnosis and Substance Classification

Chapter 4

Twelve Profiles of Using, Misusing, and Addiction

INTRODUCTION

The *Diagnostic and Statistical Manual of Mental Disorders* (DSM), a reference book for the clarification of mental disorders, broadly divides Substance-Related Disorders into two groups—Substance Use Disorders (Substance Dependence and Substance Abuse) and Substance-Induced Disorders (Substance Intoxication, Withdrawal, or Substance-Induced Symptoms). In addition, in-depth sections on related disorders for each of the 11 psychoactive drugs are included (DSM-IV-TR, 2000, pp. 191–295).

Clinicians who diagnose look to see whether someone's maladaptive use of a substance is one of dependence or abuse. These two terms frame our current thinking and direct our choices, but there is so much more. My sense is that individuals, families, and clinicians have over-relied on these categories and that has eclipsed our abilities to creatively see what is sitting across from us. Short- and long-term treatment is then compromised. Out of ignorance or a lack of imagination, anxiety or fear, exhaustion or a desperate need to control an out-of-control situation, we have narrowed our investigations. The DSM and the wider clinical community currently instruct us to pigeonhole people into one of these two categories. Nobody benefits from this narrow vision.

The DSM-V workgroup on substance-related disorders seems to agree. This workgroup has been meeting since late 2007 and is charged with reviewing, revising, and improving existing diagnostic categories and criteria. The new category of substance use disorders replaces the currently used categories of abuse and dependence. Twelve substance use disorders are identified, and two severity indexes are considered: moderate (2 to 3 criteria) and severe (4 or more criteria). There are 11 criteria in all. Also included are specifiers for possible physiological dependence and categories of remission status. The final reorganization will be published in the DSM-V, scheduled for release in May 2013.

The contents of this chapter are written in response to the perceived shortcomings of the DSM-IV-TR and also seem simpatico with the spirit of the DSM-V revisions. The following progressive profiles of use, misuse, and addiction are clinical descriptors designed to sharpen diagnostic thinking during consideration of treatment recommendations. When *Perspectives of Addiction* goes to press, we will still be bound by DSM-IV-TR diagnostic categories, so I include dependence and abuse in these 12 profiles. All profiles are designed to encourage more flexibility and freedom during diagnostic observations, provide more descriptive criteria during complicated assessments, and promote imaginative treatment planning.

Over the years, I have found it helpful and useful to think expansively about diagnosis, not just limit assessment to abuse and dependence. I think in terms of descriptive categories of using, nonusing, and addiction. I have observed human behaviors, organized my impressions, and developed 12 profiles that describe some of the idiosyncratic stories of our attachments and involvements with alcohol and drugs (AOD). The number of profiles has expanded over the years as a result of my own clinical observations and student input. We are bound by the DSM, yet I hope these clinical descriptors and the ideas behind them are of service to your thinking. Diagnosing should be a serious and spirited activity, and this chapter conveys the spirit of this book.

Children are experimenting too early, friends are drinking daily to blackout, and marriages are haunted by the death grip of repetitively damaging drinking episodes. We panic at what is going on around us—how bad things are becoming, how hopeless we feel, and how incapable of really reaching out and helping we have become. We feel confused, scared, and useless. During these moments of fear, anxiety, and helplessness, we seem to do one of two things in an effort to get relief.

First, we overdiagnose. We intervene in dramatic ways and prematurely label. We are sure people are alcoholics, are addicts, or have a drug problem or alcohol issue. If we know who they are, we can tell them what to do. We can get control. We insist on treatment or arrange an intervention. Overdiagnosing has a strange effect—it calms family members and incites the user. This effect cancels out any real progress. It doesn't help.

Second, we underdiagnose or imagine that the problem is not that bad. We excuse it away and thus avoid the labels altogether. For complex and tragic reasons, many seem unable to clearly and convincingly tell those they love that they are in trouble with drugs and alcohol. Some of my patients who have struggled with facing a family member's AOD problems have said, "My husband's drinking is out of control, but I guess this is what I have to accept with someone who is so intense with everything he does. You know, I just have to take the good with the bad." Another couple, discussing overreliance on Vicodin and her daily ritual of compulsively pulling her eyelashes out, commented, "You know, in this day and age everybody has something. And what we do doesn't interfere with our jobs and our lives." Finally, a repeated marital or partnership refrain about daily disturbing AOD dependence, "There is already so much going on with the children, her work, and her illness. You know, we all do the best we can."

I have seen this pattern time and time again over the years—frantically label or helplessly resign. Neither helps. The following profiles of using and addiction begin to address the problems of seeing too much or seeing too little. These profiles are guidelines to help us understand what we are witnessing and experiencing and to help to make sense of what is confusing and frightening. These are guidelines designed to encourage reflection. They are profiles for everyday conversation and for assessment and clinical treatment. They are designed to help us embrace a pleasurable and complex human drive, and the ways it can get us in trouble.

This chapter is written in an informational and informal tone. The DSM-IV-TR diagnostic categories of dependence and abuse are included within the 12 profiles. There are additional profiles of nonusing, using, misusing, and disordered using. These profiles were designed during idiosyncratic observations of many clinical cases over many years. The style, length, and presentation of these profiles reflect their unique stories. The informational tone delivers serious content for your consideration; the informal tone invites your participation. Readers are asked to identify with one profile or many, notice any overlap or back-and-forth over time, and consider them when thinking about their loved ones.

Hopefully, students will extrapolate what is useful, add to what is missing, and consider alternative descriptions. Class discussions on this topic are usually energized and exciting; conversations are meant to further explore the process of diagnostic thinking. Creativity in the design of profiles is encouraged. There is room for reorganization and expansion. The more nuanced our vision, the more thoughtful our treatment.

PROFILES/CLINICAL DESCRIPTORS

Use

Since humankind began, we have always looked for a way to escape or expand consciousness. Sometimes this is done for spiritual ecstasy and other times for fun. We have taken plants and seeds from the earth. We now know the special place that alcohol assumed in early civilizations. Wine was being made as early as 5000 BC. Ancient Romans had their god of drink, Bacchus, and the Greeks their Dionysus (van Wormer and Davis, 2008, p. 38). In ancient Egypt, both beer and wine were deified and offered to the gods (D. J. Hanson, 1995).

Ronald K. Siegel (2005) at UCLA proposes that this ancient desire is actually another human drive, similar to our need for food, water, and sex. He suggests that the urge to get high is among our basic motivations; he proposes that intoxication is the fourth drive, an acquired drive that is as powerful as an innate one (p. 208). And like all drives, desire varies. Some people have a high desire to escape consciousness, while others have medium or low drives. Thomas Szasz (1988), psychiatrist and academic, likens the contemporary war on drugs to a war on this human desire, suggesting that we are uncomfortable with our need for pleasure, escape, or oblivion. Both suggest that a war on our own nature is ultimately doomed.

A lively discussion always follows these remarks. Students' AOD habits are explored—from the last drink, to the last hangover, to the last time they said no. We discuss family and cultural habits. We look at people's emotional relationships with AOD.

I pose a question to students each semester, and the response is telling. "Would you be willing to look at or give up your own troubled AOD use for the duration of this semester?" A gasp and an embarrassed laugh usually follow. Many are not willing at first blush, and quickly they are struck by their protective and defensive response. Eventually, a sizable number of courageous students agree to examine or forgo a bothersome pleasure and write a chapter about the experience in their final paper, which is entitled "My Book of Learnings."

Voluntary Nonuse

This is a profile of people who early on and voluntarily make a decision not to include alcohol or drugs in their lives. They respond to this drive of human desire with a no, either emphatically from bad experiences, indifferently, or derived from a value. Some are influenced to make this choice as a result of what they have seen in their upbringing. These experiences range from a grandfather who drank himself to death to a mother who hid pills in the closet, thinking no one saw her take them throughout the day. Others lived in an alcohol-fueled household or with a sibling who repeatedly got himself in trouble. One who was scarred by an alcoholic parent said, "I'd rather play it safe and not drink than live on the slippery slope of a possibility."

Sometimes there is no negative influence at all, just a sense of "I don't need it to relax, and actually, it gets in the way of getting close to people." A college student with a father she has only known sober, because his dependent drinking was before her birth, chooses not to drink. She struggles with her judgmental attitudes; she considers the choice to drink a moral weakness, as giving into something and a waste of time. Others say they feel they don't need it: "I get enjoyment and satisfaction from sitting around a board game with friends, while others get pleasure from sitting around a bong pipe." One woman in her 30s, who does not drink, proudly announces, "It distinguishes me."

Many nonusers acknowledge the pressures they experience from drinkers who want them to join in their partying. "Drinkers seem to feel guilty about their overdrinking and don't want someone sober watching them." As one nonuser observed, "It's sad to see someone who is drunk reduced to a form of amusement, rather than a person."

Many report not liking the taste of alcohol from that first drink. These are often a category of people who are not affected in any way by others' responses to their nondrinking. "I don't feel I am missing anything and always have a good time with drinkers or nondrinkers. When I'm having fun, drinkers usually think I'm drunk anyway."

In my classes over the years, nonusers make up about 15% of the student population. Approximately 85% of students report using drugs or alcohol. Most of these student users report an increase in AOD use during their graduate studies. They are upset and somewhat alarmed by this tendency. It is part of our semester-long conversation on the profiles of using, nonusing, and addiction in our own lives.

Experimentation

"To experiment is to undertake, to discover something not yet known; to try out something to find out whether or not it will be effective. To experiment is to test something out; to tentatively explore" (Guralnik and Friend, 1968, p. 512).

A young adolescent girl has grown up in a family of evening parental cocktails. She watches her parents drink at dinners and adult parties. They look glamorous, happy, and relaxed. It seems to her that drinking brings comfort, ease, and fun. She feels pressured by schoolwork and parental expectations. She remembers where her parents keep their gin. She runs down to the kitchen and takes a gulping swig. She has begun experimenting.

Parents are gone all day working, and their children's curiosity is left unnurtured. These boys and girls roam the neighborhood and the streets, hang around malls all day, looking for something. They run into other kids from different parts of town whose pockets are filled with solvents, drugs, and alcohol. These are passed around. This group of children has started experimenting.

Other kids feel anxious and unhappy in their home situation. There is poverty, neglect, violence, drugs and alcohol. It helps to stay away from home as much as possible. These boys and girls are not sure what they feel, but they know they want to feel differently. Before they leave the house, they empty their parents' medicine cabinets of pills or liquids that might give them a buzz. AOD provides an immediate sense of relief and comfort. These kids on the street are experimenting.

Some students share their fears of losing control; they prefer not to explore the world of drugs and alcohol. Many test out experiences with one drug and not another. Other students like the thrill of experimenting with all of them.

A sizable percentage of individuals explore, experiment, or tentatively test what getting high feels like and what results it brings. For some, it's an unsatisfactory experience and usage comes to a halt rather quickly. Others have a mixed experience and return to it periodically. Still others are immediately taken by the danger, pleasure, and excitement and begin an ongoing search for more.

We have made experimentation into something dreadful and foreboding. Testing an unknown is not a bad thing. Sharing our response to our experimentation is a good thing. Conversations encourage ongoing monitoring of the pleasures and dangers involved in our desires to escape and expand consciousness.

Over the years, I have asked students in my semester classes and participants in my workshops the following question: How many of you have experimented with any or all of the nine psychoactives that we use to get high? More often than not, all of the students have raised their hands.

Take-It-or-Leave-It Use

A number of people have a take-it-or-leave-it attitude toward AOD. It is not a pocket of meaning in their lives. That is, it is not a habit or activity that they invest with importance and repetition. They do not pay attention to AOD; it is not a big interest in their lives and, therefore, it is not part of their planning.

A party either has alcohol or it doesn't—if it's there, fine, and if it's not, 7-Up is fine too. These people are not preoccupied with the place of alcohol in their lives; they barely give it any thought. There is no anticipation about the presence of alcohol, as there is for many who drink. There are also no regrets about one's experience with alcohol. Life feels full enough without drugs and alcohol, and life is enjoyed without the desire to get high. That being said, these folks are certainly capable of enjoying a glass of wine or a beer.

Take-it-or-leave-it people baffle many regular users of AOD. They generate envy in alcoholic or disordered users. "I watch people at a party or at a dinner and can't understand how they leave a glass of wine half full, not drink as much as they can get their hands on, or voluntarily refuse a glass of wine and choose an ice tea instead. I really can't fathom that." The drive to get high is so preoccupying to some and so incidental to others.

I conducted an informal survey while teaching a recent workshop. I asked the 50 students, "How many of you feel you belong in this profile?" One person raised his hand.

Social Use

Social drinkers are people who enjoy a drink or two in the company of others. They look forward to a night out with the girls or the boys and anticipate a relaxing glass of wine, beer, or spirits during an intimate dinner or at a festive gathering. They enjoy getting high with other people; they relish the relaxing effects. Social drinkers occasionally drink alone; they just don't make a habit of it.

Social drinkers imbibe to enhance a social event. They plan for a good time and gauge for any overindulgence. They usually do not want to lose control, ruin an evening, embarrass themselves, or feel any ill effects. They are gifted with an intuitive sense of moderation. They are fun loving and responsible. They enjoy sharing a buzz, know when to stop, and can also drive home. They are blessed with the capacity to learn from experience after that rare occasion of exceeding their limit. Their problems in life are not distorted by the effects of drugs and alcohol.

Social users like alcohol. Katie remembered, "This was a really tough week. My children and work were both too demanding. There was no time for me. All week I kept dreaming about my friend's 50th birthday party on Friday. I wanted to dress up and let go. Just thinking about the freedom and relaxation got me through the heartache of the week." Katie later described a really fun evening with laughter, friends, and acting silly. She had a glass of wine as soon as she arrived and switched to a diet coke before dinner.

All drinkers want to believe they belong in this profile. They may, or they may not. Katie seemed to.

Misuse

Sometimes we overindulge at a birthday lunch. We can later attend an evening event that same day and also drink too much. And we can do that on several occasions. Does that mean that we are on the road to alcoholism? Not necessarily. Check family history as well as the meaning behind the misuse of alcohol. Mishandling an attempt to satisfy a human desire does not justify hysterical and controlling responses.

Sally, a patient of mine, called one morning in an agitated and slightly panicky mood. When asked about recent activities, she described an unusual day of heavy drinking. It started with a farewell luncheon for a colleague at work. A designated driver invited many, including herself, to overdrink. She continued drinking at a social event with her husband that same night.

Sally's day and evening of drinking were noteworthy. She is not a regular drinker, nor does she have any family history with alcohol abuse. Her agitation was probably a result of a hangover from double-event drinking the day before.

Some misusers are "too inexperienced" to connect edgy apprehension with the withdrawal symptoms of overusing alcohol, which is a central nervous system depressant. I shared this with Sally, and she felt relieved that she was able to identify the source of her physiological panic and psychological discomfort. She could now wait it out until her symptoms disappeared.

Another student shared with the class, "I've made up this word—it's called 'time traveling.' It sounds like a symptom of misuse. Here's how it goes: I time travel when I drink too much. I wake up the next morning and remember how I started the evening, but can't remember how I got to the end of the evening. I remember the beginning and the end, but not much in between. That's time traveling." Another student added, "I do that too. I plan for a party night and I start out pounding drinks, and then I let these carry me through the evening. I feel some sense of control because I know I'm not going to drink anymore. I think that's why I remember only the beginning and end of the night." Both commented, "I hope it is only misuse. I better watch this." Many in the class smiled with recognition. More seemed alarmed by the universal frequency of this experience. There appears to be an element of choice in time traveling; this seems to distinguish it from a blackout (full amnesia) or a brownout (partial amnesia).

A social drinker feels a nice buzz, desires more, and regrets it later. A troubling pattern starts to develop. A workshop participant shared, "It's happening a little bit more than I would like." She described looking forward to a night of relaxing drinking with her friend. She liked the warm feeling of that first drink. It felt good; it calmed her down. She counseled herself, "I know I should stop and stay with this feeling of pleasure. Instead, I drink more and lose more control than I want. I am starting to get a little worried. I want to keep things at social drinking. I need to work harder at this."

Misusers are not afraid to acknowledge their mishaps and talk about their drinking anxieties. They prefer to address these, not hide them. They are not ashamed of overdoing it; it feels normal; "It's what all people do some of the time." Misusers have the ability to reverse this infrequent, but bothersome, behavior.

Abuse

The DSM-IV-TR identifies abuse as a maladaptive pattern of use leading to distress or impairment. To be diagnosed with abuse, one or more of the following symptoms must occur within a 12-month period (DSM-IV-TR, 2000, p. 199).

Abusive use

- Results in a failure to fulfill everyday role obligations
- Involves physical or psychological hazard

- Begets legal problems
- Produces health, relationship, work, family, and other problems
- Has not met the criteria for dependence

A substance abuser suffers from and lives with these sporadic negative consequences. These may include hangovers following evenings of embarrassing public displays under the influence. Sometimes it involves a fall while walking the dogs that results in an embarrassing bruise or black eye that is later lied about. "I was so embarrassed. A coyote ran down the hill and the dogs just took off. They yanked me so hard I lost my footing. They were so sweet. They stopped as soon as they saw me on the ground crying about my bruised eye."

Another incident may occur during a sporting accident while under the influence that ends up in an emergency room. The ER doctor comments and notes in the chart that there is alcohol on the breath. An executive is prescribed IV hydration for unhealthy exertion after a big night of drinking. Too many opiate nods are followed by a nap and a mom or a dad who misses another parent-teacher conference. Or a DUI arrest and a citation is issued with the subsequent required classes, videos, and meetings that shame, frighten, and terrify.

If you are abusing substances, chances are that the motivations for using are becoming more psychologically complex. Often it's no longer just about having fun or escaping. All too often, drinking occasions turn into unpredictable events followed by the abuser discounting what happened and why. Increased abuse brings worry and guilt, and an increasingly private monologue with yourself about behavior that you can't seem to control.

Problematic Use at a Problematic Time

A mom and dad with two children under 3 years old are working, parenting, and struggling with real and self-imposed impossible tasks (Obholzer and Roberts, 1994, pp. 110–118). Their lives are becoming too pressured and unfulfilling. Norris and Ann don't think they are managing well.

They invite a parent from another part of the country to live with them. They all share the same small apartment. Things become tense and Ann, a young mother with no previous interest in AOD, discovers that alcohol has become "mother's little helper" (Jagger and Richards, 1966). Occasional weekend evening drinking turns into daily habituation, beginning each evening at 5:00. Soon Ann's drinking escalates, involving hard liquor and in larger amounts. She drifts into day drinking on Saturday and Sunday. The children are vulnerable and suffering under her watch. Frightening and dangerous mishaps begin to occur. She is even missing days at work. Norris and Ann are surprised by this destructive and escalating trend and after a discussion agree that they do not want it to continue.

This nonadversarial couple increasingly lives in a panic and seeks help. There is no discounting the problem—not the existence, significance, or impact of the drinking on each other and the family (Lasater, 1988, pp. 30–31). At first blush, this looks and smells like alcoholism. After all, she has several symptoms of dependence, including tolerance, drinking larger amounts over longer periods of time than intended, and not fulfilling major role obligations. She is drinking seven days out of the week and can't imagine her life without the help of alcohol, and, at the same time, she is developing a sense that the alcohol is no longer helping.

Ann has no history of alcohol abuse or dependence, and there is none in her extended family. This couple works together as a team and wants to address the issue before it gets out of hand. They scare themselves and catch the problem before real habituation sets in. They both are internally motivated (Miller and Rollnick, 2002).

Using Lance Dodes's (2002) work, we explore ways that Ann and Norris both feel trapped. We identify drinking as the substitute action that she hoped would reverse her feelings of overwhelming helplessness. In five joint sessions, they nurtured a broader perspective while thinking about their dilemma, their lifestyle, and their choices. They began to make adjustments, and they quickly felt relief. Life soon felt more manageable, and the need to self-medicate with alcohol significantly decreased. They both became better problem solvers.

Behavior at problematic times can mimic more drastic diagnostic categories and seduce one into thinking of more draconian responses. We were able to reverse a short-lived unhealthy drinking pattern by exploring history, the current contextual demands, as well as noticing the considerable motivational strengths of each person. What looked and smelled like alcoholism was actually problematic use at a problematic time. The couple felt empowered and left therapy after four months. They greatly appreciated a therapeutic response that neither underdiagnosed Ann's problematic behaviors nor slapped on a label that was actually inaccurate.

Problem Use

According to the National Institute on Alcohol Abuse and Alcoholism (NIAAA) and other independent researchers, there are four times as many problem drinkers as alcoholics in this country (Moderation Management). This suggests that the highest percentage of people having issues with alcohol are not alcoholics. They are problem drinkers who experience ongoing problems but do not have a severe physical dependence on alcohol (Institute of Medicine). We offer the least amount of services for their nightly or weekend heavy drinking, their blackouts or brownouts, and/or their periodic or regular binge episodes. One of my students curiously commented, "Problem use seems like ongoing abuse to me." Two rather lengthy case studies reflect this oft-seen profile.

Problem drinkers are usually drinking not just for fun but also to cope. Life has gotten away from them, demands are overwhelming, and over time drinking has gotten sloppy. Difficulties mount in the financial and legal areas, as well as with physical and mental health, marital relationships or partnerships, children, and work. Honest discussions about these problems and difficulties stop working, and angry accusations abound. Despair is pervasive. A terrifying resignation permeates the household with the growing sense that there might not be a solution for this disturbing habit. Family members begin to live with a very unhealthy compromise and a destructive fantasy: "Maybe miraculously, without help and effort, things will get better; maybe the drinking will stop, and then we will no longer live in anticipatory terror of the next bad episode."

Drinking is occupying more attention in the drinker's mind. More time is spent planning for it and doing it. More often than not, the drinking is overdone and comes with a problem such as increased isolation, an angry outburst, or ignored children. The drinker defensively avoids any acknowledgement of drinking's destructions. All members of the household soon become discounters of what they see.

Agreements with a Couple

Over the years, I have attempted thoughtful responses for this complex profile. Usually one or both problem drinkers want to keep drinking, and they are not interested in Alcoholics Anonymous (AA) or abstinence. As one partner in a marriage said to me, "My problem with my drinking is that my wife has a problem with my drinking." While he admits he overdoes it, he wants to keep drinking and is not sure that help is out there for his goal. His wife is concerned that he is becoming an alcoholic. Nicholas and Joanna show up to begin therapy.

Here is a couple that seems to truly love each other. They value their marriage and their work, love their friends and their children, protect their health, and like their booze. More frequently, Nicholas's drinking comes with problems—drinking seven days a week instead of three, increased sloppiness and memory lapses, their shared fear of his inability to protect and care for the children, and his increasing isolation. He acknowledges these patterns. Joanna is worried and is haunted by growing up with an alcoholic mom.

Efran, Lukens, and Lukens (1990) introduce the notion of agreements. Simply stated, life works if you keep your agreements. We have agreements with ourselves and agreements with others. At any time, agreements are being kept, breached, or under renegotiation. Life works well if you keep your agreements; your life will not work as well if you breach them, or if you are secretly, privately, or even publicly renegotiating the terms of them. Life feels more cumbersome, edgy, and it gets messy during these times of reorganization or violation. This is a most practical mental health concept. Try it out; your life might work better (pp. 115–121).

I often use agreements with this profile. Agreements can be a useful tool with problem drinkers who want to solve their drinking problem. For starters, I want to make sure this is an ethical approach and not one that is colluding with the avoidance of the necessity for abstinence. I have developed eligibility criteria that help determine this profile's suitability. I used the following while assessing this couple:

- Is the drinking truly just problem drinking?
- Is the couple willing to be educated about what we know and don't know in the field of chemical dependency?
- Is the couple able to be nonadversarial? Do they want to problem solve together?
- Do they have pockets of meaning in their lives, other than alcohol? These are activities or habits that are invested with importance and nurturance (family, friends, hobbies, sports, work, religion, and so forth).
- Are they discounting the problem in any way?
- Do they want something so much they lose their judgment?

This couple met the suitability criteria and, with some assistance, devised agreements to address their drinking concerns.

The agreements were:

- Agreement #1: Monday through Thursday—drink Calistoga water
- Agreement #2: Friday night—drink as much alcohol as you want
- Agreement #3: Saturday and Sunday night—two glasses of wine or beer each
- Agreement #4: Directly address infractions

The couple was internally motivated and quickly rehabituated their drinking behaviors (Miller and Rollnick, 2002). They settled into a new lifestyle. The results were steady and promising, and our therapy conversations cleared up any confusions. A mishap needed some attention.

Nicholas went on a business trip during the week. It was supposed to be a Calistoga night. He was "away from home, children, and responsibilities," and he broke Agreement #1 and drank two glasses of wine. He chose to keep this breach and subsequent desire for agreement renegotiation from Joanna until our next session. She was not happy with the news, and he was embarrassed and remorseful. Life was not working well. Consequently, a new agreement was created about weekly business trips. Let's call it Agreement #1a: Two small glasses of wine while on a business trip.

Delightfully, the couple left after six months, content with their agreements. They seemed to experience therapy as a place to get down to business. He called for a session six months later. He noticed some agreement sloppiness, and he wanted to talk. We did, and he has not called since. I suspect they would return if they were unable to negotiate their drinking agreements. Not all can do this, but more can if we conduct a proper assessment and provide helpful tools. Read further.

Agreements with an Individual

Daniel was 41 years old when we began therapy. He mechanically described a neglectful and violent childhood. He started smoking marijuana and drinking at age 11. He added cocaine to the mix in his late teens. He used drugs and drank heavily for decades. Daniel went to law school, passed the bar, and decided to pass on being an attorney. He became a writer. His dream was to sell a screenplay. He married and divorced. He was surviving and enduring without much feeling or meaning. He didn't know the difference; he just knew that he liked to drink and do drugs "as often and as much as I could."

Daniel's drinking and drugging days gradually came to an end after his girlfriend, Julie, "kept making such a big deal out of all my partying. She got on my case a lot; it bugged me. We fought; our relationship almost came to an end. And then her concerns started to make sense." Daniel took to abstinence with sincerity and passion. He came to therapy weekly. He cherished his sober mind and experiences. His writing improved, he lived with more ease with his girlfriend, and he began valuing different kinds of friends. "I've never felt this clearheaded or good about myself."

Daniel occasionally mentioned a desire to drink again during his first year of sobriety, but he repeatedly admonished himself: "I want to make it to one year. I've never been sober for that long. But, eventually, I also want to include alcohol in my life. I want to enjoy it with others, but I don't want to lose control, and I don't want to lose the mental and emotional clarity that I've gained in this last year. I've talked it over with Julie, and we both agree it's worth exploring in therapy. I want to make social drinking a part of my recovery."

Daniel talked extensively about why he wanted to drink and concluded, "It's a risk I want to responsibly take on." He seemed ready, willing, and able to explore and reexamine this option (Miller and Rollnick, 2002, p. 10).

Daniel wanted to use therapy as an accountability tool. He felt able to self-soothe anxieties that had always been silenced with alcohol. He relished his developing ability to think before impulsively acting out. He didn't want drinking to interfere with his growth. He was willing to address any mishaps and return to sobriety if needed.

He was intrigued by the idea of agreements. Daniel queried me about their use with other patients. Later, he and Julie talked for hours; they designed a plan.

It would begin after a luxurious vacation to a faraway land. He did not want to drink during his travels. "I'm trying to see if I can bring drinking back into my everyday life, not my vacation life."

Daniel designed his agreements, took to heart successful and not-so-successful results, and crafted new ones. His first agreement was two drinks on one weekend night (2 in 1). He loved that first drink, the ease it brought, and the fun he felt. He sensed instantly that his experiment was probably going to work. He didn't want to get drunk; he wanted to enjoy the buzz with Julie. He was content with 2 in 1 for months, and then he wanted more. Daniel and Julie designed a new agreement—two drinks on two nights during the week (2 in 2). This also went well for months.

Toward the end of that first year, Daniel went to Las Vegas. He willingly succumbed to the enticement of this extravagant partying environment. He broke his 2-in-2 agreement. He got drunk for the first time, very quickly recalled being an everyday drunk, and didn't like it. He suffered through the forgotten feelings of a hangover. It took days for his head to clear. He hated the ill health he felt. "I kept dreading talking about this to you in therapy."

The results of our Vegas postmortems brought a new agreement—one the reader might not imagine. Daniel continued to relish clear-headed moderation, but he also wanted to enjoy the pleasures of drinking a few nights out of the week. He believed he had gotten drunk in Vegas because "to tell you the truth, two drinks have never really done it for me. I'm 6 foot 4, you know." He voiced a new desire—"I want to experiment with getting a real buzz and see how I do. I really think I'm ready for this and can handle it, and I want to see how it goes." His new agreement was three drinks on two nights during the week (3 in 2).

Daniel developed a capacity not always seen in alcoholic drinkers. He was excited by risk yet also valued responsibility. He successfully and comfortably abided by his 3-in-2 agreement for quite some time. We regularly tracked the relationship between his moods and his agreements. He periodically stopped drinking when it was interfering with everyday problem solving and enjoyment in living. Daniel felt very good about his ability to make this decision and stick to it. I'm always comforted by Michael Eigen's wisdom, "We must always give our patients space to do their best or their worst" (Personal Communication, 2008). This applies to some of our problem-drinking patients as well.

Shadow Use

Forme fruste is an unconventional medical term used to describe an incomplete expression of an illness (Ratey and Johnson, 1997, p. 33). These two doctors identify shadow syndromes as mild or subtle forms of otherwise serious mental disorders (p. 36). The more disabling symptoms of a diagnosis may not be present, but enough appear and cast a shadow over one's life. This incapacity impairs one's enjoyment of love and work. These syndromes serve as shadow expressions of some of the diagnostic categories delineated in the DSM-IV-TR, including substance dependence and abuse.

This profile identifies persons whose lives are going relatively well. They have jobs, friends, children, and homes. They pay their bills, and they show up for life. They also drink or drug nearly 365 days of the year. They never miss a beat, and AOD on the surface seems under control.

Over time, some underlying tensions may emerge. Increasingly, the user is less interested in participating in family activities, or if he does, he is always under the influence. Nights of drinking or drugging are never missed, conversations among family members decrease, and the distance between and among family members slowly increases. Traveling becomes problematic and cumbersome. The first stop after arrival is a liquor store or a dealer. While all seems okay on the surface, this once-benign intruder is now robbing family members of vitality and spontaneity.

The distance and lack of connectivity take their toll, and eventually someone in the family starts drawing attention to himself, better known as acting out. Help is sought, and in the mix of investigative and reparative efforts, the shadow using begins to get some attention. Ideally, this invites reflection into the meaning of this intoxication ritual, including its impact on the user and his family.

One of my patients, Sam, who is in his 40s, is attached to a substance on a daily basis and is a shadow syndrome user. He is married with three children, ambitious and financially stable, exercises regularly and works very hard at being a provider, husband, and father. He is also psychologically dependent on his daily relaxant. He openly discusses his "marijuana maintenance program" with his wife, and together they are ever watchful that this entrenched pattern does not get in the way of their relationship, evening duties, and the children. He wants to avoid any escalation of using, and he also doesn't want to stop his nightly ritual of 3 one-hitters (miniature smoking pipe designed for a single inhalation, or "hit," of cannabis or tobacco) over a four-hour period.

Sam increased his use during a very stressful period of time. Graduate studies overpowered his emotions and his judgment. He felt unable to cope with multiple pressures, and convinced himself that his increased usage was only temporary. We engaged in a very focused exploration into the meaning of this escalating every-evening ritual. Sam uncomfortably, but willingly, considered the avoidance function of his shadow syndrome use. Overwhelming demands felt frustrating, expectations felt threatening, his inability to experience the pleasures of fatherhood felt troubling, and his increasing secrecy with his wife felt even more so. His nightly reliance was no longer primarily about relaxing.

Sam begrudgingly faced the dysfunction of his increased daily dependence. He was able to be more truthful with himself, talked more with his wife, and sought out his sober marijuana friends. He explored different patterns of using, was defensive and protective for a while, faced a habit that had become invasive and consuming, and decided to stop using. He is content with his sobriety and values his emotional reawakening. He periodically announces, "One day I want to return to social using." We talk. I encourage him to continue letting his experiences build without AOD interference. He agrees.

Not all shadow syndrome users are able to arrest or reverse the insidious creeping destructive potential of this profile of using. Not all are able to reverse these troubling patterns. Some escalate into deeper trouble. Sam and his wife are a nonadversarial and nondiscounting couple. They value their passions and nurture each other and their lives. They finally saw what they didn't want to see.

Ratey and Johnson's (1997) original book cover was designed with a question above a round plastic mirror. The question was, "Do you know someone with a shadow syndrome?"

Psychological Dependency, Not Yet Physical

Alcohol, the opiates, and the sedative hypnotics have the potential to produce physical and psychological dependency. Increased use disturbs, disrupts, and resets both the mind and body's homeostatic balance, or resting point. The problem user becomes dependent on maintaining this new normal. In this profile, physical addiction is being held at desperate bay. Just enough of the drug is used to stave off the symptoms of physical withdrawal, and to quiet the escalating sense of helplessness and frustration from the permeating recognition of psychological dependency. The user senses that total loss of control is looming. Family and friends are both frantic and silenced.

The AOD use is secretly and tragically consuming more of the person's time. Life's tasks are about endurance, not meaning and fulfillment. The only hope is to complete them so that drinking and using can resume. People are desperately functioning while using increasing amounts of AOD. Pockets of meaning are discarded, isolation increases, and a sense of despair overwhelms. The possibility of not using is incomprehensible. Each night of heavy drinking is deathlike, and upon awakening, a new day of resurrection feels miraculous (Szasz, cited in Levin, 2001, pp. 213–214). This grim path is followed until it no longer can be.

The Dilaudid (and opiate) user does not want to be dope-sick at work. Shira is convinced that she is cleverly avoiding physical collapse with careful strategic dosing, just enough to take care of any physical withdrawal. Her real desire is to psychologically prove she is beating addiction, as well as self-medicating away the ever-frightening realization that life with this opiate is surely coming to an end.

The busy attorney's ambition is increasingly and frenetically focused on rearranging appointments, getting the minimum accomplished, avoiding every other attorney at both work and social engagements. The point is to get his work done and get home to drink. By now, most of his drinking time is alone. He drinks quickly and repeatedly functions in a blackout. His hope is that he did not use the phone during his alcohol-induced amnesia (see James in Chapter 12, p. 267).

Eventually, both are forced to fold into physical or psychic collapse. The final hours and days are lived in withdrawal from everyday functioning with close to around-the-clock using and passing out.

Friends or family frequently find these persons in some degree of intoxicated incoherence, often near a coma. The next step is an emergency room, likely in preparation for rehabilitation treatment. After awakening in the ER, most in this profile are silenced with terror and the realization that it is finally time to end this tortured life of isolation, secrecy, intoxication, and deep misery. Most often, this profile results in a life of abstinence and sobriety.

Dependence

The DSM-IV-TR identifies dependence as a maladaptive pattern of using, leading to distress or impairment. To be diagnosed with dependence, one demonstrates three or more of the following symptoms, occurring at any time, in the same 12-month period (DSM-IV-TR, 2000, pp. 197–198):

Dependent use

- Produces tolerance—an increase or decrease in the amount of the substance needed to achieve the original effect
- Results in withdrawal and more susbtance use to medicate this uncomfortable state
- Involves using larger amounts over longer periods of time than intended
- Results in failed attempts to reduce or control usage
- Begets an increased preoccupation—the substance becomes the central organizing principle in the addict's life
- Results in a failure to fulfill role obligations
- Produces problems

The person in this profile is using AOD 24/7. His psychological and physical dependency requires this. He is often waking up, having a swig or a hit before or in his coffee. He continues nipping throughout the day and evening. This continues into weeks, into months, and, for some, into years. Concerned pleas are ignored or angrily responded to, and friends feel alienated and exhausted. Family talks are often met with the addict's hardened desire to continue using. The dependent person feels fated to his existence; he imagines that he will use, and live this way, for the rest of his life.

To avoid over- or underdiagnosing in this profile, I have designed three additional criteria to add to the DSM list of dependent symptoms. These somewhat quirky and imaginative terms and concepts have sharpened my assessment capacities over the years. They warn me of upcoming psychological and/or physical dependency, or confirm their presence.

Use of these terms solidifies my clinical hunches and prepares me for the possibility of direct interventions that authoritatively propose abstinence (Molino, 1998, p. 128). A clinician needs this confidence to guide someone who is aggressively ambivalent about his escalating dependency. Testing positive for all three criteria authoritatively suggests that surrendering to this weary and futile battle is necessary, that abstinence is the unavoidable and best course of recovery.

These terms are described below; a clinical question is posed and their application is demonstrated in a clinical case:

The Mess Factor (Is it high, medium, or low?): Truly dependent individuals don't have problems due to using—they have messes. They live in a world of financial, health, family, physical, and work disasters. A work mess collides with a financial one. A health mess collides with a family one. Life is about dodging these messes and figuring out a way to stay high.

A high mess factor suggests that wanting and needing drugs and alcohol so much have severely incapacitated any kind of judgment. The addict is tragically unable to anticipate and address life's responsibilities and difficulties. Feeding his physical and psychological dependency is paramount, staving off the consequences of withdrawal and his messes a mainstay. The addict's collapse is his final mess. Abstinence is needed to reverse this destructive trend.

The Length of the Moratorium (Is it long, medium, or short?): Leon Wurmser (1978), a psychoanalytic addiction psychiatrist, proposes that all addiction is about a moratorium on the development of age-appropriate skills. During this developmental time-out period, the addict repeatedly uses AOD to assist in problem solving. This overreliance on an external substance results in a severe deficiency in the establishment of psychological and behavioral coping skills. Users are unable to face everyday distress, and are incapacitated by their incapacities.

The length of the moratorium measures the years people have used AOD to address or avoid emotional difficulties and everyday problems. During this time, alcohol and drugs have resided in the addict's back pocket, always available and ready to be pulled out and used in times of upset or stress. The constant return to this choice prevents the development of necessary life skills. A medium or long moratorium begs for abstinence. Without it, it is too tempting to rely on that back pocket again and again to repeatedly dodge facing reality. Abstinence forces the alcoholic and addict to draw on his own internal and external resources in ways never used before. Psychic capacity is then built, and new problem-solving skills are developed.

Pockets of Meaning (Are they decreasing? Is there only one left?): This lovely term, very loosely adapted from Jay Efran's work, is also diagnostic (Efran et al., 1990, p. xv). I have previously defined *pockets of meaning* as passions that are invested with importance. These are the things that are valuable in a person's life, the things people pocket and protect. These may include children, family, friends, hobbies, religion, or work. There is only one pocket of meaning in the world of the dependent alcoholic or addict. Life is about survival, and the substance is perceived as the only thing that can ensure that. Other pockets of meaning have long since been discarded.

This loss or lack of interest in protecting ongoing pockets of meaning or discovering new ones strongly suggests that people are paying attention to AOD too much, and for the wrong reasons. Courageously letting go of this perceived pocket of survival allows abstinence to become the primary pocket of meaning. Sobriety delivers time, and with it, a chance to discover new meanings and passions.

Dean—Messes, Moratorium, and Meaning

A 27-year-old man calls for appointments over a six-month period. During one brief phone conversation, he hesitantly reveals an alcohol problem that started at age 13. Dean either cancels scheduled appointments or does not return my calls. His ambivalence is obvious. Finally, gastritis, pancreatitis, elevated liver enzymes, severe pain, an emergency room visit, doctor's orders, and family pressures alarm him. He arrives at my office. He was able to stay off alcohol for two weeks and then began drinking again. "Nothing really changed in two weeks." He added, "I just don't want to be an alcoholic."

And so a relationship is forged, he reporting that "things" are bad but not that bad, and me searching to find him in his hiding place, in order to provide the right level of care. The room temperature is a relaxed sense of urgency.

Dean keeps drinking, increases his physical isolation as well as his psychic retreating (see Chapter 11, pp. 205–210). He stops surfing, seeing friends, and talking with his family. He stops working. He has no money. His family believes he is sober while in treatment; he comes to a few sessions, smelling of alcohol. Suggestions to attend AA meetings, undergo intensive outpatient care, and involve his parents in his treatment are given polite lip service and then ignored. As I begin to think and plan for an in-patient treatment option, he is planning an exotic trip to a tropical island. What a mismatch. It has been three months of twice-weekly sessions and I begin to feel uneasy. The growing attachment between us felt right; however, the level of treatment for him felt wrong.

Let's reflect on messes, moratoriums, and pockets of meaning and use these clinical descriptors to determine the best level of treatment for Dean. Remember, testing "positive" for all three strongly suggests both physical and psychological dependency with its necessity for abstinence.

Dean's mess factor was high. He had overwhelming difficulties with his family, his friends, his ability to work, his finances, and his physical health. The length of his moratorium was long; almost half of his young life had been preoccupied with drinking. Very few age-appropriate skills were nurtured and developed during his years of overreliance on alcohol. Pockets of meaning were rapidly decreasing. These positive test results suggested that Dean needed a level of treatment that would protect him from his incapacities and promote the beginning days of his abstinence.

Higher levels of care conversations are always anxiety provoking and difficult. A clash of wills is likely to develop; things can get very messy and go very wrong. There is always the risk that a caring therapeutic relationship can get blown apart.

I consulted Los Angeles psychoanalyst and dual-diagnosis medical service treatment director Ron Sager and received some sage advice: "It sounds like you are worried about Dean and feel that a higher level of care is the right thing to do." I agreed, and Sager offered, "Trust your gut, do what you think is right, and see what happens" (Personal Communication, 2008). This is profound wisdom for everyday life, and is very useful while making assertive treatment decisions for addicts and alcoholics who have tragically and destructively lost their way in life. I heard my gut, listened to what it had to say, recommended my sense of the right level of care, let it go, and let Dean decide.

Dean was hostile and abusive. He also wanted to hear more about my suggestion. Our discussions took place during very emotionally intense therapy sessions or agitated phone calls afterward. I asked Dean to involve his parents, to let them know of our mismatched plans and my suggestion for a higher level of protection and care. Over two phone calls, I reflected back to him his words from his hiding place that he had shared with me in previous sessions: "I'm drinking too much and drinking too often. I'm in trouble. I'm lost and alone. Nothing is getting better. Tell me what to do. I'm scared and I know that what you are telling me is right. I'll listen to you, doc."

Dean bargained and pleaded with me. I simply said, "It's time." I repeated, "It's time for your parents, time for more care, and time for more protection. Let's meet with your mom and talk. Let's tell her that you're still drinking, even after your pancreatitis attack, and that you are having a really hard time listening to your physician's orders. Let's tell her that you are worried—let's ask her for her help."

I strongly urged him to call his mom, and I reminded him that for legal and ethical reasons, I might have to do so. He panicked, I became weary, we unraveled a bit, and he cried out, "Don't I have any recourse?" I lost my "balance" and replied, "Dean, you don't have to accept my recommendation." He asked, "Can I fire you?" I felt my relief, his relief, and our relief, and responded, "You always have that choice." He quickly shouted back, "You're fired!" and hung up.

Panic, anxiety, regret, and second-guessing immediately flooded my mind. For days I worried and sought out more consultation with Ron Sager. With support and perspective, I reclaimed my gut and knew that my recommendation for a higher level of care was the right thing to do for this patient. I reaffirmed this, as well as his decision to terminate treatment, in a letter. He did not respond.

Half a year later, his parents called me, concerned about Dean's isolation and excessive drinking. I informed them that I would be willing to talk but I could not disclose anything until I received their son's permission. Read Chapter 10 to learn of further development in Dean's treatment (p. 178).

CHAPTER SUMMARY AND REFLECTIONS

Summary

The current "discipline of diagnosis" is filled with shortcomings, uncertainties, and intimidations. This chapter considered these confusions and proposed 12 descriptive profiles of using and addiction that have been observed over 20 years of recovery treatment. Out of ignorance and anxiety, there is a tendency to overdiagnose or underdiagnose. These profiles encourage creative responses to the diagnostic complexities of addiction. Hopefully the material in this chapter will enhance diagnostic thinking and sharpen level-of-care decisions for our patients. Readers are encouraged to continue developing their own descriptive profiles as they advance in their professional treatment careers.

Reflections

Before leaving this chapter, make sure you have:

- Comprehended the meanings behind the development of these descriptive profiles
- Explored their uses and limitations
- Considered your own profile or profiles of using
- Understood the ethics as well as the creativity involved in diagnosing this complex phenomenon

Chapter 5

Eleven Classes of Psychoactive Substances

INTRODUCTION

This chapter introduces the reader to the 11 classes or types of psychoactive drugs that we ignore or enjoy, abuse or misuse, become destructively dependent upon, and then, if fortunate, refrain from using. Oftentimes the 11 psychoactives are clustered into categories, such as depressants, stimulants, or analgesics. This chapter considers each individual psychoactive as identified in the *Diagnostic and Statistical Manual of Mental Disorders* (DSM-IV-TR, 2000).

People repeatedly seek out nine mood-altering AOD (alcohol and other drugs) psychoactives and often seek out psychotherapy for their troubles with them. These nine (alcohol, amphetamines, cannabis, cocaine, inhalants, hallucinogens, opiates/opioids, phencyclidine [PCP], and sedatives, hypnotics, and anxiolytics) are the focus of this book, as well as this chapter. Caffeine and nicotine are included in this chapter's reference charts to complete the 11 types of psychoactive drugs.

There are more than 15,000 texts written on substance dependence and abuse. All of them cover the 11 classes of psychoactive substances in varying degrees of depth. Scientists, treatment providers, and academicians devote anywhere from 11 paragraphs to 11 pages to 11 chapters to these mind- and mood-altering substances. Topics for each psychoactive may include:

- Historical, medical, and recreational uses
- Legal issues
- Methods of administration, absorption, distribution, biotransformation, and elimination
- Pharmacology and side effects

- Neuroadaption, tolerance, and dependence potential
- Withdrawal features
- Short- and long-term impacts on the digestive, cardiovascular, endocrine, reproductive, emotional, and neurologic systems
- Pharmacological treatments
- Current and future research

Our understanding of the pharmacology, brain interactions, and medical complications of each of the psychoactives is rapidly evolving. The field is indebted to, indeed, dependent upon on, the writers of scientific texts. They devote a substantial amount of time and research toward updating this body of knowledge. They provide a generous gift to treatment providers, addicts and their families, and students.

Most of us don't have the education or background to easily comprehend the science of how the 11 psychoactives enter and leave our brains and bodies, the physical damage they cause, or the pharmacology of their treatment. We are dizzied and derailed by the details and soon become disoriented and disinterested. Eyes glaze. The mind feels dull. The task of learning appears daunting, and we soon give up trying. We don't know where or how to start. This chapter is designed to provide such a start—to present the basics of these drugs of pleasure or prescription in, hopefully, a blessedly brief and useful form.

This chapter is divided into two sections. *Basic Neuroscience* begins with a simple explanation of how and why psychoactives work in our brains and how naturally occurring endogenous highs are adulterated by ingestion of these. *Reference Charts* includes 11 easy-to-use charts of the psychoactives. These charts provide the key points necessary to develop a foundational grasp of these mind-altering substances, and are also useful for both clinical assessment and treatment. Reference texts are highly recommended to further one's own knowledge, provide answers to perplexing questions, offer guidance during clinical emergencies, and, more importantly, assist our patients and their families in their own education process (see Further Study section at the end of this chapter, p. 70).

BASIC NEUROSCIENCE

To understand how drugs and alcohol work, let's review some basic neuroscientific information about cells, neurons, and neurotransmitters. We begin with the cells of the brain called neurons and the communication signals that are passed on from one neuron to another. Neurotransmitters are the chemical messengers that carry these communication signals. They leave one cell, move across the synaptic cleft, and are introduced to another cell through receptor sites. These endogenous neurotransmitter messengers play important roles in mind-body regulation (Erickson, 2007, pp. 42–44).

Here are a few examples. Serotonin levels determine our feelings of depression or well-being; dopamine affects the experience of pleasure and pain; norepinephrine regulates many bodily functions, including growth and digestion; acetylcholine activates muscle tissue and gland activity; endorphins are involved in both pain regulation and feelings of euphoria; and endocannabinoids also influence mood and pain control. In addition, the amino acids glutamate and GABA (gamma-amino-butyric acid) act like neurotransmitters. Glutamate excites or agitates, while GABA inhibits or relaxes (Erickson, 2007, pp. 42–43).

The chemical structures of basic drug molecules are similar to endogenous neurotransmitters. Consequently, once in the brain, the drug molecules are able to join ongoing neuronal activity. They introduce a new message that increases or decreases existing neurotransmitter communications (Erickson, 2007, p. 42). This produces a high, a low, or something in between (Inaba and Cohen, 2007).

The fundamental point here is that natural mood- and mind-altering neurochemical pathways exist in the central nervous system. Endogenous molecules travel from neuron to neuron on these pathways, attaching at a specific receptor site. They give the new cell directions that influence our physical and emotional state of being. The more salient point here is that drugs and alcohol work on these existing pathways—they do not create new ones (See Table 5.1). They work on what is already working. They modify normal neuron functioning of the

Table 5.1 The Relationship Between AOD and Neurotransmitter Systems

Drug	*Neurotransmitter or Amino Acids (aa) Directly Affected*
Alcohol	GABA (aa), Glutamate (aa)
Benzodiazepines	GABA (aa)
Marijuana	Endocannabinoids
Opioids	Endorphins
Hallucinogens (LSD, PCP)	Serotonin
Cocaine and Amphetamines	Norepinephrine, acetylcholine
Ecstasy	Serotonin, dopamine, adrenaline
Inhalants	Dopamine, GABA (aa), glutamate (aa)
Nicotine	Acetylcholine, serotonin, dopamine, Norepinephrine, epinephrine
Caffeine	Dopamine, norepinephrine, GABA (aa)

Source: Erickson, 2007, pp. 42–45; Schuckit, 2010, pp. 279–288.

brain; they strengthen or weaken a potential that already exists. Psychoactives affect each of us because they amplify or decrease, mimic or disrupt ongoing neurotransmitter messages in the body (Doweiko, 2009, p. 46; Erickson, 2007, p. 42).

Simply put, psychoactives (drugs and alcohol) cannot create sensations and feelings that don't have a natural counterpart. Again, this implies that human beings are able to naturally create virtually all of the sensations and feelings we try to get through drugs. There are four big differences: (1) the drug or alcohol experience is a more intense one; (2) the timing of their impact is more predictable; (3) drug or alcohol effects weaken with repeated use; and finally, (4) drugs or alcohol carry deleterious side effects (Inaba & Cohen, 2007, p. 61).

So, for example, let's look at the natural ways our neurotransmitter messages work on the brain and how these allow AOD molecules to produce mind- and mood-altering results.

Good teaching requires a tremendous amount of energy. Many a professor, preparing for an 8 a.m. class, panics after a sleepless night. She gradually learns that her "fight" response will release the neurotransmitter norepinephrine, also called noradrenaline. Despite exhaustion, she will suddenly feel more aroused and alert. She will benefit from her "natural" production of speed. Her teaching will feel energized. The psychoactive stimulants work on this same neurotransmitter system.

Regular daily joggers benefit from a runner's high. Natural endorphins are released, and the runner feels euphoric. Ongoing psychological and physical pain is diminished. Consequently, the serious daily runner thrives in this altered state of well-being. This often fuels tremendous output and accomplishment. It is imagined that these endogenous pain relievers mitigate the psychological and physical suffering that accompanies these high levels of productivity. Heroin and other opiates also influence this endorphin neurotransmitter system.

Working the overnight shift in a psychiatric hospital or emergency room results in overwhelming and uncomfortable fatigue. This sleepiness often produces visual and auditory hallucinations. This natural trip is initiated by endogenous serotonin activity. The hallucinogens work on this neurotransmitter system as well.

Finally, relaxation exercises such as yoga and meditation calm the individual through increased release of the amino acid GABA. It takes discipline, effort, and time to achieve these natural, soothing benefits. The antianxiety medications, the benzodiazepines, also relieve stress and panic. The results are felt in 20 minutes. This speedy and predictable response, unfortunately, entices too many in the United States, and others around the world.

These introductory neuroscience notes provide a rudimentary and working background for using the reference charts that follow.

REFERENCE CHARTS

The charts on the following pages are quick, easy, and useful reference guides. They are designed to include the key content necessary for understanding the basic essentials of each of the psychoactives listed in the DSM-IV-TR. The material has been gleaned from multiple sources—reading and studying technical texts on chemical dependency, teaching and listening to student stories over decades, and listening to and learning from my patients. The historical and factual materials have been gathered from the texts identified in the Further Reading section in this chapter. The number of featured categories is intended to neither overwhelm nor underwhelm the reader with AOD facts. This selective grouping is a concise guideline for assistance during treatment.

The categories are described below.

- Material in italics: A factoid of historical interest
- Group: Examples of the pills, powders, or liquids in each psychoactive class and their effects on the mind and body
- Pattern of Use: Method of administration
- Natural History: The likely number of years and patterns of using AOD (Vaillant, 1983, pp. 107–180)
- Potential for Dependence: Physical and psychological dependence potential—high, medium, or low
- Withdrawal: Short- and long-term physical and psychological symptoms that appear after a dependent user stops using
- Points to Ponder: Selective clinical considerations and salient features

(1) ALCOHOL

A part of human culture since the beginning of recorded history. Making sense of alcohol's place in human culture engenders avoidance and conflict.

Group

- Beer, wine, liqueurs, distilled spirits
- These are central nervous system depressants.

Pattern of Use

- Oral

Natural History

- 25 years to a lifetime of dependent use
- 15 years of problematic use
- 15 years of poly, or mixed, AOD use and experimentation

Potential for Dependence

- Physical—High
- Psychological—High

Withdrawal

- Initial acute withdrawal of 24–96 hours includes the following symptoms: hyperarousal, anxiety, irritability, insomnia, tachycardia, delirium tremors, agitation, sweating, vertigo, alcohol hallucinations, muscle weakness, excessive fatigue, irritability, incontinence.
- Alcohol has a 2-year protracted withdrawal period with decreasing severity and frequency of symptoms.
- BAC (blood alcohol content) over 0.35 signals danger of overdose.
- Alcohol overdose or death results from suffocation on one's own vomit or respiratory failure.
- Treatment of overdose involves hospitalization with respiratory, hydration, and vitamin monitoring and support.

Points to Ponder

- Alcohol is the most popular psychoactive pleasure in the world. It isn't easy for people to learn how to enjoy, not exceed, this central nervous system relaxant.
- The health benefits of alcohol depend on a person's age, gender, and overall medical history; used intelligently, alcohol can relieve stress (Erickson, 2007, p. 131).
- Alcohol releases a neurotransmitter called GABA, which results in euphoria, slow reaction times, and impaired muscle control. The brain then releases a stimulating chemical called glutamate. When alcohol is cut off, glutamate remains high and causes irritability and discomfort. The brain craves another drink to relieve this irritability. Campral, a newer pharmacological treatment, helps the brain resist these cravings by checking the production of glutamate; it brings brain chemistry back into balance (Erickson, 2007, p. 69).
- Alcohol recovery always involves the working through of anxieties about interpersonal closeness and intimacy.

(2) AMPHETAMINES

Scientists have discovered ephedra plants thought to be 60,000 years old. The Chinese used ephedra for medicinal purposes 5,000 years ago. Ephedra was used for asthma in 1930. Amphetamines were synthesized as a result of ephreda's high demand.

Group

- Dexedrine, Desoxyn (meth), Ritalin, Adderall, Ephedrine, diet pills, Ecstasy
- These are central nervous system stimulants.

Pattern of Use

- Oral
- Intravenous (IV)—into a vein
- Intramuscular (IM)—into a muscle
- Nasal inhalation
- Smoked

Natural History

- 25 years to a lifetime of dependent use
- 15 years of episodic and binge using
- 1–5 years of poly drug use and experimentation

Potential for Dependence

- Physical—Debated in the literature
- Psychological—High

Withdrawal

- Withdrawal is most intense for 3 to 5 days but remains in decreasing intensity for weeks and months.
- Symptoms include craving, irritability, agitation, aggressiveness, restlessness, insomnia, fatigue, depression, and anhedonia (inability to experience pleasure).

Points to Ponder

- Amphetamines massively increase the amount of dopamine in the synaptic cleft. Amphetamines work through this release, as well as from blocking the reuptake of other neurotransmitters (Erickson, 2007, p. 41).
- It is estimated that 60–80% of amphetamine users simultaneously drink alcohol (Schuckit, 2010, p. 140).
- Repeated use can temporarily decrease the number of dopamine receptor sites and severely damage the brain's pleasure centers. There is some evidence of reversal after long-term abstinence.
- Amphetamine-acting substances are found in many over-the-counter products. They provide easy responses to fatigue, stress, and depression.
- Amphetamines enter the bloodstream very quickly when smoked or injected. This leads to a rapid high and to a greater likelihood of toxicity.
- When used carefully, Ritalin can be very effective for the treatment of attention deficit hyperactivity disorder (ADHD) and does not necessarily predispose the child to drug dependence.

(3) CANNABIS

The industrial, medical, and recreational use of the cannabis plant has a long history, beginning in 8000 BC.

Group

- Marijuana—unprocessed leaves, dried flowers, seeds, and stems of the plant
- Hash—processed from the resin of the plant; cakes/lumps—hashish; oily liquid—hash oil
- THC (tetrahydrocannabinol)—the active chemical in cannabis resin—the primary mind-altering agent
- Cannabis produces variable effects—stimulant, depressant, relaxant, psychedelic.

Pattern of Use

- Smoked in a pipe, joint
- Eaten in food
- Drunk in tea
- Ingested from a pill

Natural History

- 25 years to a lifetime of dependent use
- 15 years of a pattern of on-and-off use—on during the weekend or nighttime, off during the week or daytime
- 1–5 years of poly drug use and experimentation

Potential for Dependence

- Physical—Low
- Psychological—High

Withdrawal

- Symptoms include irritability, restlessness, mental confusion, anxiety, depression, cravings, insomnia, and agitation.
- No documented case of fatal overdose exists (Earleywine, 2002, p. 11).

Points to Ponder

- Marijuana is the most commonly consumed illicit drug, with 200 to 300 million users worldwide (Earleywine, 2002, p. 47).
- The experience of marijuana is influenced by one's mindset and one's physical and emotional setting; it is referred to as a set/setting drug.
- Strength of preparation of hemp depends on the resin content; some strains produce a great deal of resin; others do not.
- With increased use, tolerance develops. People learn to adapt to being high—they soon can perform normal activities while under the influence. Consequently, using marijuana 24/7 is not uncommon and is an extremely hard habit to break.
- The concept of marijuana as a gateway drug is seriously questioned (Earleywine, 2002, p. 64).
- Marijuana has many established medicinal purposes—from serious medical problems to mild ailments.
- The federal government is waging an intense fight against medical marijuana use in certain states.

(4) COCAINE

Derived from the pulped leaf of the South American coca plant. Cultivated by natives of South America for thousands of years. Chewed daily throughout parts of the world.

Group

- Coca leaves, coca paste, cocaine hydrochloride powder, cocaine alkaloid
- These are central nervous system (CNS) stimulants.

Pattern of Use

- Coca leaves are chewed.
- Coca paste is smoked.
- Cocaine hydrochloride powder is snorted or injected.
- Cocaine alkaloid is smoked or injected.

Natural History

- 1–5 years of daily, dependent, and dangerous use
- 5–30 years of a mix of daily use, episodic use, and binge use
- 1–5 years of poly drug use and experimentation

Potential for Dependence

- Physical—Debated in the literature
- Psychological—High

Withdrawal

- Acute withdrawal of 36 hours includes symptoms of anhedonia, craving, paranoia, agitation, fatigue, chills, nausea, headache, vomiting, and muscle tremors.
- Post-acute withdrawal of 7–10 days includes symptoms of fatigue and flulike symptoms.

Points to Ponder

- Cocaine increases the amount of dopamine in the synaptic cleft by preventing its reuptake.
- It is estimated that 60–80% of cocaine users simultaneously drink alcohol (Schuckit, 2010, p. 140).
- Beware of crack cocaine's consumptive powers. It can rapidly take over one's life and result in death.
- Speedball is a street name for a combination of a CNS stimulant and a CNS depressant.
- Rapid intake can result in increased heart rate, respiratory arrest, and death.
- Remember, crack and freebase cocaine are chemically the same—both are altered forms of cocaine hydrochloride powder. The smoked product is usually 40% more pure (Schuckit, 2010, p. 141).
- Crack—cocaine mixed with baking soda and water over a hot flame. The substance, which is 90% pure cocaine, is then dried. The soapy-looking substance that results can be broken up into rocks and smoked. These rocks are about five times as strong as cocaine. Crack gets its name from the popping noises it makes when it is smoked. One puff of a pebble-sized rock gives a high for about 20 minutes. The user can usually get 3–4 hits off the rock before it is used up (Doweiko, 2009, p. 137; G. R. Hanson, Venturelli, & Fleckenstein, 2009, pp. 268–269).
- Freebase—produces a stronger high, and the process eliminates cutting agents. It is made with cocaine hydrochloride (street market cocaine). It is dissolved in water, and a solvent (usually petroleum ether or ammonia) is added to release cocaine alkaloid from the salt and other adulterants. A stronger base (baby laxatives) is then added to neutralize the acid content. The solvent rises to the top, where it can be filtered or drawn off. As the solvent evaporates, the cocaine salt oxidizes, and what is left is cocaine base. Freebase cocaine is water soluble and can be smoked or injected. These methods get rid of all possible cuts in cocaine (Doweiko, 2009, p. 137; G. R. Hanson et al., 2009, pp. 268–269).

(5) INHALANTS

Inhaled substances altering perceptions of reality can be traced to ancient Greece. Currently, inhalant abuse is a worldwide problem.

Group

- Volatile substances—glue, paint, paint thinners
- Volatile nitrites—amyl nitrite, butyl nitrite
- Anesthetic gases—nitrous oxide, ether, chloroform, halothane
- This group produces intoxicating, stimulating, and stupefying effects on the central nervous system, as well as euphoric giddiness, loss of inhibitions.

Pattern of Use

- Inhaled from a container, rag, or canister ("huffing" or "bagging")
- Boiled to inhale fumes

Natural History

- 5–8 years of mixed use—daily, episodic, or binge
- 1–5 years of poly drug use and experimentation

Potential for Dependence

- Physical—Low
- Psychological—Low

Withdrawal

- Symptoms include mental confusion, disorientation, ringing in the ear, headache, fatigue, and muscle weakness.

Points to Ponder

- Inhalants are breathable chemicals that were never meant to be used as recreational drugs.
- One-time using of inhalants can result in sudden sniffing death syndrome. Learning disability symptoms develop with increased inhalant use.
- Children who regularly sniff solvents develop tolerance to them. This sniffing habit can be difficult to break.
- Medical disorders associated with inhalants include cardiac irregularities, hepatitis and liver failure, kidney toxicity, transient impairment of lung functioning, skeletal muscle weakness, and peripheral neuropathies (Schuckit, 2010, p. 245).

(6) HALLUCINOGENS

Hallucinogenic plants have been used since long before recorded history.

Pattern of Use

- LSD (lysergic acid diethylamide), *Salvia divonorum*, morning glory seeds, psilocybin mushrooms, peyote, mescaline, ibogaine, Ecstasy, DMT (dimethyltryptamine, "the businessman's LSD")
- This group alters perceptions and consciousness; an intensifier of experience.

Pattern of Use

- Oral—pill, cubes, capsule, tablets, seed or plant, drink
- IV—rare (LSD)
- Smoked
- DMT—injected, IM, sniffed, or smoked

Natural History

- 25 years to a lifetime of episodic or ritualistic use
- 5–10 years of planned monthly hedonism
- 1–5 years of poly drug use and experimentation

Potential for Dependence

- Physical—Low
- Psychological—Low
- May be the psychoactive that results in the lowest potential for abuse and dependence.

Withdrawal

- Flulike symptoms, depression, fatigue, and anxiety

Points to Ponder

- Drug seekers search for sensual experimentation and ritualistic use.
- Hallucinogens are set/setting drugs; the mindset and one's setting greatly influence outcome. Predictability is reduced, thus long-term interest decreases.
- Many "bad trips" are related to dose and quality of the drug.

(7) OPIATES/OPIOIDS

Used in religious rituals, and cultivated as a crop as early as 10,000 years ago. Narkoticos—the Greek word for numbing or deadening.

Group

- Naturals—the opium poppy, morphine, codeine
- Semisynthetic—derived from the naturals: heroin, Vicodin, Percodan, Dilaudid, OxyContin
- Synthetic—produced in a laboratory: demerol, darvon, methadone, buprenorphine
- These drugs are analgesics and reduce physical and emotional pain. They provide a euphoric rush, lower anxiety, and increase an overall sense of well-being.

Pattern of Use

- Oral
- IV
- IM
- Subcutaneous—between the layers of the skin (skin popping)
- Snorted
- Smoked
- Mucous membranes of mouth, nose, or rectum ("bootie bumping")

Natural History

- 25 years to a lifetime of dependent use
- 15 years of daily periodic or episodic use
- 1–5 years of poly drug use and experimentation

Potential for Dependence

- Physical—High
- Psychological—High

Withdrawal

- Initial acute withdrawal of 48–72 hours of withdrawal includes symptoms of nausea, vomiting, gooseflesh, intestinal spasms, abdominal pain, kicking movements, diarrhea, irritability, violent yawning, sneezing and runny nose, restlessness, and increased heart rate and blood pressure.
- The opiates have a 2-year protracted withdrawal period with decreasing severity and frequency of symptoms.
- Opiate withdrawal is not usually fatal unless the person is medically compromised by a serious condition such as hypertension or heart disease.

Points to Ponder

- Prescription pain relievers all too often become drugs of dependence and abuse.
- Beware of the opiates' daily seductions as mother's, or father's, "little helper."
- Buprenorphine (Suboxone, Subutex) has been approved by the FDA and seems to have replaced methadone as the treatment for opioid dependence. It is unique because its therapeutic effect plateaus at certain levels; addicts are less likely to get high (Erickson, 2007, p. 237).
- Chipping—occasional use of heroin or another drug.
- A heroin high is a most pleasurable sensation, usually considered more powerful than an orgasm.
- Addicts become experts in finding new veins.
- Chronic use of these drugs does not produce organ pathology as with alcohol.

(8) PHENCYCLIDINE (PCP)

Introduced as a surgical anesthesia for humans in 1957. Discontinued in 1965. Discontinued for veterinary use in 1975. Illegal in the United States.

Group

- PCP and ketamine
- These produce dissociative states. Users feel detached from the body and from external reality.

Pattern of Use

- Oral
- IV
- IM
- Smoked
- Snorted

Natural History

- 5–8 years of mixed use, including periods of daily use interspersed with episodic or binge using.

Potential for Dependence

- Physical—Low
- Psychological—Low to Moderate

Withdrawal

- Mixed evidence about withdrawal symptoms.

Points to Ponder

- PeaCe Pill is the street name for PCP.
- As a drug of abuse in the United States, its popularity waxes and wanes. PCP is considered a set/setting drug; mindset and setting greatly determine outcome.
- Levels of intoxication range from mild to induced psychosis.
- Rash of scare stories about PCP may reflect society's need to have "devil drugs."
- A toxic reaction to PCP can be one of the longest lasting produced by any drugs of abuse. Recovery progresses into a 2- to 6-week period (Schuckit, 2010, p. 226).
- PCP's structure resembles a depressant (Schuckit, 2010, p. 226).

(9) SEDATIVES, HYPNOTICS, AND ANXIOLYTICS

In 1960, a new class of antianxiety drugs replaced reliance on the barbiturates. Benzodiazepines (BZs) are the most prescribed psychiatric medications in the world.

Group

- Barbiturates—Seconal, Nembutal, Amytal, chloralhydrate
- Benzodiazepines—Librium, Xanax, Ativan, Klonopin, Restoril, Rohypnol
- Drugs that act at BZ or melatonin receptor sites—Ambien, Lunesta, Rozerem
- Other sedatives-hypnotics—quaalude, GHB (gamma hydroxybutyrate), meprobamate (Miltown).
- This class of drugs reduces anxiety and induces relaxation. They can also promote sleep and a sense of well-being.

Pattern of Use

- Oral
- IV

Natural History

- 25 years to a lifetime of daily use
- 15 years of periods of daily use
- 1–5 years of poly drug use and experimentation

Potential for Dependence

- Physical—High
- Psychological—High

Withdrawal

- Initial acute withdrawal of 24 to 72 hours includes symptoms of apprehension, anxiety, insomnia, stomach cramps, sweating, fainting, nausea, restlessness, agitation, a sense of paranoia, depersonalization, and impaired memory. Acute withdrawal can last 15 days and into months.
- The benzodiazepines have a 2-year protracted period with decreasing severity and frequency of symptoms.

Points to Ponder

- These medications are thought to increase function of GABA and suppress unnecessary anxiety and insomnia.
- Sudden cessation will produce withdrawal symptoms. Tapering of dependent use is strongly recommended.
- Be wary of alcoholism-sedativism. The effects of daily heavy drinking are mitigated with nightly benzodiazepine use.
- Watch for increased daily usage as antidote to fast-paced anxious society.
- Likely increased use with anxiety of living longer through medical hardware, multiple surgeries and treatments, and medications.
- Increasingly used as a recreational drug that may lead to possible dependency.
- The risk of fatal overdose with benzodiazepines is small if they are taken alone. High dosing causes prolonged sleep and memory impairment.

(10) NICOTINE

References to nicotine are etched into Mayan stone carvings from 600 AD. Nicotine was used during transcendental ceremonies to ward off evil. In the 1500s, tobacco was used to treat a number of ailments, from headaches to colds. It was called the "holy plant." In 1828, the psychoactive ingredient in tobacco was named nicotine. Medicinal prescriptions ended in 1890.

Group

- Cigarettes, tobacco, snuff, nicotine gum, nicotine skin patch, cigars, pipe tobacco, and salves
- This class of drug decreases anxiety, calms, and decreases appetite.

Pattern of Use

- Smoked
- Chewed

Natural History

- 25 years to a lifetime of dependent use
- 25 years to a lifetime of chipping or episodic use
- 1–5 years of experimentation

Potential for Dependence

- Physical—High
- Psychological—High

Withdrawal

- Symptoms begin within hours and peak on days 2 to 4, and last up to a month.
- Symptoms include increased craving, increased appetite, irritability, anxiety, difficulty concentrating, and restlessness.

Points to Ponder

- In the 1960s, 40% of U.S. adults were smokers. Today, this is down to 21% (Kuhn, Swartzwelder, & Wilson, 2008, p. 174).
- Family studies reveal a twofold to fourfold increased risk for smoking if parents or siblings are smokers (Schuckit, 2010, p. 290).
- 80% of men and women who are alcohol dependent currently smoke (Schuckit, 2010, p. 211).
- Prenatal and postnatal effects include oxygen depletion, resulting in smaller head circumference; compromises in verbal and mathematic abilities; and hyperactivity (Kuhn et al., 2008, pp. 181–182).
- Nicotine may prove helpful in the treatment of ADHD and schizophrenia.
- There are two sources of smoke from cigarette smokers; the smoke they exhale (secondhand) and the smoke rising off the lit cigarette (sidestream). Sidestream smoke has a higher concentration of carcinogens than either secondhand smoke or the smoke taken into the lungs through a cigarette filter (Kuhn et al., 2008, p. 181).
- A fatal overdose of nicotine is quite rare, but it is possible. Symptoms include nausea, abdominal pain, diarrhea, vomiting, decreased heart rate, and dizziness (Kuhn et al., 2008, p. 172).

(11) XANTHINES (CAFFEINE)

Origins of tea are traced back to China in the fourth century. Coffee was first cultivated in Yemen in the sixth century. By the 1600s, coffeehouses spread rapidly in Europe. Specialty coffee shops and cafés developed on the West Coast in the United States in the 1980s and continue to be highly popular meeting places around the world today.

Group

- Coffee, tea, chocolate, soft drinks, energy drinks, over-the-counter pain relievers, stimulants, and medications
- This class of drugs enhances concentration, alertness, and attention; calms; and decreases fatigue.

Pattern of Use

- Oral

Natural History

- 25 years to a lifetime of dependent use
- 25 years to a lifetime of episodic use
- 1–5 years of experimentation
-

Potential for Dependence

- Physical—High
- Psychological—High

Withdrawal

- Symptoms develop between 12 and 24 hours after the last dose of caffeine.
- Symptoms include headache, fatigue, yawning, and nausea.
- Nonprescription pain relievers to relieve headaches are used during withdrawal.

Points to Ponder

- It is estimated that more than 50% of Americans drink coffee every day.
- Prenatal and postnatal effects include reduced chances for pregnancy and lower birth weights (Kuhn et al., 2008, p. 69).
- Caffeine disturbs, stresses, or interrupts functioning in the heart, eyes, kidneys, and digestive, reproductive, and respiratory systems.
- Caffeine causes constriction of blood vessels, and this is a likely reason why it is effective for migraine headaches (Kuhn et al., 2008, p. 71).
- Overall, caffeine is fairly safe if consumed by a healthy person in moderate amounts.

CHAPTER SUMMARY AND REFLECTIONS WITH FURTHER STUDY

Summary

This chapter was designed to be blessedly brief and clinically practical. It provided readers with some neuroscience as well as some comparisons between the natural mind and the one adulterated by alcohol and other drugs. Salient features were included in 11 easy-to-read charts that serve as a ready reference guide for clinical work or emergency situations. This chapter provides a recommended reading list for further study. These books contain additional information about each drug, more in-depth clinical applications, and current research focus and findings. Readers are strongly encouraged to buy updated editions each year.

Reflections

Before leaving this chapter, make sure you have grasped:

- Some basic neuroscience about how alcohol and other drugs work in our body
- The differences between each of the 11 psychoactives that we can use, misuse, or become addicted to
- The importance of further study of scientific or medical discoveries about each of the psychoactives

Further Study

Doweiko, H. E. (2009). *Concepts of chemical dependency* (7th ed.). Belmont, CA: Brooks/Cole.

Earleywine, M. (2002). *Understanding marijuana: A new look at the scientific evidence*. Oxford: Oxford University Press.

Erickson, C. K. (2007). *The science of addiction: From neurobiology to treatment*. New York: W. W. Norton.

Hanson, G. R., Venturelli, P. J., & Fleckenstein, A. E. (2009). *Drugs and society* (10th ed.). Sudbury, MA: Jones and Bartlett.

Inaba, D. S., & Cohen, W. E. (2007). *Uppers, downers, all arounders* (6th ed.). Medford, OR: CNS Publications.

Kuhn, C., Swartzwelder, S., & Wilson, W. (2008). *Buzzed: The straight facts about the most used and abused drugs from alcohol to ecstasy* (3rd ed.). New York: W. W. Norton.

Schuckit, M. A. (2010). *Drug and alcohol abuse: A clinical guide to diagnosis and treatment* (6th ed.). New York: Springer.

Part III

A Perspective on Models of Treatment and the Suffering Behind Addiction

Chapter 6

Ten Models of Treatment

INTRODUCTION

This chapter was originally developed from the article "Treatment Implications of Chemical Dependency Models: An Integrative Approach," written in the *Journal of Substance Abuse Treatment* in 1989 by Brower, Blow, and Beresford. The article identifies basic (single-focused) and integrative (multi-focused) models of chemical dependency treatment. Etiological assumptions, addictive identities, treatment goals, strategies, and caveats, as well as advantages and disadvantages of each model, are suggested.

This article delivers a classic contribution to the field; the presentation of models is comprehensive and also concisely organized and cogently delivered. The features and uses, strengths and vulnerabilities of each model are freely shared with the reader. These 10 pages provide a very useful overview of the most widely used treatment models, along with suggestions for clinical application. The treatment provider is encouraged to mix and match models and model parts with their clinical style, as well as with the needs, wishes, and beliefs of the addict and alcoholic.

What follows builds on Brower et al.'s very substantial work, still useful for conceptualizing and treating contemporary addiction problems. These models have been developed and expanded after years of clinical application and teaching. The thinking and doing of our treatment has evolved since 1989; new ideas, new programs, and new approaches have been included.

Models of treatment organize our thinking about the complex human problem of addiction. They enhance our understanding. Models serve as a standard or example available for imitation or comparison. A model is a hypothesis that proposes a provisional theory to explain a certain class of phenomena (Costello, 1997, pp. 644, 843).

The models presented here do not delineate a truth about the field of chemical dependency. Instead, they propose a conceptual coherence. They are guides. Each reflects a point of view about the cause or causes of addiction and suggests treatment options that would best address these. The 10 models of treatment provided in this chapter reflect most of the current treatment thinking in the field.

The philosopher Isaiah Berlin's essay titled "The Hedgehog and the Fox" quotes the Greek poet Archilochus: "The fox knows many things, but the hedgehog knows one big thing." The hedgehog's life is organized around a major preoccupation—the location of the fox. The fox's interests and concerns vary. In his essay, Berlin (1953) divides writers, thinkers, and philosophers into two types of people: Hedgehogs are thinkers who are captivated by a single large and all-embracing idea as the key to understanding complex phenomena. Foxes, on the other hand, entertain multifarious ideas as key.

The substance dependence/abuse field is populated with hedgehogs and foxes. Hedgehog thinkers are single-focused in their beliefs (monists) about the causes of chemical dependency and its treatment. As an example, the medical model states that diseased behaviors are directly related to genetic and biological influences. These result in an irreversible loss of control over substances (Schuckit, 2010). The treatment recommendation for this incurable incapacity is abstinence. Fox thinkers are multi-focused and look at multiple causal sources (pluralists), and thus they suggest varied treatment approaches. A biopsychosocial model of addiction recognizes the biological, psychological, and social factors contributing to chemical dependency. Multiple treatment responses might include abstinence for the disease, psychotherapy for the suffering, or improved coping responses for the environmental stresses. A decision to be a hedgehog or fox treatment provider should be based on study and reflection.

Our patient population is also divided into hedgehogs and foxes. Each arrives at our door with an intuitive sense of which models will work best for him. "I'd like to try to figure out a way I can drink better" suggests a disinterest or rejection of disease model treatment, with its insistence on abstinence. Rather, a patient may be interested in addressing the underlying causes of his destructive behaviors, reducing the harm of his problematic using, or learning new cognitions. Family members terrorized by a son or daughter's drinking may hold another view and only want a path of complete sobriety. Others have a strong sense that a depression drives their using and are receptive to psychopharmacological support. Some hope that a clinician will abide by their spiritual journey of Alcoholics Anonymous (AA) recovery and also help them more deeply address pervasive patterns and troubling conflicts.

Treatment providers are encouraged to listen for and respect the patient's choice of recovery. We may start with the patient's wish, and it may be the approach that works. Often, an alternative model is needed to save a life or provide a more effective level of care. The decision is best made within the relationship.

This chapter is designed to introduce the reader to the field of treatment and further understanding of different approaches to recovery. It provides the key content necessary to develop a workable and reflective grasp of treatment modalities in the field. It is designed to furnish the most pertinent information about each model with the least amount of unnecessary complexity or redundancy. Students and clinicians are encouraged to develop a discerning sense of the model or models of treatment that are simpatico with their conceptualization of chemical dependency, as well as intuitively in sync with their clinical style.

The 10 models of treatment discussed in this chapter are outlined in the diagram below. There are 5 basic, or single-focused, models and 5 integrative, or multi-focused, models. Key features of each are presented, followed by some advantages and caveats; selective considerations and concerns are proposed, as well as speculations that may generate further discussion during classroom conversations. Hopefully, what follows will help readers identify and clarify their treatment approach of choice.

Figure 6.1 Models of Treatment

SINGLE-FOCUSED	**MULTI-FOCUSED**
MORAL	AA (Moral, Learning, Disease)
LEARNING	DUAL DIAGNOSIS (Disease, Self-Medication)
DISEASE	BIOPSYCHOSOCIAL (Disease, Self-Medication, Social)
SELF-MEDICATION	HARM REDUCTION (Learning, Disease, Self-Medication, Social)
SOCIAL	MULTIVARIANT

SINGLE-FOCUSED MODELS

Single-focused models are designed for hedgehog treatment providers. Chemical dependency is conceptualized as originating from one causal source. Recovery addresses this.

The Moral Model

A moral model suggests that chemical dependency occurs as a result of moral weakness. The chemically dependent person has an evil, weak, or bad character. This weakness of will and character results in a person who is unable or unwilling to stop destructive and hedonistic use of substances. Treatment for this "condition" includes spirituality, religion, or the military. God or a strong arm is the only solution. Both inspire the willpower needed to resist the evil temptations of the substances.

This model, with its reliance on religion and authoritarian approaches, strongly encourages responsibility for the consequences of using. It advocates the reconsideration of values and ethics. Many a sober chemically dependent person deeply regrets the malfunctioning of his moral compass during his using days. A return to religion, spirituality, or discipline often repairs this.

While most believe that this punitive and harsh model is outdated, this approach is actually the underbelly of the entire field. All of us are prey to moral model thinking. It insidiously creeps in during upsetting interactions with alcoholics and addicts. We are not as highbrow as we think. Even the Supreme Court defines alcoholism as willful misconduct (*Traynor v. Turnage*, 1988).

Treatment providers may inadvertently slip into a moral model style. Working with the actively using addict feels perilous. A sense of helplessness overwhelms; exhaustion and panic set in. Suggestions repeatedly rebuffed produce frustration. A direct approach fails; an overly controlling one feels necessary. A power struggle develops. The clinician delivers this message, "You're in trouble, and you're doing it the wrong way." The addict responds, "I am not in trouble, and I'm doing it the right way." Moral model thinking incites a battle between good and bad.

Living with someone with an AOD problem can be an exhausting experience. Initial conversations with a family member are often filled with love and concern. There is hope, and a willingness to listen to the addict's point of view. People give chances. This willingness often gets eroded after too many disappointments. Hurt and fear too often produce anger, bitterness, and desires to control. We stop thinking of the addict as vulnerable and in trouble and begin to see him as bad, evil, and weak. A desperation sets in, and so do harsh judgments. A punitive tone delivers a message even during our most heartfelt appeals for increased care.

A morally loaded asymmetrical relationship develops. "We, the family, are right, strong, and good . . . . You the addict are weak, evil, and bad." The suggestion here is that *we* know the kind of help that *you* need, and *we* know that *you* need it now. Early concerns turn to antagonism and condescension. This tough love approach reflects moral model thinking at its worst—we know best, and you do not; we have the right answers for your life, and you have the wrong ones; we are living well, and you are not.

The insidious creep of moral model thinking takes another turn. A chemically dependent person is often unable to be truthful. We reserve the words deception and manipulation for the addict. Hypocritically, exhausted and frightened family members often resort to similar tactics. These include sleuthing around in a son's room to check his stash, diluting vodka bottles with water, checking pockets and pocketbooks, cars and wallets, e-mails and messages. These discoveries are later used as collateral evidence during a "confrontation for your own good." Our justifications swell from moral model thinking—"We are right to violate your privacy because your using is violating our lives." The battle between who is right and who is wrong now dominates family interactions. This, sadly, precludes real conversations about real concerns. Ironically, most would adamantly deny their moral model thinking and refuse to believe how much it is a part of the degradation of family relations.

Contemporary society seems to sanction more aggressive, judgmental, and controlling approaches if all else fails. It is the trump card that we feel ready to use at that certain point when the frustration is too great, the fear too paralyzing, and the disappointments too numerous. This choice is saturated with moral model thinking. Its adoption all too often tantalizes family members, terrorizes the user, and reverberates throughout our treatment industry. Its dichotomous separation of good and evil creates enemies to be avoided, not team members talking.

When considering the moral model, remember it is ideologically complex. It deserves reflection before "use."

The Learning Model

The learning model suggests that chemical dependency arises from the learning of both maladaptive behaviors and faulty cognitions. The chemically dependent person is a tabula rasa, or a blank slate. Unhealthy habits and thinking patterns, behaviorally and cognitively imprinted, drive destruction. A decision to drink or drug every night is a remembrance of the numbing rituals of childhood. This learning and repeating goes on without reflection for years and decades. This blank-slate-of-a-person is not bad; he is woefully misdirected by poor parental or family modeling.

Salvador Minuchin, the renowned family therapist, implies that addiction results from an absence of good, healthy problem-solving skills in families (Minuchin, cited in Garner and Garfinkel, 1985, p. 282). The thinking and doing of drinking substitute for the thinking and doing of problem solving.

Some have suggested that drug and alcohol problems are bad habits that are repeatedly reinforced and become embedded in a lifestyle (Peele and Brodsky, 1991). While hard to reverse, these habits can be altered or even extinguished if one is ready, willing, and able (Miller and Rollnick, 2002, p. 10). There is optimism. What you learned, you can unlearn and learn again (Brower et al., 1989).

Learning model approaches hold people responsible. Treatment encourages the development of new cognitions and behaviors, better coping responses, as well as healthy lifestyle adjustments. Education is stressed. Moderation Management (MM; Kosok, 2006) and Self-Management and Recovery Training (SMART) are examples of learning models (Horvath and Velten, 2000). Weekly groups identify specific goals, provide support, and attempt to hold people accountable.

Some of these learning models stress behaviors, cognition, and skills that embrace abstinence (SMART). These work for many. Other models encourage the development of self-control skills for the learning of moderate behaviors (MM). Controlled drinking is the hope and dream of many. Some succeed in successfully rehabituating their drinking, as seen in several clinical cases described in this book (Nicholas and Joanna, p. 43; Daniel, p. 45; and Dean, p. 137). The decision to address problem using with self-control requires very careful scrutiny. It may work; it usually requires ongoing effort. For some, it may be a setup for disaster and heartache. No amount of hoping, wishing, or trying can reverse a fundamental inability to pace the use of AOD. Repeated embarrassing incidents suggest that some people have no business drinking or drugging. Fantasizing about an ability that doesn't exist can delay the inevitable need for abstinence.

In either case, these treatment options allow people authority and choice over their own lives. They value new learning and encourage experimentation. They also encourage responsibility for the discovery and execution of healthier options in living. Learning models are not punitive, blaming, or shaming.

When considering a learning model, remember the Hippocratic Oath, "Above all, do no harm."

The Disease Model

The disease model suggests that chemical dependency occurs because someone is sick or ill. This is often referred to as the Medical Model. Alcohol and drug problems have been characterized as chronic illnesses for centuries. In 1784,

Dr. Benjamin Rush wrote a pamphlet defining frequent drunkenness as a disease (Thombs, 2006). Alcoholics Anonymous, founded in 1935, stressed alcoholism's disease nature. The American Medical Association (AMA) recognized alcoholism as a disease in 1956. In 1960, Edward Jellinek's book *The Disease Concept of Alcoholism* furthered the legitimacy of it as a medical condition.

Simply put, the disease model states that alcoholism is a chronic, progressive, incurable disease characterized by an irreversible loss of control over alcohol (American Society of Addiction Medicine). The alcoholic is sick with an illness and needs treatment and care. A lifetime of abstinence is the recommended course of recovery. In the current Zeitgeist, this is by far the most dominant model of treatment in the United States. It is entrenched and established; endorsed and embraced by the majority, funded for treatment and research, and politically correct.

The disease of addiction is considered progressive, and its evolution is displayed in Figure 6.2. The predictable course leading to dependence is most likely inherited from and influenced by two forces—40% is attributed to genetics; 60% is attributed to the environment (Schuckit, 2010). Its followers say, "Be wise, o ye traveling on this oft-seen course. Accept your disease, and decide now on abstinence before complete destruction sets in." Some listen and stop drinking. Others want to keep drinking and are able to reverse the progression from problem drinking back to social drinking, from binge drinking back to experimentation, or resist daily habituation and resume social drinking. Still others keep drinking and convince themselves that they are reversing bad behavior, when actually the progression is continuing.

Figure 6.2 Progressive Continuum of Disease Model

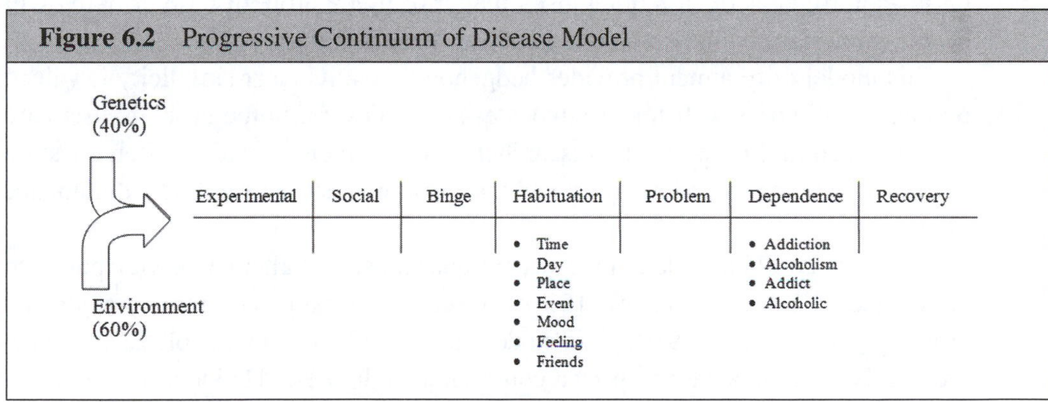

Source: Visually adapted from Schuckit (2010) and Inaba and Cohen (2007).

Genetic and biological factors are considered of paramount determinant importance in understanding the disease of chemical dependency. While the etiology of alcoholism is unknown, the country is assured that one day science will prevail. One day, we will find a gene, a chromosome, a marker, or molecular mechanisms of dependence that will prove precisely what causes addiction. Abundant research is being conducted toward these findings. Studies are exciting, promising medical and biological answers for our confusions about addiction. A pervasive pattern, however, seems to exist—Study A identifies an important discovery, and Study B fails to document the same results. While all this research has yielded scientific suspicions, we still don't have conclusive proof of very much (Doweiko, 2009, p. 35).

In the absence of this scientific proof, some say the disease model has served as a wonderful cultural metaphor. It has allowed people to get treatment with dignity in either a medical setting, a spiritual fellowship, or some kind of therapeutic treatment modality (Doweiko, 2009, p. 35). This model has challenged the notion of addicts as weak-willed people, has removed some stigma and some notions of moral depravity. It is neither punitive, nor blaming, nor judgmental. The emphasis is on disease treatment through abstinence and not through self-control, new learning, or immorality's repair. The disease model encourages accountability and responsibility.

Disease model thinkers and treatment providers are watchful for the ever-present threat of relapse. This begins when the once solidly abstinent person starts entertaining notions that drugs and alcohol can be managed and should be a part of his life again. A shaky recovery path will continue if this distorted thinking stays hidden.

If fantasies, urges, and vulnerabilities are denied or dismissed, it is only a matter of time before an actual relapse will occur. Relapse, according to this model, occurs when one drinks again. It is important that a lapse into drinking after abstinence be looked at seriously. While the first return to drinking may not result in an out-of-control episode, it's often just a matter of time before disease drinking will occur again. Family and community support are essential.

This model of treatment provides hedgehog focus; its clear simplicity is valued by many and works well for its advocates and believers. Some problem users are not interested in this approach. Researchers and treatment providers often question its singular authority, and many around the world wonder at its political dominance in our culture.

There are conflicting data, unanswered questions, and alternative viewpoints to be considered. For example, 5%–15% of "diseased" drinkers return to asymptomatic drinking (Brower et al., 1989). This model cannot explain them. Harold E. Doweiko, previously cited, is a well-respected contributor to the field. He identifies researchers that have concluded that Jellinek's classic work, which still defines and drives disease model enthusiasm, was seriously flawed. A survey was used as a method of data collection for analysis. A return rate of 6% is rarely accepted as the foundation of a research study (Doweiko, 2009, p. 23). Others found that the progression of alcoholism develops in only a minority (25% to 30%) of cases, suggesting that alcohol-dependent individuals do not follow a single progressive pattern (Doweiko, 2009, p. 27).

Dr. Ed Khantzian and Mark Albanese (2008), also well regarded in the field, suggest that disease thinking and biological mechanisms cannot alone explain why addictions are so compelling (p. 11). George Vaillant (1983), in his classic *The Natural History of Alcoholism*, suggested that alcoholism is often dexterously "shoehorned" into medical model thinking (p. 4).

This dominant model of treatment has strong supporters, detractors, and doubters. Honest conversations in classrooms and homes about patterns and problems of drinking and drugging shed much light on our clinical understanding of addiction. My own thinking and conceptualizing has greatly evolved from studying the idiosyncrasies of individual cases, as well as from student stories and collegial exchange. Anecdotal clinical data combined with research is likely to provide more understanding as well.

"*No matter how you look at it, addiction remains a most curious disease*" (Doweiko, 2009, p. 26).

The Self-Medication Model

The self-medication model says that addictions arise from untreated psychological suffering. During the 1970s and 1980s, Ed Khantzian (1999) at Harvard did much to humanize addiction and its treatment. He and others debunked the popular and prevailing notions that addiction resulted from hedonism, sociopathy, or self-destruction. Khantzian, in his classic paper on the self-medication theory in 1985, suggested that addicts attempt self-medication for a range of psychiatric problems. They use drugs and alcohol to help alleviate the unresolved pain of their histories; to relieve the symptoms of another primary mental disorder such as depression, anxiety, or schizophrenia; or to compensate for psychological incapacity. They self-medicate for intense suffering; they are not morally weak, driven by a disease, or recipients of poor parental modeling. They have psychological problems, have found a solution in AOD, and need psychological help. The goal of treatment is to improve mental health. The strategies include psychotherapy and psychopharmacology.

This model is not punitive, blaming, or shaming. It encourages discovery of the underlying psychological causes of chemical dependency, as well as arresting ongoing consequences. Regular therapeutic work may clarify any overlap. Working through both may relieve much suffering.

This model hints at a return to drinking. It suggests that if psychological suffering is understood and relieved, the chemical dependency or abuse would dissipate.

Self-care and self-soothing capacities would reduce the need to self-medicate. Using would not be driven by the desperate need to alleviate unbearable suffering. This certainly is the case for some who are able to return to asymptomatic drinking (Vaillant, 1983, p. 235); however, it usually requires a lifetime of labor-intensive scrutiny. Others alleviate much of their suffering and strengthen their psychological capacity but their return to self-regulated drinking does not work. Sometimes no amount of psychological or spiritual repair can reverse some unquenchable psychic thirsts.

Chapter 7 is devoted to further exploration of this model of treatment. Theories of suffering are explored, and suggestions for treatment are considered.

When considering the self-medication model, always ask the question, "What is the drug or alcohol doing for you?" (Khantzian and Albanese, 2008).

The Social Model

A social model of addiction links the stresses of social living to addictive consumption. The emphasis is on sociocultural influences, not individual psychopathology, biologic or genetic derivatives, moral failings, or the introjection of destructive habits and faulty thinking. Chapters 1 and 2 were written to deepen our grasp on these influences.

Social distresses that drive chemical dependency include discrimination and economic anxiety, drug availability and peer pressure, a sense of urgency pulsating in big cities and a sense of despair languishing in our rural towns, family chaos and dysfunction, and work pressures and exhaustions, as well as living above our means and greed. These disturbing social influences are vast. It feels almost impossible to isolate and identify their specific contributions to addiction. We then feel helpless and unable to reverse these impacts. We choose to deny or dismiss them instead.

Treatments support social adjustments—recognizing and altering destructive forces in one's environment, as well as identifying and improving coping responses for the day-to-day stresses of living in contemporary culture. The socially chemically dependent person, at all sociocultural levels, feels trapped by his environment. Group support, individual therapy, or reliance on religion may help reverse this sense of helplessness. These may provide a lost perspective and help locate lost courage. Avoiding the evening bar crowd, mixing up social relationships, spending more time alone, staying away from destructive environments, and testing out healthy skills in interpersonal relationships may feel more doable with the support of a support group.

Many social addicts feel victimized by societal forces that seem beyond their control. An overwhelming sense of futility brings tragic resignation and increased destructive behavior. Immobilization sets in. Irvin Yalom's (2002) work on the assumption of responsibility may provide empowerment here (pp. 139–140).

Long-standing societal oppressions cannot be eradicated. Ongoing daily stressors cannot always be satisfactorily soothed. Yalom's relentless advocacy for the here-and-now responsibility may prove applicable here. He proposes a formula that, at first glance, feels simplistic and seems naive. It is not at all; rather, it is quite profound. This formula may provide a potent response to the entrenched social influences of chemical dependency. It just may reverse some feelings of despair.

Yalom (2002) imaginatively asks us to consider: "Ninety-nine percent of the bad things that happen to us may be someone else's fault." He strongly encourages us to consider embracing the other one percent—those things that are more under our influence than we want to admit, things that we have the capacity to adjust or alter, even just a little bit, to produce some feelings of relief." Yalom urges treatment providers to imaginatively brainstorm or free-associate with our patients, encouraging an ownership that has been dismissed and overlooked. This is an extraordinary challenge; if met, it may empower in previously unknown ways. It's worth a try (pp. 139–140).

Still, some may feel excruciatingly overwhelmed by their environment. They live within extreme isolation and may be internally ill-equipped in the face of extreme external pressures. They may tragically feel that the only option is to drink or drug their lives away. Early on in my career, one psychiatrist left a lasting impression with this remark: "Some of them, Margy, we just can't help." I have always remembered these solemn words. I find it particularly relevant when working with social model addicts.

When considering the social model, watch out for being entrapped by a sense of overwhelming helplessness and negativity.

MULTI-FOCUSED MODELS

Multi-focused models are designed for fox treatment providers. Previously discussed single-focused approaches are woven into one. Recovery addresses the multiple causal factors of an integrated conceptualization of chemical dependency.

The Alcoholics Anonymous (AA) Model

This model contains aspects of the moral, learning, and disease models.

AA embraces and incorporates each of these single-focused models. A spiritual path to recovery is encouraged. Acknowledging powerlessness over the disease of addiction is strongly suggested. This paves the way to abstinence. Meetings, 12-step work, moral inventories, service to others, fellowship, apprentice learning, being sponsored, and, later, sponsoring combine to support long-term sobriety. AA meetings are available around the world and 24 hours a day. Alcoholics

Anonymous has believers and doubters. Many people in the field have written about its utility and effectiveness as well as its stranglehold and serious limitations (Rotskoff, 2002).

AA was founded in 1935. Somewhere, I read this joke. A man asks another man, "How does AA work?" The response, "It works very well, thank you."

George Vaillant (1983), the longitudinal alcoholism researcher, and Jerome Frank (1963), the renowned psychiatrist, imaginatively and thoughtfully propose an understanding of the mysterious workings of AA. Both recognize the power and importance of natural healing forces in recovery processes. Frank's work on hard-to-comprehend diseases in contemporary history and Vaillant's analysis of the defense mechanism of reaction formation are useful in understanding all that goes on in the rooms of AA. Their works, explored below, shed more light on human responses to unintelligible suffering.

Hard to Comprehend Diseases: The Integration of Lourdes and Alcoholics Anonymous

In the early- to mid-1800s, western Europe was plagued with illnesses, diseases, infections, and inflictions that overwhelmed the medical community. In 1858, an apparition appeared to a young girl, Bernadette Soubirous, in Lourdes, France. She was told where to dig for a spring. She delivered this news to the local town leaders. From this vision, the modern Shrine of Lourdes was created with its grotto of healing waters. Since that time, people have made pilgrimages to Lourdes in search of healing for ailments that are confusing to modern medicine. Cures of several illnesses have occurred there. These are exceptionally well documented and have undergone careful scrutiny (Frank, 1963, p. 67).

Alcoholism is a hard-to-comprehend disease. What has mortified and separated families, exhausted and isolated the sick, baffled science, and mystified medicine is embraced in the rooms of AA. People talk of a miracle. Alcohol and drugs, once loved and cherished, are suddenly rejected and hated.

Lourdes and AA, created by the people, offer a spiritual, social, and behavioral support and recovery community for defeating diseases. The suffering sick enter these communal settings with a surprising sense of renewed hope, abide by prescribed healing rituals, and soon thrive in a spiritual fellowship.

Persuasion and Healing (Frank, 1963) and *The Natural History of Alcoholism* (Vaillant, 1983) ponder the healing powers of Alcoholics Anonymous rooms around the world, as well as the wondrous waters in the grotto at Lourdes. Both suggest that participation in these rooms and bathing in these waters provide the wounded and the weary with a *relief of suffering* and also maximize an *attitude change* that produces some kind of healing.

AA and Lourdes are emotionally charged settings that feel miraculous and convince the afflicted to begin a new path of recovery for illnesses once believed intractable. This heightened morale carries the patient's mind to new beliefs, which encourage new behaviors. The sufferer feels connected to others and empowered within. He chooses to live in healing with his handicap, not be devastated or destroyed by it (Frank, 1963, p. 69).

Lourdes and AA *relieve suffering* because both (Vaillant, 1983, pp. 287–289):

- Reduce overwhelming fears about an intractable disease.
- Instill hope and raise expectations about lost-cause cases.
- Move people from the periphery of their families and communities to the center of a new, resource-rich support group.
- Stress service to others rather than preoccupation with self.

Lourdes and AA produce *attitude changes* because both (Frank, cited in Vaillant, 1983, pp. 287–289):

- Indoctrinate the sufferer into a coherent ideology about the etiology of his illness.
- Replace medical bafflement with the all-certain belief in a prescribed path of recovery.
- Reinforce new beliefs through repetitive customs and rituals.
- Provide opportunity for identifications with fellow sufferers—"If they can heal, so can we."

The relief of suffering and sustained attitude change seem to begin a natural healing process of recovery for these cunning and baffling illnesses and disorders. In both Lourdes and AA, intense emotional arousal in a setting of abundant human and supernatural encouragement seems to provide a hope that is healing (Frank, 1963, p. 72).

Reaction Formation: More AA Mystery

A reaction formation is a defense mechanism that seems to be utilized by most sober AA members. It is manifested by the abrupt reversal of what was once cherished and loved into what is currently rejected and hated. Addicts engage in a passionate lifelong love affair with the pleasures of their alcohol and drug use. They hold the desperate conviction that using drugs and alcohol is the only way to respond to the perceived persecutions of their internal and external environment.

It appears that participation in the fellowship of AA seems to mysteriously reverse these entrenched notions. These beliefs actually turn into their opposites. Alcohol and drugs, once sources of instant relief and gratification, soon cause pain and regret. Other reaction formation reversals occur. One rather quickly moves from a preoccupation with blaming and externalizing responsibility to a fervent desire to "own your powerlessness" over alcohol and drugs. This invites a sense of responsibility, leading most to accept the necessity for abstinence. Previous massive denial of any sense of problems or troubles with the substance becomes a public, almost exhibitionistic "presentation" of the messes of addiction and the unmanageability of one's life. Excessive self-preoccupation is replaced with service to others. Finally, it is not uncommon for people to identify themselves as an alcoholic before they tell you their name (Vaillant, 1983, pp. 203–204).

It is fascinating to observe the human creation of ritualized, spiritual communities of persuasion and healing that embrace complex human conditions.

The natural healing powers of an emotionally charged setting give birth to a healthy defense mechanism that may be responsible for so, so much.

The Dual Diagnosis Model

This model contains aspects of the disease model and the self-medication model.

The dual diagnosis model of treatment has reverence for two disorders. One is the disease of addiction and the other is a mental health disorder, such as depression or schizophrenia, generalized anxiety, or a personality disorder. Both need diagnosis and attention. Both are considered primary, and both exacerbate each other. Both involve denial and an element of loss of control. Both can be life threatening, and recovery usually involves lifelong attention. Treatment options include AA and other support groups, psychotherapy, outpatient or inpatient programs, and medications.

The reality is that the most dominant model of treatment in the field is not the disease model, but rather some form of a dual diagnosis model. Most addicts choose a life of addiction as a result of unresolved trauma or emotional distress, or as a symptom of untreated mental illness. Therefore, it is essential for clinicians and family members to grasp and value the interactions between these co-occurring disorders. Clinical clarity develops slowly; it takes time to register mutual impacts and correctly diagnose the untreated psychiatric distresses driving one's addiction.

Identifying these underlying disturbances sheds light on the severity of use and also reduces shame and offers alternative sources of care and additional types of treatment. Discovering the existence and influences of coexisting disorders greatly enhances conversations about treatment decisions—abstinence, moderation, pharmacology, psychotherapy, spirituality, or support groups. Diagnosing during active using is difficult. A strung-out alcoholic or addict may present as a person with an anxiety disorder. Symptoms of depression may actually be the apprehension and dread that come from nights and days of alcohol intoxication. Insomnia may not be related to the stresses of living but to the distresses of using. Thought disturbances and severe paranoia may be a symptom of AOD withdrawal, not schizophrenia or psychosis. Extreme mood swings, instability, omnipotence, and anger may be from the lability of ongoing AOD use, not a cluster B personality disorder.

Continuing diagnostic confusion is reflected in a premature diagnosis of depression, anxiety, or an adjustment disorder. Apprehension and anxiety, irritability and argumentativeness, despair and sadness, sleepiness or sleeplessness, inability to concentrate and make decisions—all may be a normal reaction to adjusting to a new sense of self as well as a completely new way of living. Time and good assessment skills will determine if these symptoms actually signal the onset of a more formal diagnosis of depression or anxiety. These may need psychopharmacology treatment or psychotherapy, or both.

In addition, it's extremely important to detangle the relationship between drugs and alcohol and other compulsive disorders. Alcohol's abstinence may exacerbate bulimia; cocaine's removal may escalate sexual compulsivity; gambling may become less exciting as drug and alcohol use is reduced; workaholism may increase with increased sobriety. It takes time to see how these destructive appetites influence and define each other.

Finally, a new category in our understanding of dual diagnosis is proposed—the disease of chemical dependency and the predicament of an unbearable life and lifestyle. Increasingly, people self-medicate for mismatched or distressed marriages or partnerships; for relief from an unrelenting pace; for jobs that are too demanding, overwhelming, repetitive, tedious, unsatisfying, and demeaning; as well as for a life that goes on too long as a result of modern medicine. Many feel unable to address these issues and resign themselves to a life that doesn't feel good. Drugs and alcohol do.

The very real stresses of our economic lives bear down on our being in frightening ways. We feel trapped in dread and terror. Drugs and alcohol provide a solution that temporarily untraps us and provides some illusion of hope.

Others are tortured with conflicted feelings about parenting. It's hard to develop emotional coherence around such extreme feelings and desires—love and hate, pride and resentment, joy and terror, togetherness and separateness, inclusion and exclusion, protection and avoidance. All too often, the children's homework and bedtime rituals are made more tolerable with mind-altering pills, powders, or liquids. For some, relief begins much earlier in the day.

The disease of chemical dependency is driven by so much more than biology.

The Biopsychosocial Model

This model contains aspects of the disease, self-medication, and social models.

This fox treatment provider values the interactive influences of three single-focused models in her treatment of the chemically dependent person. She subscribes to the disease model and its emphasis on biological derivatives of addiction. In addition, the self-medication model, which stresses the importance of diagnosing and treating coexisting psychopathology and emotional distress, is considered imperative. Finally, the social model, with its emphasis on family, cultural, and environmental influences, sheds even more light on the external influences driving addiction.

Treatment for the biology may include abstinence and AA, or moderation and psychotherapy. Treatment for the psychological suffering is likely to include pharmacology and psychotherapy. Social recovery strategies may include group support, AA meetings, improved coping responses, and adjustment or alterations in the environment.

This is a likely choice of treatment for many.

The Harm Reduction Model

This model contains aspects of the learning, disease, self-medication, and social models.

Harm reduction began as a grassroots movement in the Netherlands and northern Europe, and was eventually adopted as a form of treatment in the United States (van Wormer and Davis, 2008, p. 59). It is a recent addition to the models of chemical dependency treatment. It seems a particularly suitable approach for adolescents and young adults who are unable to fathom a lifetime of abstinence.

Alan Marlatt (1998) called harm reduction Compassionate Pragmatism (pp. 56–58). This model of treatment takes a realistic approach to AOD use. It embraces Ronald K. Seigel's (2005) suggestion that the drive to get high is a universal one in humans (pp. 206–227). This desire for pleasure needs understanding and support, not punishing responses. Some are able to temper this desire; others overdo it. This model's strategies are geared to reducing the harm for those who overdo it—with themselves, among their family and friends, and within society.

Harm reduction begins with recognizing the validity of the patient's own preferences and strengths. Treatment options and decisions are designed within the treatment relationship. Harm reduction does not hold abstinence as a necessary precondition for recovery. Rather, problem users may become more responsible users if given the chance to do so. Strategies are varied. Any reduction in harm is considered a step in the right direction.

This model believes that treating a problematic user, addict, or alcoholic with respect and dignity pays off. Compassion invites a collaborative treatment relationship, which may eventually encourage the adoption of abstinence, if harm reduction efforts have failed.

Harm reduction approaches creatively consider alternatives to immediate sobriety and practically propose ways to reduce harm. Needle exchange programs, methadone maintenance, and its newer alternative, buprenorphine (Suboxone), are all more concerned with the physical dangers and dependencies of the opiates than with the insistence on complete abstinence. Agreements as alternatives to abstinence may be adopted for the development of moderate drinking habits. Drink diaries encourage identification of the problematic emotional states that drive one to drink or drug in excess. Avoiding weeknight drinking may reduce reliance on drugs and alcohol as the only coping response to the daily stresses of balancing work and life (Tatarsky, 2002).

There are a variety of harm reduction strategies, including designating a driver during a night of social drinking, alternating alcoholic and nonalcoholic drinks during an evening's entertainment, and soliciting the support of friends during periods of problematic using. Finally, the purchasing of alcoholic goods and services must be carefully monitored. It's best to avoid large discount stores that sell massive quantities of alcohol at reduced prices. These generously stock our refrigerators, shelves, and wine cellars in dangerous ways.

When choosing a harm reduction model, be aware that reducing harm, while extremely valuable, does not mean that the problem is solved.

The Multivariant Model

This model embraces features of all the basic and integrative models of treatment.

A multivariant treatment provider values the components of both single-focused and multi-focused models. She believes in the sensibilities and sensitivities of the addict. She tends to study each model and appreciates the idiosyncrasies of each. She continually searches for a good treatment fit.

A multivariant clinician develops a sense that at some point a discussion of values, ethics, and morality may be extremely helpful. A clinician may appreciate harm reduction approaches yet also be clear when abstinence needs serious consideration. The psychological forces driving addiction are as valued as the cultural and social stressors in the environment. Medication for psychological symptoms may reduce suffering from untreated psychiatric disorders. Destructive drinking may be decreased with the learning of new behaviors and the adoption of healthy cognitions.

This fox treatment provider values the mix and match of each approach.

CHAPTER SUMMARY AND REFLECTIONS

Summary

This chapter provided a reflective perspective and comprehensive overview of 10 models of treatment that currently populate or predominate the American recovery industry. It was designed to furnish the most pertinent information about each model with the least amount of unnecessary complexity or redundancy. Students and clinicians were encouraged to consider the model or models of treatment that are simpatico with their conceptualization of chemical dependency, as well as naturally in sync with their clinical style. Remember, most of our patients arrive at our door with an intuitive sense of which model of treatment will work best for them.

Reflections

Before you leave this chapter, make sure you have:

- Thought about and discussed each model of treatment
- Assessed the strengths and weaknesses of each
- Discussed their clinical utility
- Considered your treatment model(s) of choice

Chapter 7

Self-Medication, Psychoanalytic, and Psychodynamic Theories

INTRODUCTION

During the 1970s and 1980s, Dr. Ed Khantzian did much to humanize addiction. His 1999 classic, *Treating Addiction as a Human Process,* gave the field its heart, and this chapter is the heart of this book.

He and others debunked the popular and prevailing notions that addiction resulted from hedonism, sociopathy, or self-destruction. Instead, Khantzian suggested that alcoholics and addicts suffer more intensely and with greater difficulty than most. He proposed, in his classic paper on the self-medication theory in 1985, that they use alcohol and other drugs (AOD) to self-medicate for these disturbing emotional states, as well as for a range of psychiatric problems. In many cases, this has led them to discover that the short-term effects of their drug of choice help them cope. Continued use gets them in a lot of trouble. Psychological treatment can be helpful here (Khantzian, 1999, 2011; Khantzian and Albanese, 2008).

Since the mid-1980s, psychiatrists, psychologists, and social workers have been moved to understand and explain addiction from the point of view of psychological suffering. They have drawn on psychoanalytic theory; examined vulnerability, dependency, attachment, and self-soothing capacities; and have also looked at self-disturbances and emotional dysregulation. They have tried to understand the relationship between widespread contemporary addiction and psychological distress. They all suggest, and in different ways, that people self-medicate with drugs and alcohol because they are unable to self-care (Khantzian, 1999, pp. 335–356).

This chapter presents material that has been respected and valued by students and further developed over 20 years of teaching. The following theories are from a self-selected group of addiction and psychoanalytic writers who value connecting psychological and emotional vulnerabilities with the development of substance dependence and abuse problems. I have also included several renowned psychoanalytic thinkers and specific aspects of their work. Their contributions deepen and further our understanding of the psychological suffering driving the need to self-medicate.

The work of each contributor has been reviewed and studied. I have attempted a clear and straightforward synopsis of selected aspects of their work. I have used discipline, imagination, and creativity in my interpretations of their contributions to the field. These theorized essentials are followed by discussion ideas, brief clinical vignettes, and suggestions for their use in recovery treatment. The length of each theoretical presentation varies, dependent very much on my capacity to succinctly apply its applicability to the world of addiction and recovery. Each theory stands alone, yet together they provide a rich understanding of the relationship between emotional pain and the need for relief through AOD. Many of these theorists have made classic contributions in their fields of study. While references may be dated, their contributions continue to provide a deep understanding of the psychological suffering behind addictive symptoms.

Class discussions are strongly encouraged, and students are urged to further their study with additional research and reading.

SELF-MEDICATION THEORISTS

Lance Dodes

Lance Dodes (2002) is a psychiatrist from Harvard University. He has worked in the field of addiction for over 20 years. He proposes that true addiction, or the "heart of addiction," is fundamentally psychological in nature. Addiction exists when there is a psychological need to perform the addictive behavior (p. 74). Dodes straightforwardly highlights the transient nature of physical addiction, and urges us not to confuse its consequences and complications with the problem of addiction in general. He sharply suggests that "physical addiction is surprisingly incidental to the real nature of addiction" (p. 76). These symptoms are largely a medical problem attended to during the early hours of withdrawal. Most people can be safely detoxed in a matter of days or weeks. His emphasis is on addiction's psychological nature, not its physical complications (pp. 3–9).

Content of addiction: People often feel trapped in a problem or dilemma. This results in feelings of helplessness and powerlessness.

Drive behind addiction: Being and feeling trapped creates rage. The rage at feelings of helplessness is the irresistible force that drives addiction.

Purpose of addiction: To reverse feelings of helplessness and powerlessness. Addiction provides a false sense of empowerment, seducing the addict into believing that he is in control of his emotional experience, as well as his life.

Addiction as a substitute action: All addiction is a substitute action because another, more direct response to one's helplessness does not seem possible or permissible.

People may feel hopeless, helpless, and thus trapped in many areas of their lives. These include:

- Relationships and marriages
- A gender
- Raising children
- Illnesses
- Emotional inability
- A body
- Caretaking
- Depression
- Work
- Expectations
- Financial pressures
- A mood or an anxiety

Feeling trapped often results from living with a rigid or anxious perspective about any of these issues. Nicky, a patient who is actively using, tells me she has had a rough 24 hours with a recurring relationship problem. "My partner Lisa, once again, doesn't get it. She'll never get it. How many times do I have to tell her? I'm furious and all alone in raising our children." Nicky felt trapped in this perceived dilemma of over-responsibility, pain, and isolation. She felt hurt by her partner's abandonment and righteous about Lisa's perceived parental delinquency. Nicky was drawn into recalling the details of her sorrow and anger in repetitive and distressing ways. These surrounded her mind and soon immobilized her body. Nothing seemed helpful; no action seemed comforting. She felt stuck on a wish, caught in an emotional standstill. She was breathless; no air seemed available. Agitation and frustration set in. She found a Vicodin and ingested it without thinking.

Dodes suggests that addiction is often the only action that feels available at these moments. Again, it is a substitute action in an effort to reverse the terrorizing feelings of helplessness; it provides an illusion of control in a situation that feels out of control.

The work of recovery involves helping addicts reconsider their substitute response to a problem, and start to consider a healthier, more direct response. This begins by understanding and embracing the patient's sense of helplessness and gently offering a broader perspective. I encourage people to consider *TOES,* that is, to learn to *T*inker *O*n the *E*dge*S* of a problem and to work with the many layers involved in human emotions, behaviors, and dilemmas. It takes time to learn that a fantasized wish is not the only solution that feels good.

Use of *TOES* released Nicky from her righteous and omnipotent rumination—"My partner doesn't get it. Nothing is going to feel better until she gets it, and she needs to get it right now." Nicky felt trapped by her thinking, lost in its repetition. She withdrew, isolated, and eventually felt worse. She panicked at their increasing distance. She felt stuck and rageful; she had taken herself down with her narrowing perspective.

I reflectively listened and heard her yearning for her partner. I recommended a couples session for the two of them. She angrily responded, seemingly convinced that their busy schedule could not accommodate it, "She has no time for a session; don't you get that?" I didn't respond. We both sat in silence. In a matter of seconds, she replied, "I never even thought of that." I could see and feel the relief in her.

Nicky's expectation for satisfaction was exclusively tied to "My partner has to get it." She was unable to imagine any other relief until a couples session was proposed. The *TOES* suggestion invited her to think on another level, to consider connecting rather than stewing.

I try to help patients feel the value of tinkering around the perimeters of a problem. *TOES* is a tool that shifts perspective and encourages an affective appreciation of these incremental shifts. Actively broadening a perspective opens up an opportunity for reflective and creative thinking, and often allows for healthier choices. Thinking is something you can build a tolerance for, that is, something you want to do more of. Over time, it feels better than taking drugs and alcohol.

Dodes's work reminds us to avoid the trap that "my fantasized solution is the only avenue of true satisfaction." This misguided hope results in a frustration and sense of helplessness that beckon the illusionary soothing capacities of a drug high.

Ed Khantzian

Ed Khantzian (1999, 2011) is the founder of the self-medication theory of addiction. His early theories in the 1970s and 1980s challenged the prevailing notions that addicts were weak-willed, and thus doomed to forever capitulate to hedonistic desires. For decades, he has been moved to look at the psychological suffering of addicts. One of his earliest theories looked at the relationship between an individual's emotional suffering and his choice of drugs (Khantzian, 1999, pp. 69, 117–119).

Motivation to use: Not self-destruction, sociopathy, or euphoria.

Purpose of addiction: To turn uncontrolled or passive suffering into controlled or active suffering.

Addicts: Are sitting on an affective storm of chaotic emotions. People live with the sense that something is wrong but are at a loss as to how to explore this. This is passive suffering.

Choice of drugs is not random: People choose a specific drug because it predictably and reliably works on their internal storm. It quiets or animates the storm. Returning to this relief again and again results in addiction. This is active suffering.

Most addicts did not get a good emotional education. As a result, they live with a limited number of words for feelings. In this condition, emotions feel both big and small, intense or absent, and often collide together. The addict's psychic capacity is compromised; this is a handicap to problem solving. Something feels off and wrong, but one lives with a sense that this discomfort and frustration is just a part of life. This causes a tremendous amount of suffering. Addicts don't know how or whom to ask for help. AOD relieves this passive sense of suffering.

The choice of drugs or alcohol is important here (Khantzian, 1999, p. 59). Random experimentation quickly loses its appeal as soon as the addict discovers that something works, that a specific mind-altering substance changes this feeling of passive suffering. The drug of choice quiets, dulls, deadens, silences, or conversely enlivens, animates, excites one's chaotic emotional storm. The sufferer finally feels a solution to his pain. Returning to this experience again and again becomes a way of life. The result is addiction.

This feeling of passive suffering is replaced by the active suffering of the addictive process. One hasn't always known or understood one's emotions or feelings; but one now knows what it is to be an addict. It brings unwanted attention from family and friends, but it feels better than living with a chaotic and confusing emotional storm inside one's psyche. Actively suffering with addiction and its consequences feels better than passively suffering with an unknowable internal world (Khantzian, 1999, pp. 117–119). True addicts don't use to escape life; rather, they use to find a place in life (Zoja, 2000, p. 15). The rituals of addiction give the passive sufferer's life a purpose. "I can do life, while addicted." Sadly, many, many people live in this compromised solution.

The recovery work here includes expanding one's emotional vocabulary, helping people locate the place and name of feelings in their body, heart, and spirit. A user who is "upset" feels frustrated inside and frustrates those around him. Global feelings need deeper exploration. The process of working through upsetting emotional states is a painstaking task. It takes time, patience, endurance, and tenacity. Recovering addicts can develop the capacity to explore emotions at greater depths. This ultimately turns passive and active suffering into active thinking, problem solving, soothing, and living. This is a good deal.

A woman in her 50s is going through a divorce and has also just begun a very exciting and satisfying relationship. She was emotionally and physically abused by her father. Her pattern has been to abandon herself and her feelings in the face of male demands. Her drug of choice was alcohol. She's in her first year of sobriety.

Her soon-to-be ex-husband is demanding and threatening. She also doesn't want to disappoint her new boyfriend. Her extended family sees her as a troublemaker, and her children are withdrawn. Pressure is mounting, and life is heating up. She walks into my office, short of breath, holding back tears, and, I quickly see, feeling numb. She confirms the passive sense of suffering that accompanies being numb. She is willing to do some work, and we pull out a feeling chart. She circles 32 words in her chaotic, undifferentiated emotional storm and is shocked that "all that was going on." She agrees to redesign her day, make room for some journaling, and calls later in a much more comfortable spot. "I now know what I feel certain about, and I now know what I am not sure of." Alcohol would have quieted and dulled her emotionally anxious storm. She might have temporarily relaxed, but drinking would have prevented her from learning from this experience. She would not have gained an understanding of her distress.

Ed Khantzian With John Mack

A hallmark contribution of Ed Khantzian with John Mack (Khantzian, 1999, pp. 335–56) is the discovery that addicts self-medicate because they are unable to self-care. Self-care functions are ego functions developed through the process of internalization. Responding to a child's needs and fostering healthy dependency over time build his ego capacities and skills. These are necessary to live well. Self-care ego functions serve to warn, guide, and protect individuals from hazardous or dangerous involvements and behaviors, including drug addiction and alcoholism, unhealthy and violent relationships, impulsive choices, and destructive situations. Khantzian looks at self-care deficiencies as a way to explain a range of troubled human behaviors (Khantzian, 1999, pp. 335–355).

Addiction is about two things: Problems of control and psychological suffering in four areas.

Problems of control: Addictions are troubled and destructive behaviors. People have lost choice and lost control. Addicts are unable and thus unwilling to make healthier choices.

Psychological suffering in four areas:

1. A chaotic affect from the experience of qualities and quantities of feelings that are either too intense or too vague, nameless, or confusing

2. A pained sense of self with little or no confidence
3. A wish to make contact and have relationships with others, but it is a wish filled with a sense of hazard and impossibility
4. An inability to desire self-care for oneself

Self-care functions: Early and responsive caregiving results in self-care functions that produce:

- An energized sense of one's value and worth. A feeling that one is worthy of care and protection either from self or others.
- An ability to listen to anxiety that says some kind of trouble is approaching, with the desire and ability to anticipate, as well as attend to, the danger.
- An ability to control impulses and renounce pleasures whose consequences are harmful.
- An enjoyment of appropriate levels of risk, in which dangers are realistically measured.
- An accurate and real knowledge about the outside world and oneself sufficient for survival.
- The ability to be self-assertive or aggressive in order to care for and protect oneself.
- Important relationship skills, especially the ability to choose friends and loved ones who ideally enhance one's sense of value and worth and encourage one's self-care and protection. The ability to rebuff and avoid people who interfere with and jeopardize one's sense of value, self-care, and protection.

Human nurturing comes with limitations, and thus none of us got enough of these ego functions. We all can make poor choices without them. Not all of us choose AOD to compensate for their absence. Addicts do, as a result of marked deficiencies in their nurturing experience. They lack a sense of value and feel unworthy of protection. They are unable to say no to everyday dangers. They self-medicate with drugs and alcohol without these ego functions of protection and care.

The good news is that these deficiencies can be repaired. When people call me and ask me if I charge for the first session, I think of this theory and respond in my mind, "Hell yes." As soon as a patient sits down in my office, I vest him with my libidinal or life force energy of interest, curiosity, and wonder of his life. My clinical intention and hope is that my energy of interest will be taken in by him and, over time, will transform into his own vitalized sense of self-interest, worth, and value. All good caretaking is about the transfer of this investment energy, as any clinician, teacher, or parent knows. An energized interest in self is a key ingredient for living a full life. Drugs and alcohol feel necessary without this sense of vitality.

Patients in ongoing psychotherapy gradually internalize these ego functions of self-care. The recovering addict starts to feel consistently more valuable and worthy, and thinks in terms of his own care and protection. He asserts and risks, and he chooses friends that encourage more of the same. Self-care vitality starts to expand his sense of possibilities. His world starts to feel more pleasurable, and also more rewarding, than AOD ever did.

Ego functions of self-care are valuable for everyday psychological management. Students and patients like working with these functions. Addicts really like it. All their lives they have been called selfish. To learn that valuing and protecting oneself is not selfish, but rather an act of self-care, is a most exciting notion and a welcome relief for those suffering with addictions. I often warn that we will never execute these capacities perfectly. We will, however, catch a failure or deficiency in these needed guidelines for healthy living much sooner.

Donald Rinsley

Donald Rinsley, a psychiatrist who wrote in the 1970s, focused on what is missing in the psychological structure of people with a borderline personality disorder. He was struck by their inability to self-soothe. Addicts lack the same capacity (Rinsley, 1988).

Soothing introject: An element of psychological structure that allows one to identify, monitor, and modulate the emotional shifts that occur throughout a day. It is missing in addicts. They are unable to soothe feelings of frustration and helplessness.

Reason addicts use drugs: To self-medicate as a coping mechanism for this deficit in psychological structure.

Infants and children are dependent on caregivers for food and care, as well as the development of emotional capacity. Rinsley focuses on one's ability to self-soothe. His work suggests that addicts are unable to internally soothe themselves, and thus they look externally for this function in AOD (Rinsley, 1988, p. 3).

One internalizes a soothing introject in several ways. Some opportunities can occur during the preverbal periods in a child's life. Often, he is carried around by a caretaker or parent who is doing double duty. She (or he) is both attending to the child and also attempting to identify, figure out, and calm her own upset about other life events. The parent patiently works through nameless emotional states in an effort to calm her distress.

The child in her arms takes in and learns from her effort to self-soothe. Hopefully, he internalizes her success. He learns that mom can feel bad, clammy, and cold when anxious. He learns that soothing takes time, and that eventually we are able to quiet ourselves. He senses that frustration can be modified, either through emotionally clear thinking or support from other people. The mom's ability to self-soothe is taken in and becomes a part of the child's psychic structure. During this introjective process, he is developing a capacity to eventually soothe himself.

Another opportunity for internalizing a soothing introjection occurs when a child expresses concern or fear to the caretaker, for example, about going to the dentist. The child is soothed if the mom stops what she is doing, listens to his concerns, and engages in a conversation addressing his worries. The child takes in her skills.

In both of these healthy examples, the external function performed by the caregiver is likely to become an internal function of the child's. Repeated external soothing develops internal calming capacities. The adolescent, and then later the adult, will then be poised to draw on himself in times of stress or discomfort, rather than reach outside for soothing in the form of AOD or other compulsive behaviors. Self-soothing capacities take time to develop and more time to trust. Eventually, they become the instinctive go-to tool. These skills greatly enhance self-confidence. Repeatedly using these capacities is gratifying, eventually much more so than taking drugs or alcohol.

Therapists and Alcoholics Anonymous (AA) sponsors do a lot of soothing during the very early days of sobriety. These needed functions are then internalized. They are essential for long-term recovery.

Karen Walant

Karen Walant (1995) is a social worker from Katonah, New York. For decades, she has been interested in attachment and addiction. Walant suggests that a denial and devaluation of merger moments throughout the life cycle has increased the likelihood of addiction. She proposes that premature autonomy and independence have been encouraged at the expense of attachment needs. She applied this interest to her own version of the theory of self-medication and addiction (p. 2).

Merger moments: Transformative experiences between a parent and dependent child that result in the child developing a cohesive sense of self.

Normative abuse: When parents and caretakers do not honor a child's healthy dependency needs, but instead honor the cultural norm of independence and separation.

Normative abuse results in: A child, adolescent, and then later adult who is disconnected from his needs and desires, and thus lacks a cohesive sense of self.

At the heart of addiction: A detached, alienated person looking for pseudo-merger with AOD.

Figure 7.1 The Flow of a Merger Moment

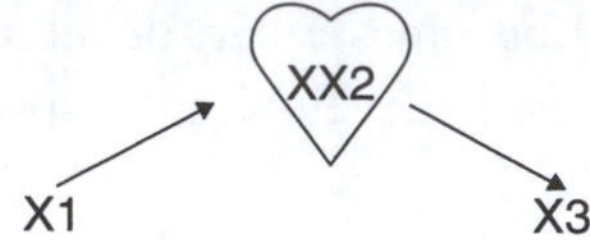

Walant suggests that merger moments are necessary experiences for the child. This is best understood by a diagram (see Figure 7.1). A fearful child with a healthy dependency need is represented by X1. Let's say the child is concerned about going to a birthday party with children he doesn't know. He approaches his caretaker, and if she is responsive, they merge together in an intimate relationship characterized by healthy dependency, talking, and problem solving, represented by XX2. When this moment is over, the child is transformed (Walant, 1995, p. 112). His anxiety is now soothed. This is represented by X3.

The child figured out his response to the birthday party dilemma. Healthy dependency and merger increased his confidence. The child learned three things from this experience of transformation. He learned that dependency is good, that it's okay to ask for what you need, and that it is possible the universe might provide it. He senses there is a solution to his fears. This feels good, and life feels doable (Walant, 1995).

Walant also postulates that, particularly in America, there is a tendency to deny or become fatigued with a young child's repeated dependency needs. When this happens, we often urge him to be a big boy and remind him that "Johnny down the street doesn't have a problem with birthday parties."

Walant suggests that the loss of these merger moments produces a child who is detached and alienated from himself and his needs, and thus at a loss as to how to respond to them. He is in a dilemma when problems arise. The child is then poised to look for pseudotransformation in unhealthy merger experiences with his thumb, his navel, his twirling hair, his bottle, fetishes, or other secret solutions. The child, adolescent, and then later adult continues this pseudomerger with drugs and alcohol. He then becomes dependent on these ungratifying compromises to soothe life's distresses. They create a temporary sense of feeling better, but provide little or no opportunity to learn from experience. Nonetheless, they become a way to deal with life.

In very early recovery, the sensation of merger with another person or therapist is often a new and profound experience. If repeated often enough, there develops a growing expectancy that merging with people is safe and desired, that healthy dependency needs should not be ignored and dismissed, and that drowning them in AOD is undesirable and unsatisfying. Addicts start to feel more connected to who they are and what they need, and look for healthy ways for the universe to respond to them—relationships, hobbies, teaching, and writing. A sense of self-cohesion and self-order is reborn.

Heinz Kohut in Jerome Levin

Jerome Levin (2001) is a major contributor to the field of addiction theory and treatment. His work, *Therapeutic Strategies for Treating Addiction*, includes Heinz Kohut's psychoanalytic theory of self psychology. Kohut sees narcissistic, or self-disturbances, as central to the psychopathology of the addict. Internally, the addict feels empty, fragmented, and unorganized. Alcoholic drinking is the pathological compromise that attempts to make up for this depleted sense of self.

Therapeutic relationships that foster a sense of self-cohesion are essential in recovery. Addiction doesn't inhabit individuals with a sense of self-cohesion and life purpose (Kohut, cited in Levin, 2001, pp. 71–97).

Selfobjects: Important others in the life of a child who are experienced as part of the self or in the service of the self.

Selfobject needs: Specific, empathic responses that the child needs in the areas of grandiosity, idealization, and likeness.

Selfobject experiences: Occur when parents provide needed responses to the child. These parental responses assist in the building of his self-structure. We seek similar experiences throughout our lifetime.

Transmuting internalization: Occurs when needed aspects of important selfobjects are internalized. Functions of the parents are taken in and transmuted into the child's sense of self and self-worth.

The experience of the addict: An inner emptiness is felt as a result of an absence of an internal self-structure. This is experienced as a void that addicts try to fill with AOD. It cannot be done. This effort is "futilitarian."

Motivation to use: All human beings strive toward health no matter how disturbing their behavior. Use of AOD is an attempt to preserve and protect a fragile and fragmented sense of self.

The need during recovery: A relationship with a person or persons that can build and replace deficient and missing selfobject capacities in the areas of tension regulation, self-soothing, and self-esteem regulation.

Kohut (in Levin, 2001, pp. 71–97) sees the self as present at birth. Hopefully, parents feel it and respond to an infant's initiations, assertions, and joys. These empathic responses provide early selfobject experiences for the infant.

According to self psychological theory, the self of the child has needs that must be responded to in certain ways for healthy self-development. These responses provide necessary functions for the child. Self-structure is then internalized from these selfobject experiences.

Kohut identifies three sets of needs or three poles of self-structure. The first set of needs pertains to the grandiose sector of the self-structure. The child needs to receive confirming and mirroring responses from others regarding his greatness, specialness, and importance. If all goes well, this sense of greatness translates into healthy ambitions and goals.

The second set of needs pertains to the idealizing sector of the self-structure. The child needs to extensively idealize selfobjects in his world. This idealized merger allows for vicarious participation in the perceived strength and calmness of the other during anxious or fearful times. A child eventually translates this borrowed capacity into his own; he can self-soothe.

The third set of needs pertains to the twinship sector of the self-structure. The young child needs selfobject relationships with others that create a sense of essential sameness. These experiences provide a sense of "My needs are okay, and I am like other people." This translates into a sense of belonging and self-confidence.

The child internalizes early empathic responses to these three sets of needs. They become a part of the child's sense of self. A cohesive self-structure is formed that is filled with a sense of vitality, tension regulation capacities, self-control, and self-confidence.

Gross empathic failures to these three sets of needs result in deficits in the child's self-structure. These result in a sense of self that lacks vitality and cohesiveness, that feels fragmented, empty, and enfeebled. This failure of internalization, with its feelings of being lost, can lead to addiction.

Kohut sees this disturbance of self as central to addiction. Addicts' core difficulty is the absence of internal structure. Again, this results in deficits in the self's capacity for tension regulation, self-soothing, and self-esteem regulation. These missing parts of the self are experienced as a void. It's an inner emptiness that addicts try to fill with drugs and alcohol, food, or other compulsive behaviors. Addiction is a desperate attempt to compensate for missing parts of the self. It cannot be done. Whatever is compulsively taken in goes right through, like pouring water into a sieve. It is a "futilitarian" effort. What is missing can only come from other people, from a certain kind of relationship that can be internalized.

For many recovering addicts, a therapeutic relationship is a very good start. The work of recovery and repair takes time and involves the use of transferences to reverse lifelong empathic failures in relationship experiences. Therapeutic skill is required to reawaken the addict's desire for people, long replaced by drugs and alcohol. This first flourishes in the form of a selfobject transference to the therapist. The therapist's essential skill here is not to interfere with the development of this need. Beware, as this is often bungled through lack of awareness or training, as well as anxiety. Once the selfobject transference is in sway, the patient, by psychic necessity, will ask the therapist to function as part or parts of the patient's missing self-structures (Baker and Baker, 1987).

The functions the recovering addict looks to the therapist to provide through this transference experience will most likely be related to one or more of the three major selfobject states from Kohut's theory of self-development:

- The grandiose self—the recovering addict needs to experience his essence as interesting, valuable, and worthy of others' attention.
- The idealized parent imago—the recovering addict needs to merge with the calm, strength, wisdom, and greatness of the therapist in order to join in his perceived strength and calmness.
- The alter-ego twinship—the recovering addict needs to feel that he is like another, to develop a comforting sense of his essential sameness and belonging.

An important task of the therapist is to discern which type of selfobject response the patient needs at which point in treatment. When the right selfobject transferences have formed, the patient is ready to resume the development of the self, fueled by what Kohut calls the Zeigarnik phenomenon (Kohut, cited in Chessick, 1992, p. 152). This is the wonderful, delightful human tendency to complete interrupted tasks of development if given a chance to do so.

Over time and by transmuting internalization, psychic structure is built. The therapist serves as a selfobject that provides needed functions. These then become internalized and self-structure is rehabilitated to new levels of health, strength, and maturity. The recovering addict is then able to seek out important selfobject experiences and relationships with other people in his own life. He begins to learn that drugs and alcohol actually interfere with the richness of these experiences.

Wilfred Bion

Dr. Wilfred Bion, a British psychoanalyst who wrote in the 1950s, made a major contribution to our understanding of how we as a people learn how to think.

Bion (1967) considers tolerance of frustration an innate factor of our personality (pp. 110–119). In other words, we can face frustration if our mother (caretaker) helps us. When she accepts, contains, and modifies these overwhelming and upsetting feelings, she turns them into what Bion calls our apparatus for thinking thoughts. She acts as a soothing container for difficult emotions. We learn, from her, how to face life's upsets. We learn the pleasures of thinking and, thus, don't need the gratuitous satisfaction that comes from AOD (Fetting, 2009, p. 7).

Deficiency in the addict: The apparatus of thinking thoughts.

Causes of deficiency: Lack of reverie from his childhood caretaker. Reverie is maternal containment of a child's frustrations. It often results in repeated experiences of transforming painful sensations into tolerable states of being, via the mother's thinking and soothing functions.

Motivation to use: To avoid dealing with frustration. Frustration is repeatedly felt as an overwhelming emotion that needs to be evacuated at all costs. This frustration and upset is discharged during repetitive addictive behaviors. It brings temporary satisfaction.

Addict's need: A relationship with someone who has the capacity for reverie. The recovering addict can then internalize this person's capacity to think through and soothe frustrations. He is then less likely to act them out in addictions.

An infant is frustrated and cries; mom responds and enters a mental state that Bion calls reverie. Reverie is emotional availability, fueled by fierce maternal instincts. A mother takes in and takes on the baby's frustrations. In the process, she tolerates them and tries to figure them out. Her instincts keep her focused until she determines his relief. After the baby is held and if all goes well, sensations are transformed—frustration is now satisfaction, emptiness is now fullness, pain is now pleasure, isolation is now company, anxiety is now calm, and dread is now hope (Fetting, 2009, p. 7).

The baby starts to sense, via the mother's capacity for reverie, that he can handle these upsetting feelings. He begins to internalize her capacity to think through and soothe his frustrations. It gradually becomes his capacity. His instinct is to face frustration, not avoid it. Thinking feels better than acting it out. It brings better results.

Without these repeated experiences of reverie, a child, adolescent, and then later adult is left unequipped and uninterested in facing life's everyday frustrations in healthy ways. The individual is left with one solution, and that is to avoid them. Addiction becomes a reliable avoidance strategy, and a way to discharge the tensions of frustration. While one feels temporarily relieved, the path of addiction usually results in the degradation of one's life and relationships. Lack of capacity to think through frustration moves one toward addiction, and the lack of capacity to think through the tragic and harmful consequences keeps one in addiction.

A major part of recovery is in the development of the capacity to think, to learn how to take in and take on one's frustrations, worries, and fears and to reflect on them. Reverie is a learned state. Thinking brings its own pleasures. People gain confidence in thinking things through rather than impulsively acting them out.

Christopher Bollas

Christopher Bollas is a British psychoanalyst and writer. He has written on many topics, including free association and unconscious communication. He also has drawn on the classical notions of fate and destiny, as well as on D. W. Winnicott's ideas about the true self and the false self. Together, these notions are very helpful in understanding some of the deeper self-medicative purposes behind addiction (Bollas, 1989, p. 8).

Addict's vulnerability: The addict's object world (parents, caretakers) did not provide the right conditions for the child to evolve and articulate his idiom. This person feels tragically fated and unable to experience life as conducive to the fulfillment of his destiny.

Purpose of addiction: To remove the suffering that comes from living the fated and reactive life of a false self; to self-medicate the suffering that comes from feeling unable to achieve one's true destiny.

The need during recovery: A relationship with a person who hears the faint murmurs of a true self with its desire to express its idiom through its destiny.

Idiom: The unique nucleus or defining essence of each individual.

Sense of fate: A person who feels fated has not experienced reality as conducive to the fulfillment of his inner idiom. Such a person is frustrated at the very core of his being. A false self becomes his guide through life.

Sense of destiny: Refers to the urge within each person to articulate and elaborate his idiom, a form of a life instinct in which the person seeks to come into his own true being through "an experiencing" that releases his potential.

Bollas (1989) helps us comprehend why some people seem destined to live a life of meaning and fulfillment and others seem fated to live a life of endurance and survival. It goes back to those early days.

If all goes well, an infant, child, and later adolescent experiences his mother as reliable. She enables him to come into contact with and experience his true self or his inherited potential. The child establishes his personality and feels real, alive, and capable of fulfilling his inner idiom, or his defining essence. He is then poised to ruthlessly select objects in his school, peer, and cultural world that facilitate the development of his unique destiny. People of destiny are passionate about what they are doing in life and how they relate to others. They feel strong about what they want. They are not selfish or self-centered. They are in touch with their idiomatic desires (Bollas, 1989, pp. 7–47).

If all does not go so well, an infant, child, and then later adolescent lives in a world of commandments. These are experienced as drastic demands dictated by his caretaker. These commands most often have nothing to do with the child's true self or inner essence. He feels required to adopt a certain way of thinking, choose certain friends, attend certain schools, and dress in certain ways. These declarations feel topsy-turvy to the child's sense of self, but he feels fated to follow them. The child is alienated from the experience of his true self and his idiomatic desires. He is then poised to feel despair and hopelessness about the world. He loses all interest in the search for objects that will help him experience his true self and unique destiny. A sense of emptiness shadows his life. He feels fated to live a life that he is not really connected to. Without this connection, he is unable to steer for himself. A false sense of self serves as his guide. He despairingly moves forward. He knows no other way (Bollas, 1989, p. 45).

Drugs and alcohol provide much comfort for the fated individual. He ruthlessly selects them as a reliable source of soothing and reprieve for these feelings of nameless dread (Bion, 1967, p. 116). AOD seem the perfect complement to a fated life with no imaginable future. "I can live in this rudderless world if I'm protected with Vicodin or alcohol." Henry David Thoreau said that so many individuals in our culture live lives of quiet desperation. They also live with addictions.

During recovery, the work is both directive and psychoanalytic in spirit. Addicts in their early days of sobriety need direction, guidance, and support. They also need attentive listening by important others. Their true self is searching for a connection that hears their essence and their destiny desires. If that listening occurs, a formerly fated addict can soon begin to live an unimaginable life of his future. It requires the fortune of staying drug-free, as well as focused determination, and a long, steady road of very difficult work with some healthy assertion and aggression to get what you need.

Lisa Director

Lisa Director looks at omnipotence in the psychoanalysis of substance users. Living in a state of omnipotence suggests that one desires a sense of complete control or influence over the self, an object, or others in the outside world. Dr. Director (2005) describes elements of omnipotence that are present in drug use. These include a dominant wish, a focused drivenness with an insistence on pleasure (pp. 567–587).

Addict's vulnerability: Addicts live with a pervasive and disturbing sense that one's needs cannot be met by self or others. This sets into play an aggressive and destructive search to meet them through AOD.

Instrument of omnipotence: Drugs, alcohol, and the world of ritualized addiction provide the addict with a sense of omnipotent control. The use of drugs and alcohol promises that needs will always be met.

The need during recovery: A relationship with a person who has the capacity to hold and contain the addict's defensive feelings of omnipotence. The function of this state of mind can then be more easily explored and discussed.

An infant regularly fed and attended to develops a sense of healthy omnipotence. With this comes a sense of trust that the universe and the people in it can satisfy basic needs. D. W. Winnicott calls this a "moment of illusion." This experience provides an infant, child, adolescent, and then later adult with a faith that other people can provide support during overwhelming times (Winnicott, cited in Director, 2005, p. 575).

Addicts seem to live a very pained life without this internalized sense of illusion. Many have been dramatically and repeatedly disappointed in childhood, adolescence, and, later, adulthood. They live in a state of frustrated need without a clear sense of what to do or how to help themselves. Director and others suggest that addicts aggressively and rather exclusively seek out drugs and alcohol to satisfy these frustrations. They discover that they work, and over time, the AOD becomes the central organizing principle in their lives.

They develop a love affair with this omnipotent provider. The sense of ever-present provisions brings with it tremendous feelings of security and safety. While it is akin to the moment of illusion of the early infant when breastfed, it is a miscarriage of reality based on a perverted relationship with a dangerous object. This relationship provides neither a healthy relational back-and-forth nor satiation. Its pleasure lies exclusively in its control (Director, 2005, p. 575).

Director (2005) goes on to highlight the frustrations experienced by persons in the life of the addict. When the addict is ruthlessly devoted to control of the drug experience, he pushes people to the periphery with aggression and hostility. Family members, loved ones, and even therapists know too well the experience of feeling devalued and unimportant to the addict, even hated, particularly if his using feels threatened. Unconsciously, the addict pushes others away as ruthlessly as his needs were pushed away as an infant. The addict's omnipotence belies his terror; feelings of uselessness bring much suffering to his loved ones (pp. 567–587).

Certainly it is critical for a therapist to contain this omnipotence if it should reappear in early recovery. It requires much tact and patience to listen to an addict's overbearing enthusiasm and sense of certainty about his plans in his early days of sobriety. This certainty has a brittle protectiveness to it. Many times, it prevents real contact with therapists or loved ones, and many times relapse occurs. It is not uncommon to feel as irrelevant to a newly sober person as one did during his days of using.

Omnipotence needs to be addressed, and the deeper reasons behind pushing people away understood. This is very delicate; it takes time and patience. Adam

Phillips (1994) says it best for the plight of the recovering omnipotent addict: "Hell is not other people, but one's need for other people" (p. 45). Learning to trust others without the use of omnipotence is a daunting undertaking.

CHAPTER SUMMARY AND REFLECTIONS

Summary

This chapter presented a self-selected collection of addiction and psychoanalytic theories that shed light on the etiology and psychological suffering behind addiction. A concise synopsis of selected aspects of these theories was presented using discipline, imagination, and creativity. These nine unique, yet overlapping theories proposed that untreated human psychological suffering drives some people to self-medicate their pain with alcohol and other drugs. Each theory presented provides the reader with an insightful and useful perspective on what might cause this suffering. These theorized essentials were followed by discussion ideas, brief clinical vignettes, and suggestions for their use in recovery treatment. Class lectures enrich clinical understanding and invite more personal student participation.

Reflections

Before you leave this chapter, make sure you have:

- Studied each theory
- Further studied those of personal and clinical interest
- Recognized the uniqueness of each theory and the overlap among them
- Considered returning to this chapter again and again

Part IV

A Perspective on the Treatment Path of Addiction With Clinical Cases

Chapter 8

Stephanie Brown and an Integrative Treatment Model

Figure 8.1 Identity Reconstruction Chart

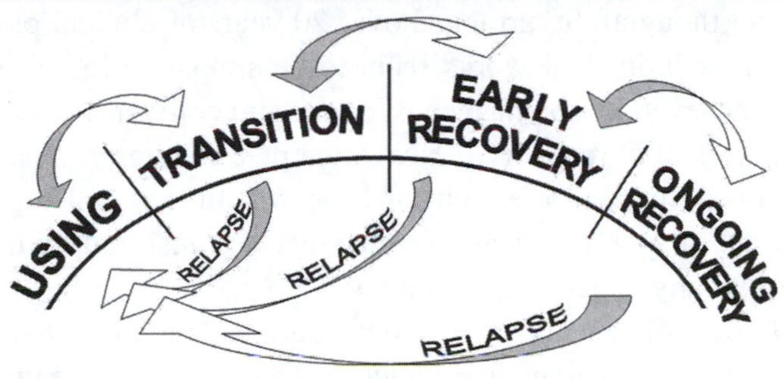

INTRODUCTION

Dr. Stephanie Brown is a major contributor to the field of addiction. She has written several books, including *Treating the Alcoholic: A Developmental Model of Recovery*. She cofounded the Stanford Alcohol Clinic in 1977 and has published in the areas of addiction psychotherapy and the process of recovery, including individual and family treatment. Dr. Brown was intrigued by the question, "What happens to adults when they stop drinking?" This led to the creation of her developmental model of treatment that heralds the importance of the addict's construction of a new identity, highlights the evolving needs and processes of each "timeless" stage of recovery, and identifies the deeper work required for the achievement and maintenance of a sober identity and the evolution of a healthy lifestyle. I have valued, studied, treated from, and taught this model for over 20 years. Students, addicts, and their families seem to value it as well.

This chapter provides an overview of Brown's stage-driven developmental model of alcoholism recovery. This overview is followed by four chapters that highlight some of the work of each of her stages of treatment, identify the tasks of therapist and addict, and propose additional avenues of growth and development for both members of the therapeutic dyad. This section is the meat of this book.

Brown's substantial body of work is cogently and selectively presented. Her writings reflect her allegiance to the disease model of addiction. She has created an abstinence-based developmental model of recovery. It is a model of treatment that is quite structured and also invitingly flexible. Over the years, I have discovered that her model welcomes and easily incorporates other treatment theories and strategies. As an assimilative thinker, I have included writers, psychoanalysts, social workers, psychologists, addiction specialists, and educators to support the work of each of her stages. Their inclusions have been intuitively selected, and thoughtfully arranged over 20 years of clinical psychotherapy and teaching. Their individual works seem to be simpatico in spirit and substance, and together they seem to enhance, support, and enliven Brown's very solid and dependable model of recovery. I have attempted to interpret each person's work with both discipline and creativity. I have woven them all together in an integrative model of treatment and recovery that was inspired by the yearnings and needs of my many patients and families.

The field of addiction and its treatment has a bad rap in contemporary culture—skeptics often say, "Manipulative addicts and alcoholics are treatment resistant and bound to relapse. Nothing really works." This section is an invitation to reconsider this reputation. The integrative model reflects a treatment vision from a group of diverse and creative thinkers, all uniformly dedicated to emotional recovery and growth. It has had many good successes, some missteps, and always valuable learnings. It continues to grow and fills me with a sense of pragmatism and optimism about the field. I hope you find it valuable.

OVERVIEW OF BROWN'S STAGES OF RECOVERY WITH AN INTRODUCTION TO AN INTEGRATIVE TREATMENT MODEL

Stephanie Brown's model of treatment can be explained in one sentence: Recovery is about an identity reconstruction, nurtured over four stages of development. Dr. Brown's emphasis on an identity reconstruction is absolutely essential for the achievement of abstinence, but also applicable for any of the profiles of addiction discussed in Chapter 4. To sustain change in any of these troubled behaviors, the addict or problematic user has to fundamentally shift how he sees himself and how he sees his world (Brown, 1985).

Identity Reconstruction

Brown's focus on an identity shift is imperative, and to grasp this profound task is to have reverence and respect for anyone who attempts recovery. One has to dare to say, "Enough," even hesitantly, to a sense of self that lived a life preoccupied with the habitual and excessive use of alcohol and other drugs (AOD). And one has to dare to say, "Welcome," even begrudgingly, to a life without the destructive thinking and behavior patterns of addiction. This is the crux of Brown's model, and this is the crux of recovery.

Most simply, recovery involves what Michael White (1995), the recently deceased Australian social worker, calls the migration of an identity—actively moving away from how one has known oneself and the world (the drinking or false self), with a desire to experience self and the world from a new and different place (the recovery, or true self). This involves moving away from "I am not an addict, it's not that bad, everyone is out to get me, and who cares anyway?" and moving toward "I see that my difficulties with living are related to using, people are caring and not controlling, and I care and want to do something about this" (p. 99).

Migrations are always hazardous, and the traveling takes more time than anticipated. This journey involves a courageous willingness to continually chip away and discard a defensive or false identity driven by the need for avoidance, protection, and endurance. It also requires the addict to tenderly build and reinforce a true identity based on facing and enduring conflict, risk, vulnerability, and growth. This is a frightening and painstaking process that relies on thoughtful ongoing support.

Recovery for the addict is fueled by his devotion to the task. Treatment by the provider is fueled by the deep recognition that recovery will flow from the continual support of the user's identity reorganization. In psychoanalytic parlance, this dual devotion closely mirrors the mother-infant relationship. The infant striving for his being is supported by the "boundless, unknown support" of his mother (Eigen, 2009, p. 23). The addict striving for healing relies so preciously on the same support from an analyst, a therapist, or a sponsor; a fellow addict; or a family member. These relationships are critical for recovery. The depth and strength of these attachments make all the difference.

Nurturing Interest and the Prevention of Relapse

The British psychoanalyst Adam Phillips (1998) suggests that passionate living is dependent upon an energized interest in one's true self. Fundamentally, recovery is about engaging in a more authentic relationship with oneself and one's world, and keeping this interest ever-present. Unfortunately, many recovering addicts start to disregard this new sense of self, and think it's okay to let this interest drift away. The business of getting to know oneself without alcohol and drugs gets frightening and tiresome. Life gets stressful, demands increase, family members become impatient, and pressure mounts. That old endurance and survival self is called into action, and relapse is not far behind. While it is often blamed on stress, that's only part of the picture.

The integrative model presented here builds on Marlatt and Gordon's (1985) classic work on relapse prevention. The proposed treatment model suggests that relapse occurs because people stop taking their new sense of self seriously. They grow weary and lose interest in staying connected to the reawakening of their true self, including their fragile recovering identity (Phillips, 1998, pp. 3–36). One patient announced, "I'm so tired because I'm recovering from my life, you know."

Fatigued and impatient family members, therapists, and sponsors can lose interest in supporting this process as well. This forgetting is lethal, which will be emphasized again and again in this section. Nurturing, sustaining, and maintaining the return of a childlike curiosity, with its unbridled interest in self, is the key to long-term recovery. Relapse will occur otherwise. And relapse has made a mockery of a treatment industry that has not conveyed this message to the recovering consumers and their families, and the public in general.

Four Stages of Development

Brown's developmental model of recovery includes four stages. The stages begin while one is actively drinking or using and move through transition, early recovery, and ongoing recovery.

Her model provides a progressive mix of ingredients, including characteristics and features of each of the stages, identity tasks for the alcoholic or addict, and recovery responsibilities for the treatment provider. These together essentially define the work of recovery and treatment.

Prochaska, DiClemente, and Norcross's (1993) well-regarded stages of change complement Brown's developmental progression and highlight the painstaking and courageous preparations involved in the addict's recovery work, and the consistency of treatment needed to solidly support the addict's identity evolution.

Return to Figure 8.1. It diagrams the addict's journey through the four developmental stages of recovery. Growth is not linear; thus the arrows move back and forth between stages. Some parts of the self move forward into a new stage, while other parts remain in or return to a previous stage. Integration of these selves takes time. A conflicted or unintegrated identity sometimes invites relapse. Simply put,

"The addict forgot who he was." Please keep this in your mind as you learn about the work of each stage.

Part IV journeys through each of Brown's stages, chapter by chapter. I have also included many other well-established theories and theorists, new ideas, and creative formulations to deepen and widen Brown's suggested developmental journey of growth and recovery. Each chapter identifies the primary tasks of each stage and is infused with a psychoanalytic sensibility that suggests additional clinical concepts and interventions that are useful for the ongoing treatment of identity reconstruction. These encourage a deeper therapeutic relationship through the use of transference and countertransference. A holding relationship allows the addict to open up to previously unfelt emotions and experiences. The capacity to recognize and face unresolved childhood conflicts is enhanced, and the addict is able to assume deeper individual responsibility for sobriety and self-development.

I have found the inclusion of this attitude extraordinarily helpful for the addict as he moves away from a life dominated by impulse and defense. The analytic concepts presented invite deeper therapist and patient self-awareness and self-reflection as well. Psychoanalytic thinking is a hospitable and valuable addition to contemporary addiction treatment approaches.

Clinical case studies are presented that are representative of the challenges, opportunities, and struggles of each stage. Treatment theories and psychoanalytic concepts are practically applied to these struggles in *Therapeutic action moments*. These clinical excursions spawn from the pains and passions of so many, most poignantly from my patients and most passionately from the writers and thinkers presented in this book. As always, I encourage use of your own intuition and experience as you explore the fit between theory and practice.

Reading Guidelines

The next four chapters identify a mix of treatment theories and concepts, therapeutic skills, and clinical caveats that are useful to understand and also apply during the addict's travels through each stage of recovery. This mix of concepts, skills, and caveats is for treatment providers to match with their own intuition, their own clinical style, and their patient's particular path. Past and ongoing clinical cases put theory to practice in therapeutic action moments. A clinician prepared for the primary and secondary tasks of each stage invites the addict to do the same. Study these ideas; make them useful in your own life, and also yours to use during recovery treatment; develop a tolerance for the unfamiliar; and go at your own pace as your mind struggles and then rests.

These reading guidelines will reappear in the introduction of each chapter in this section.

CHAPTER SUMMARY AND REFLECTIONS

Summary

This chapter provides a cogent overview of Stephanie Brown's cognitive, behavioral, and dynamic model of recovery. The reader is further introduced to the ideas that will be presented in the integrative treatment model presented in Chapters 9 through 12. Brown's developmental model is infused with a psychoanalytic sensitivity that proposes additional treatment concepts and tasks for both therapist and addict. Therapeutic action moments highlighted in the case studies of these chapters put theory to practice.

Reflections

Before you leave this chapter, make sure you have:

- Started to understand the addict's developmental journey of recovery through four stages of treatment
- Considered returning to this chapter in order to keep your clinical bearings

Chapter 9

The Integrative Treatment Model

The Drinking and Using Stage

Figure 9.1 The Using Stage

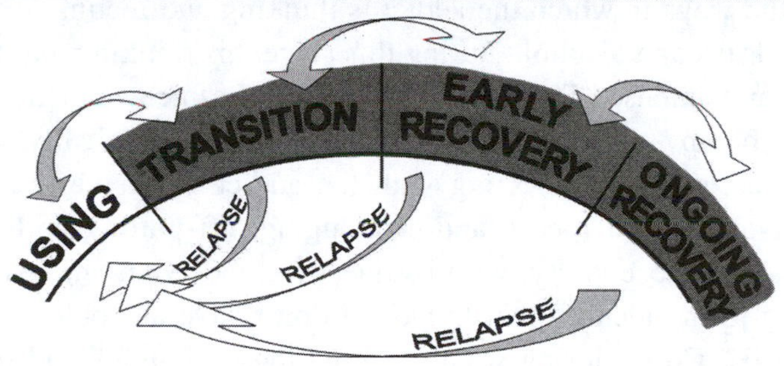

INTRODUCTION

The using (drinking, drugging) phase of treatment is about establishing a meaningful relationship with a person in trouble with drugs and alcohol, not conquering an addict or alcoholic. There is nothing more to do than create this relationship, and doing this is doing so much. The field, including its addictive families, too often becomes obsessed and preoccupied with a campaign or conquest, not with a connection. We are lost and misguided without the establishment of a relationship that is receptive to the alcoholic's way of being and point of view. Many of our "difficulties" working with alcoholics and addicts are because of this relational confusion. We need a meaningful connection, not a victorious conquest.

While this focus is not the immediate priority during encounters with hostile drunkenness or a terrifying, life-threatening emergency, the establishment of this real experience of connection with a person in trouble with alcohol and other drugs (AOD) is always primary. Alcoholics and drug addicts so desperately need to experience therapists, psychiatrists, social workers, or counselors as a receptive presence. This is a presence preoccupied with listening, not controlling or coercing. Without this, treatment providers are perceived as a threat, like everyone else in the addict's life.

Fatigued and weary family members plead with loving concern, yet understandably their motives are often about controlling the addict and his frightening behavior. This approach leaves no room for the addict to safely connect. He is repelled and runs the other way. A person coming into treatment during the using stage hopes for another chance, and a different experience. A receptive attitude is essential for the development of a therapeutic attachment during an office visit or an intervention. Holding on to this attitude may be one of the greatest ongoing challenges in addiction treatment.

Establishing a working relationship means making contact with the user's identity, the ways in which the addict is thinking and feeling about his relationship with drugs and alcohol. During this stage, his thinking and feeling are both confused and intense. The clinician needs assessment and treatment skills in cognitive therapy, as well as capacities to work dynamically with many contradictory emotions. Connecting with the addict's evasive, hostile, or aggressive ambivalence is slippery and challenging, off-putting and bedeviling, and also necessary. Receptivity, with its quest for understanding, paves the way for connecting to the identity that thinks, "I don't have a problem, and if I do, it's not that bad." Co-exploring what's behind these thoughts and feelings leads to an attachment between therapist and patient that encourages embracing an identity that begins to believe, "I have a problem, and I'm ready to do something about it."

Using's primary tasks are:

- **Establishing a relationship** with a using identity that feels persecuted and omnipotent, anxious and misunderstood, terrified and hopeful, desperate for help and fiercely protective of his relationship with drugs and alcohol
- **Comprehending the dual nature of addiction** as a thinking, or cognitive, disorder as well as a doing, or behavioral, disorder
- **Incorporating clinical concepts** such as *identity reconstruction, discounting, blind eye, natural history, reverie, totalization of identity, detotalization of identity, authority, harm reduction, receptivity, ambivalence,* and *registering impacts*

This chapter is divided into three sections. *Clinical Concepts with Brief Clinical Cases* introduces the reader to theories and interventions that are useful for initiating and developing a treatment relationship. *Clinical Cases* demonstrates their application in therapeutic action moments. The relationship is the vehicle that transports the identity migration over four stages of recovery (M.White, 1995, p. 99). Initiating and nurturing a robust therapeutic connection are needed to foster this journey. The process of identity reconstruction needs safe travel, as it is the crux of recovery.

The concepts presented have been creatively borrowed from many, and imaginatively adapted over years of clinical treatment and teaching. Some are adapted from researchers, writers, and clinicians in the addiction treatment world. Others are clinical concepts from psychoanalytic literature. I have found the psychoanalytic attitude to be both energizing and utilitarian. Their applications greatly facilitate and reinforce the addict's identity evolution, the anchor that stabilizes his recovery. The concepts and ideas used during this stage encourage thinking before activity, contemplating rather than compulsivity. They also deepen the therapeutic relationship.

Cognitive Theory with Brief Clinical Cases introduces the importance of cognitive work in recovery treatment. Identifying and challenging addictive beliefs are necessary to change behavior as well as to shift identity. Clinical cases are used to identify and demonstrate cognitive interventions.

Reading Guidelines

This chapter identifies a mix of theories and treatment concepts, therapeutic skills, and clinical caveats that are useful to understand and also apply during the addict's travels on using's terrain. This mix of concepts, skills, and caveats is for treatment providers to match with their own intuition, their own clinical style, and their patient's particular recovery path. Past and ongoing clinical cases put theory to practice in therapeutic action moments. A clinician prepared for using's primary tasks invites the addict to do the same. Study these ideas; make them useful in your own life, and also yours to use during recovery treatment; develop a tolerance for the unfamiliar; and go at your own pace as your mind struggles and then rests.

CLINICAL CONCEPTS WITH BRIEF CLINICAL CASES

Identity Reconstruction

As has been said in Chapter 8, recovery involves an identity migration over four stages of treatment. The using identity is composed of a mix of self-states. Two contradictory ones frequently appear. One is fiercely protective of its drinking/

drugging and fiercely private about its worries. Another state is dreaming about a better solution to one's life and yet unable to imagine this possibility.

The therapist during the using stage receptively listens for the addict's hidden wishes. She also needs to be actively ready to intervene if imminent danger threatens the addict's life. These therapeutic sensibilities invite attachment.

Most addicts and alcoholics begin treatment while actively using. Some are ready to let go of their AOD identity, others are immobilized by their ambivalences, and some are very reluctant to relinquish this way of living. The therapeutic work of the using stage is to develop a relationship with this confused sense of self. The relationship contains the addict's worries and wishes. Identity reconstruction work can then begin, and migration through the using stage becomes possible.

Discounting and Blind Eye

The using phase of treatment is focused on addressing denial. Arguably, the world of addiction and recovery has hijacked this word and coveted its use. In reality, we all live in some form of denial much of the time. T. S. Elliot, the poet, elegantly confirms this when he writes, "Humankind cannot stand very much reality."

I use the word *discounting* when working with an addict's denial (Schiff, cited in Lasater, 1988, pp. 30–31). The *American Heritage Dictionary* defines the word *discount* as "(v.) To underestimate the significance or effectiveness of; (v.) to make allowances for; (n.) a reduction from the full or standard amount of a price or debt" (1985, p. 403).

Addicts discount in four ways. First, they discount the very *existence* of their addictive behavior. Many actually live with little or no conscious connection to their AOD problem. It is built into the fabric of their day-to-day world of endurance and survival. A 41-year-old recovering alcoholic and cocaine addict said to me, "I went to bars and got drunk every night. I thought everyone else that was home with their kids or their family was missing out on what life was all about. I knew I had the real secret to living while I was in these bars." Next, many also discount the *significance* of their problem. Addicts are often unable to make a causal connection between their pained life and their problematic using. This reflection promotes too much unmanageable anxiety and is thus avoided.

Additionally, alcoholics cannot bear to take responsibility for the *impact* their using has on the lives of their loved ones. This is aggressively defended, excused away, or dismissively justified. A 56-year-old father of three proudly announces, "It's all so different now that I'm not using." It's hard for his wife and children to trust this statement. They have lived through multiple relapses over 18 years. No one is sure from one day to the next if he is drinking or sober, abstinent or relapsing. The family's watchfulness is perceived as obsessively controlling to him; he deflects their pain. Finally, most addicts live in the problem and only dream of a solution. This causes them to discount their *capacity to repair anything at all* about their using. Persons in trouble with AOD often feel stymied and stuck between knowing that they have a problem and defending and protecting its continuation. This paradoxical bind of knowing and not knowing, sensing trouble but not wanting to address it, often called turning a blind eye, leads to immobilization (Steiner, 1993, p. 129). The person is unable to imagine a change that would make a dent of any kind.

The user has blind-eye vision, and the using phase is peppered with discounting in all four areas. Embracing these concepts facilitates a more fruitful assessment, encourages patient reflection, promotes flexible discussions, and gradually allows for more individual ownership of the problem. Patients are able to parse their denial—separate it out into different components. For example, "I now see that since I discount the existence of my drinking problem, I have to minimize its harmful impact on my family." Conversations get going when we use *discounting* instead of *denial*.

Natural History

A cold has a natural history of five to seven days. You can make it better or worse; everyone has a choice. For example, first you have to acknowledge that you have a cold, not pretend that it doesn't exist or wish it away. Then you have to decide what to let go of in your schedule, how to attend to your responsibilities, how to redesign your life to allow for some healing space, and then communicate these adjustments to everyone effected. This all requires accepting the hard realities of illness and recovery. Accepting these involves embracing an identity of vulnerability and healing. If you ignore this path, a common cold could lead to bronchitis or walking pneumonia. If you work with your natural history, it will be over in a shorter amount of time.

George Vaillant (1983) is one of the most respected longitudinal researchers in the field of addiction. He looks at the natural history of alcoholism, that is, the path or course of one's distinct relationship with AOD, as well as one's path or course of recovery (pp. 107–180). Everyone's natural history is unique, and it's imperative that each is understood. One of the first things I do in the using phase is get a sense of the patient's "location" in his natural history. Where is he in accepting this dual identity of sickness and healing? It is important to both embrace and challenge that place. Addicts feel respected by this effort.

Identifying a patient's natural history aligns a clinician with the rhythm of the addict's current relationship with AOD. To understand this is to grasp his readiness to acknowledge some difficulties or his preference to pretend them away. Does the addict recognize his "cold" and know some adjustments in living will further natural healing? Does the person ignore all the telltale signs with a wish that by looking the other way, the cold will spontaneously disappear? Or does someone attack his cold with an infusion of his own homegrown remedies and stubbornly keep on going anyway?

Natural History One

There are two natural histories that appear during the using phase of addiction. The first involves people who are paying increasing amounts of attention to AOD. They are beginning to get into some troubles and tensions with self, work, family and friends, or health. Things haven't spun out of control, and there is a hope and belief that they will not. While an experienced or caring eye can sense potential disaster ahead, the addict does not. He is unable to constructively utilize feelings of impending doom. He hopes that he can keep getting away with his troubled behavior. He imagines more time and usually wants to take it. Treatment interventions are meant to provoke conversation and reflection about a complicated and conflicted habituated relationship that the alcoholic/addict does not want to let go of. A few clinical examples will shed light on the utility of this concept during this stage.

Larry

Larry is a 17-year-old senior in high school. His parents worry about his difficulty with directly addressing problems that arise with friends or in making plans. He avoids facing his anxieties and concerns. Plans turn into messes. His friends are increasingly frustrated, and Larry gets more anxious and angry. He starts smoking marijuana every day and drinking at parties. Larry's outbursts and using are upsetting to the family. His parents insist on therapy.

His mom and dad hope I will work wonders with their son. Larry, on the other hand, is not a willing or happy patient. "The patient pressured into treatment" phenomenon is a regular feature in this stage of recovery. Larry believes his parents are overreacting and says that his marijuana and alcohol use is "normal, and no more than others. I see people in trouble and that's not me." He insists that he is dealing "just fine with my schoolwork, my girlfriend, and my family. If I smoke too much marijuana, I skip a day. I don't want it to affect my workouts or my chances of getting into college."

Larry shows up to our sessions "to honor my parents," and, not surprisingly, he misses most of them. We have a conversation about his absences and his feelings about therapy, and he says he doesn't want to be forced to talk. I listen and also suggest that therapy might help with his tendency to avoid difficult discussions and situations. He says he is not interested. He feels burdened by parental pressure, and he says he wants no part of any help. He pleads, "Would you tell my parents that forcing me to talk is not going to work?" I listen and also remind him that we have started a therapy relationship and if he ever wants to talk in the future to give me a call. I share with his parents, "While there are live issues here, your son does not want to talk. It is not his time or I'm not his type, but he knows how to reach me in the future."

I choose to respect Larry's natural history, not aggressively confront it. This choice has risks; real physical and psychological dangers may erupt. After all, a cold could turn into bronchitis. I sense that his using is more problematic than he imagines, and it is worth examining and understanding. I suspect he is discounting the existence, significance, impact, and repair capacity of his issues with marijuana. I also sense he feels unable and unwilling to address any of these at this time.

The concept of natural history is useful. Therapeutic interventions become more meaningful and memorable if we work within the addict's location, not insist on telling him "where he needs to be." This thoughtfulness feels inviting and fosters the addict's attachment to the clinician. This is often followed by some willing reflection on his behavior. Avoidance and defensiveness are reduced. This proved true a year later.

Larry gave me a call and said that he needed to talk. His first year of college had been a disaster: "I didn't attend classes, I drank a lot, I had trouble with my girlfriend, I fooled around with other girls, and I stayed in my dorm room smoking dope most of every day. I felt depressed and slept too much. It was bad." When he arrived at my office, he seemed a different person than the year before. He was concerned and worried, reflective, not defensive. He wanted to talk, not avoid, and he seemed to fully grasp the difficulties of his first year in college. He "felt" inside of his own skin. He wanted to grow from "my mistakes." Larry was earnest and sought reassurance—"I don't think I've blown it all, and I hope I can regain what I lost during that first year?" Here was a natural history ready to work. His call demonstrated once again that the "risk of respect" seems to make a memorable long-term impact. Try it out.

Sarah

Sarah is a woman in her late 40s. I have seen her on and off for years. She is a single professional in a very demanding field. She works hard and "needs" two martinis every night. They seem to get her through. We have talked about the meaning and functions of this evening ritual. We have explored her anxieties about her work, her desire for a relationship, her loneliness, and their contributions to her drinking. It's "something I need to look at, and my good friends are concerned about my drinking as well." Over the years, these conversations were started and never finished. I encouraged their continuation. Her natural history thought otherwise. I chose not to engage in a "confrontation game." She drifted in and out of her life, as well as our therapy.

Then she had a brain tumor and gave me a call. She was ready to work: "I'm scared and have been 'asleep.' I hope it's not too late. I've talked in therapy, but I've never done anything with the talking. I want this time to be different."

During our early conversations, she talked more about her relationship with alcohol than her brain tumor. I noticed this natural history shift. She spoke more freely about her need to drink every night. She was vigilant about her alcohol stash and always knew if her supply was running low. She would stop at the liquor store on her way home. "I would never miss a day. It got me through. I would close my apartment door and pour a martini. I tried to wait until after my shower. That never worked. I would have a drink, eat a snack, and have another martini. I would pass out. The same thing happened night after night. I didn't want to look at this until now. I guess the brain tumor woke me up."

Sarah was advised not to drink after her surgery. However, in less than a month, she was drinking wine several nights a week. Her relief was filled with discounting: "I feel good that it's not vodka." She missed her martinis, "but knew better than to start that again, yet I don't think drinking two glasses of wine is all that bad? After all, a doctor once told me that it's only a problem if you have three to four drinks every night, not one or two like me."

Common sense sometimes trumps medical advice. Best to avoid drinking during recovery from a brain tumor. I did not engage in a vociferous campaign about the dangers to her health. She did not want to "hear" that; she wanted her glasses of wine. Yet I was struck with how much more, in our brief time together, she was talking about her drinking. She hesitantly volunteered in a later session, "I am not sure I want you to hear this, but there is a part of me that wants to stop drinking altogether." I asked her what was behind her thinking. She continued, "It's not healthy, it burns out brain cells, and it keeps me asleep." Her natural history and identity had shifted. Her need for discounting diminished. She seemed to sense that her relationship with alcohol was separating her from her inner world of feelings and preventing her from living her life. As we continued to discuss her drinking patterns, I strongly suspected that the time had come for her to deal with this issue. I also suspected that respecting her natural history over the years had paid off. Our relationship was now a safe one to attach to—to explore past issues that were driving her drinking, as well as to develop more understanding of her current relationship with alcohol.

Reverie

Alex

People call for an appointment and we meet a first time. I wonder what is troubling them and if we are going to be a good fit. Alex is a 52-year-old who comes into my office, saying, "I'd like to get some advice on yet another knockdown, drag-out fight with my narcissistic father." We have a conversation, and I sense a wounded man at the hands of an abusive and neglectful father. He tries hard in his life—he works at his marriage, perseveres as a professional, and is a struggling writer. He tells me he has "done a lot of work in therapy over the years" and only wants an occasional visit about his current predicament. I continue to listen.

Two months passed and we now meet another time. It is 1 p.m. After 15 minutes of conversation, I sense that I smell alcohol in my room and on his breath. This confirms the alcohol odor I thought I smelled in the waiting room. I am always powerfully impacted by this olfactory rush, and immediately I start thinking about how I'm going to work with this and address it. It's always difficult in a new and tentative therapeutic relationship. Often, I doubt my perceptions, and it takes a bit of time to confirm them. This day, I decide to finish our session and conduct my "smell check test." I shut my office door as we headed to the suite exit. After he left, I returned to my office, opened my door, and found the information I needed. My office reeked of alcohol. I then felt sure that "day drinking" was occurring and, more importantly, alcohol may have been needed to come to therapy. I began thinking about what I might say if he called again.

Alex did call, and we set up another appointment. It is 3 p.m., and once again, there is the odor of alcohol. I receptively listen to his words about his father and his pain. He is uncertain whether "to confront him or just let the relationship drift away." I am also pondering a similar dilemma—do I address the alcohol odor or let my concerns temporarily drift away. Here is a person I have seen only three times in two months, and he came to me for issues with his father, not issues with his drinking. Nonetheless, the alcohol was in the room.

I sat there listening to Alex in a state of reverie. Wilfred Bion, the eminent psychoanalyst, describes this maternal state of caregiving with an infant. The caregiver takes in and on her child's frustrations and fears; pondering what and how to respond to them. Reverie is a receptive, not prematurely active state, fueled by emotional availability and fierce maternal instincts. The mother functions as a thinking container for the infant's desires and frustrations, and transforms hunger into satisfaction, pain into pleasure, and loneliness into company. Therapists are encouraged to inhabit this state as well. We take in and on what our patients present or "give" to us, and we "dream" a response. It is a difficult state of uncertainty, but staying with and in it usually brings good results (Bion, cited in Grinberg, Sor, and de Bianchedi, 1977, p. 39).

My reverie worked, and it came to me. I asked him, "You are going through a lot of pressure and stress about your dad now. Often, people in a difficult time have trouble with sleeping, eating, drinking, or sex. I was wondering if you were experiencing behavioral changes in any of these areas?" His response was very quick, too quick. "I do have a problem with drinking, but that is a separate issue. I need to talk to you about that at some point. For now, I'm okay."

Later in the session, I shared, "I wanted to ask about your current drinking habits because I thought I smelled alcohol on your breath in our last session, and even today. I wanted to see if you were experiencing any changes or difficulties with your drinking during this very rough time." We gave each other firm eye contact, and then he quickly moved on to another topic.

I went back into reverie about this interaction as we continued talking. At the end of the session, I followed up, "I wasn't sure how to address the alcohol odor in this room, but I wanted to check it out with you." His response had an edge, "That's fine, and as a matter of fact, I did have a couple of glasses of wine with a friend at lunch earlier today." He left and said he would call me soon for another session.

My reverential instincts told me that this direct but nonconfrontational attitude was the right approach. I respected his natural history by not pushing it, yet I also wanted to respectfully comment on his drinking prior to our therapy session. I thought it useful for him to start thinking about his current relationship with alcohol. Brown suggests that this is a confrontation within a therapeutic alliance (Wyatt and Yalom, 2007). The seamless inclusion of day drinking into one's life reflects a behavioral and thinking distortion that portends increased difficulty.

My respect for Alex's natural history worked for him. He called periodically for sessions. The concerns were always about work, his father, his health, or his wife, and caretaking. At some point during each of these conversations, he would say, "Eventually, I have to do something about my drinking. I do too much of that." Alex didn't want to say much more, but he may have found a place for his natural history when it is ripe for healing.

Natural History Two

People are paying much more attention to AOD in the second natural history of this stage. The using has dangerously escalated; chaos and unpredictability are the norm, families are terrorized by bad decisions, and physical and mental health are seriously deteriorating. Time is running out, and life is threatened. This natural history can end with devastation or with opportunity. Interventions are more action based, unlike the more cognitive and reflective interventions of Natural History One. A few clinical examples will shed light on this and other concepts.

Totalization of Identity, Detotalization of Identity, Authority, and Harm Reduction

Melinda

Melinda is a 30-year-old "floppy stoner mom." She arrives at her first therapy session under the influence and tentatively announces her desire to stop smoking marijuana "eight times throughout the day." She has a medical marijuana prescription and has discovered that pot gets her through the pressures of mothering, the stresses and humiliations of living with a verbally abusive and domineering husband, and the pain of unresolved conflicts of childhood. As we begin talking, she asks me, "Do you think I'm an addict, or do you think maybe I could learn to moderate my marijuana use?" She continues, "You know, I don't really want to be an addict; I just want to be less of a stoner mom." These are common sentiments heard during the using phase. A majority of people in trouble with drugs and alcohol have just as much trouble with the label of addict or alcoholic.

While some revel in the term alcoholic, as well as the notion of disease as identity, others are truly mortified by these terms and concepts. Michael White (1995), the recently deceased Australian social worker, makes a valuable contribution here. He believes we are tragically obsessed with labels in America. White suggests this is a shaming cultural practice. We call people alcoholic and addict, bulimic and anorexic, or shopaholic. He continues that these labels totalize one's sense of self or identity. The alcoholic often feels morally weak, behaviorally bad, or mysteriously flawed. Pathological feelings totally dominate the addict's sense of self (pp. 43–59).

White continues that this totalization of one's identity is particularly harmful. This hyperfocus on a label dismisses so many parts of the self that are not at all "contaminated" by the symptom of drinking and drugging. Yes, an alcoholic under the influence can be self-destructive and frightening, defensive and hostile. And, yes, an alcoholic may also be thoughtful, caring, gentle, hardworking, devoted, creative, and passionate when not in a state of excess.

Our country's obsession with breaking the addict's denial regretfully galvanizes our most intimate conversations with the person in trouble with AOD. In the process, the healthier aspects of the alcoholic are ruthlessly bypassed and overlooked. The user begins to think of himself exclusively as a "big bad alcoholic or addict." He is overwhelmed with feelings of shame, guilt, humiliation, and embarrassment. The addict's self-regard plummets, and brittle defensiveness is called on to prevent both awareness and integration of these difficult feelings. This negative self-evaluation monopolizes his feelings about self; any pride or positivity about embracing recovery quickly evaporates.

It is imperative to be curious about, make contact with, and explore all facets of a user's identity. This is most important work during the drinking stage. Addicts and alcoholics need to be detotalized. They need to feel that people are interested in other parts of their being, and value all aspects of their personality. They need to know, like all of us, that we are more than our problems. This interest goes a long way in softening defensiveness about their addiction. The safety necessary for attachment is fostered, and relationships among therapist, family members, and users are increasingly tolerated.

Back to Melinda, I hear a natural history that is terrified to acknowledge a cold and isn't interested in a label. "I hate the term addict. It implies so much weakness. I think I have some control. I have just gotten myself into some bad, bad habits." Melinda is not interested in the disease model and abstinence; however, she acknowledges problems and seems to have some willingness to explore them. I work with her location on her natural history and suggest a harm reduction approach.

This modern treatment, discussed in Chapter 6, proposes working with a patient's strengths and availabilities, as well as his natural history. Harm reduction does not immediately insist on abstinence, but rather on everyday action steps that reduce one's harm while using. I discuss this with Melinda: "This approach is like a research project. The data collected from your action steps will both demonstrate and help us determine if you can achieve your goals of 'stopping marijuana' in outpatient therapy, or if you might need a higher level of care, possibly intensive outpatient groups or an inpatient setting."

Melinda is enthused by the harm reduction concept, and she begins a program of reducing her marijuana and alcohol intake, as well as reducing the strength of the marijuana she currently smokes. She was ready, willing, and able (Miller and Rollnick, 2002, pp. 10–11) to change and adjust. "My smoking of Mary Jane that causes me to really hate myself—when I smoke first thing in the morning, or when I'm with the kids, or when I am driving the kids, or when I am chasing a pot crash and the kids want to go to the park, or when I just keep doing it and doing it. These are situations I want to change, and I feel ready to change them." She is quickly able to drop from smoking eight times a day to three times a day. She and her husband drink a bottle of wine every night, "but I am staying away from the hard stuff." She feels good that she is trying, and she feels good about her reductions.

Melinda continues talking about her long-term goal of stopping marijuana altogether. Her ambivalence responds, "I don't really want to stop, and I don't think I can. My husband asks me to throw my stash into the ocean. I can't. If I think about stopping on my own at home, I think I would just sleep and drink to get over it." We compare her painful approach with detox in an inpatient facility. The former leaves her in a hangover and a haze and without any support. The latter has Melinda in a protected setting, medically supported, and beginning the work of recovery. She seems to get the difference. "I think I am headed toward going to the hospital. Our harm reduction is working well in many respects, but I am not stopping. I think I need a hospital, but it's so hard to go away and leave the kids. It's embarrassing. What do I say? Right now, I still want to work with harm reduction."

Melinda's goal of abstinence remained. We continued our work on harm reduction. I heard her ambivalence yet challenged her discounting. Eventually, she acknowledged, "Therapy isn't working. I'm not able to stop. I'll call you when I am ready."

Michael White (1995) also reminds us that all people, including addicts, are authorities on their own lives (p. 86). No matter how out of control addicts look, they do have definite ideas about what's going on in their world. I'm not quite sure of all the reasons why, but over the years we have divested addicts of this authority. Some of this undermining is a natural response to the life-threatening aspects of addiction and its ever-present sense of terror and helplessness. "If addicts are not aware of their out-of-control behavior, they must be ignorant about other aspects of their being as well."

More often than not, family members and clinicians enter conversations with addicts convinced that they know what is the best course of treatment. They lead from their authority, reinforcing their talking points, and stop listening to the addict's authority and his preferences. Connections are aborted, conversations are eclipsed, and treatment suffers. The addict feels detotalized when others respect his life and his authority over it. This often enhances his sense of dignity and encourages his adoption of a recovering identity (M. White, 1995, pp. 82–111).

Melinda did call me four months later. She had remained in treatment with her psychopharmacologist. Her medical marijuana card had recently expired. She tapered off from what remained and stopped completely on her own. Her authority revealed, "I just got sick of it, and sick of the whole thing. I am doing okay but still have the same problems with my husband and taking care of my children. I thought it would be a good idea to go to the inpatient facility we talked about. I just need to get away from my husband, my children, and my life. I felt I could stop on my own, and I did. I woke up this morning and instantly thought about Vista Del Mar [a dual diagnosis treatment facility]. I'm grumpy, I'm worried about my marriage, I need more help and want more support. What do you think?"

I thought it was a natural history ready to work, and two days later she entered Vista Del Mar in Ventura County, California, for two weeks of intensive outpatient treatment.

Receptivity

Larry, Sarah, Alex, and Melinda show up during their using stage. All are traveling through their own natural history with their drug of choice. All have a unique cold and are filled with uncertainties about how to respond. A primary treatment goal during the using stage is to receptively and respectfully locate the addict on his path. The attitude of receptivity seems a key one during the using stage. Patients have to feel that we are truly open to their sense of their distress. I have an index card on my desk that reads, "Be receptive; interpretations may intrude." This index card is helpful, and I read it several times a day. Being receptive and open to natural rhythms, rather than being confrontational and controlling, paves the way for developing and sustaining a safe and therapeutic working relationship. Remember, this relationship is often nurtured "in waiting" for that moment when an alcoholic or addict decides it's time to deal with his using.

Ambivalence

Someone in the using stage is in trouble. Family members start to worry; there is increasing concern and desire to talk about it among themselves or even with a therapist. These conversations are important, and the attitudes and sentiments of the clinician and family member are key. How we think about someone influences how we treat him (Gottman, 1995). One's thinking about the user can either foster constructive conversations or end up in disappointment and frustration.

An aspect of Miller and Rollnick's (2002) seminal work on motivational interviewing is helpful here. They remind us that an addict is not a liar, manipulative, resistant, or in denial. Rather, if you tickle or scratch an addict's psyche, you will find it is filled with worry. Scratch or tickle another part, and you will find that it doesn't want to stop. Addicts' hearts and minds are filled with ambivalence (pp. 13–19). They love and hate their relationship with drugs and alcohol. It's been a best friend, and now it's becoming an enemy; it's been trustworthy, and now it's no longer reliable; it's saved a person from utter despair, and now it brings about disgrace, humiliation, guilt, worry, and tension; it's prevented them from suicide, and now it's causing thoughts of suicide; it's had some predictability, and now it has almost none.

All this back-and-forth is not the stuff of a good friend—a good friend consistently cares about you; drugs and alcohol don't (RonSager, Personal Communication, 2008). Exploring the realities of this ambivalent relationship is imperative. It takes finesse and time. Addicts shift their identity when they are able to talk about their love affair and its dangers.

Registering Impacts

Michael Eigen (1998), the renowned psychoanalyst and writer, repeatedly encourages us to register the impacts of both our everyday relationships and ongoing life experiences (pp. 61–79). In intimate and therapeutic relationships, interactions feel energized and focused if we allow the impact of our beings to receptively wash over each other. "I take in what it feels like to be connected to you, and you take in what it feels like to be connected to me." These impacts can feel good and invite self-expansion, or they can feel bad and invite self-restriction. Eigen reminds us that we live with the "shock" of these relational and experiential impacts all day long, and it is important to take these into account. Registering them helps us understand what is going on inside of us, as well as what is going on between us.

He suggests, "One gets a little better at working over impacts and letting impacts work on one, so that one gets something more out of living" (Eigen, 2004, p. 142). This registering capacity is woefully underacknowledged. Emotional confusions are often cleared up when this concept is introduced and examined in therapeutic work with patients. It is particularly useful with addicts (Eigen, 1996, pp. 143–144).

Many alcoholics were damaged by early experiential and relational impacts. For them, these felt too much or too little, too harsh or too empty, too rejecting or too indulgent. They were overwhelmed and often without a language of understanding. Not surprisingly, young children, and then later adolescents, denied themselves certain experiences and dismissed closeness with people. They searched for impacts elsewhere. AOD provided some relief from the emptiness of their incapacity and the pain of their aloneness.

Being open to impacts is essential when working with someone in the desperate stage of using. An addict's intense ambivalence is cloaked in many unattractive emotions. These impacts often overwhelm, and the confusion is difficult to register. Clinicians shut down in defensive protection. Addicts bear the brunt of our anxiety and inability. We tune them out, talk over them, and attempt to coerce them and tell them what to do. This is not an exchange that invites connection. Rather, it encourages resistance. They tune us out, withdraw, and become angry, and then we lose them. They often relapse as well. A connection begins when we take in their hostility and belligerence, protectiveness and omnipotence, stubbornness and fear, arrogance and evasion, and deeper wishes and desires for caring, connection, and help. "But it is to the impact the analyst returns, an affective core of experience, which gives birth to images, which gives birth to symbols, which gives birth to ideas" (Eigen, 1998, p. 63).

When we make the effort to take them in, we are less preoccupied with their brittle and righteous arrogance and are more connected to their fear, anguish, and aloneness. Addicts feel the impact of this receptivity. They then risk being receptive to us as well. A treatment relationship is preciously forged.

Therapeutic relationships have to compete with drugs and alcohol in this capacity. They have to, and can, provide the same excitement. They have to, and can, offer a connection that feels as good as being intoxicated. The mutual registration and discussion of impacts is the cocktail that provides this "high."

Many of us need to acknowledge that we have failed addicts and alcoholics in this regard. It takes a consciousness to kindle and rekindle our desire to take "all of them" in, and it requires a therapeutic presence to "deliver" this experience back to them. This relational back-and-forth feels both promising and hopeful to someone who long ago gave up on the pleasures of human contact.

On to more clinical cases, to see how this mix of treatment concepts, therapeutic skills, and clinical caveats has been applied in therapeutic action moments.

CLINICAL CASES

Dr. Conrad Park

I receive an emergency call from the wife of a couple I have seen periodically. He is a physician and a patriarch. He drinks too much and hides and denies it. They've battled this for years. She tells me that he is drinking a lot and has gotten more aggressive and hostile; the kids are fed up, and they want to put him in a treatment facility. I ask her if he wants to go into treatment. She replies no and says his response is "I'd rather die drinking." I hear the final days of Natural History Two and suggest a conversation in my office. She's not sure how to get him there but thinks their daughter may help. It's all very frantic sounding, and the family feels in a panic.

The daughter arrives on time, we talk, and she is anxious and terrified. She reports that her father is hiding liquor, spending $400 a week on vodka, and drinking and driving. She is not sure if he is drinking while working or drinking around the clock. I am rather sure he is doing both. I suspect physical dependency has set in, and he is drinking just enough to stave off withdrawal, just enough to marginally keep functioning. This is something that happens often during Natural History Two in the using phase. Family members seem unable to grasp the utter lack of choice involved when physical and/or psychological dependency sets in. If one's body and mind are physically and/or psychologically dependent, one drinks—end of story.

Dr. Park shows up 15 minutes later, and I smell alcohol. This confirms my suspicion that he is drinking 24/7. He is bleary eyed, trembling, and unsteady in his gait. He is tragically and poignantly dressed in physician scrubs, reflecting his desire to hold on to a semblance of normalcy to the bitter end. He sits down and seems embarrassed, disoriented, frightened, and sullen. He doesn't want to be in my office.

Dr. Park's daughter is in tears, begging him to go into treatment and get help. She chokingly assures him of his family's love. She gently reminds him that everybody needs help sometime and that now it's time for him to get help. She reminds him of the times he has helped her in college. She's nervous and pleading; he is withdrawn yet tolerant. His discounting is painfully obvious.

I listen and observe this exchange for a while. I go into reverie and decide I want to directly address him. I want to intervene and interrupt the family's controlling and coercive sense of authority about what they perceive is best for him, and instead tap into Dr. Park's authority. I purposefully decide to reverse the family trend of pleading, imposing, and begging. I also decide I want to use Eigen's work on impacts. I want to take in what he is thinking and feeling, as well as what he wants. I want to register his impact and his authority and have those both wash over me. I want him to register me taking him in and respecting his authority. I want him to hear my professional recommendation and authority. This swap of registering impacts felt imperative here—it is useful in all stages of treatment. It creates a visceral connection and an emotionally truthful bond. These are essential in the work of relationship building and recovery.

I turn my chair toward Dr. Park and look him in the eye, receptively and respectfully. I ask him, "How do you think you're doing with your drinking?" The look in his eye is softly murderous. His hateful hold reflects a combination of sentiments including "I hate you," "can't stand you," and "get out of my face." And at the very same moment is an expression of "I hope so much you're not afraid of me, you're not bullshitting, and you can actually stick with me to help me out of this mess I'm in." He looks back at me, and I sense he sees I am taking him seriously. He seems to get on some level that I am allowing his hatred and hope to wash over me as I take the experience of him into my being.

Dr. Park noticeably calms down and says, "I am not doing so well now." I reply, "I see that." I continue, "So you're a physician; you get this dependency thing. I'm sure you know that you're not doing so well with drinking as a result of your physical dependency on alcohol. We both know you need this stuff so as not to get sick from withdrawals." He nods in agreement and seems okay with our talking. I ask him what he wants to do about this; does he want to go into a treatment facility? He says emphatically, "No," and adds, "I want go to a motel, and stop drinking over a three-day period. I can handle this by myself. I don't need anyone to help me. I'm a physician, and I know what I'm doing." I see that he wants to take matters into his own hands, design his own detox program.

I again look Dr. Park in the eye and say to him with kind authority, "You know, you don't have to be so mean to yourself. That's a cruel and old-fashioned way to help you get through the shakes, sweats, and nausea of physical dependency. There are hospital settings in town that provide detox with medical support. The current treatment industry offers different levels of support. There are places designed to help you through detox without trying to rope you into a 28-day stay. There are places designed to get you through this crisis period and allow you to be somewhat responsive to your own pace. There are facilities geared to accomplish what you want without the pain, as well as the isolation of a motel room. There is a way to clean out your body and mind without the torture of a cold turkey detox."

We were both engaged in the ongoing registering of impacts. It was tense and intense as we took each other in. He looked at me and said, "I'll think about it." I asked, "What does that mean?" He responded with a hostile tone, "I hear you and I will think about it, and now I want to leave." I also felt I wanted to say something about how alone and desperate he must have felt. I looked him in the eye again and said, "I'm going to say something that feels difficult. When you leave now and go down to your car, I understand that you need to drink. I understand going for that bottle of vodka on the backseat of your car. If you can, just remember our conversation now and know that you can consider another way to detox, that there is a safer and kinder way to get through this." He got up, stumbled out of my office, and left my suite.

I went back to my office and talked to Dr. Park's daughter. She was relieved and cautiously hopeful. She was incredulous that he seemed to listen. I told her that I thought he was in serious trouble and she should go get him. She said she would do that. She also called her mother and told her to wait at home. The daughter asked me if I would contact the hospital. I told her that I would call, set things up, and let her know of the admission process. I gave her my "professional" recommendation: "I think it's best now to go get your dad and start driving up to Vista Del Mar, regardless of admission possibilities. I'll call and inform you of their bed availability, but for now, my unofficial suggestion is to go buy a bottle of vodka, get him, and start driving."

They did just that. Dr. Park agreed to get in the car. They drove and he drank. His admission was delayed. He was admitted to a local ER while his blood alcohol content dropped to levels that matched Vista Del Mar's medical capacities. After that, he furiously walked into the facility, but he walked in voluntarily. At that moment, he stopped discounting. The healthy side of his ambivalence was victorious; his natural history was ready for help. His wife called me at midnight, joyous about "the miracle." She thanked me profusely.

Dr. Park stayed in Vista Del Mar for five days of medical detox and was discharged with a recommendation for further treatment. He chose not to. His wife called two weeks after his discharge and left a message saying that he was better but still drinking. She hoped he would call and said, "He still needs help, and I hope you can help him again."

This is a classic example of authority clashes in families. The family authoritatively wanted him to go into treatment, and he authoritatively did not. This tension prolonged his using as well as their distress. This man clearly wanted to continue drinking; letting go of alcohol seemed an impossibility. I identified his location in his natural history and respected his choice, despite the life-threatening aspects. We came together the moment we began registering each other's impacts in the office. He knew that I believed he needed medical detox. I knew he wanted to keep drinking. This mutual respect of authority created a connection. He was able to hear my recommendation, think about it, and eventually walk into a dual diagnosis treatment facility voluntarily. Use of these clinical concepts facilitated his admission and subsequent successful medical detox. I consider this a life-saving intervention.

I thought about Dr. Park often. A year and a half later, I ran into him in a neighborhood deli. He carried a sober countenance. I was beside myself with excitement. He volunteered some family facts. I registered his impact, and he mine.

I asked him, "So how are you doing?" He looked me in the eyes and said, "Life is good. I am sober, and have been for about a year." I responded with a warm smile, "I thought so." We do what we can, and a natural history works when it is ready.

Dean and His Family

Dean on the Run and Parental Fear

A young man of 27 comes into my office with pancreatitis (refresh your memory about Dean in Chapter 4, pp. 51). Dean was told to stop drinking by his physician. He stopped for two weeks and felt "nothing is really changing."

He starts drinking again. I concentrate on building our relationship. I work with the concepts of discounting, ambivalence, authority, self-care, and the mutual registering of impacts. His drinking gets worse, and I recommend a higher level of care. He fires me to ensure that I will not pass on my recommendation to his parents. He moves to another part of the world. His natural history suggests that serious troubled drinking is ahead. I worry for him—I like him and hope I hear from him again.

Half a year later, Dean's parents call in a panic and for an appointment. I respond that I would be willing to meet with them, but I can provide only general information and direction. I inform them that I can give no specifics about their son without his permission. We agree and meet on these terms.

The parents are extremely concerned about e-mails they have received from Dean's friends. They are very frightened about his excessive drinking and alcohol-induced mania. I describe the intense ambivalence of a person in trouble with AOD—"An alcoholic knows he's in real trouble with alcohol, but he has no idea how to live without it." Initially, they had trouble understanding this. His father pleaded to me in anguish. "I don't get it. How can you have a problem with alcohol and not stop? That's baffling to me. How could that be?" We talked about alcohol and self-medication, alcohol and a love affair, alcohol and desperate survival. Eventually, they seemed to comprehend both the acute and chronic nature of their son's issues with alcohol.

They were able to grasp that his "need" for alcohol was so strong that he ended up in the emergency room with severe pancreatitis. They vaguely understood that he was self-medicating for psychological suffering. "Well, he was depressed and anxious in high school and college." "He disappears often and spends a lot of time in his room." "He seems uncomfortable talking to us." "He never seems happy. He always looks worried and preoccupied. We walk around him on eggshells."

By session's end, Dean's parents had developed a growing sense that their son was desperately searching for a way to relieve his anxiety and despair. They seemed to understand that alone, and without emotional problem–solving skills,

Dean probably believed that he had no choice but to return again and again to alcohol for survival. Without a set of brakes and some judgment, he is likely to get into serious trouble again. They "got" the extreme danger of this situation. They went to Indonesia on the first plane they could book. The plan was to find their son in this remote part of the world and bring him home.

We all agreed that inpatient and outpatient treatment should be explored. His parents hoped he would resume psychotherapy. They planned to let him know that his friends had e-mailed them about his escalating drinking and his unusual behavior. They would say that they met with me to discuss general concerns about his drinking and the content of the e-mails, as well as to get some guidance and direction on what might be the best way to handle this type of situation.

They found Dean in Indonesia. He was shocked, defensive, and protective of his drinking. He was also polite to them and able to register their honest fear. They talked and were able to listen to each other. (Remember, in the last year, he fired me, ran away from home and his parents, and drank in excess.) That night, some of the discounting was over; his natural history was ready. Dean begrudgingly agreed to return home, reconnect with me, and consider inpatient treatment. He said he needed some time alone that night. He would meet them the next day. Dean later told me that night he consumed massive amounts of alcohol and drank to blackout. He called me before his blackout and left a message: "I'd like to set up an appointment to catch up, just for one time."

They all returned home and did what many families do after they get through such an acute crisis. They each scattered in different directions and dropped "the intervention ball." The parents went on a trip and assumed that Dean was following up on "the plan." Dean, on the other hand, met up with friends and continued partying.

Both parents were traumatized and worried, as well as frightened and incapacitated. This was a family that lacked the ability to calm themselves and each other and also remain emotionally connected and cohesive during the implementation of this life-saving plan. The trauma of it all was too much; they "had" to disperse in avoidant and destructive ways. Brown (in Fetting, 2011) refers to the trauma of recovery, when family members don't know what to expect and don't know what to do next. Family therapy is often as essential as individual work during the using stage, particularly in times of crisis (see Chapter 10, pp. 168). Everyone's thinking and behavior are impaired. Families need information, coaching, and support.

Relationship Repair

My immediate focus, however, is on reconnecting with Dean. He arrives at our first appointment, furious and ambivalent. He is furious about our relationship rupture. He is furious I spoke to his parents and that they came across the world to find him. He is furious he got caught and is being forced to deal with his drinking. He also came home, so he is probably hopeful that someone will help him.

We repair and begin again. He is exuberant about his travels, mad at his parents, and drinking a lot. He blames his drinking on being stateside. His parents leaving town sends a confusing message to him. "What's going on with my parents? They make this big deal to fly all over the world to tell me to stop drinking, and then they disappear. They don't even know what I'm doing, and I don't know what I'm supposed to be doing. So, I'll keep drinking."

Dean cancels several appointments. When we do meet, he appears angry and adrift, and he admits that his alcohol intake has gotten worse. He avoids in-depth conversations about his drinking, insists that he has been making progress over our treatment break, and doesn't want to be like one of those "alcoholics." His discounting feels tragic, and his extreme hatred of the alcoholic label is telling. He feels brittle and faraway; connecting or making contact with him seems impossible. I suggest that we meet together as a family and follow up on the agreed-upon plan to explore inpatient treatment. He wants no part of this and says his parents don't deserve it because they have betrayed him. He keeps stalling for time.

I am worried a clash of defensive authorities will reappear, that we will start fighting. I'm worried that I will "insist" on a higher level of care and he will "insist" that he is doing better than anyone thinks. I dreaded a return to our stalemate of six months ago. I seek out Los Angeles addiction psychiatrist and psychoanalyst Ron Sager for some consultation. I was worried our relationship would fail. My sense of helplessness was identified. I was terrified that I could not influence this person whose drinking had caused a life-threatening episode of pancreatitis. Sager asked, "Are you planning to cooperate with his suicide mission?" There was the intervention, just waiting for the right moment (Sager, Personal Communication, 2008).

I went into reverie. In our next session, I remind Dean that his drinking resulted in an emergency room visit with life-threatening pancreatitis, that his doctor strongly advised him not to drink, that he was killing himself, and that he had agreed to go into treatment. I looked him in the eye and respectfully acknowledged that I would not collude with his suicide mission. He took me in and sat in stunned silence. His body collapsed. He seemed frightened by the notion that he was actually killing himself. This was a transformational moment between us, involving an impact swap as well as an honest exchange of authorities. He agreed to visit an inpatient facility the next day. Although he was not interested in attending, it began a deeper relationship between us. We searched together for a level of care that matched his authority with my authority.

I continued my reverie, "This is a young man that is loath to identify with being an alcoholic. His sense of humiliation and shame is palpable. It seems intolerable at this point in his natural history to acknowledge that alcoholism may be a possibility. His discounting needs parsing and finesse. He needs to be detotalized."

Self-Care Works

I use the work of Dr. Ed Khantzian, the founder of the self-medication theory of addiction (see Chapter 7, p. 96). Khantzian suggests that alcoholics are neither sociopaths nor hedonistic pleasure seekers. Rather, addicts self-medicate for the psychological suffering they feel as a result of deficiencies in their ego functions of self-care. Together, Dean and I walk through my self-medication handout, and he perks up with interest. This sounds very appealing to him. He can think of his drinking problem as a lack of self-care. He stops discounting the existence of a problem, and his identity starts to shift. He begins using the phrase *self-care* often, and his authority is interested in developing his own treatment program around this concept. We're not fighting each other. I sense the relationship is working and that Dean is encouraged and hopeful. He is so encouraged that he stops drinking on his own. The next time I see him, he is two days sober.

Dean represents a treatment trend that I have seen often in the past couple of years. It involves drinkers who drink to crisis, have a big scare, have financial means, and have a skeptical attitude toward Alcoholics Anonymous (AA) and the recovery community in general. They have their own plans in mind, and they want to follow them. The recovery world, despite good intentions, often imposes its authority on them and suggests that they suffer from "terminal uniqueness." I suggest that we listen harder to their authority and somehow make room for their niche. This is a treatment trend that will likely continue. We need to pay attention to this.

I refer Dean to a psychiatrist, who prescribes both Campral, an acamprosate calcium used to restore chemical imbalance and seemingly reduce cravings in an alcohol-dependent brain, and the antidepressant Lexapro. We design a treatment program that includes a schedule of daily exercise, yoga, chores at home, and sessions with me three times a week. He seems invested in staying sober and working within this plan. I say, "It is a plan with limited support and full of risks. You are sober and want to do it, so let's try it and see what happens."

Struggles with a Label and Loneliness

Dean reluctantly counted the days of sobriety and hesitantly showed up for treatment. Despite his defensive reserve, I could tell that he was very pleased about not drinking. I sensed that he felt both surprised about his ability to say no to alcohol and accomplished that he could follow through. His measured pride fueled those early days of recovery.

In time, however, his fascination wore thin, his loneliness surfaced, and confusion set in. His mood was starting to spiral down, and his anger was increasing. The symptoms of an isolated journey of recovery were starting to appear. The risks of doing it without a community were becoming obvious to me. I started a conversation about the stresses of his withdrawing and retreating during recovery.

I reminded him of James Taylor and his wonderful comment about his own journey of recovery: "Things got good for me when I finally got out of my own way." He listened but shrugged off its utility. Dean still needed to do some things in his own way.

The challenge was to figure out how to create an attraction to a community of support. We began talking more about his lifelong habit of retreating, the value of connecting with others, and AA. I was both receptive to and respectful of Dean's discomfort with the AA community. I also imagined that AA could be a wonderful support system that would challenge his defensive isolation. I felt he would benefit from identification with other young men and women on a similar courageous journey.

"Your decision not to enter more intensive treatment means that you are without connection and community support. We said we would talk about the risks of that choice, and I'm now worried that your isolation is going to work against you, make things harder for you." I continued, "You know, there is a logic behind the design of these 28-day programs that include meetings, groups, motivational supports, and education. These experiences boost one's sense of purpose and create affinity and camaraderie among other addicts. I get that inpatient treatment is not for you; I also get that we need to find a way to fill in the gaps. Community support can do some good. Too much isolation may erode your spirit. It may become too much for you alone; you may destructively retreat and destructively consider drinking again." I remind him that "speaker meetings in Alcoholics Anonymous are large, and a wonderful way to truly be anonymous. One can come and go, pace their level of involvement. The experience of connecting seems to give people an energy boost and a sense of purpose." I remind him of the boost he gets from our conversations. I suggest that part of his despair and frustration is because he feels so alone on his difficult journey. He listened but looked sullen.

Dean struggles with the alcoholic label and its perceived sense of humiliation and shame. He is trapped in its embarrassment. Use of the term alcoholic debases his sense of self. He cannot identify. He so desperately needs to hear from others who do not feel totalized by their alcoholic identification. These interactions could move him out of his isolated funk and further his search for his own definition of his problems with alcohol. Dean, however, feels unable to do this at this moment.

While our therapeutic relationship is intact, it feels strained. I feel shut out and useless. I sense that Dean is a psychic retreater (see Chapter 11, p. 205). He prefers withdrawing and figuring things out alone. He doesn't see the value of community. The challenge for Dean and many retreating addicts is exquisitely stated in a quote by the psychoanalyst Adam Phillips (1994): "Hell is not other people, but one's need for other people" (p. 45). Dean and I struggle together. I need to keep registering his brittle impact, not shut down in frustration. I need to continue my ongoing reverie. I want to respect his authority yet also converse about its potential difficulties in his current journey of sobriety. As pen goes to this paper, he is considering AA. Read about his continued progress in Chapter 10 (p. 178).

Penny

Self-Imposed Impossible Tasks

Penny has been in solid ongoing recovery from alcohol for nearly 20 years. There has never been an alcohol relapse from that moment in my office when she stated, "I can do therapy, yoga, Buddhism, meditation, and I can bargain and make agreements. My drinking is a problem, and it needs to stop now." She has not had a drop since. She lives with this success and other struggles. She suffers with the eating disorder, compulsive overeating, and stresses from a big L.A. life. She and her husband, Roger, have two children, big jobs, and a bountiful world. She wives, mothers, and runs the household. He is a lawyer and mediator.

They are both driven and imprisoned by their own self-imposed impossible tasks (SIITs). Vega Zagier Roberts (Obholzer and Roberts, 1994) defines these as tasks that are impossible not by their nature but by the way they are tackled (pp. 110–118). The rigid approach chosen is designed to meet internal, unarticulated, unconscious, and persecutory needs. The tasks increasingly feel impossible. People feel trapped by them and drive themselves into a life of expectations and endurance. Folks find satisfaction through the narcissistic reflection of how much they are able to get through and accomplish, rather than in the qualitative experience of a meaningful task. Penny and her husband are not the only ones caught in the psychological and cultural trap of SIITs. Drugs and alcohol can soothe this painful lifestyle. Penny has been vulnerable to this form of self-medication.

As is often the case with some long-term therapy clients, people come and go—they do periods of intense work and then "leave and live life." Penny worked intensely with me in her first year of alcohol recovery. She left therapy, married, and had children. Appointments were intermittent, with "check-ins and tune-ups" during struggles with depression or her eating disorder, and with everyday self-imposed impossible tasks.

Confusion During Intermittent Therapy

Penny strives to be a perfect mother and wife. My understanding and sense of her is that she is persecuted by feelings of worthlessness and shame, and her unrelenting pace attempts to prove otherwise. Over the years of not drinking, there have been somatic complaints, perplexing physical illnesses, surgeries, and symptoms of depression and chronic fatigue. She battles with her food and is tortured by her body. There have been multiple prescriptions filled for insomnia, anxiety, and depression. There have also been prescriptions for pain. These have all been prescribed under the care of a well-respected psychiatrist. Dr. Ashley and I have shared many patients over the years. He and Penny have always informed me of any medication adjustments or additions, as well as changes in dosage. A lot of things fall through the cracks during intermittent therapy work.

One year, Penny called several times in a panic, "I feel more irritable, aggressive, and depressed than ever." She was sullen and withdrawn from her husband and impatient with and agitated by her children. I asked Penny how her sobriety was going. She replied, "Drinking is not an option." I felt a sense of clinical unease talking to her over the phone and suggested that we meet in my office. Something felt off and confusing.

Penny also met with Dr. Ashley, and he and I spoke on the phone afterward. We both had a shared sense of clinical mystery. He suggested that her symptoms might be characterological in nature. We both agreed she was not suffering from depression or in a depressive episode. We diagnosed a massive lack of self-care. Dr. Ashley encouraged her to return to therapy with me as well, and she did. We spent a session catching up. I felt that the persecutory pull of a self-imposed impossible task was in charge of her being. She felt strained and angry. My mind entered a confused state of reverie after our first meeting.

While I had not seen this woman regularly, I remembered her preference for the opiate Vicodin. She had been prescribed a benzodiazepine for anxiety in her first year of sobriety but found "the Vicodin prescribed for my back pain works better. It calms a lot of my anticipatory worry." My reverie was starting to work. I asked her if Vicodin had been "useful" to her lately, and she responded, "Yes, and it is worrisome, but I'm watching it." She assured me that it had been prescribed over the years for pain following her multiple surgeries. She reminded me that she had also been recently prescribed several benzodiazepines for anxiety and insomnia.

So here's where the confusion and possible collusion occur. Penny, her husband, Dr. Ashley, and I were watchful for an alcohol relapse. During those years of intermittent work, conversations addressed cross-addiction as well as the potential for use, misuse, and overuse of prescribed benzodiazepines and opiates. These conversations, while brief, seemed to have allayed everyone's concerns.

Physical pain, exhaustion, and anxiety from SIITs continued, and more prescriptions were filled. Worries of misuse were again touched upon and talked about, and we all moved on. These were followed by intermittent calls filled with angry agitation and reports of some incidents of loss of control with the children. Penny described periods of "hiding in my room with no support from my husband."

My reverie musings about the current situation continued to feel baffling and uneasy. Addiction's first tugs often feel vague and veiled, especially when working with a 20-year sober alcoholic. Is she drinking again? Is this prescribed cocktail of medications problematic? After a month of her "returning to therapy," including both individual and couples work, I felt more and more that Penny was in the uneasy grip of addiction. I had a hunch that her discounting was the source of my confusion.

Using While in Ongoing Recovery

There was another surgery. My focus sharpened. Penny felt edgy and elusive. The cumulative exhaustion, physical pain, surgeries, fatigue, and erratic upsets were taking their toll. Her distance from her husband and irritability with her children were all starting to make sense. The mystery of a prescription addiction was unfolding in front of my clinical eyes.

One day, in a revelatory moment, Penny talked about her increasing use of Vicodin to "ease this crazy pain and power through." She haltingly told me of her worries but assured me that it had all been prescribed. I firmly and delicately reminded her of the psychological and physical dependent potential of the opiates. "Let's talk about what's going on here, Penny."

Opiates ease physical pain as well as emotional distress. They often soothe emotional storms filled with rage and shame. As Ed Khantzian (1999) says, the choice of drugs is not random. Drugs are chosen because they do something predictably and reliably to an internal feeling storm. They deaden, dull, or quiet the storm; they puncture, sever, or obliterate it. They animate, enliven, or resuscitate the storm (pp. 145–152). Either way, life feels more doable.

It clicked just then: This 20-year recovering alcoholic had been living a life of self-imposed impossible tasks and residing in an emotional world of relentless shame and smoldering rage. The rage masked a fragile sense of worthlessness and drove her into a world of inescapable, exhausting endurance. Opiates quieted and dulled her storm.

I went into reverie: This woman is an opiate addict, a chipper, or an occasional user with a ravaged body and a tortured mind. She lives alone in a secret world filled with distant doctors, truncated care, intermittent therapy, and plentiful prescriptions. I recalled, "It is a joy to be hidden, but disaster not to be found" (Winnicott in Epstein, 1995, p. 38). I think I just found her in her opiate and benzodiazepine domicile.

Penny sobbed, "I've been really scared and worried for a long time. I want help, and I want to stop." She finally stopped discounting her discounting. As we talked, I sensed both her relief and terror. We spent some time discussing the logistics of her care, which were going to be challenging with approaching travel, family, and holiday demands. As she prepared for an annual family trip, I reminded her of her vulnerability, and she replied, "I want to be done with the chipping, and I'll use the benzo only for sleep. I'll call you if I get in trouble."

I sensed that we were getting closer to the truth of Penny's using. I also knew that "this intervention" was going to stretch out over time. Her natural history seemed ready, willing, and able for bits and pieces only. Her need for self-medication continued.

After the holidays, Penny called from her bed. She was wailing. She sounded exhausted, depleted, and angry. Something felt off again. I bluntly asked, "Penny, have you relapsed?" And then it came out. It had been four days of hazy swirling and sleeping with her daughter's prescribed post-op liquid Vicodin, as well as with the benzodiazepines, Valium, Xanax, and Klonopin. She had taken to her room in resignation. She had screamed at her girls and avoided her husband. "I am a mess, a real mess." She was overwhelmed with her life and finally with her addiction.

"Penny, we need to look at this like the alcohol. Remember 20 years ago when you said something like, 'It's a problem and it has to stop'?" She sobbed, and cried in fear with words of self-hatred, embarrassment, shame, and fear. We sat there together on the phone for several minutes. I asked her what she wanted to do; she said, "I don't know." I asked if her husband was home. My directions were clear: "Go get him and talk to him. You need to let him know what is going on." She was quiet again, and then she said, "I'm ready." The next day, the two of them came into the office and she began her opiate and benzodiazepine recovery. "Using while in ongoing recovery" is not uncommon. Read more about Penny's progress in Chapter 10 (p. 169).

COGNITIVE THEORY WITH BRIEF CLINICAL CASES

Addiction is of a dual nature. It is a cognitive or thinking disorder as well as a behavioral or doing disorder (Brown, 1985, p. 83). Both keep the using going. Over the years, treatment providers have overfocused on the doing and underfocused on the thinking. We have done this because behavior is visible. We have also done this because many addiction clinicians don't know how to treat addicts and alcoholics with cognitive interventions.

This overfocus and underfocus dilemma has produced many problems in treatment—it sets up behavioral power struggles; we miss addressing half of what drives and sustains the addict and alcoholic's identity, and we deny addicts the sense of dignity and empowerment that comes with the realization that addictive thinking contributes to the embarrassing and shameful behaviors of addiction. It's not all about behavior and loss of impulse control. It's also about recognizing the distorted thinking that causes destructive drinking.

Stephanie Brown heralded the importance of understanding and working with the dual nature of addiction. She stressed the importance of cognitive work in the identity reconstruction of the recovering alcoholic. Many others have developed and advanced cognitive interventions in the work of recovery. Aaron Beck, the cognitive psychiatrist from the University of Pennsylvania, has broadened his trademark focus on depression and anxiety to include work with substance abusers (Beck, Wright, Newman, and Liese, 1993).

Helping people examine the cognitions that govern their destructive actions is essential. Shifting an identity requires shifting one's thinking about one's using. Changes in beliefs invite changes in behavior. Both continually reinforce the identity shift necessary for recovery. An example works here.

Lily

Lily is 35. She comes into therapy concerned about her drinking alone at night. She drinks to blackout (full amnesia) or brownout (partial amnesia). She doesn't want to stop drinking, "I just want to have a place to talk about it." In a using stage session, Lily initially tells me, "My drinking wasn't that bad last night." At a later time in the same conversation, I hear, "I don't remember parts of a phone call with my friend. I hope I didn't say anything stupid."

There is a mismatch here between thinking and behavior. While Lily thought she didn't drink too much, I suspect she was in a blackout while talking on the phone. Her thinking said her drinking wasn't that bad, but her behavior was symptomatic of alcoholic drinking. This mismatch invites a discussion about the incongruent relationship between Lily's thinking and Lily's drinking. Her thinking says one thing, her behavior another. Cognitive work in the using phase begins with listening for this glitch between thinking and drinking, followed by exploring these contradictions in a respectful discussion.

I asked for clarification, "What made you think that you might have said something stupid on the phone?" She replied, "I don't know, I was kind of tired, and we kept talking and talking about something we disagreed on. It was getting late, and I think I was kind of falling asleep. I don't remember much after a certain point."

I pursued, "You mentioned at the beginning of the session that you didn't drink that much last night." She nodded and said, "I didn't." I continued, "What does that mean?" She responded with obvious pride, "Well, rather than gulp my drinks, I spread my cosmopolitans out over a couple of hours." I responded, "You seem to feel good that you spread them out. Did that seem to make a difference in your buzz?" She hesitated, "At first it did; I didn't feel so drunk. But, as we are talking now, I remember I purposefully made a very strong drink at the end of our conversation because I wanted to be able to fall asleep after we finished talking." I asked, "How do you think that drink affected you?" She paused and responded, "Maybe more than I thought."

Our conversation continued. She and I dissected the thinking and drinking of that night. Lily wants to keep drinking; her using identity thinks it's not that bad. As we talked, she became more aware that her thinking said, "It's not that bad," and her behavior involved "blackout forgetting." She looked rattled as she felt that contradiction. Therapy provided her with an opportunity to "hear" a relationship between a belief and a behavior that would have remained private and unexamined. Her thinking and her behavior were at odds. At that moment, she didn't want to stop drinking, but said, "I want to keep thinking about this. I've never made a connection between what I think about my drinking and how I really drink. I never talk about what I am thinking. I always keep things private and in my head. Now I want to think about this. Let's talk later."

Belief, Behavior, and Identity Shift

This cognitive intervention contributed to a belief shift and identity evolution in Lily. She started talking more about bad nights of heavy drinking alone and saying to me, "I am concerned about that blackout. I tried so hard not to end up in one, but I did." Lily began moving away from a sense of self that said, "My drinking is not that bad, and I don't have a problem" toward an identity that felt, believed, and said, "My drinking is bad, and I think I have a problem."

The cognitive contribution is obvious here. Treatment providers encourage patients to identify the unexamined addictive beliefs that govern and sustain addictive behaviors. Contradictions between beliefs and behaviors are explored in conversation. Old beliefs are challenged and discarded, and new beliefs are considered and adopted. When addictive beliefs are examined and replaced, healthy behaviors can follow. When beliefs and behaviors shift, so does one's identity; as one's identity shifts, so do more beliefs and behaviors.

The following pages go into greater detail about a cognitive intervention during the using stage. The work of Dr. Aaron Beck supports and deepens the work of Dr. Stephanie Brown. Theoretically, the field appreciates cognitive work; practically, it is not something that many clinicians effectively utilize. A clinical case study is presented that highlights the value of cognitive assessments and interventions.

Kathy

A Turbulent Year with Brandy and Milk

A 55-year-old woman attended one of my licensing lectures on substance dependence and abuse. The California Board of Behavioral Sciences requires this for clinical licensure. She called for an appointment. During our first session, Kathy told me about a very distressing, turbulent year full of painful events that included a divorce after 28 years of marriage, loss of her home, several unsuccessful minor surgeries, and loss of regular contact with her son. She also began a love relationship with a married woman who remained in a heterosexual marriage. She lived alone in a studio that prohibited her beloved animals. I asked her how she was surviving and she said, "That's why I'm here today. I have discovered brandy and milk, and it's causing me problems." No discounting so far.

Kathy continued with the logistics of her life. She was an administrative social worker, responsible for site inspections. She spent her days in the field and had considerable control of her time and schedule. Kathy finished her inspections early in the day, returned home, and in the last year began a drinking ritual that was causing her some anxiety. She would arrive at her studio apartment at 2 p.m. and begin drinking brandy and milk. The two glasses she gulped put her to sleep for several hours. Upon awakening, she would do the same thing and continue this in three or more cycles before retiring for the day. During these periods, she would fight with her lover, obsessively ruminate about her son, and drink through brownouts and blackouts. She was beginning to wake up with a bad hangover, including considerable shaking and sweating.

Kathy called me for an appointment after she noticed a new and disturbing trend—her drinking ritual began at 11:30 a.m. "Booze is the only thing that stops the shakes and calms me down. I can barely get through my early appointments. I can't wait until 2 p.m. anymore."

Cognitive Considerations

During those early sessions, I focused on the dual nature of addiction—the thinking and the doing. As she shared more details about her life, I began hearing addictive beliefs that guided and governed her using. Aaron Beck identifies certain beliefs and cognitive ideas that influence one's decision to use and contribute to the continuation of problematic drinking and drugging. He proposes specific cognitive filters to adopt when listening to patients' struggles with their addictive behavior. These filters help to decode sentences, stories, and behaviors into the addictive beliefs that enable the addict's using (Beck et al., 1993, pp. 38–41).

Beck et al. (1993) suggest that all alcoholics and addicts have ideas about pleasure seeking and using, problem solving and using, relief and using, escape and using, and permission giving and using. In addition, they identify dysfunctional ideas that perpetuate troubled using. These include (p. 38):

- A belief that one needs the substance to maintain psychological and emotional balance
- An expectation that the substance will improve social and intellectual functioning

- An expectation that one will find pleasure from using
- A belief that the drug will energize and provide increased power
- An expectation that the drug will have a soothing effect
- An assumption that the drug will relieve boredom, anxiety, tension, and depression
- A conviction that if craving is not satisfied, it will go on forever

Beck's guidelines are etched into my brain. I've used them during cognitive interventions with alcoholics and addicts. I asked Kathy to tell me what brandy and milk does for her, how it "works" in her life. I listened for the addictive beliefs that drove her using as she described its purposes, functions, and meanings over several sessions. These included statements such as, "It calms me down"; "It is something I look forward to"; "I count on it at the end of the day"; "It's my reward for getting work done"; "I feel so anxious, upset, and alone about the divorce and brandy and milk helps me forget it all"; "I don't know what to do with myself. Feelings scare and overwhelm me"; "It's warm and calming"; "I'm not as scared"; "It makes it easier to talk to my son and my lover"; "It helps me to do boring tasks, and it helps me sleep"; "It's fun"; "It's my life"; "I feel less lonely when drinking, which is good because loneliness hurts"; "I'm nervous around people, so if I drink brandy and milk, I forget my people pain"; "It calms down my mind"; and "Everything seems a lot better with brandy and milk in my life, even if I drink too much and blackout."

Using Beck's list, I translated Kathy's sentiments, purposes, and meanings into addictive beliefs. I had them in my mind as I listened to her over several sessions. I waited for her behavior to contradict these beliefs. It usually does with addicts. The essential skill involved in doing cognitive work with addicts is threefold: decode stories into addictive beliefs, store them in one's listening mind, and wait for a behavior to belie a belief.

In Kathy's case, I identified the following addictive beliefs that drove her into drinking and kept her drinking going throughout her day. She believed, or had ideas, that brandy and milk would:

- Be soothing
- Help her stay in balance
- Provide comfort
- Reduce anxiety and worry
- Relieve tension
- Serve as a deserved reward after a hard day at work
- Circumvent her loneliness problem
- Reduce nervousness with her lover and her son
- Drown out her pain

- Make life more tolerable
- Provide some fun

Contradictions Appear

Kathy paged me on a Saturday at 9 a.m. I was jogging, so it took me 15 minutes to get to a phone. She was livid, and she was drunk. She screamed obscenities at me and accused me of being unprofessionally late. She was hostile, insulting, aggressive, and critical of my abilities to "help her." She fired me over the phone and hung up. That was an upsetting call on a Saturday morning.

I eventually calmed down and made a decision that I did not need to call the Psychiatric Emergency Response Team (PERT), as Kathy would most likely fall asleep. Prior to her nap, she left four more drunk, abusive, insulting, and hostile messages on my voice mail. I received a sober phone message from her at 10 o'clock that night. She said, "I'm so upset. I think I left several messages on your voice mail today that were insulting and rude. I think I was drunk and don't remember what I said or how many times I called. I took some notes, but I can't read my writing. I apologize for anything I said, and I'm fearful that I fired you. If I did, I did not mean that. I'm worried now, and I suspect that you're going to fire me. When you get a chance, give me a call."

I heard and appreciated Kathy's message. I did, however, feel rather beaten up by the events of the day. I decided not to return her call so late on a Saturday night. I wondered if there might be repercussions. I wondered if her anxiety would cause her to drink. Unfortunately, there were repercussions. Early Sunday morning, I received four more drunk and angry messages. Five silent hours passed, a sober message followed with a request to keep our Tuesday 1 p.m. appointment. I did call her back, "See you Tuesday."

I took some time in reverie, imagining Kathy's feeling states over the weekend as well as reflecting on my reactions to all that had transpired. The impact of her lashing out was hurtful, her potential danger to herself was frightening, and the fatigue of the back-and-forth was wearing. Working in the using phase always stirs primitive emotions. I registered these impacts, and reflected on cognitive interventions the day before our session. Reverie created receptivity.

Cognitive Intervention

Kathy was in my waiting room three hours early. I later learned that her anxiety drove her there. She said, "I've wanted to be sitting in your office ever since we talked on the phone. It felt like a safe place to be." My own anxiety had driven me to reflect on her addictive beliefs. We began the session. She was visibly upset as she began sharing her litany of apprehensions and regrets. She reported that she had been physically sick most of the weekend, both from a hangover and from worry. She continued that her lover was very annoyed with her "out-of-control outbursts" and she mentioned that her son had called, knew she was drunk, and hung up. She feared that I was going to "fire her," and several times said that she was very nervous to see me. She was now even more worried and frightened about her drinking. She had not had a drink since Saturday. She seemed embarrassed, guilty, and remorseful.

I receptively listened to her feelings and words. My reverie over the weekend joined my current state of reverie. I felt ready to make a cognitive intervention using her beliefs and her behavior, as well as her agitation and her distress about what she described as the consequences of this past drinking weekend.

"Let's try something, Kathy. Let's talk about why you like to drink." Together, we pondered over her sentiments described in detail on page 149. I then asked her to consider something. "You told me, over several sessions, all the reasons why drinking was a good idea for you and all the reasons it was helpful during a stressful year. You also told me it calmed you down, it reduced tension, and it was comforting. And yet, your painful descriptions of drinking this past weekend fly in the face of your hoped-for comfort. Do you know what I mean?" Kathy sat in thought.

I continued, "You once said brandy and milk was soothing, but you don't seem soothed; rather, you seem kind of agitated and upset. You said it relieved tension and anxiety, but, sitting here now, you seem very stressed and worried. You even said it drowned out pain, and now this weekend of drinking seems to have caused much pain and remorse." Kathy seemed to grasp the disconnect between her intended wishes for drinking and the actual outcome. She "got," for the first time, that while her early days of brandy and milk had resulted in some relaxing experiences, her more recent drinking episodes resulted in unintended outcomes and painful, regretful emotions. The conversation was difficult but tolerable for her. She left with some real insight about her thinking and her drinking. She said, "I really don't want to go through this again. I don't want to drink like this anymore. I hope I am done."

The Pause Factor

One respectful and powerful cognitive intervention does not result in dismantling addictive beliefs or producing consistent changes in behavior. Rather, what occurs is what I call the *pause factor,* and it happened here. That night, as Kathy went to fix herself a brandy and milk, she paused before she poured a drink and thought instead about our conversation. The pause lasted an hour. She tried to think about why she wanted to drink, particularly after such a distressing weekend. She wondered what the experience might result in and if she could consider doing something besides drinking. Her thinking felt agitating, so she drank anyway. Over the next couple of weeks, this "thinking prior to drinking" continued. There were a few satisfying drinking episodes, but mostly there were disturbing ones. Over time, the pauses grew longer, and during these pauses, nondrinking beliefs began to replace drinking ones. These included the following new ideas: "If I drink, I will probably lose control. If I drink, it will make my life tougher. If I drink, I will probably embarrass myself. If I drink, I will regret it." This belief replacement process continued, and eventually Kathy's mind was filled with beliefs that supported a decision not to drink. She ended her relationship with brandy and milk.

Being in therapy greatly supported and assisted Kathy's decision making. Each week, she was able to talk about her drinking behavior, as well as examine her thinking. Each week, as Michael Eigen says, she was able to "care about her own destructiveness, care enough to struggle with it" (Personal Communication, 2009). Therapy supported her struggle and led to her decision to stop her self-destructive behavior. She and I worked together on understanding and managing the considerable stresses of the past year without alcohol. We did some good work for about six months, and then she decided to leave therapy. I've always wondered if those addictive beliefs ever resurfaced.

Cognitive work is no substitute for the deeper recovery work of understanding and working through the suffering behind one's using. It is, however, a clinical intervention that can enhance treatment during the using and transition stages. It supports identity reconstruction, the crux of recovery. Patients gain a sense of empowerment when they understand how their thinking influences their drinking and drugging. As addictive beliefs shift, they begin to feel a capacity for choice where none was felt before.

CHAPTER SUMMARY AND REFLECTIONS

Summary

This chapter introduced the reader to the using stage and highlighted its focus. The development of the treatment relationship with a hostile yet hopeful addict, alcoholic, or troubled user requires patience and finesse. Clinical concepts from many addiction specialists and psychoanalytic thinkers were presented as suggestions for the development and nurturance of this relationship. A psychoanalytic attitude of receptivity, prior to interventions of activity, was encouraged. A mix of analytic ideas and clinical interventions, as well as Aaron Beck's cognitive treatments, was introduced. These encourage and support the addict's desire for a therapeutic connection, recovery, and growth. Clinical cases reflected the fear, anxiety, and hope residing in therapist, addict, and family members during this frightening stage. Therapeutic action moments integrate theory into practice.

Reflections

Before leaving this chapter, make sure you:

- Know the primary and secondary tasks of the using stage
- Have a solid understanding of the key theories and concepts presented
- Have examined their individual merit and critically analyzed and discussed your intuitive clinical responses to their application in therapeutic action moments in the clinical cases of this stage
- Have begun to design your own integrative treatment approach for this stage
- Are willing to read and reread this chapter

Chapter 10

The Integrative Treatment Model

The Transition Stage

Figure 10.1 The Transition Stage

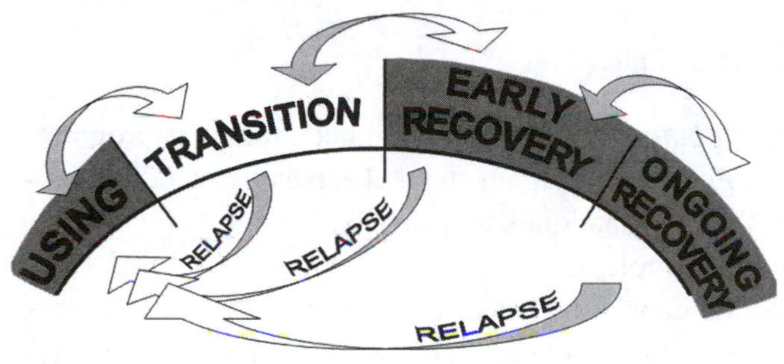

INTRODUCTION

No addict wants to stop using. Acknowledging his behavioral folly and facing what is underneath seem utterly incomprehensible. There is no ability and no will. So many addicts and alcoholics use until they have damaged themselves and most good things in their lives. They use until they have run out of most forms of currency—spiritual and emotional, relational and financial, and physical and psychological. They use until their bankruptcy forecloses around them. Addicts then do the unfathomable—they stop, or they reconsider. They enter the transition stage of recovery.

Transition marks a change in the addict's relationship with drugs and alcohol. It begins with an unconscious wish, followed by a conscious desire. Next are cognitive reconsiderations and changes in behavior. Much needs to take place.

The addict's ambivalence, for the first time, tips toward not using. A crisis forces him to stop, or the threat of a crisis forces him to reconsider. This crisis has to be subjectively experienced by the addict—nothing changes otherwise. There is a freedom for the using identity that surrenders. There is entrapment for the using identity that remains in conflict. Either way, things will never be the same again. This chapter is about the straight and crooked path of a developing transition identity.

Transition's primary tasks are twofold:

- **Fostering a sober identity** and **nurturing interest** in the interests of the true self
- **Incorporating clinical concepts** such as *transition's identity reconstruction, transition's time, transition's primary tasks, the transition moment, transition moments revisited, interventions during transition, authoritative versus authoritarian hints, hovering and hinting rather than possessing and ordering, the interests of transition, trauma, relational home, resurrective ideology*, and *families in transition*

Other tasks include:

- *Codeveloping* the design of the addict's recovery program
- *Supporting* the management of the messes of addiction—legal, relational, work, health, emotional, and financial
- *Attending* to relapse
- *Exploring* considerations of using again
- *Including* clinical concepts and treatment interventions from Chapter 9

This chapter is divided into two sections. *Clinical Concepts* describes the theory behind the tasks of transition and *Clinical Cases* demonstrates their applications.

Clinical Concepts introduces the reader to theories and interventions that are useful in furthering the process of the addict's transition identity reconstruction, as well as the reawakening of interest in the self. A psychoanalytic perspective enriches the work of this stage. An attitude of receptivity and respecting the addict's use of defenses greatly reduces the power struggles between therapist and addict that are likely to occur during this stage. *Clinical Cases* demonstrates the application of these ideas in therapeutic action moments.

I am passionate about helping patients find useful residence in transition; addicts struggle to enter and stay in this most pivotal stage of recovery. Often, they leave because of relapse, and many times they return for further treatment. Transition is the foundation of recovery. The addict's sense of self is rediscovered without the ravages of destruction. Every minute, every hour, and every day count. Reverence for this stage is critical; we fail our addicts and alcoholics if we don't strongly encourage this high level of attentiveness.

Penny (p. 142) and Dean (p. 137), introduced in Chapter 9, successfully migrated from the using to the transition stage of recovery. Both weathered agonies and missteps. The therapeutic relationship strengthened as a result. Penny and Dean struggle with ownership of their transition identity and toil to define their sobriety and incorporate it in their lives. They confront surgeries, weddings, parental visits, and family expectations. They struggle, I struggle, and we struggle together.

Two new cases are introduced as well. Angela had just entered her transition stage when our work began. Mark's twisted and torturous path through transition is explored.

Reading Guidelines

This chapter identifies a mix of theories and treatment concepts, therapeutic skills, and clinical caveats that are useful to understand and also apply during the addict's travels on transition's terrain. This mix of concepts, skills, and caveats is for treatment providers to match with their own intuition, their own clinical style, and their patient's particular recovery path. Past and ongoing clinical cases put theory to practice in therapeutic action moments. A clinician prepared for transition's primary and secondary tasks invites the addict to do the same. Study these ideas; make them useful in your own life, and also yours to use during recovery treatment; develop a tolerance for the unfamiliar; and go at your own pace as your mind struggles and then rests.

CLINICAL CONCEPTS

Transition's Identity Reconstruction, Transition's Time, and Transition's Primary Task

Identity Reconstruction

Transition for an addict is based on a deconstruction of an identity. This involves an unconscious and conscious wish to shed the using sense of self that was unwilling to know its own trouble and became isolated in slow disintegration instead. It also involves shedding an identity that felt that using drugs and alcohol was the only and best answer to life.

Transition is also based on constructing a new identity—an identity that wants to be free from the intoxicating highs and quick fixes that made life seem easy. This new identity is forged from a desire to face things, no matter how painful. This new identity is also infused with a precocious self-interest that evolves through the Zeigarnik phenomenon. This is self psychologist Heinz Kohut's term for the wonderful, delightful human tendency to complete interrupted tasks of development if given a chance to do so. Growth resumes without the interruptions of alcohol and other drugs (AOD; Kohut, cited in Chessick, 1992, p. 152).

Addicts in transition begin the sobering journey of identity reconstruction. As you recall from Chapter 8, each stage beckons a new sense of self and requires completion of specific developmental tasks. Migration from stage to stage depends on this evolution. Recovery is secured as identity is solidified. If you know who you are, you know what you're doing.

Transition's Time

Transition is a time of fits and starts, focus and exhaustion, distractions and detours, gains and reversals. There are good days and bad days, and good hours and really bad ones. The addict can't count on anything, as it's all so new. His identity has wobbly legs and needs the most careful attention and support. This critical stage requires desire, focus, humility, a willingness to listen to others, be open to their suggestions, and even take direction. This all takes transition's time.

Time, for the addict, has been about using, recovering from using, or preparing to use again. This urgent "use" of time has not allowed for an openness to other experiences or opportunities with people, nor for thinking and reflecting. Wilfred Bion (1992) identifies an addict's difficulty with time when he states that drugs and alcohol are substitutes employed by those who cannot wait . . . for time's unfolding (p. 299). The question of what to do with time is a critical undertaking during this stage in recovery. Transition's time is best reflected in a quote from Michael Eigen (1996, pp. 193–194):

> Time is God's most precious gift;
> God's most pervasive filter.
> To do away with time is to do away with life.
> The psyche needs time to work,
> the mind needs time to think,
> the soul needs time to feel,
> and life needs time to evolve.

This time is now available to be discovered, to be used for experiencing, learning, problem solving, and healing. Therapeutic "holding" is imperative during the addict's struggle to make sense of time's newfound dimensions. A surrendering addict is willing to be held before he knows what he is being held for; a conflicted addict is not willing to be held if he doesn't know why. Embracing this gift of time takes time.

Transition is also a frightening and overwhelming time as the addict begins to recover from the wreckage of the past—destruction is everywhere after years of excess and disregard. The messes of addiction are often huge, and the addict in the early days of transition is usually not in good shape. He's been defeated and forced to surrender the illusionary confidence of his drinking and drugging days. It's hard to clean up a mess with no confidence. The relationship between therapist and addict, or sponsor and alcoholic, can provide containment and direction for this time-consuming transition task.

Transition's Primary Tasks

The using stage's primary task is relationship building. Transition's primary task is twofold—fostering a recovery identity and nurturing interest in the real self. The first is addressed in the next two sections on transition moments. The section on the interests of transition addresses the latter.

The care and protection of a sober identity requires an every-day, all-day focus. Adam Phillips is a British child psychologist, psychoanalyst, and prolific writer. His work suggests that the addict embrace this task as a personal and ethical morality that requires devotion to the developmental needs of the moment (Phillips, 1998). These needs often feel as taboo, foreign, and unacceptable as they did in childhood. A warm therapeutic relationship starts to reverse the addict's antipathy toward his own caretaking. This relationship encourages a new listening. The addict's responses to what he hears determine the direction of his identity evolution, as well as the likelihood of relapse. His transition identity will either take, rest, or reverse itself throughout this stage.

The Transition Moment—For Addict, Treatment Provider, and Their Relationship

Transition Moment for the Addict

Transition begins with a bang or a whimper. It is the most critical stage of treatment. It is also the most tender. The addict needs chutzpah for the critical and grace for the tender. Arriving at transition has been both treacherous and exhausting. Its first hours and days bring agitated relief and numbing terror. The addict momentarily possesses a startlingly clear sense that the drinking and drugging behaviors have to change. This revelation is often grasped from an emergency room gurney, from a rehab bed, in a family intervention circle, or on a therapist's couch.

This transition moment is terrifying. The addict meets this moment in those first hours, and he is challenged by its reappearance throughout this stage of recovery. The transition moment is a question for the addict—"Will my identity grow forward into my recovery, will I languish and lose some vigor along the way, or will I move backward into using?"

A deep and calming resignation that the fight is over and defeat is victory brings recovery (forward). A halfhearted acquiescence suggesting that the fight continues and defeat is only temporary begets hesitant movement (languish). Overwhelming emotions and feelings of extreme alienation from others often invite a return to destruction (backward). The path of transition is often shaped during this period of early awakening. Does the addict embrace a transition identity based on knowing that the gig is up and it's time to let go? (Move forward.) Does he hold on to a using identity based on fantasizing that by cooperating now, he can quietly resume drinking or drugging later? (Languish.) Does he flatly refuse to enter transition's gates? (Move backward.) These responses determine the direction and momentum of transition's early development and movement.

Is the addict able to be emotionally truthful? Is he capable of facing feelings of utter vulnerability with its terrifying need for others, as he lies baffled and alone in a cold emergency room or huddled on the bathroom floor of his home? Or is he incapable at this time of facing feelings of surrender and healthy dependency and instead suits up in the costumes of either superficial compliance or hostile omnipotence to get through these early transition hours?

An addict's location in his natural history greatly influences the direction of this transition moment. The response and receptivity of therapists, nurses, friends, and family are also influential. Together, they determine if this becomes a transformational experience for the addict or another worrisome misstep during transition.

The transition addict surrenders, hesitates, or refuses.

Transition Moment for the Treatment Provider

Most treatment providers have been patiently and purposefully waiting and working for this transition moment.

Is the therapist able to be emotionally truthful? Is she capable of facing the utter powerlessness of this intense moment? Can she accept that all her hard work, idealism, and hopefulness are utterly inconsequential? Or does her ego, own history of addiction, or professional reputation take over? Does she try to possess the moment and force a direction?

Is the therapist able to grasp that this is the addict's moment, not hers? Is she able to provide a challenging environment, not a controlling one, in the midst of all this danger, fear, and hope? Analytic hovering or listening gives the addict room to live his natural history, as well as to decide what he wants to do in his moment. A thinking treatment provider gently embraces the addict's surrender into the transition stage or patiently provides a containing berth for the addict's hesitancy or reassertion of control.

The transition therapist is receptive or possessive.

Transition Moment for the Relationship

A simple explanation of this transition moment between addict and therapist is proposed. There are three experiential options. Entry into the transition stage of recovery is more likely if the addict is able to surrender to vulnerability, and the clinician is able to submit to utter powerlessness. This first experience brings the addict and clinician together in the shared emotional truth of a transition moment that grows forward.

Hesitating during a transition moment occurs when the addict overtly complies, yet covertly defies. He feels unable to articulate his real ambivalence, and the therapist is unable to read or connect with it. This second experience reflects unspoken interpersonal anxieties that result in a developmental pause.

Return to the using stage of recovery is more likely to occur if the addict cannot tolerate dependency on another and the clinician tries to force it. This third experience reflects a friction between the patient's natural history and the clinician's overzealous wishes. This experience feels tense and aggravating to both, and, for the time being, the addict's identity moves backward.

Treatment providers must be more sensitive to the relational influence of this transition moment and be willing to address their own anxieties that interfere with and obstruct the addict's identity evolution. Listening with receptivity is extraordinarily difficult in the midst of a terrifying life-and-death emergency. Each therapist must find a way to gently hold and firmly challenge the addict during this momentous decision period. After all, the addict has been waiting for this his entire life.

Addicts and clinicians are exquisitely sensitive to the impacts of each other during this moment. The British psychoanalyst Christopher Bollas (2007) says, "Indeed, it is unconscious to unconscious" (p. 13).

Transition's Moments Revisited—Identity Forward, Resting, or Backward

Transition's beginnings are unique to each individual. For some, the path feels a glorious launch into the wondrous unknown. There is excitement, hope, and relief. This journey is open to possibilities. For others, the path is entangled by doubts and hesitancies, refusals and reversals. Conflicts ensnare possibilities. There is often begrudging or destructive movement. On any of these paths, the recovering addict will revisit transition moments again and again. These are critical forks met along the way. Every transition moment begs a challenge: Will the addict venture into recovery's infinity? Will his growth plateau in hesitation? Or will he resubmit to addiction's authority? These moments arise again and again during transition.

Sometimes, transition moments invite practical, everyday questions: Will I listen to myself? Will I take the time to hear my struggles? Can I handle what is next? How will this undertaking affect my recovery? Should I take it on, or does it feel too much? Am I overwhelming myself? Do I need to reach out to others, to support systems? Does something feel right or wrong? Can I start to trust my gut?

These questions irritate the newly sober transition addict, who is often driven to make up for lost time. Facing the truth of his limitations feels humiliating. Yet ignoring these questions invites suffering and anguish, identity reversal, and relapse. Cultivating a watchfulness for these transition moments is a major part of the work at this stage. Patients feel cared for when recovery therapists attentively hover around these questions and answers and nurture the importance of their responses. Attending to this private, personal morality promotes a forward identity development, encourages adjustments in living, and greatly reduces, if not eliminates, relapse.

Interventions During Transition, Authoritative Versus Authoritarian Hints, Hovering and Hinting Rather Than Possessing and Ordering

As has been suggested, a psychoanalytic attitude can enhance addiction treatment. It provides a way of listening and relating that is both unintrusive and empowering. It encourages a self-experience that values psychological reflection and thinking. It allows the addict to wait for time's unfolding (Bion, 1992, p. 299). It adds merit to a field that tends to be overcontrolling, possessive, too directive, and prematurely reassuring. It has its place in the four stages of recovery. Its use, however, requires judicious discernment. Sometimes, it operates in the forefront, and sometimes it needs to be waiting in the background.

Some tasks of transition require more active and direct interventions. These save a life, resolve a crisis, and redirect momentum. These are necessary interventions for persons overfamiliar with survival through the use of drugs and alcohol, and underfamiliar with the use of clear thinking and healthy day-to-day coping strategies. Transition's messes are substantial and the addict's capabilities fragile. Friends and family, therapists, and sponsors want to pitch in, and sometimes take over. Subsequently, guidance and direction giving have become overly institutionalized in the world of recovery, especially in transition's early days. This approach has a time and a place. Its benefits are many. Other styles of responding are also important to consider.

Adam Phillips's (1998) work on hinting is extremely useful in both the development and delivery of transition interventions (pp. 75–117). Psychoanalytic practitioners listen through attentive hovering. Hovering suggests that one lingers or waits close by in an uncertain condition or stays suspended or fluttering in the air near one place (Guralnik and Friend, 1968, p. 705). Hinting after hovering provides the transition addict with some helpful guidance as he learns to make decisions based on his own truth.

The *Oxford English Dictionary* defines a hint as "an occasion or an opportunity; a slight indication; a suggestion or implication conveyed covertly but intelligently" (Phillips, 1998, p. 90). Hints give a person room and are more likely to be freely taken. They start things off and get things going. Good hints are not felt as compromising, but rather as some kind of release. Hinting is like borrowing—taking something of somebody else's for your own use. The good hint is always in the eye of the beholder. Hinting and hovering help dignify transition's direct interventions (Phillips, 1998, pp. 75–117).

Phillips differentiates between authoritative and authoritarian interpretations or hints. An authoritative hint delivered after hovering allows for two possibilities: It gives the addict room to make something of his own of it, and it also gives him space to dream something up from it (Molino, 1998 p. 128). The clinician who uses her authority with an authoritative hint honors the addict's authority as well.

An order is the opposite of a hint. An order is authoritarian. Its message is confining; there is no room for dreaming. The addiction field is dominated by orders. These invite retaliation or compliance. Neither reaction is useful for the urgencies of this stage or for the evolution of the real self.

Remember, the transition addict is preoccupied with the repair of past destruction, and at the same time driven by the desire for new discovery. These tasks and passions overwhelm the fragile recovering identity. A transition therapist hovers around the addict's authority and gives it time to unfold. She holds his initiatives and confusions, desires and anxieties. No doubt he will flounder during the reworking of his interior and exterior worlds.

At these times, an active intervention may feel necessary if the patient is dangerously reversing identity development, and thus potentially in the path of relapse. A hovering hint feels better than an order. Hints delivered without possession are often received with welcome. Respect for the addict's authority encourages healthy surrender to his truth. The therapeutic relationship thrives, and the addict's identity evolves. For the time being, transition's path is moving clearly forward.

The Interests of Transition

Adam Phillips isn't a specialist in the field of addiction. His profound writings on childhood interest and curiosity, however, endow us with a deep understanding of addiction's etiologies, as well as powerful propositions about what is necessary for addiction's recoveries. He sheds light on the dual concerns of the transition stage of recovery—the securing of a sobering identity that eventually invites the return of the addict's interests in his real self. Listening for an addict's interests and encouraging their further exploration are key tasks of transition. They also secure long-term recovery.

A creative foray into aspects of Phillips's (1998) work is helpful here. Freud felt that the child's profundity was in the quality of his curiosity. Children know what they are interested in—where babies come from, the differences between the sexes, and parental relationships. These curiosities are not options for children; they are urgencies. "The child is addicted to, driven by what he doesn't know" (p. 11). He loves his questions and initially is both unfazed and unbaffled by his parents' fatigue of them. Children want to know about parental and sibling sexuality, but most grown-ups tell them that they need to know something else. They are instructed to move away from what they are really interested in and encouraged to become occupied with some kind of substitute (pp. 21–36).

Children quickly learn that their parents and their schools sanction and support official and safe habits of inquiry, and discourage unofficial and more spirited aspects of curiosity. Civilization's standards foreclose on the child's real interest (Phillips, 1998, p. 23). His pleasures feel rejected and mocked. The child feels humiliated. For a long time, he valiantly fights to hold on to his own self-education—keeping up with his interests, rather than society's dictates. Tragically, this heroic effort cannot sustain itself. The child lets go of his insistence on exploring what seems exciting.

There are costs to losing interest in what is interesting. These appear in symptoms of anxiety, depression, and despair. The child, adolescent, and then later adult begins to develop pathologies. The *Diagnostic and Statistical Manual of Mental Disorders* (DSM) is full of diagnoses that, at heart, stem from a loss of interest in what interests the real self. As Lance Dodes (2002), of Harvard, says, addiction is always a substitute action, because another way of being does not seem possible or permissible. Alcohol and drugs mask the agonies of lost interest, excitement, and passion.

Early transition days are about moving away from the crisis of using, clearing up addiction's wreckage, and doing physical repair. Transition growth soon sparks the reawakening of the interests of the real self. Phillips so wisely encourages us to analytically hover and listen for the reappearance of those childhood wonders that got stuck, and later sublimated in the ravages of alcoholism and addiction.

Phillips's contribution here is one of the more exciting and hopeful additions to the world of recovery treatment! A selection from Chapter 8 (p. 116) identifies the relationship between interest and relapse:

> The integrative model presented here builds on Marlatt and Gordon's (1985) classic work on relapse prevention. The proposed treatment model suggests that relapse occurs because people stop taking their new sense of self seriously. They grow weary and lose interest in staying connected to the reawakening of their true self, including their fragile recovering identity (Phillips, 1998, pp. 3–36). One patient announced, "I'm so tired because I'm recovering from my life, you know."
>
> Fatigued and impatient family members, therapists, and sponsors can lose interest in supporting this process as well. This forgetting is lethal, which will be emphasized again and again in this section. Nurturing, sustaining, and maintaining the return of a childlike curiosity, with its unbridled interest in self, is the key to long-term recovery. Relapse will occur otherwise. And relapse has made a mockery of a treatment industry that has not conveyed this message to the recovering consumers and their families, and the public in general.

The transition addict is very interested in his experience of life without AOD. At first, he may sense how frightened and scared he is; later he may notice how little and small he feels as well as how big and overwhelming the world seems. Watching what others are doing and saying, connecting with others in recovery, and discovering his feelings and preferences are filled with childlike wonder. These early interests and curiosities are overwhelmingly frightening and threatening. They haven't been listened to for years; they feel foreign and odd. There is a chilling fear that they are unimportant and irrelevant, and certainly not critical to the tasks of transition. It takes time to realize that interest in one's true self needs to become a lifelong interest.

Transition addicts need someone behind them. They need to be in a relationship with someone who listens for and helps keep alive their discovery of their real interests. This may be a sponsor, a therapist, a psychoanalyst, or a member of Alcoholics Anonymous (AA) or another support group. Without this champion, disinterest reappears and relapse will surely follow. Relapse occurs when one ignores the nuances of need in those early, bewildering days of transition.

Again, the work of Phillips on interest heralds in a new point of emphasis in the work of addiction recovery, and specifically in the stage of transition. Sobriety is a priority, and so is self-discovery. Hovering and listening provide a safe space for the addict. These quietly encourage self-experience and reflection, long lost to the ravages of addiction. Mike Eigen (2006) reminds us that experience is the garden that always needs tending (p. 107). Childlike curiosity returns when the addict returns to his garden. Attention to abstinence (or moderation) and devotion to a deeper interest in the self requires dedication during transition.

A gentle caveat: Sometimes, the addict's interest and recovery path separate him from his family, friends, or AA. Sometimes, this invites relational conflict. The separateness of self-interest is often equated with the selfishness of addiction. Family members confuse the addict's self-assertion with resistance, denial, and difficulty. They interpret his independence as willful. It reminds them of using struggles. They are suspicious of these new preferences. Their fearful responses often intimidate, and the guilty addict is tempted to capitulate. He may give up his interests like he did in childhood. Relinquishing his newfound vitality beckons a loss of self that may lead to relapse.

Recovery is a creative endeavor. It requires energy and commitment. All family members must participate. The task is to discover, negotiate, and respect differences in interest, separateness, and connectivity among all members of the newly recovering family system. This takes waiting time.

Trauma, Relational Home, Resurrective Ideology

Robert D. Stolorow is a renowned psychologist and psychoanalyst. His work on trauma and its impact on everyday life helps here. He posits that the developmental trauma experienced in early relationships crushes the human spirit and leaves in its wake unmetabolized affects that haunt emotional life (Stolorow, 2007, pp. 4, 14). The child, adolescent, and then later adult looks for a way to relieve this unnamed pain. Drugs and alcohol do the trick for a while. If lucky enough, this trick stops working and a healthy solution is found. Stolorow's (2007, 2009) work on trauma and its repair are extremely useful in the transition phase of recovery.

A little background is useful here. Parents or caretakers consider children's needs all day long. They can either regularly attune, or malattune, to a child's longings, as well as his painful and joyful feeling states. With attunement, the child feels good, connected to, and curious about his feelings. He is poised to understand that the back-and-forth of good feelings and bad are a part of our everyday experience and ongoing existence. The child grows to accept and embrace this fact. He discovers that relational connections soften the emotional blows of everyday life (Stolorow, 2007, pp. 1–6).

With malattunement, the child feels bad, isolated from others, and shameful of his feelings. He loses the innocence of curiosity, as well as a faith that the relational world will support him during difficult days and uncomfortable times. He feels lost and, with it, a sense that "something is always wrong" (Eigen, 2009, pp. 77–79).

The malattuned child goes into action and methodically chooses to present himself to his world without these bad and defective aspects of his being. He contorts a coherence on himself that excludes the parts that feel wrong. The child, adolescent, and then later adult denies and restricts much of his emotional experience. This brings alienation from self and isolation from others. Life doesn't feel good, either inside the self or with other people. The malattuned child does not understand why (Stolorow, 2007, pp. 1–6).

He soon discovers that drugs and alcohol alleviate this pain and alienation. With seamless effort, this numbing ritual becomes a part of everyday existence. Stolorow (2009) calls this ritual a resurrective ideology (pp. 5–11). The alienated adolescent or adult is resurrected into the world of addiction, with all its false promise and temporary empowerment. It relieves people of feelings of estrangement and loneliness. Drugs and alcohol provide the illusion of self-satisfaction as well as a false sense of enjoyment and comfort in the company of others. This resurrective lifestyle creates a misguided sense of safety and invincibility that sustains the addict for many years. This compromise can produce careers, marriages, and children. It is built on deception and exclusion of the true self. The mythology of this solution eventually collapses in often violent and destructive ways. The addict then enters the stage of transition. He needs support for both the exterior and interior reorganization that will follow.

Stolorow reminds us that emotional trauma originates in an interpersonal context. A relational home also becomes the context for repair. This therapeutic space provides support for the tasks of transition, cultivates the registering of impacts, covets the sacredness of transition moments, and nurtures the therapeutic relationship. Initially, it is a shelter to survive detox and design the next levels of care, as well as to begin the terrifying steps of digging out of the messes of years of addiction. It supports the development of an addict's new identity—the most enduring task of recovery. Early on, this means focusing on the behavioral truth of the next steps in recovery. For most, this means behavioral abstinence. For some, this means behavioral adjustment (Stolorow, 2007, p. 26).

As soon as possible, relational home therapists should consider attentive hovering in addition to behavior monitoring. Being fully receptive to the perceptions and interests of a newly sober addict feels counterintuitive. After all, most have little lived experience with discussing real feelings, thinking things through, negotiating relationships, and problem solving. Perceptions and cognitions have been colored by alcohol.

Creating relational space for the addict to reflect on his inner experience begins to rebuild a lost gut, and with it some much needed self-confidence. The transition addict begins to draw on himself in ways previously felt unfathomable. Encouraging this self-connection builds psychological capacity. This interior remodeling can start sooner than we think in our work with addicts and alcoholics. We don't always have to hold our breaths with them for fear that they will return to using. There is much to do between exhaling and inhaling.

In time, transition's relational home becomes a container for intimidating and overwhelming feelings. It becomes a sacred space to dare to connect with the loneliness and sadness, rage and alienation that drove the addict into such a destructive and illusionary resurrective ideology. It becomes a place to experience and express these terrifying emotions, to develop a new reverence for thinking, and to rework early trauma (Stolorow, 2007, 2009).

The relational home must be returned to again and again. This is not at all easy for a person wounded by early trauma and omnipotently suspicious of the utility of people and relationships. Persistence gives birth to rewarding interpersonal experiences. The addict tentatively begins to search for more of these. Residing in a relational home prevents relapse.

Families in Transition

If family is involved, most members begin the transition stage caught between emotions. They feel exhausted and invigorated, hopeful and terrified, grateful and resentful, willing and reluctant. Many are dreaming of a new life without the ravages of addiction—its sleepless nights, endless fights, confusions and deprivations. Their wishes and repair fantasies need realistic support.

Family members, sometimes referred to as co-addicts, often feel left out and confused, ignored, and silenced during transition's early days. They are often baffled by the addict's recovery. They are bewildered by his transition path. They do not comprehend the limitations of a person who just months ago managed events and activities without a glitch. They forget that drugs and alcohol fueled his smooth sailing. They often do not understand the necessity for temporary withdrawal periods that foster identity restoration. These feel eerily reminiscent of drug-using isolation; it takes time to trust that these retreats are healthy. Families feel held hostage by the addict, even in recovery.

Family members need attentive hovering to know they are being listened to and that they matter. The family needs to be "held" as well after the crisis of using. They also need to be actively involved. Yes, family members need to learn about the addict's recovery stages. Most importantly, they need to learn about, actively value, and embrace their own recovery. Their work is just as important as the addict's. Years of addiction and family avoidance have taken a toll on everyone. Family members are encouraged to attend Al-Anon meetings, elicit the help of a recovery coach, participate in their own psychotherapy, and seek out community support. Each member needs to embrace his own self-care while supporting the addict's recovery. This is a foreign concept. Family members are used to ignoring and abdicating their own needs. This message requires constant reinforcement (Brown, 1988, pp. 205–289). Many addiction specialists are passionate about family members' involvement in their own recovery.

Stephanie Brown, Terrance Gorski, Peter Steinglass, and others deeply value the importance of family recovery. Dr. Brown reminds us that every member is involved in an identity reconstruction and precariously rests on his or her own pair of wobbly legs of growth and development. She has developed a four-stage model of treatment that supports the co-addict's migration through his own recovery. Each family member is encouraged to advocate for his own status as an identified patient and relinquish his role as an appendage to the addict. Family members can be supportive of others' recovery as long as they believe that their own individual recovery comes first (Brown, cited in W. L. White, 2011).

Steinglass and Gorski have also spent much of their professional lives dedicated to the alcoholic family. Gorski and Miller (1986) suggest that the addict is the first family member to seek treatment. Family members are initially hyperfocused on the addict's sobriety. It often takes a while for them to identify their part in the family's distress. It takes even more time for them to decide to put energy into their own recovery. Steinglass, Bennett, Wolin, and Reiss (1987) have developed a Family Life History (FLH) model suggesting a comprehensive approach to recovery that includes family of origin and multigenerational concerns. Their phase-driven recovery model addresses the "invasion" of the family regulatory behaviors by alcoholism and the characteristic developmental "distortions" adopted as a result (p. 335).

Transition's immediate goals are to prevent the addict's relapse and soothe overwhelming family confusion. The long-term goal is the sustaining of recovery for each family member, as you have seen in the case of Dean and his family during the using stage (p. 137) and will see in the cases of Penny and Mark. You will also read clinical cases that do not include family members.

Transition is not the time for normalcy. Rather, it is a focused and persistent time of rebuilding. This often brings a deep disappointment and resentment for family members who have endured so much and just want to move on. Moving on is a recipe for disaster.

And now on to clinical cases to see how this mix of treatment concepts, therapeutic skills, and clinical caveats has been applied in therapeutic action moments.

CLINICAL CASES

Penny

An Unfortunate Event: Surgical Relapse

Penny was now 65 days abstinent from the opiate Vicodin and the benzodiazepines, Valium, Klonopin, and Xanax (refresh your memory about Penny in Chapter 9, p. 142). She designed her individualized treatment program, which included between three and four days of individual therapy, couples therapy, and phone support as needed. She did not want inpatient rehab, and her wish was working so far. She embraced the beliefs of a sober transition identity. She respected its wobbly legs. She wanted her husband's understanding and involvement. She was interested in herself, and she was doing well.

A most challenging transition moment confronted Penny. It extended over eight days. She was required to have dental surgery for acute tooth decay and pain. The surgery was expected to include a major amount of cutting in the gums and required some grafting. Post-op pain was expected; opiates and benzodiazepines are usually prescribed.

Penny was filled with agitation and dread. She feared that physical pain would overwhelm her. She doubted her capacity to tolerate it. Would she try to get some emotional relief as well? Would she lose her sobriety?

I encouraged her to talk to her dentist and get as much information as possible about the surgery, as well as the realistic amounts of pain expected. She volunteered, "I'm going to tell him I'm a recovering addict and I cannot take opiates or benzodiazepines." Her declarations suggested a transition identity at work; I strongly supported her and hinted, "Let's create a support team—you, me, and Roger. We can talk and make decisions together. I think that will help you with your fear." She agreed.

Penny decided to manage her post-op pain with Tylenol or Motrin. "I don't want to get near opiates." Her dentist suggested that if the surgery proved more difficult, he would prescribe a very small amount of the semisynthetic opiate Percocet, which is used for severe pain. All agreed that Roger would hold and dispense the Percocet. It would only be given if Penny was in extreme pain.

We briefly talked about Tramadol, a non-narcotic pain reliever for mild to moderate pain. Theoretically, it produces less dependency and is prescribed to many recovering addicts. Penny insisted on relying on Motrin and Tylenol for the moderate pain and Percocet if it became more severe. "That's what the doctor told me." In retrospect, I should have insisted on Tramadol. The speed of events interfered with my own clarity.

I talked to Penny on the telephone after the surgery. I was extremely distressed to hear that the surgeon had administered the benzodiazepine Halcion. Best intentions had failed. When I asked Penny about the Halcion, she replied that the surgeon had told her that it was sleep medication. I responded, "You've been addicted to similar medications; that's unfortunate that it was prescribed." I warned her that psychoactive drugs were swirling around in her brain and the call for more drugs was most threatening right now.

She said she was okay with Motrin. She felt preoccupied. My attentive hovering increased.

I began listening for the sedating and disorienting effects of this benzodiazepine. I also began listening for her brain's desire for opiates. It came in the form of pain complaints. She repeated several times that her dentist said that the infection was the worst he had ever seen. "He told me that he had to do much more digging than he thought." She began questioning Motrin and Tylenol's effectiveness. I sensed that the Halcion was altering brain chemistry, influencing her thinking. Already, it seemed to lower her resistance to pain and to increase her desire for more intense medication. She started to sound confused. She also felt distant. Her words and affect hinted at an unconscious, if not conscious, desire to return to drug use.

The next day, I learned that in the late evening she approached her husband in "excruciating pain." She assured him that the pain was real and that she needed the Percocet. They had a long talk; he agreed. He gave her one and locked the bottle away again.

Penny and I talked about her experience of taking an opiate after 65 days of sobriety. She claimed to be okay and said, "It was for pain relief only." She felt distant from me and seemed a bit too confident and self-assured about this experience. Sober addicts are terrified about surgery, pain medication, and the potential loss of their sobriety. They are ambivalent and agitated. Penny was not. I registered the difference. I sensed her using identity was returning.

How would she handle this? How would we? Here was a transition moment. Will Penny's identity continue to shift backward, or will she surrender to vulnerability and truth and express her confusing desires? Will she seek healthy dependency with Roger and me, or will she return to the omnipotent solution of drug use with its denial of need? Will I try to possess this moment or surrender to my utter powerlessness? The moment is hers. If Penny wants to use drugs, she will find a way. All I can do is hover and hint. I was unsettled but thought we might be on the right track.

Over the next couple of days, she reported that she was filled with pain, that she could not sleep, that her face was swollen, and that her ears were throbbing. She kept repeating, "This whole experience is very upsetting. I mean, I'm in a lot of pain. I need relief. It's gotten so complicated." She was engaged in a campaign of convincing herself that more medication was needed. She wanted my vote as well. Hesitancy and ambivalence seemed to be driving her transition moment responses.

Assessing and negotiating the need for pain medication is an overwhelming task during the early days of transition. Postsurgery discomfort is real; it warrants medical attention. It is also fraught with unconscious yearnings for the old days of drug comfort, as well as relief from the drudgeries of early sobriety. Penny, Roger, and I spoke often during medication decisions. Is there pain? What is the pain about? Is the Motrin sufficient? Why not? Are there "ice cubes clinking" (our code words for brain chemistry that is calling for drugs)? Does the pain warrant a Percocet? Should we use Tramadol instead? This process is always emotionally grueling. We all seemed to be looking forward to the day her suffering would be over.

On the eighth day, I noticed that she was edgy, sad, and withdrawn. I commented that her irritability and agitation felt familiar. I asked, "Are you taking Percocet instead of Motrin?"

There was a long silence. She burst into tears, "I've been lying to you." She told me that on the third day postsurgery, she woke up wanting more Percocet. She needed to manage her own dental discomfort. "I convinced myself after the late-night Percocet that Motrin wasn't working anymore. I didn't want to talk to the team, humiliate myself in front of Roger, convince him that the pain was real, beg to be believed."

Penny had called the dentist and complained of excruciating pain. She requested more medication. The doctor apparently forgot that she was a recovering addict and prescribed 12 more Percocet. Penny picked them up that day. She now had her own stash and didn't need to involve her husband in pain assessment or relapse prevention. With that decision, she began self-medicating her emotional distress. With that decision, she interrupted over two months of sobriety.

As she was crying, she stated, "The whole thing got to be too much, and then I began to feel and remember the warm relief that comes with taking an opiate. As soon as I connected with that feeling of opiate ease that first night, I just wanted more." Penny told me that her secret plan was to take the Percocet until they were gone. After that, she would return to her recovery program. She felt that neither Roger nor I understood her pain and that she had to take matters into her own hands. She answered a transition moment question with backward movement. Her using identity returned and was in charge. As she sobbed, she told me that she now knew how much she was back in the grip of the psychological urgency of addiction. She was blinded by the comfort of Percocet. She continued, "My plan worked for a while, and then I couldn't tolerate the deceit."

The guilt of lying to herself and her treatment team crowded in around Penny. It brought her to her senses. She said, "I've been so upset about lying to you. You are my lifeline to recovery. I lit a match to the cord that is between us. I kept thinking that I would put out the fire before I destroyed the cord." She wept and said, "If I don't have that cord, I have nothing." She continued that she was terrified to talk to me but needed to face her relapse. She was ready, willing, and able to return to her recovery (Miller and Rollnick, 2002, pp. 10–11).

Several long conversations followed. Penny was humiliated and ashamed, uncertain how to move forward. She was truly frightened but also very willing to take some direction. I consulted her psychiatrist, Dr. Ashley, and assured her that no detox was required. That night, the team spent a long time going over the events of the previous week and the overwhelming feelings that went unaddressed.

As discussed, surgeries, legitimate pain, and dispensing of medication are enormous challenges during the early days of transition. An insidious process takes over. Desire is restimulated, the possibility of relief so near. Fear and confusion abound. Addictive beliefs replace recovery beliefs. Identity waffling occurs. Addicts soon forget their wobbly legs. They suddenly feel very sure-footed. They lose interest in themselves, and they lose interest in talking to people. Omnipotent solutions start to feel logical. Isolation and solitary choices follow.

I saw Penny in my office the next day, and she seemed remarkably lighter in spirit. Her unconscious ambivalence toward her recovery was activated as soon as Halcion, the sleep medication prescribed, got into her system. This triggered drug-seeking wishes and drug-taking behavior. Her using identity overpowered her recovering identity. She secretly used and was filled with shame, terror, and remorse. Penny reclaimed a transition moment, and growth moved forward again. She resumed her transition identity with greater unconscious commitment and a new sense of clarity. She felt relief. Her ambivalence had been exposed, acted out, and redirected toward the side of recovery. Penny felt reinvigorated, yet humble, and she muttered, "I'm terrified of being cocky in any way." This relapse put a searchlight on the challenges of the transition days ahead.

A Visit with Mom—Preparation

Penny was nearly eight months sober, which included her eight-day surgery relapse. At times, the household felt more manageable, the children more containable, her husband more on board, and there was room for some friends. She did not want to self-medicate with drugs. She embraced her abstinence but deeply struggled with bringing her new sense of sober self into her own being and into her life as a mother and a wife.

Penny dismissed her own feelings and wishes with disgust. We identified this tendency and understood its origins. We knew what we were up against. Penny was a Munchausen by proxy child. Munchausen by proxy parents (often the mother) have a symbiotic and overinvolved attachment to their children. The mother unconsciously encourages a sick role, exaggerates symptoms, and convinces children that their illness needs special care (Cantor, 1996, p. 194). Penny's own interests were violently rejected, as she was possessed by another. We had to work hard to create a sense of legitimacy about them again. This reversal was at the heart of her recovery work. She would have to fight to feel her life's value, to listen to what really interested her, and to struggle even harder to have it drive her day-to-day existence. She had to fight for a place called self (Brown, 2004).

Penny was very determined. And she wanted to make up for lost time. She struggled with overcommitting; she would then collapse in fatigue. She tried to learn from these experiences. It didn't always sink in. Her desire for more sometimes got the better of her. It sometimes engendered imaginative fantasies.

Penny called her mother to come for a visit. She had a vague sense that it was a dangerous move and that the visit might threaten her recovery. She also had a deep wish "to finally face her, to get it over with, to finish it with her, to not have to deal with her for the rest of my life." In a matter of hours, her transition identity began to putter out and lose momentum.

An equestrian analogy is applicable here. Penny over-faced herself. A horse in this condition is in a vulnerable spot. An owner asks his horse to perform feats that the horse is physically, emotionally, and developmentally unprepared to handle. The horse, being a creature who wants to please, succumbs to his owner's demands. His willingness is crushing to watch. In faith, the horse performs things that he is constitutionally unable to accomplish. At the end of his valiant effort, he is left in a horrible state. His body is cramped and tight. He suffers shortness of breath. He is sweating profusely and excreting from every orifice in his body. He is also massively depressed.

An addict during the transition stage of recovery all too often unwittingly over-faces his transition identity. The humiliation of years of addiction violently drives him. He asks himself to do things that he is unable to handle. His hopefulness and enthusiasm belie his capacities. His willingness to destroy himself is also crushing to watch. A transition therapist must attentively hover around this unbridled and omnipotent desire. She hints at its potential destruction to recovery. She must decide the nature and tone of her interventions. Should she educate, contain, or more aggressively intervene to detangle confused thinking, protect sobriety, and promote peace of mind?

The days following Penny's decision were filled with exhaustion and despair, anxiety and dread. She had lost her transition footing and mistreated another transition moment. Her development languished. She displayed symptomatic consequences from over-facing herself—she took to the bed, fed herself erratically, and withdrew into her interior. She grew weary and lost interest in nurturing and protecting her fragile recovering identity. Penny's wishes overwhelmed her capacity.

Our conversations were no longer about transition's tasks but about the terrors of her mother's six-day visit. Penny was numb. "I don't know where I am anymore." She dismissed her recovery identity; she was driven by old expectations. She could not get out of bed four days before the visit. Her mother was trumping her life and her being, as she had when Penny was a child. Penny could only allow that then; she forgot that she had a choice now. She was far away from her true self.

We had an emergency phone session. Penny was panicked. "I can't hide like this when my mom is here. I'm afraid I won't be able to get out of bed tomorrow, much less next week. I want to go get my husband, Roger. He needs to be in on this conversation." Omnipotent solutions were becoming less interesting. Penny increasingly desired her husband's involvement in decisions that would affect the family's recovery. A transition moment forward.

Roger got on the phone. I quickly sensed he was overwhelmed with his own life and frightened about his wife's. Roger's own therapy was intermittent; it was hard for him to recognize his need for more. He struggled without this support.

Roger seemed braced for another transition stage emotional meltdown. I felt his agitated fatigue immediately. I also felt his hostile and perturbed projections land on and in me. They felt as if he were saying, "You're the f---ing therapist, do you know what you're doing? Why is this crisis happening again? How long is this recovery going to ruin our lives? I am paying you money to handle this. You professionals are the problem in all this. Just leave us alone."

I remained calm, and it was a hard conversation. I felt the need for an authoritative transition intervention. I hinted, "I'm about to make one of those more direct interventions here. We all know the work both of you have been doing during Penny's recovery. This visit has the probability of being completely overwhelming. And we now know that this cannot be powered through by taking a pill. With several days to go, you both still have a choice. Is this visit something you both want to take on at this time in your family's recovery? It's probably going to be extremely draining. There are many ways to work with this. You can reschedule, you can have your mother stay in a hotel, or you can cancel the visit altogether." I provided my best wisdom within a hinting spirit. They reluctantly listened, and they went ahead with their original decision. A transition moment backward?

Mom's Arrival

The day of her mother's arrival, Penny called me at 7:30 in the morning. She was in an angry panic: "I feel terrible. Roger is being such a jerk. I asked him to help me. He doesn't seem to get what's going on. I'm so scared we are going to get into a fight. He doesn't seem to want to talk. I sent him an e-mail last night with a poem. He hasn't said anything about it. I'm not sure why. I am so angry that he is not responding to my feelings in the poem." Penny's powerful poem was unfortunately delivered at an unreceptive time.

"I Feel"
like this is such a crucial moment
like I am coming face to face with my most painful truth
the thing that made me drink, take pills

numb myself, not trust myself, despise myself, drive myself to perfection at the
expense of myself and those around me,
question and doubt myself,
abhor myself
And I feel my belly swell and I feel raw
and vulnerable and braced for something I have spent years trying to
change or avoid, and now it awaits me and I am filled with dread
Not of this old woman, but the pain and suffering she embodies
and there is nothing I can use as a barrier—no drugs, no alcohol.
I feel exposed and sad
I feel tired and afraid

Penny was probably more agitated by the upcoming visit than by Roger's lack of response. It was not, however, the time for couples work. I sensed her drowning in fear and regret about an ill-timed transition moment decision.

It was a time to provide perspective, to put this visit in the frame of her recovery and wobbly-legged transition identity. It was a time for another authoritative transition intervention. My hint was more direct. "Penny, I'm going to cut to the chase here and ask you to consider the following thoughts and ideas: Neither you nor Roger seem to want this visit, and it probably shouldn't be happening at this time in your recovery. But it is, and we will get through it as a team. The most important thing is to maintain your sobriety. This visit is probably not going to look pretty all the time, and your mother may be critical of your actions. You probably won't live up to her expectations, but you can manage her visit in a way that honors your recovery. Your mom will be drinking all weekend, and she has no idea of your history of addiction and your recovery. But you and Roger know the work you've been doing, and you know that this weekend is a real challenge to that work. You both may limp along, and Roger may not be there for you. I will, however, and now that the visit is here, we can only do the best we can to honor your sobriety."

She immediately replied with relief, "I get it, I get it," and she continued, "Your words got me out of my fog. I'm ready to begin the day, and already I've changed my expectations for myself and for Roger." Her mother's visit was scheduled for six days and so were evening phone sessions.

The first two days were "hallucinatorily" successful. Penny was able to navigate her mother's visit in ways that surprised her. Then on day three, she hit a wall. Her voice was edgy, her mood despairing, and her patience tattered during one of our evening sessions. For the first time during our eight months of very intensive transition recovery work, she said, "I have to get off the phone. Talking to you is making me too agitated." It was time to tap into family support; Roger needed to get on board. I authoritatively suggested, "He needs to know that you are hitting a wall, and you need his support."

My head was spinning after the call to Roger. I left him a message, and I wondered: Was I going to surrender to powerlessness? Was Penny going to relapse? Was it happening already? Was Roger too overwhelmed? Were Penny and Roger going to work it out together? Was growth going to develop forward, move backward, or languish?

Mike Eigen encourages respect for the patients' absolute Otherness. They are on their own search. He suggests that we listen for and follow the patients' instructions of living. He dares us to give them space to do their best—or their worst (Personal Communication, 2008). These words comforted me the next day and night when I didn't hear from Penny or Roger. It was the time to give them space for their best or their worst. There was nothing to possess, only to reflectively and receptively wait. This is always hard. Therapists are emotionally invested in patient growth.

Penny and I did not talk on day five. I sensed she was pulling away. She called and left a message, "I'm just trying to get through, hour by hour."

The number of houseguests had expanded: there was her mother, her mother's caretaker, her sister, her niece, her niece's four sons, and occasional friends. The house was filled with intoxicated individuals. Her children were stressed and exhausted. Guests ravaged her home. Her husband's support was inconsistent. Her mother was insulting. The violations were mounting. Penny was beside herself, and with nowhere to go, it all crowded in around her. She developed a rash and a migraine. She took a Benadryl. She went to bed early that evening and, unfortunately, was unable to sleep most of the night.

Mom's Departure

The morning of her mother's departure was torture. Penny could not bear being in her presence. Her mother's caretaker, Mena, was biting and told Penny she felt "burdened" by the visit and "shocked" by Penny's fatigue and stress. Mena repeated several times, "Our time here was tense and uncomfortable." Penny felt both numb with incredulousness, and punched in the gut with criticism and contempt.

Her mom and caretaker returned home, and Penny immediately developed bronchitis. She went to bed early that night. We were unable to meet or talk. I wondered about her response to the visit and the state of her recovery. Our relationship felt strained and drained by this transition experience. I gave it time and space.

Penny put some of her self-care ego functions to use during her recuperation, specifically those of Khantzian (see Chapter 7 in this book, p. 96). She valued parts of herself, and had some ideas about how to protect herself from danger. Over the next couple of days, she repeated, "I know what I need to do for myself. I need to rest and sleep and do what I can with my girls. I know what I need to do. It's a good sign that I know how to take care of myself." She was proud of her work and strongly identified with her recovery. Her attention to herself, her interest, and her care slowly returned.

During a couples session, Penny anguished, "I will never be a normal person able to function in the world like everyone else. I feel stuck in this pattern. I try to do what I can for my family; I try to do my best and make it all good. It gets to be too much. I barely get through, and when I do, we are all miserable and I have to return to my room, my bed."

Roger's own recovery led the way that day. He reminded his wife that the fatigue and exhaustion they both were feeling was to be expected. He reminded her of our discussions before her mom's stay, "Margy said there would be a before, during, and after period to this visit, and now we are experiencing the aftermath." He shared his perceptions about the depths of her mother's mental illness, her passive-aggressive ways, and her inability to do anything other than try to destroy Penny's confidence and well-being. He seemed to grasp the emotional violence that had transpired. He seemed to grasp how it had taxed Penny, her recovering identity, himself, and his recovering family.

Later, I asked Penny how it felt to listen to her husband. She paused for a moment and reflected, "On one level, it felt okay. I never realized how much he got my mother and saw how she treats me and what she does to me. On the other hand, I think he missed the point. There's something here I don't quite understand, something I don't think we understand." Continue reading about Penny's journey of recovery and growth in Chapter 11 (p. 210).

Dean

Drinking at a Wedding?

Dean never made it to Alcoholics Anonymous (refresh your memory about Dean in Chapter 9, p. 137–142). He continued, "I just don't want to have a problem or be a problem to my parents. Coming here three times a week, considering AA, and taking all these prescribed medications makes me feel like I am crazy. Can't we change this schedule? It makes me feel weird around my friends. None of them need this much therapy or medicine. I'm not going to go to AA; I am just not going to do it."

As he begged for session reduction, he kept saying, "You're the boss, doc, and my family and I listen to what you have to say." He wanted out of his problem, and he also wanted to hold tight to our relationship. Despite hostile ambivalence, his transition identity kept showing up in our relational home.

Dean was obsessed with being "normal." For him, this meant no alcohol problem, no depression or anxiety, no medications, and no therapy three times a week. I suspected that all this talk of being normal had to do with an upcoming wedding—and Dean's own relationship with alcohol. It was his first wedding since his sobriety.

Dean had done good work in therapy. He stopped drinking, avoided party buddies, and worked on his relationship with his parents. He thought a lot about his drinking years and drinking habits. "It was something I really looked forward to at the end of the workday. I did it because I could, it was easy, and it helped me forget my problems. I knew I drank more than others—I didn't care. I knew that I was out of control. I imagined one day that I would get some help. Eventually, I knew I had to stop. I didn't see how I could back then."

Dean slowly stopped isolating in the months prior to the wedding. This was quite a risk for a young man who favored retreating in his room, rather than venturing out into the world (see Chapter 11 on psychic retreats, p. 205). He preferred the often-inhospitable company of his own mind over the company of people. Nonetheless, Dean now risked social events, holiday parties, travel with family, dinners with friends, and business lunches, all with no drinking. He anticipated these with painstaking anxiety. His participation was limited and guarded. But he stayed sober. He got through with some pride but always with shame, embarrassment, and exhaustion about his "alcohol problem."

The wedding celebration included a number of close friends. I suspected that Dean's agitation and ambivalence about therapy masked his inability to talk about his desire to drink. I asked if this was the case. He adamantly responded, "I don't want to drink." I doubted his response. The growing distance between us was troubling; an edge of avoidance surrounded us. We couldn't get around or through it. We persevered.

Weeks later, Dean managed to interject, "I've been thinking something different lately. I'd like to drink at this wedding. I just want to be normal. I don't want to get drunk. I don't want to act stupid. I want to drink and want to see how I will handle it." My authoritative hint reminded him of his pancreatitis attack of a year ago, his family intervention in Indonesia six months later, and the short duration of his sobriety, "There is a lot of risk here." He quickly responded, "I know, I know, but I think I can handle drinking now."

I encouraged elaboration and conversation. Why drink? Why is drinking important now? What does drinking mean? What will you gain and lose by drinking? What will you gain and lose by not drinking? He retreated instead. I sensed that he had already made his decision to drink at the wedding. I sensed he felt misunderstood and attacked. We continued to struggle with our distance.

A transition moment is revisited, and lots of questions surfaced in my reveries. Will his identity grow forward, move backward, or languish? What will he choose, and what is the best way to support his decision making? Will he surrender to his fears? Will he deny their existence? Will his need to drink override thoughtfulness? Will I try to possess the moment? Will I overeducate? Will I punitively tell him that he is out of his mind or expand the scope of his inquiry? I can only provide a perspective larger than his. I can only encourage him to take an interest in thinking it through, to continue to take an interest in this painstaking examination.

As Dean was leaving my office, the last session before the wedding, I intervened with a direct transition intervention question: "What are you going to do with alcohol?" He said, "I'm leaning on not drinking." Dean knew my concerns, and it was time to give him space to do his best or his worst. He went to the wedding and called and left a message as he drove home from the airport after the trip. "Well, it all went okay, and I behaved well for the most part. I'll talk to you when I see you."

The Morning After

Dean looked different when he arrived in my office. His usual overall impression is of a handsome and sensitive young man who looks physically guarded and feels preoccupied and brittle. Dean's impact is a constricted one—his loving sensitivity is overshadowed by his rigid self-protection. One gets the feeling that he is holding back, holding in, and holding on. Dean lives in a retreated mind.

Dean looked confident, calm, self-assured, and relaxed, and he felt considerably lighter in gait and movement after the wedding. His impact felt easy. He wasn't holding himself back. Dean described a wedding weekend of some drinking. He was forthcoming in spirit and manner. "I waited all day. I thought about what I was doing. I thought about our work. I didn't want to blow all the work we'd done. I decided to drink at the rehearsal dinner. I wanted to take it easy and not get drunk. I had a shot of Cristall [vodka]. I later nursed two beers over the evening. I kept watching myself, feeling for my buzz. I didn't want to get wasted. I didn't want to stay late. I didn't want to hang out with the big party people. I haven't had a drink since, and I think I did very well." I soon understood—he finally felt "normal," and this is why he looked so good.

Many who experiment with drinking after a period of abstinence are unwilling to give the first drinking experience so much scrutiny, much less share it with others. Most keep the experience to themselves. Dean did not. He had suffered a harrowing, near-death experience with alcohol, he had been abstinent for four months, his commitment to a completely sober recovery was reluctant, and his desire to drink a reality. I was very apprehensive about his return to drinking; the decision felt off. I was also trying to stay receptive to his point of view. I wanted him to keep talking, to keep up his watchfulness. He seemed interested in doing the same.

Dean and I had discussed how we might include his parents in his experimentation with drinking. They were very involved in his recovery. Their concern about their son's drinking brought them to my office, led to a trip to Indonesia, and ultimately a family intervention. They insisted on treatment. They were willing to support this member of the boomerang generation, who had left home and later returned. He was dependent on their generosity on so many levels. He was also put off by their adherence to the disease model, with its insistence on abstinence. At first he bristled with conflict and wasn't sure how to involve them, but later he agreed that, "if I drink, they should know."

During one of our morning-after conversations, I asked if he had told his parents about his wedding experiment. He responded with a sense of accomplishment, "I've already told them." I asked, "What was their response?" He responded that they were "okay and glad I felt in control. They also asked, 'What did Fetting say?'"

Clinical Reveries

This may be one of the more difficult considerations of contemporary recovery efforts. The treatment industry and the country are very ambivalent, if not skeptical and hostile, to a "return to drinking" option. This is understandable after years, even decades, of AOD disruption and deceit. Encouraging open, ongoing discussions about this wish feels soft, dangerous, wrong, and enabling. It is easier to stick with abstinence; it certainly guarantees no harm. For many, sobriety is inarguably wiser and the drinking option should never be reopened, much less reconsidered. For others, wisdom is packaged in unorthodox ways. Not all have to quit their problematic behaviors. Some can learn to make better choices along the way. The reality is that many wish to drink again.

Whether alone, in a relationship, or in a family, talking about the desire to drink again is essential. A containing forum needs to be established for ongoing discussions. It is imperative to reverse the patterns of secrecy, discounting, and covering up that occurred during those problematic and harrowing days of using. The addict needs support for his wishes, and the family members need space to voice their concerns. This contemporary clinical reality deserves a comprehensive treatment response.

Hope and dread, wishes and concerns, and blind spots and realities need room for exploration. Some addicts, even once-sloppy drunks, after a period of sobriety want to take on the responsibility of talking about the possibility of responsible drinking. They want to submit to labor-intensive discussions of the "whys" beforehand and the "whats" afterward. They accept that a serious scrutiny of their drinking will be an ongoing part of their lives. They want to be truthful. They are willing to learn from experience. They are ready to make adjustments. They deserve a chance to learn how to drink well.

Others, after a period of open and ongoing exploration, acknowledge that their return to drinking fantasy has failed and that they are unable to manage their behavioral choices. Sometimes this recognition follows a harrowing period of experimentation. Other times, it comes with less destruction. Many times, the "failed" results are ignored. The outcomes are varied, but the chance to responsibly explore one's preferences is always useful. The experimenter deserves the chance to decide.

Dean and His Ongoing Scrutiny

Dean was humiliated by his pancreatitis attack and more humiliated by its cause. He couldn't bear the feelings of weakness it engendered in him. This blow caused him to retreat from the world and his friends. I wondered how he would tolerate talking about his progress with drinking after the wedding and how we would proceed in therapy. Dean informed me that he wanted to drink on special occasions only. He said that he did not want to drink regularly and start back on something that got him "in so much trouble." He continued, "I have no desire to drink every night or on weekends. I want to leave it for special occasions and keep bringing it up in therapy."

So, we began. Dean tolerated a number of purposefully probing questions about his wedding experience and his return to drinking after four months of sobriety. Some I asked that day. Some I held for later discussions.

"How did it feel to have that first drink? What did the high feel like? Did you want to get drunk? What's wrong with not drinking at a wedding? What was going through your mind before, during, and after that first drink? How did drinking affect your experience of the wedding weekend? Did you think about day drinking? Did you want to drink on the plane home? How do you envision your return to drinking? What do you think is going to stop you from old patterns? Why is drinking so important to you? Why are you taking this on at this time in your life? How did you make sense of drinking after such a scary bout of pancreatitis and after such an intense intervention?"

We had a long back-and-forth. He was often humiliated by the scrutiny; he acknowledged that it was the cost of a return to drinking. "The drinking felt good. I think I handled it very well, even telling my parents. I tried hard. I watched every move. I was scared. I was thinking of you, our work. It felt so good to be normal. I don't want to get in trouble again." He exuded a sense of relief. He was delighted to feel like a "normal" drinker and even more delighted to belong again to his peer group. He finally asked me, "So, what do you think?"

I had been living in a state of reverie about Dean and was ready to share my thoughts. "You know, Dean, you are 28, and I know you want to be normal and drink like everyone else. I also know at a very young age you got yourself in a lot of trouble. I have developed a hunch that has proven true, sometimes in situations like yours. I call it my 'grand way' theory, developed from years of experience in recovery work. It has guided me and influences my thinking about you and others. I may have mentioned it to you before. When people get in a lot of trouble with drinking and drugging, they often lose control in a grand way. They end up in an embarrassing situation; their out-of-control behavior is exposed; they may end up in a hospital. Other people are pulled into the situation—to help out, to respond to their crisis. Your drinking landed you in the hospital with pancreatitis. Your family was scared and concerned. They begged you to begin therapy. We started working together shortly after your hospital visit. You started drinking again, and it got worse. I recommended more care. You moved to a different part of the world. Your parents came to get you.

"A desire to return to drink after such a grand loss of control is highly suspicious. Anybody would say that. Most other addiction specialists would call me crazy. You might even agree on some level." Dean listened intently.

I authoritatively continued, "My professional sense is that you are taking on a very big and dangerous risk that could either end well or end in a very bad disaster that might show up before you know what you're doing." Our eyes locked; we sat silent. "But Dean, you are here, and you are in treatment and we are talking. This is a risk you want to undertake, and you want to take it on in treatment. All you can do is be truthful about your drinking so we can figure out if your desire to be 'normal' will work out for you or, eventually, if you need to consider something else." He didn't say too much; he didn't need to. His wish was now his reality, and he felt good about the way he was handling it.

Drinking was back in his previously sober treatment. We continued to maintain our now twice-a-week outpatient schedule, and he continued to push for less. I encouraged him to get through this period, and we would discuss schedule changes later. He agreed. We trudged on. He voluntarily returned to sobriety. He said, "I'm okay with not drinking daily. I don't want to. I want to keep it to special occasions."

Special Occasions

Several weeks after the wedding, Dean went to visit his girlfriend. He opened up our session with a long discussion of his recent job search efforts. Eventually he talked about his weekend, and I asked, "What did you do with alcohol?" He quickly responded, "Oh yeah, I wanted to tell you about that. I forgot to tell you about that. Sorry." Dean then reported that during that weekend visit to see his girlfriend, they shared a bottle of wine on Friday night, and he drank two beers on Saturday afternoon and half a glass of wine on Saturday night. He continued, "I just forgot to tell you this."

Dean informed me that he had done well with alcohol that weekend, that it was different, and that he didn't want to get drunk. He talked for a while. I listened and eventually hinted, "Dean, remember after the wedding, you said you only wanted to drink on special occasions." He begrudgingly nodded.

"Bear with me on this, Dean. When people like yourself attempt a return to drinking, I listen carefully to their original wishes about how drinking might fit into their lives. I listen to their thinking and follow their behavior. I try to figure out if they match or mismatch. So, remember our discussions after the wedding?" He nodded. "Remember you said how pleased you were with how you handled yourself, that you didn't want to drink regularly, that you only wanted to drink on special occasions?" He said, "Yes." He paused in reflection and seemed to register where I was going with this. "Well, this weekend, you drank—it wasn't a wedding, a birthday, an anniversary, a funeral, or a national holiday. You said you were going to limit your drinking to special occasions, and now we have something different here. It seems your behavior this weekend is contradicting your original thinking, wishes, and desires. What do you think, Dean?"

His first reaction was blatantly hostile and defensive. "I'm pissed. Now you are insulting me. Are you saying that my first weekend with my girlfriend after our breakup wasn't a special occasion?" I looked at him with an endearing smile, and said, "Now, Dean, do you want to think about what you are saying here? Are you now parsing the use of the words special occasions? Do you really consider weekend activities as special occasions?"

Dean almost immediately calmed down and gave me a look that said a lot, including, "Okay, okay. I know I'm off here, and you got me. I'm glad you did. I know you are behind me. What you're saying makes sense. It's worth thinking about and talking about." He requested, "Let's talk more."

Ron Sager's words echoed in my mind, "Children racing out of the house both love and hate to hear these words. 'Remember, don't run out into the street!'" (Personal Communication, 2009). It seemed Dean loved this conversation.

Eventually I repeated my ongoing concern, "You know you are doing something with alcohol that is very challenging. You got yourself into some serious trouble with your pancreatitis, and then you ran away from your family and didn't return until they chased you down halfway across the world. All this happened because you drank destructively and you didn't want to deal with it. Since sobriety, you have worked very hard in therapy. You have faced many things. You also want to be 'normal.' For you, this includes drinking. So, if you tell me one thing and do another, then we have a contradiction to talk about, a potential problem to address before alcohol's insidious ways get ahead of you. Do you understand what I am saying here?"

Dean took this in. He got it, and he liked it. He understood the thinking-and-doing link of drinking. We talked at length about his desire to return to drinking, his wish to be normal, his belief in himself. He also talked about its threat to his health and well-being, and about his desires. "I really want to do this. I think I can. What you said today helped me. I kind of know where you stand, and I also get that you are with me on this." We both tried hard in these conversations. I was respectful of his wishes and authoritatively truthful about my professional expertise. Transition moments were moving forward. Time would tell.

Dean's Way

Dean voiced his commitment to his own recovery but also said, "Dr. Fetting, I really would like to try to reduce the number of weekly therapy sessions. I want to work, but it is really depressing to have to come in here so often." I heard his desire and again remembered Eigen's words—"Listen to the instructions of our patients, and give them space to do their best and their worst" (Personal Communication, 2008). Incongruously, it felt intuitively right to start reducing the number of weekly sessions. Over the next month, we moved from twice a week to once a week.

The reduction had a noticeable effect on Dean. He came into sessions more animated, clearly feeling less pathological about himself. His desire for less defied a certain treatment logic; it also provided him with personal freedom.

Clinical Reveries

Regular, ongoing support is absolutely essential during the first year of recovery. We also have to listen to our patients and what they express about the pace of their newly discovered dependency needs. Dean's early days of sober pride were short lived. After four months, he wanted to enjoy a human pleasure. He wanted to drink—to feel normal and belong to his peer group. His sense of abnormality overtook him. He wanted to approach his recovery his way—to recognize his problems with alcohol and consider alternatives to abstinence. He wanted to drive his life, his drinking, and his therapy. He wanted to define his own sobering identity.

Many in recovery, and particularly the young, cannot tolerate the narcissistic wound of not drinking like their peer group. It feels a stunning defeat that needs defeating. Victory is in drinking again. Dean was caught between a rock and a hard place. He wanted to stay connected to me to work on his "shaming" alcohol problem, but he also needed the approval and acceptance of his peer group—even if only in his mind. He continued coming once a week, and we continued talking about his drinking in every session. He wanted to learn from his mistakes. He wanted to drink, and he knew he couldn't be cavalier. He was developing a capacity to face reality. He was proud of what he was doing and how he was doing it. I delighted in his maturation.

Another Girlfriend Visit

Our work rhythm felt in sync. I asked him about an upcoming visit with his girlfriend. "What are you thinking about drinking?" He quickly said, "I'm not planning on drinking. I don't think I want to drink," and then added, "but I don't know why I can't. I mean, it's just a drink, and I know I don't want to get out of control. I just want to drink like most people on a weekend. What's wrong with relaxing with your girlfriend?"

I followed up, "You've got a lot of different ideas going on here, Dean. They feel like they are conflicting. Let's try to figure them out. What are you really thinking? Do you want to drink, or not?" I paused, and then continued, "If you say you're not going to drink and then you do, then there is that contradiction again. It suggests that your thinking and drinking are at odds. Do you know what I mean?" He nodded, and I continued, "We are looking at your drinking wishes and words, thinking and doing. These conversations are to help you get clear with yourself; in many ways, they are to help you learn how to drink well."

Dean paused in silence for minutes and said, "That's helpful, and I get it. Here's what I've come to: I don't want to drink this weekend and that is my real intention." I asked how he came to that. He replied, "I can't pretend my troubles didn't happen. It was serious, it is serious, and I have to deal with this." A transition moment catapulting forward. Dean had embraced his "humiliating" reality, and it now began to drive his treatment decisions. He was able to be vulnerable and open with himself and me.

Our treatment relationship breathed another sigh of relief. We had been distant at times, determined more often, and at courteous odds for weeks. Dean was at odds with himself about his relationship with alcohol. He wanted to face his drinking problem, and he also wanted to return to drinking. I was at odds about his desire. Was it utter danger to entertain Dean's wish, or was it movement toward his healthy assertion? He sensed correctly that I felt sobriety was the smartest way to go; he also sensed my receptivity. We had finally figured out a way to talk.

Dean clearly wanted to protect himself from another crisis; he also wanted to be a 28-year-old drinker. As a transition therapist, I wanted to get him through a number of "sober firsts"—first bouts with a myriad of emotions, family fights, social occasions, holiday parties, breakups, and frustrating job searches. He had accomplished all without drinking. We both felt good about these sober successes. Then Dean wanted different things. He wanted a reduction in therapy sessions, as well as the right to manage his own negotiations with alcohol. He wanted both on the table; I had to hear him, and he had to hear me. Courteous odds eventually became cooperative understandings.

As months moved on, Dean became much more comfortable with therapy. He developed a transition identity based on moderation. His own brand of ownership of his alcohol problem reduced his shame considerably. As a result, he was able to discuss more openly his drinking history and its destruction, the frequency of his consumption, the debilitating side effects, the fear of not knowing what to do, the loneliness, the isolation and lying, the terror of it all. Dean was becoming more vulnerable before my very eyes. Indeed, a remarkable show of courage for this wounded and sensitive young man.

Dean also talked more freely about his current desire to drink. Together, we explored every little nuance of the before, during, and after of a drinking event. Dean's healthy beliefs drove his moderation identity. He wanted to feel good about his life choices, and he wanted to include drinking in his life. He did not want to repeat the past. He did not want to lose control. He was not interested in getting drunk or, for that matter, drinking too much. He did not want to embarrass himself or live with regrets.

Dean was designing a new life that included a once-abused pleasure. I asked him, "So how do you feel about these discussions about your drinking experiences?" He responded, "I hate them and I like them; for sure, they're not easy, but I know they are absolutely necessary and what we need to do together—and what I need to do if I want to drink."

Dean developed a real interest in his own ideas as well as a responsibility for his own choices. He wanted to drink, recognized the risks, and worked hard to mitigate them. He became a surprising exception to my grand way theory.

Clinical Reveries

This is slowly becoming a "classic" problem in the world of alcohol treatment, particularly with persons in their teens, 20s, and 30s. Today's youth do not want to embrace a lifetime label of alcoholic; nor do they want to think abstinence is the only solution. Many of them have trouble viewing alcohol problems as a disease and are suspicious of AA's dominance, but they are willing to acknowledge drug and alcohol problems and want to be co-creators in a solution. Forcing "the way" on them engenders rage. It also fosters a disconnection in the treatment relationship—the most important ingredient in addiction treatment, particularly during the using and transition stages of recovery.

Dean continued drinking well. He did not drink daily, or even regularly—actually, he became that special occasion drinker he had originally talked about. He risked being more open and real with his family and friends. He and his girlfriend grew closer. He found a job that fit. He sent me a check for his treatment with this letter:

> Dr. Fetting…
> Dear Margy,
>
> I wanted to include this note to remind the both of us how much great work I have done with your wonderful help. I have been and continue to nurture myself through persistent self-care. This self-care has become a mentality and a part of daily life. I want to sincerely thank you for all the care that you have given me… so far. I will call soon to update you and plan our next meeting. Until then, take care and know that I think about our times together often.
>
> Sincerely,
> Dean

Transition's primary recovery tasks are to maintain interest in the reality of one's issues with drugs and alcohol and to develop an interest in the real self. Regardless of the profile, diagnosis, or label, the most important thing is to face the AOD problem, develop a solid recovering identity, and retain a truthful connection to the work of the particular healing choice. Therapists who foster a receptive environment allow room for the addict to find his own transition identity and his own recovery way. The newly curious addict is then likely to embrace an ongoing interest in the path of his own growth and development.

Dean and I talk periodically. Many aspects of his life have matured, and he consistently reports he is a moderate, special occasion drinker.

Angela

Treatment Before Formal Treatment

Angela, age 31, arrived in my office from a regularly referring psychiatrist, Dr. Rod Rajan. Angela was in the transition stage of recovery after a year of several inpatient and outpatient treatment programs, including a week of relapse. She was now almost four months sober. Angela vacillated between a manic excitement about what she was discovering without drugs and alcohol and a dismal sense of despair. During the latter, she slept, watched TV, and withdrew and retreated in her apartment with her dog (see An Overview of Psychic Retreats, Chapter 11). She called these lost days and weekend "funks." She made an important connection during a pharmacology session with Dr. Rajan. "Talking with him, I began to understand that what I called a 'funk' was actually depression. You know, it came to me one day in my apartment as I lay on the couch with the shades pulled down. This must be what depression is like for people. Oh crap, I think I've been depressed all these years, and these things I call 'funks' are actually periods of depression."

Angela arrived for her appointments with an eager curiosity to understand what had led to her years of alcohol, crystal meth, cocaine, and opiate abuse and addiction. Heroin was her drug of choice. I developed an early working sense that her recovery identity was solidly in place. She had clearly responded to transition moment questions with an affirmative desire for growth forward. She was fiercely interested in herself and her sobriety. I felt a conscious/unconscious coherence in her that suggested some smooth transition terrain ahead. Time would tell.

Angela's History and Some Treatment Before Treatment

In our early work, Angela reported that her addiction began when she went away to college. "I would go to parties, and I would drink there, and I would find people who smoked a lot of pot, and we would always get high together." She recalled that these early days of drinking usually involved drinking to get drunk. Angela managed to get through undergrad and applied to business school. She drank and smoked pot on weekends during her first year of graduate school. During her last year, she found friends who encouraged crystal meth and cocaine. She partied on the weekend and noticed a dangerous trend, "My friends would party, and I would leave them, go find a dealer, get some cocaine, and stay up for days at a time, doing lines all by myself." Nonetheless, she reported, "Somehow I was able to get through school and made the dean's list half of the time."

Angela reported that she returned home after grad school and quickly became agitated by her dysfunctional family. "I needed to get out of Ohio, and I needed to get out as quickly as possible. I visited a friend in San Francisco, and several months later, I moved there. I was fortunate that I didn't have to work the first few months in San Francisco. I had been working odd jobs for my mother while in Ohio and ended up stealing a fair amount of money from her. That large sum got me through my first months in San Francisco."

Angela's drug use escalated. She was no longer partying on weekends with friends. She was getting high every night. She became a regular in the club scene in San Francisco. She liked Ecstasy, cocaine, GHB, and crystal meth. She temped as a corporate secretary. Her drug life began to trump her dreams of becoming an executive.

After a year and a half of this lifestyle, Angela recalled moments of clarity; "I have a drug problem." Her friends agreed, "You party different than the rest of us. You just don't stop." She noticed that it was hard for her to show up for work, and she was often not asked to return after temporary assignments. Angela decided to try to address her drug problems. She removed herself from the San Francisco scene. "I realized I needed to do this because I was unable to say no to my friends and dealers in San Francisco." So, "I moved to L.A. to remove myself from this situation. While I didn't stop the drugs altogether, I confined my cocaine use to weekends."

I listened and observed that some of Angela's thinking and behavior reflected her desire for more healthy living. She was deeply into drugs and yet able to embrace some transition moment questions and move her recovery identity forward. She started her treatment before any formal treatment. This revealed her tenacious temperament. Her prognosis felt promising. Back to her history . . .

A year later, she met Mike. "He had lots and lots of pills. Mike and I spent a lot of time together, and even more time swallowing pills. We used OxyContin, Dilaudid, and Vicodin." "Mike found a pharmacy that was willing to provide him with an endless amount of pills. He always returned with a lunch bag full of amphetamines, pain killers, and muscle relaxants. We did pills day in and day out, and at the time, I was still able to function as a corporate secretary."

"After two years, I knew that both Mike and I were dependent on opiates. Things got even scarier when Mike moved from pills to shooting heroin [intravenously injecting]. Our friends started getting worried." Angela remembered that she was interested in intravenously injecting heroin, but Mike forbade it. He told her, "I want to protect you from needle marks." So he taught Angela how to insert a needleless syringe of heroin in her rectum. "It's called booty bumping. I was a booty bumper. I liked putting heroin up my ass. That's the way I did it, day after day." Very quickly, they lived a life of injecting and inserting heroin all day long.

Mike's ex-wife became increasingly worried about his use, and she arranged an intervention. Mike entered treatment. He stayed for 30 days, returned to Angela, and they both continued injecting and inserting. Her treatment before her treatment revealed itself again. Angela became extremely frightened about her using and investigated rehabilitation recovery facilities. She entered one and stayed for five weeks. When she returned home, Mike was still using; Angela began using again. "For me, all I need to do is see the stuff. As soon as I saw it, I started using. Just like that. It's so quick. I don't even think."

Within a month, Angela reentered a treatment program, and this time she took it seriously. Over a nine-month period, she moved from inpatient to intensive outpatient to group work, as well as regular ongoing therapy. She attended 12-step meetings. She separated from Mike. She continued drinking but was sober from opiates and other recreational drugs.

Angela drank alcohol on a date. She drove home and needed to go to the bathroom, and found her way to Mike's apartment. She was overtaken by memory and immediately began searching for drugs and, "As soon as I found them, I used." Angela partied periodically for a week and then called a counselor from her last rehab. She decided to be more serious; to approach treatment differently, she upped her commitment to recovery—no drugs and no alcohol. When she came to see me, she was approaching her fourth month of sobriety from her relapse. She had been diagnosed with a mood disorder and was stabilized on several medications. She was ready to work on the tasks of transition.

Transition's Work

Angela took delight in taking herself seriously. She seemed driven to understand; she was full of childlike curiosity and was interested in herself. She repeatedly teared up whenever she experienced a new self-discovery. "It feels so tender to know this about myself. When I feel tender, I cry. I never got to know myself as a child. It feels great to give myself a chance."

Angela writhed in pain as she described life with her physically and emotionally abusive mother. She wept with incredulity that she would "hurt her own daughter that way. I don't understand. I don't understand how a mother could do that to a child." She continued, "Every night, I was scared for her to return home after work. As soon as she opened the door, I felt her mood. I knew how to read it instantly, and I knew what I was up against. She yelled at me most nights about whatever upset her, and more often than not, she beat the crap out of me. I didn't know what to do then. I felt so bad. I was all alone. It was just me. I either sat in the corner of my bedroom with my hand around my knees and my head down, or I fell asleep in tears."

Angela was also extremely ambitious. At the end of her first year of recovery, which included her weeklong relapse, she entered a rigorous master's program to supplement her business degree. I had a hunch that she was over-facing her transition identity. I hinted at this as well. Her bubbly and eager (manic) nature wanted to get through school, wanted to do deep work in therapy, and wanted to stay sober. Supporting all three of her wishes was therapeutically challenging, a possible recipe for relapse.

Healing Time or Making up for Lost Time?

School was not intrinsically meaningful to Angela; she was proving something to herself. She lived with the stress of a self-imposed impossible task, and stressed her recovering identity as well. She tolerated classes and procrastinated on homework. She compared her performance to others', and agitatedly wondered about her lackluster study habits. She persecuted herself with her perceived mediocrity. She attacked herself, like her mother used to, with the high heel of a stiletto shoe.

Angela started talking as soon as I greeted her in the waiting room. She walked through the suite hallway into my office. She was restless and upset. She gestured and writhed in self-torture as she paced into my office. "Get with it, Angela, you are so stupid, how dumb you are, why are you doing this to yourself . . . Stupid, stupid, stupid!" She circled in self-hatred and disbelief. "I can't believe how much I procrastinate. I need to be doing homework and studying. All I do is watch TV. I think I am a TV addict. I'm just a no-good lazy bum. Why am I doing this? And why am I picking at my face, my chest, and my arms? I can't stop myself. What is going on? What am I going to do? I'll never get through school. I'm amazed that I don't drink."

Another session, she entered my office and proclaimed, "As I was driving here, I knew what I wanted to do as soon as I walked into this office. I wanted to go over to your couch and do this." She kneeled into the corner of my couch, buried her head in the pillow, and stuck her buttocks up in the air. (Interesting, same position as booty bumping.) She screamed into the pillow, "What am I doing? What is going on? I can't do anything! I am stupid and no good."

Reverie's work held her tortured and isolated mind, as well as her frustration, shame, and despair. I also held her over-faced transition identity. She was living beyond her capacities, she lost self-interest and her focus, she forgot her recovery, and she disconnected from her real self. I swirled in and around her impacts during our sessions, and hours after.

Clinical Reveries

Angela was not alone. So many in transition are very deeply overwhelmed with regret and sadness. They rush to catch up with what has been lost during their drug and alcohol existence; it feels easier than feeling their sorrow. They lose track of themselves in their manic repair. Their wobbly-legged recovery identity is dismissed. It feels impossible to face up to how "little" one feels during early transition days. It's too humiliating and shameful to face the despair and destruction of one's earlier life. Transition addicts often choose overextension instead; collapse soon follows. Working through this mania and exhaustion is a big part of transition's work. A relational home provides helpful hints.

Drugs and alcohol are the central organizing principle during the using stage. Recovery has to become the same in transition. The love affair with AOD has to be replaced with a deep reverence for healing and growth. The fragile transition identity needs to be listened to and protected. Transition therapists must focus on this focus and encourage its prioritization. It's a part of transition time and requires continual reinforcement. We always have to remember because patients forget.

Angela needed these continual reminders. She often forgot to fathom, hold, and cherish the goodness of her healing—discovering life without heroin. She overlooked its importance. Too often, it felt more important to deny the reality of her recovery and drive herself instead. She brutally neglected and abused herself, as was done to her in childhood. As many in transition, she expected much of herself and lived tortured within these demands.

Early transition work with Angela involved a combination of recalling childhood memories, drug life remembering, investigating her choices about day-to-day living, assessing and adjusting psychopharmacological therapeutic effectiveness, continually challenging her perspective, and always, always reminding her not to forget her current life's focus. She grew from this containment. She found her transitional relational home. "It helps so much that you, Dr. Fetting, understand what this is all about—this transition time. I mean, I want to do it myself and make my own decisions, but I always feel better after we see each other and talk. I get a better handle on my confusion and a better sense of what's going on in my recovery and in my life."

Continue following Angela in Chapter 11 (p. 229).

Mark

Managing a Transition Crisis

Mark is a 47-year-old very successful businessman. He entered another transition phase of treatment after 10 harrowing years of erratic, secretive, and turbulent use of alcohol, cocaine, gambling, and women. Alcohol is Mark's drug of choice. He is married to Lacy, and they have four children.

Mark was referred to me by a colleague in the addiction field. He called and said, "I've been working with this couple, and I feel the husband needs an expert." That comment catches my attention and creates some apprehension. It often means the patient has been through several treatment attempts and is very challenging.

I liked Mark and immediately recognized a sensitive soul. "I should have been living in the 1950s with a loving wife waiting for me after work; no Internet, cell phones and technology, or overscheduled athletic weekends for the kids; and a much slower pace so we have room to connect."

Adam Phillips (1998), the British psychoanalyst, captured Mark's dilemma: "All our stories are about what happened to our wishes. About the world as we would like it to be, and the world as it happens to be, irrespective of our wishes and despite our hopes" (p. xiii). "We have gotten further and further away from those things that matter most to us" (p. 31).

Complex internal and external forces interfered with the fulfillment of Mark's dreams and wishes. He had a "lovely" wife, family, and home. He had professional and financial accomplishment. These brought him no joy. He felt trapped in demanding and unfulfilling expectations. He thought he was going after the right things, that he was providing a noble life for his family. He, like many others, turned to drugs and alcohol to compensate for the emptiness he felt, the feelings he did not understand.

Lance Dodes (2002) posits that all addiction is a substitute action because a healthier action does not seem possible or permissible. It's frightening to observe so many trapped Americans—successful exterior shells, vacant interior lives, drinking and drugging every night and all weekend to soothe this mismatch. The lucky ones find a way to face their truths, end the destruction, and reconnect with their wishes. Sadly, too many keep drinking and give up on their dreams.

Mark and I met once weekly for two months. He reported sobriety. It felt too glib.

Mark's History

During the previous decade, Mark's hidden and excessive drinking resulted in two visits in rehab, three intensive outpatient programs, AA, and individual therapy. In each case, he remained sober for a few months and always returned to drinking. He started with a beer or two during lunch in the neighborhood pub. "I really like to go there and just connect with the locals. It feels so good to be talking to the people. There is no pressure. It's easy. Then I return home and help Lacy with the kids."

Lacy eventually smelled alcohol on his breath. She was upset. Mark bargained with her to drink openly at homes and parties. She reluctantly agreed. This resulted in embarrassing drinking episodes, public humiliation, harrowing fights, and blackouts. Another rehab or treatment attempt followed. It was a house full of frustration on many levels.

Mark was interested in recovery approaches other than AA. We had exchanges about alternative paths to recovery. We were getting to know each other, building a relationship. Then I smelled alcohol on his breath at 10 in the morning. I "reveried" a direct transition intervention and waited for the right time.

During the next session, I followed up on our conversation, and hinted, "You know, Mark, we don't know precisely what causes addiction; nor is there agreement on the best approach to recovery. However, there are profiles of using that we see regularly and treat often. These profiles help us with all this uncertainty." I then briefly shared my grand way theory. "If somebody loses control of drugs and alcohol in a grand way, he is probably best served by staying away from the stuff." He agreed and told me that's why he is sober. I then acknowledged, "Well I have a tough question for you. I thought I smelled alcohol on your breath during our last session, and I wanted to ask you if my perception was true." He looked stunned, embarrassed, and angrily said, "Yes." He was defensive and enraged, but we were able to talk about his wishes and their risks. His transition identity still wanted to drink.

A Family in Distress

Tragically, Mark's drinking drastically escalated, his work life deteriorated, his recreational binges became more lavish, and his wife, Lacy, became frantic. She kicked him out. He got a studio apartment. His sense of tension increased, and so did his drinking.

Lacy called me on a Saturday at 5 p.m. Mark was in a full-blown relapse. He was gone, money was gone, and she was panicked. She asked if I could help. We had not yet met, but I was most willing to help her husband, who was in severe danger. Listening to a patient's family member describe an impending deadly disaster, without revealing confidences, is one of the more complicated aspects of addiction treatment. Some ethical considerations for family calls during a transition crisis include:

- For the family members—listen, get the facts, provide general support, encourage Al-Anon meetings and/or psychotherapy, and reiterate ethical allegiance to the patient
- For the patient—call him, share the family member concerns, request a session
- For the treatment provider—research higher level of care treatment options

That night, I tentatively secured a bed in a local treatment facility. As is often the case, that bed waits empty for weeks. Mark's did. During this time there were belligerent, drunk, and stoned calls as well as cancelled appointments. There were also frantic calls from Lacy. An emergency session was called. The three of us agreed to meet at a local restaurant near the University of Southern California. It was a softer version of an intervention, more accurately, an intense transition moment conversation. Lacy and I agreed on a tone that was filled with concern and limits. She could take no more. She wanted and needed him to get more treatment. Her own therapy was working.

Mark asked Lacy, "If I go into treatment, will you be there for me?" She responded, "Mark, you have to want to do this for yourself." He stormed out of the restaurant. Lacy and I awkwardly debriefed, as this was the first time we had met face-to-face. Nonetheless, I shared a bottom line with her: "My hunch is that Mark will either call you or me later to enter treatment or he will begin a big bender and possibly kill himself in the process." She said, with calm exhaustion and in tears, "I know."

Thankfully, Mark embraced this transition moment and moved forward toward recovery. They both called me later that night. Mark entered a 45-day rehab. His recovering identity had resurfaced. His transition stage of recovery had started again.

Omnipotence During Transition Treatment

Mark's stay in treatment was as harrowing as his drinking. He never seemed to strongly connect with a forward-moving transition identity and settle into his stay—he lived in agitation and was ambivalent about recovery. Much of this, understandably, was fueled by Lacy's filing for divorce during his second week in rehab. Lisa Director (2005) describes the infant, and, later, addict, who has no faith that the world will meet his needs (see Chapter 7, p. 108). The addict finds an omnipotent solution in drugs or alcohol. The drinking may stop; often the omnipotence continues during one's recovery.

Mark attempted exclusive control of his treatment stay as he had taken exclusive control of his drug and alcohol use. He continually challenged the rules, pushed away everyone, engaged in manic monologues, and pressured people to listen to his latest diatribes, written on pages and pages of yellow legal pads. He overwhelmed other patients. He showed no interest in taking in another human being, engaging in impact swaps, or listening to others' experiences. The treatment team prescribed bipolar medications. He needed more containment, as well as more medication. My first task was to try to make real contact with this terrified man.

Mark agreed to psychiatric medications for sleep and mood stabilization, and he reluctantly continued treatment with me. The treatment facility delivered him to my office once a week. I felt he needed more; his transition identity was absolutely not interested. He attended AA and seemed to tolerate and benefit from the community connection and support. Our therapy was part of his discharge plans in theory only. When we met, I struggled to break through his pressured speech. I asked if he was interested in continued treatment. He said, "Oh yeah, it's just I'm so busy now, and I'm trying to figure everything out. I'll give you a call." I felt pushed to the side and could only say, "Treatment is important to your recovery, and I'm here to continue our work."

Over the next couple of months, Mark attended AA meetings and saw me infrequently and sporadically. I had worked passionately to arrest Mark's destructive relationship with AOD. I had worked tirelessly with his panicked and exhausted wife, Lacy. I had been on call and was ready to step in as often as I was able. I had put in so much, with little satisfaction in return. Mark's omnipotent solution to recovery excluded me. It also hurt.

This is a particularly difficult experience for a treatment provider. Working with the projections and omnipotence of a recovering addict feels extremely frustrating, rejecting, and debilitating. The feeling of a shared journey is absent; a sense of hopelessness and uselessness, dismissal and devaluation dominates the clinician's mind. It is odd to be working so hard while consumed with so many feelings of worthlessness. Consultation helps. Ron Sager helped me sort through Mark's projections and pointedly asked, "Do you expect him to thank you?" (Personal Communication, 2009). I realized I was luxuriating in therapeutic possessiveness. Thinking resurfaced, and a new sense of receptiveness kicked in. I was able to hold Mark's overwhelming senses of fear, powerlessness, worthlessness, and hopelessness.

I went into reverie about Mark's sense of helplessness and omnipotence. I imagined the pain he felt as his fragile identity soberly walked into so much rejection, and with no chance for repair. Divorce's doors clamped down on him like a prison gate. I imagined him sensing the loss of all that he worked for over many years. I imagined his panic and terror. He was doing all that he could with these overwhelming emotions. I understood his need for omnipotent protection. I was able to reorganize his projections and restore my balance. I waited, not knowing what would happen. Brown (2011) reminds us that transition addicts often get more out of AA slogans and fellowship than individual psychotherapy. The evolving identity searches for its own comfort level.

Couples Work During Transition

Then Mark called for some couples sessions. I agreed with the idea. Family support during an addict's transition stage is always helpful. I quickly realized, however, that this couple was struggling to communicate through competing agendas. Mark was aggressively engaged in couples counseling in hopes of marital reconciliation and a possible reunion. Lacy was pleadingly engaged in family therapy, in hopes of co-parenting repair. I hinted that we use these sessions to help with communication during the divorce. It, at least, framed the work.

The sessions were stormy and turbulent. Agendas could not come together. They stopped attending couples therapy, Mark slowed down on individual therapy as well as AA. During one of our infrequent sessions, I asked him about his drinking. He said, "I'm sober." I sensed he was lying. I said, "Are you sure about that? I get the feeling that something else is happening." He quickly responded, "It is. I am drinking, but I don't want to lose control. I can't." I asked him to tell me about his drinking, how he was doing it, what it was doing for him. He described a familiar pattern. "At the end of the day, I am all alone in my tiny apartment. Lacy gets the home and the kids, our house and our life. Nothing much has changed there, but so much has changed for me. I can't stand being alone. So, I go to the local pub and have a few beers and talk. It just helps me calm down, so I can eventually go to sleep at the end of the day."

Mark sheepishly continued, "I have a new girlfriend of sorts. She's sweet and nice, but she is married. I like her, but I know it's no good. I'm a home wrecker. It's going nowhere, but it does feel good to lie in her arms after sex. It just feels good. And I'm in pain a lot. The booze, the pub, and the girlfriend help me."

Mark halfheartedly acknowledged, "I probably shouldn't be doing any of this. It's the same pattern. Crisis, sobriety, and then I start it all over again. I hope this time is different. I can't lose control, but I just can't stand being alone." I directly intervened about the potential dangers of these behaviors at this time in his recovery. We talked about continued drinking and its potential devastating outcome. He would likely lose Lacy's trust and then likely lose his relationship and connection with his children. I was authoritative in my assessment and also wanted to create room for Mark to talk about what he was doing with alcohol, his life. I wanted him to feel safe enough to tolerate examining the feelings that were driving his dangerous need for this substance.

Mark opened up. "You're saying the truth, I know it, and it's just so hard to do what is right. I hurt and I need. I am devastated by what has been lost; all I want is Lacy and my family." A transition moment forward. A vibrant athlete and businessman was now weeping in front of me. He called for appointments and showed up regularly. This man who I thought was lost in omnipotence had finally landed in his recovery—in his own way, and on his own terms. I wondered in reverie what would be next. How long would this fragile transition identity last?

Interest in the Real Self

Lacy called me a few days later in a panic. "I'm really worried about Mark. I've never heard him so low. I am truly scared. Can you help him? I think you should give him a call." I sensed a severe depressive episode. I wondered if he had stopped taking his medications, and I wondered about his drinking.

Mark and I scheduled an emergency appointment, and he appeared down and despondent. He was finally feeling pain that he had been avoiding for a lifetime. He didn't understand it, and it scared him. "What is going on? I've never been in so much pain. I don't want to kill myself, but I don't care if I'm not here. There is no one to live for. I don't have Lacy or my children. My drinking has ruined me and my marriage. All I want is her, and she is not here."

I kindly and compassionately responded, "I can't take all this pain away from you, Mark, but I can be by your side as you go through it. I suspect this is all the hurt and sadness you've been drinking and drugging over." We talked at length about his feelings, his childhood, his marriage. He sobbed, and sobbed again. We talked about his medication and his schedule. He agreed to go to an AA meeting that night and see Dr. Rajan for a psychopharmacological consult. He seemed to get a glimmer, a grasp, of what was required for the work of recovery. He seemed to understand his choice—face his emotional reality and pain or, once again, open relapse's door. Mark's transition identity was evolving forward. He finally developed an interest in staying sober.

Mark's countenance changed. He didn't look like a little boy anymore. He was a man with a mission. He showed up for appointments. He planned vacations for his kids. He liked being responsible "for all the decisions about their lives when we are together. I like being a responsible, reliable dad. I want them to know that I am there for them, that they can count on me to help them grow. I don't want to blow this now. This is my chance."

Mark was also able to let go of Lacy, and let go of his girlfriend. He didn't let go of alcohol, but his sober stretches in between a night of a few beers grew longer and longer. I suspected that if he were able to sustain interest in himself, there would be little interest in the numbing effects of alcohol.

However, I never got the chance to know what happened. Mark traveled more for work and cancelled more appointments. He said he would call to reschedule, but he did not. I have wondered about his recovery and have wrestled with calling but have not. I have told myself that he must be doing okay because Lacy hasn't called.

This case reflects transition stage work. It involves identity confusions, terrifying relapses, family crises, higher levels of treatment, grappling with the omnipotence of addiction and recovery, much reverie, and a search for the right level of aftercare.

Treatment providers put so much effort into negotiating transitional moments, igniting interest in the true self, creating a relational home while intervening in life-or-death solutions. There is a longing to be with an individual and his recovering identity during its entire migration through all four stages. Often it doesn't work out this way. But the door always remains ajar if the patient desires more travel.

CHAPTER SUMMARY AND REFLECTIONS

Summary

This chapter proposed developmental transition tasks that encourage the evolution of the addict's identity through this sobering stage. Transition moments were introduced, and the therapist was encouraged to decipher the addict's recovery growth through this clinical lens. Psychoanalytic theories and concepts were presented that guide the work of the therapeutic dyad during this stage. These include interests of the addict, hovering and hinting, trauma and the relational home, and family considerations. Remember, this turbulent stage fatigues both patient and therapist. Moving through it requires patience and persistence. Clinical cases demonstrated these hearty treatment realities in therapeutic action moments.

Reflections

Before leaving this chapter, make sure you:

- Know the primary and secondary tasks of the transition stage
- Have a solid understanding of the key theories and concepts presented
- Have examined their individual merit and critically analyzed and discussed your intuitive clinical responses to their application in therapeutic action moments in the clinical cases of this stage
- Have begun to design your own integrative treatment approach for this stage
- Are willing to read and reread this chapter

Chapter 11

The Integrative Treatment Model

The Early Recovery Stage

Figure 11.1 The Early Recovery Stage

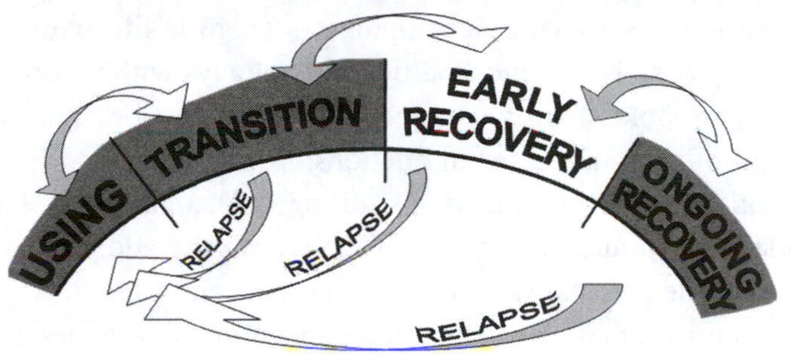

INTRODUCTION

The entrance into this stage is subtle. Early recovery moments often slip past the conscious awareness of both patient and clinician. The addict is no longer preoccupied with the prevention of relapse. The clinician is no longer preoccupied with its potential. A successfully negotiated transition stage sets up a seamless shift in identity. The alcoholic's commitment to recovery feels in place, and his capacity to probe both the state of his mind and his world finally feels possible. These commitments and capacities signal adoption of a new identity, as well as entrance into this stage. These early recovery moments are usually recognized after the fact.

The fit of the environment is examined, and the state of the addict's mind is explored during early recovery. There are days when he expands with previously unfelt joy; there are many more days when he cowers with confusion, pain, and uncertainty. He dreams of support he has never known or felt. The addict struggles through the reorganization of his internal world and the reconstruction of his external life. This is the treatment work of early recovery.

Landscape of the Environment

The lives of recovering addicts are no longer organized around not using. Life is more than sobriety. Gone is the chaos of the using stage, the turbulence of transition. Gone are constant cravings and pervasive temptations. The addict's rituals of sobriety and moderation are supported by a new lifestyle. His identity feels solid, and confidence in his recovering style has developed. There is either an increase or decrease in attendance at Alcoholics Anonymous (AA) meetings, an increase or decrease in therapy, and an increase or decrease in medications. The addict relies on his styles and choices, and these are now increasingly trusted by his family, friends, and co-workers.

There are many satisfying developments. There is life without daily drinking episodes; dinners and weekends, parties and holidays without drunken destruction; increasing household stability, more consistency in work performance, and the development of new intimacies in relationships.

These satisfying developments also bring challenges. A welcoming of a new life includes a departure from the old. The recovering addict puts his world under scrutiny—how he parents, what he does, how he enjoys, and who he spends time with are all up for grabs. There is a reorganization of so many aspects of his life. His relationships with his partner, family, friends, and work are examined. Some existing bonds are intensified and deepened; others are weakened and disrupted. There is so much going on within and between everyone in the addict's world. It is important to make room for feeling and thinking through these impact changes. The addict struggles to make sense of his longing for the familiar, excitement for new possibilities, and apprehension about the future.

The addict's sober availability to face new realities both in his external and internal worlds is severely threatened by the pain it causes. Many longstanding relationships feel off, and some existing situations feel wrong. There is regret and hope, confusion and confidence, fear and uncertainty. His sober emotional responses to these new realities and experiences feel unbearably overwhelming.

Landscape of the Mind of the Addict

The mind of the addict is saturated with alcohol and other drugs (AOD) during using. It is preoccupied with its perpetuation. The mind of the addict is busy crafting constant adjustments during transition. It is occupied with staying afloat. The mind of the addict in early recovery is neither preoccupied nor occupied. It is free to feel and then learn to think. The primary therapeutic task of the early recovery period is to listen for this mind and, upon hearing it, begin to explore and investigate its operations. What does this mind do with itself without AOD? How does this mind process everyday thoughts and feelings? More specifically, how does the newly "natural" mind experience and work with pain? It is a mind overprimed to escape suffering; it is a mind underprimed to live with discomfort and uncertainty. The ways it has responded to pain are visible for the first time in years. Attention to this activity is a primary early recovery task. This chapter proposes a lens for viewing this critical function.

Early recovery's primary tasks are twofold:

- **Exploring the fit** between a sober identity and a sober world and **determining** if a psychic retreat is the dominant response to pain
- **Incorporating clinical concepts** such as an overview of *psychic retreats, structure, treatment*—a retreated mind becomes visible and a retreated mind speaks

Other tasks include:

- *Reinforcing* methods for achieving sobriety or maintaining moderation agreements
- *Assessing* dual diagnoses, as well as establishing and adjusting psychopharmacological supports
- *Conducting* family work as needed
- *Including* the cohort of clinical concepts and treatment interventions from Chapters 9 and 10

This chapter is divided into two sections. *Clinical Concepts* provides an in-depth description of psychic retreats. *Clinical Cases* demonstrates the application of this treatment concept in therapeutic action moments.

John Steiner (1993) is a member of the British Psycho-Analytical Society and a former consultant psychotherapist at the Tavistock Clinic in London. Theoretically and clinically, he was challenged by patients who appeared stuck in their psychotherapeutic or analytic treatment, and with whom meaningful contact was difficult. Steiner needed to understand why. He developed the concept and theory of psychic retreats (pp. 1–13).

Clinical Concepts asks the reader to consider a complex aspect of the mind that is camouflaged while under the influence and makes itself known during early recovery. It is proposed that a clear understanding of the functions and facets of a psychic retreat is needed to truly grasp the struggles of this stage.

New conflicts live within the addict's mind and between his relations with others. There is so much suffering, and years of using hark back to instinctive avoidance. Psychic retreats become the drug of choice for many. The addict's "use" of his retreat prevents clear thinking about his conflicts. It also stalls therapeutic work, disturbs relations between the sponsor and sponsee, and disrupts communications among family members.

Understanding a retreated mind and grasping its function become very useful clinical tools when working with a psyche prone to escape human pain and then compound this escape with drugs and alcohol. An evasive and confusing treatment relationship is then comprehended. A connection, which might otherwise remain elusive, deepens. It adds a much-needed dimension to the work of early recovery treatment.

Furthermore, introducing the concept of psychic retreats into the world of addiction treatment is extremely useful in understanding the mental and emotional antecedents of relapse. Grasping its complexity and befriending its operations require therapeutic skill and tenacity. Patients usually respond with curiosity and appreciation. Most grasp the idea, relish its precision, and are soon able to engage in ongoing conversations about their mind's retreated operations.

Clinical Cases demonstrates the application of this concept in early recovery treatment. The first clinical case highlights the murkiness, frustration, and prolonged agony involved in putting pieces of a confusing recovery puzzle together. It took months for me to discover that a retreated mind was directing Penny's last days in transition and her beginning days of early recovery. This discovery led to higher levels of treatment, influenced the direction of Penny's recovery work, and created a more viable treatment relationship.

The second clinical case illustrates a slightly less cumbersome identification of the dominance of a retreated mind in the early recovery stage. Angela's historical and current use of her solution to pain was more obvious; its accessibility less difficult.

We see in these cases that discovering and discerning a retreat's operation is often clouded by the circumstances and complexities of the addict's history, as well as the demands of his current recovery world. Penny needed to integrate sobriety into an established yet distant marriage, the uncertain expectancies of motherhood, the family's habits and expectations, and ongoing social obligations. The pain was overwhelming; her ability to deflect it through the use of a psychic retreat was very sophisticated. Angela, alone and younger, was not as restrained by the habituated demands of her existing environment. She had less to protect; her hiding place was more visible.

Reading Guidelines

This chapter introduces a new treatment concept and includes a mix of theories, therapeutic skills, and clinical caveats that are useful to understand and also apply during the addict's travels on early recovery's terrain. This mix of concepts, skills, and caveats is for treatment providers to match with their own intuition, their own clinical style, and their patient's particular recovery path. Past and ongoing clinical cases put theory to practice in therapeutic action moments. A clinician prepared for early recovery's primary and secondary tasks invites the addict to do the same. Study these ideas; make them useful in your own life, and also yours to use during recovery treatment; develop a tolerance for the unfamiliar; and go at your own pace as your mind struggles and then rests.

CLINICAL CONCEPTS

An Overview of Psychic Retreats

Addicts in early recovery go through periods of evading real connection. Protection is more important than contact. Changes feel overwhelming, growth pain feels unbearable, and moving through it all seems impossible. The work of recovery can start to lose its appeal. Many addicts in treatment decide to stop the work. The therapeutic dyad starts to feel stuck. Steiner's work on psychic retreats is useful here.

As has been previously mentioned, the early recovery identity is very secure. Addicts are no longer plagued with thoughts of using. They want to stay sober or keep their moderation agreements. They are instead preoccupied with challenges of everyday living on both an emotional and task level. These might include "being" in time, facing and living within a world that was constructed while using, and more deeply feeling difficult emotions as well as navigating old connections and discovering new intimacies. These experiences are all potentially overwhelming.

Psychic retreats beckon as a protective response. These are well-worn internal structures of the mind that were organized and deployed during an addict's infancy and childhood (Steiner, 1993, p. 105). These were the mind's way of offering shelter during early overwhelming trauma and neglect (p. 8). Retreats both camouflaged suffering and caused suffering during adolescence and early adulthood. AOD provided ongoing relief. Many retreat-prone individuals develop addiction problems.

The addict, in the early recovery stage, often starts to rely again on this sober psychic haven after transition's busy days of early abstinence. The fluttering glow of new fellowship and new sobriety no longer inoculates pain, particularly the pain of vulnerability. Pulling in and around these agonies brings relief. Pulling away from others feels right. The addict enters his sanctuary of protection with affection and anticipation. Residing in this retreated space feels familiar and safe. A sense of security temporarily provides complete satisfaction. Consequently, the retreated addict is difficult to connect with during this stage of treatment.

Structure

All people psychically retreat at times. Not everyone repeatedly relies on a psychic retreat as a pathological form of survival. Psychic retreats, as states of mind, are highly structured systems of primitive defenses, including projective identification and splitting (Steiner, 1993, p. 2). The former gets rid of unwanted emotions; the latter keeps difficult ones apart. In either case, emotions remain inaccessible, and therefore not useful.

Retreats are also tightly organized networks of object relations that seduce parts of the personality. Dependent and destructive parts of the self are projected onto a group of internal objects (Steiner, 1993, pp. 4, 13, 54). This "organization" of internal objects has a character or "feel" (pp. 47, 53). Retreaters describe it as a mafia gang, a choir of young boys, a table of statisticians, a group of leprechauns, military commanders, an island, a glass room, a force that powers through, a light bulb, *Charlie and the Chocolate Factory*'s great glass elevator, a cave, a warm humming sound, or a fortress. The individual mind determines if these objects protect with vengeance or shelter with warmth (p. 8).

Retreats are also tightly organized networks of object relations that seduce parts of the personality.

A Faustian deal is entertained. This organization of the mind hates human weakness and vulnerability, truth, and growth. The individual or recovering addict is afraid of these. The organization offers a promise: "We will take away your fears, if you honor our hatred of truth and don't listen to yours." The individual signs on, "I will give you omnipotent power over me, if you protect me from my fear of vulnerability and provide a shelter that prevents exposure of this." A family business is born.

Retreats provide an area of the mind where reality does not have to be faced, where fantasy and omnipotence can exist unchecked, and where growth and development are sacrificed (Steiner, 1993, p. 5). They are alternately felt as a refuge of relief and resignation or a site of defiance and triumph (p. 2). They are unconsciously recalled during overwhelmingly painful moments. These refuges prevent fragmentation from feelings of persecutory anxiety experienced in Melanie Klein's paranoid-schizoid position, or state of mind. They also bypass devastation from feelings of loss experienced in her depressive position (pp. 25–39). Retreats promise avoidance of pain and reality, and this temporary protection is returned to again and again.

Treatment

Clinicians are at a real loss without the watchful sense that retreats may become the pathological organization of choice during early recovery. They are stymied without understanding the omnipotence and perversion these seductive structures provide retreat-prone addicts. The immediate safety and security they furnish obstruct contact with reality, connection with others, and ongoingness in the therapeutic dyad (Steiner, 1993, p. 5). Patients visit and depart these "sites," or dwell in and become entrapped by them.

During this stage, the dependent part of the addict is no longer saturated with AOD's protection. Reality, avoided for years and sometimes decades, presents unbearable challenges to the addict's newly sober psyche. Early recovery addicts lack experience with conflict, and its resolution with the help of people. Reliance on others feels wordlessly untenable.

The desperate and vulnerable addict soon returns habitually and excessively to this omnipotent shelter of deceptively confident internal objects. This complex organization promises unquestionable protection from pain and suffering. This lonely promise is perverse, but it is a promise. The recovering addict fastens on with tenacity. The addict is spared from exposing his fears and needs to others, yet he deeply misses and yearns for the human contact. Thus, he hides in this internal world with disappointment and veiled contempt. While safely inside, he avoids working through the suffering underneath years of addiction. This sneaky detour gives him a sense of omnipotence. The real confidence that comes from revealing truths with intimate others is sacrificed.

A Retreated Mind Becomes Visible

The addict arrogantly pulls back from any meaningful contact with his therapist. This can continue for days, weeks, months, and on and off for years. What was once warm and idealized is now a relationship filled with cold condescension. Sessions feel difficult and tricky. The dyad feels hostile and stuck. Work feels at a standstill. The relationship doesn't know what to do with itself.

Steiner (1993) supports the view that the therapist should make herself available for the patient and be open to receive his projections and communications with as little interference as possible (p. 141). This feels very difficult. Projections from the retreat are often filled with the "indulged and justified" cruelty of sadistic hostility (p. 15). At other times, communications feel polite and compliant, yet evasive and elusive. Each of these styles deflects the patient's dreaded desire for real contact. Showing vulnerability to his therapist is not an option; protection from perceived annihilation feels necessary. The retreat provides the only form of refuge from these primitive fears. The patient feels smug and protected or tragically resigned. Either way, he feels entrapped by and loyal to the organization. "It is joy to be hidden, but disaster not to be found" (Winnicott in Epstein, 1995, p. 38).

The retreated patient moves with the body of a snail and the head of a turtle. Receptive clinicians "listen" with a gentle watchfulness. They pick up both the imperceptible movement toward them, and the slightest movement away from them. These confusing moments of back-and-forth are essential to grasp. The addict must feel that the therapist understands, or is struggling to understand, the nature of his humiliation as he begins to emerge from his retreat (Steiner, 1993, p. 10; 2011, pp. 25–41). If the therapist moves too slowly, too eagerly or quickly, too harshly or aggressively, he will return to his protective haven with a hostile vengeance (1993, p. 4). Focused and sensitive navigations by the therapist provide the patient with some sense of order. If he feels held by her efforts, some real contact with her feels tolerable. The relationship can temporarily feel more hospitable for both.

The inevitable retreat brings more distance and disturbance. A therapist who is able to sustain and endure this back-and-forth provides "aggravating" safety to the patient. This jagged relationship is the truest one the addict has ever known. He hates this fact (Steiner, 1993, p. 3). Truth, however, compels him to show up against his will. "I hate this, I hate this work, I hate you, and I don't want to do it. It's not helping; I don't want to deal with you, me, the relationship, and therapy anymore. None of this is helping. I don't want to be here."

A dreaming therapist knows she is being challenged by desperate protectiveness. Her devotion to reverie and thinking allows her to be receptive and tolerant, hovering and noncombative. She moves between the patient's hard and soft edges. She waits for an opening.

The patient is drawn in by this rhythm of respect. A softening occurs. The patient glances at, and then scans, the therapist's face. Her focus feels safe, and he tentatively says, "I haven't told you this . . . ." This is followed by sharing a normally avoided embarrassment, as well as exposing a vulnerability (Steiner, 2011, pp. 25–41). The therapist's intense attunement gently responds, "I knew you were going through that, I knew you didn't want to tell me, and I knew you didn't want to talk about it. I sensed that you felt if you talked about it, you would show me your weakness."

The patient inaudibly screams, "She knows. She knows where I go; she knows how my mind works." This sense of feeling so deeply understood brings instant disintegration to the retreat walls. He can now be with the piercing truth of his own human weakness. A stunned and stunning experience of realness with another human being is tolerated. The patient is momentarily free, and he knows it. The relationship has figured out what to do with itself. It may take weeks, months, or years to understand this metamorphosis.

A Retreated Mind Speaks

The individual may always struggle with the retreated parts of his personality (Steiner, 1993, p. 13). With continued effort, the recovering addict will eventually begin to experience relief in exposing bits and pieces of his own humiliation, terror, and aloneness to his therapist (2011, pp. 25–41). Slowly, he may begin to value the tender pleasures of relating to another more than the familiar protections from his internal omnipotent family. With more satisfying experiences of relational intimacy, the retreat's habitual use may diminish. With insight and awareness of how it is created and used as a defense, its dominating power may recede. Creating a language about its operations oftentimes creates more cohesion between patient and therapist.

Below is a journal entry, written by James, a 52-year-old patient in early recovery. (See Chapter 12 for more on James, p. 267.) He worked extremely hard in therapy and was able to gain tremendous insight into his lifelong use of psychic retreats. This poignant entry provides an example of a psychic retreat's powerful place in an alcoholic's mind. It also demonstrates the tremendous loss involved in courageously letting go and moving away from the domination of these lifelong pathological protectors.

> Yesterday, I was all alone. I wanted someone, anyone. I could not tolerate my aloneness. I wondered about others' lives, what goes on in homes, how people move around each other, and experience the struggle of being with each other. Since I was a little boy, I have always felt this struggle cannot be seen or shared. It shows weakness and weakness is shameful. What if you are doing it wrong and what if you are feeling the wrong thing? You could be making someone mad about who you are, the way you are being in your life. Better to dodge contact altogether. It may be treacherous; it may bring big trouble for you.
>
> I can see how my leprechaun gang came into being. I was always alone in my mind. They reached out and told me that I'm the smartest; I have the most sensitivity and talent, the most bounce and chutzpah. I'm the one it comes easiest to; people take to me, and my enthusiasm. I always get what I want. I can see how the leprechaun gang provided me company and comfort when no one, no one was there.
>
> I always found them anytime I felt scared, mad, embarrassed, sad, or confused. They were just waiting for me. I talked about what was going on, they listened. They understood when I felt unsure and frightened. They had answers. They told me not to worry about these feelings. They told me I didn't need to talk about them to anyone. They assured me that I was just fine. They told me to keep up my enthusiasm and act like nothing was wrong. They reminded me that I get a lot of good attention from my optimistic nature. I felt I could go back into the world after our discussions. I felt like I knew what I was doing; that things would be OK. I felt their support behind me.

> They were my friends, and they are such good, good friends. They make me cry. They have been there for me my entire life. It is only with sobriety that I understand them, and how they have worked.
>
> I am crying now because if I leave them, I will hurt them so much. They will not understand why I have to go. They will be lonely and won't know what to do. They are very sad now, sitting outside in a circle around the fire; they don't want me to leave. They are so sad, and I am so sad to leave them. They are nice leprechauns, and they have only meant well. Now they feel they are wrong and are being punished. They are despondent and confused—I love them so much. But it's time for me to try something, someone else. You will be okay. Maybe you will find a nicer way. You have each other, you sweet leprechauns. Thanks.

The work of early recovery continued. A language of leprechauns brought closeness between us. The leprechauns lost their exclusive control over James, yet they continued to fight for his allegiance. He fought their pleas. Sometimes their seductions appealed to him and he was lured into hostile hiding. Other times, he was able to resist their perverse temptations. Eventually he preferred our conversations over their protections. For the first time in his life, he was able to choose dependency with another human being, over the trusted protectors of his mind. He struggled to be continually truthful to me about his experiences of vulnerability and pain. He continued to choose these over pathological protection. On to more clinical cases, to see how this mix of treatment concepts, therapeutic skills, and clinical caveats has been applied in treatment in therapeutic action moments.

CLINICAL CASES

Penny

Psychic Retreat

Penny was a psychic retreater. She learned to withdraw as a child. She relied on her retreat throughout her lifetime. Food camouflaged the regularity and frequency of its use, and later years of alcohol and drug use soothed the loneliness of the perverse protection it provided.

Penny was a sober soldier during transition. She rebounded after her surgical relapse, she was drug-free when her mother's visit finally came to an end (refresh your memory about Penny in Chapter 10, p. 169). She was a determined fighter. Her allegiance to sobriety was clear; her use of a psychic retreat was not.

I restudied John Steiner's work. I soon realized that it was the dominating force behind most of her driving and isolative patterns, some of my clinical confusion and despair, and our often distant and frustrating transition treatment relationship.

Penny, like many newly sober people, was enthusiastic about her life and determined to make up for lost time. She produced grand family events, wished to become an exceptionally devoted mother, a consistent friend, and a reliable wife. I repeatedly broached the caretaking of her wobbly-legged identity. She politely listened and repeatedly convinced me that she was fine. Her enthusiastic determinations, however, were followed by several days of collapsed exhaustion. She withdrew into her bedroom when emotions overwhelmed her, conversations disappointed her, and life felt too much.

Initially, I attributed these isolative patterns to the difficulties of the first year of sobriety. Many need a break after so much exertion and stimulation without mitigating buffers. Many withdraw to rest and reorganize. Penny repeatedly relied on this physical retreat. For some time, I believed it gave her new identity a chance to register impacts and regroup.

Toward the end of that first year, my thinking began to change. I began to wonder about the cruel repetition of this pattern of exertion and collapse. I was perplexed by a cooperative and compliant nature that was never cooperative or compliant with treatment suggestions that might help her with her choices and alleviate some of her suffering. I could not comprehend Penny's inability to learn from experience. I doubted my clinical capacities and frequently felt despair. I was baffled by her psychomotor retarded thought, affect, and speech patterns. I mistrusted her frequent requests for phone sessions and her more frequent cancellations of face-to-face meetings. I wondered about our shared weariness, our stuck and stymied therapeutic dyad.

Penny's ability to sustain this pattern of exceptional exertion followed by more exceptional exhaustion was severely weakening by the end of her first year of transition. Her "performance" time greatly diminished; her collapse time greatly increased. Her husband was losing faith, and her children were confused. A series of events would soon change the course of her life and gradually allow us to discover the retreated mind that drove this weary pattern.

First-Year Anniversary—Despair and Dismissal

The holidays were approaching, and pressure was mounting. An annual family trip was planned. Penny valiantly tried to integrate a sober identity into old performance expectations. She shopped for her children, she prepared the house for the holidays, and she volunteered. She packed clothes and gifts for the trip. She supported her husband during a stressful year's end. She was used to powering through with drugs. Instead, these efforts brought overwhelming fatigue, despair, and exhaustion. Nothing was enjoyable; as a matter of fact, life was miserable.

I asked about the upcoming trip. "How are you feeling about going away during this holiday time? How are you feeling about returning to the scene of your last days of using? How are you feeling about your first-year sobriety anniversary?" (Refresh your memory about Penny in Chapter 9, p. 142.)

Penny numbly responded, "I don't care about the trip, and I don't care about my anniversary." Her dismissal of herself saddened me; I pleaded and hinted, "Do you have to go? I don't know how you're going to do it in such a state of depletion. It seems an impossible undertaking. It seems cruel." I heard her utter hopelessness, "I have no choice. I have to."

The trip was completely overwhelming for Penny. She took to the bed, and her family took to the slopes. Misunderstandings led to fights, and pained confusion ended in anguish. This was a family on the brink. Despite this, her husband, Roger, seemed to grasp the desperateness of the situation. He told her that he loved her and was there for her. She cried inside, "You mean you're not going to leave me? You mean you don't think I am a bad person?"

Not surprisingly, Penny went into some mild mania upon her return. Temporarily, it protected her from facing her complete sorrow, from facing the fact that her life was not working, that she felt completely incapable and was overwhelmed with feelings of terror and despair. A depleted state soon followed. Penny's bed became home base. She did what she could for her children and then returned to collapse.

Higher Level of Treatment

I began talking to Penny about a higher level of care. Twice over the previous year, during similar circumstances, I had suggested inpatient treatment. Twice my recommendations were taken in, thought about, and rejected. I felt a failure that I could not help her want more for herself. I picked myself up and abided by her choices and her suffering. Her determination and deep desire for sobriety and growth kept me faithfully by her side.

This time, however, I sensed that Penny would not and could not continue dismissing or denying her overwhelming pain, fatigue, and collapse. She and her husband could not ignore or overlook her utter lack of functioning. I sensed they were ready to accept realities that had previously been rejected.

For the first time ever, I heard Penny say, "I am not functioning. I am not living. All I do is take care of my children, overdo it with family events, overextend myself with friends and my children, and then return to my room. My life is not normal. I don't go anywhere or do anything. I eke out what I need to do and go into hiding. Every part of my body is aching, my stomach is more bloated than ever, and my head is throbbing, I can't sleep, and this is not normal. I can't keep doing this." I asked her, "How much longer are you going to destroy yourself? I feel like I'm watching someone march to the guillotines. You can't keep this up for much longer. You know your life is at stake here." I sensed she was finally willing to work within the reality of her own lived emotional experience (Ogden, 2005, p. 95).

Penny softly uttered, "I know, and I have to stop. Yes, I have to go into a hospital. I need help. I have to do this now or never." She had nothing defensive left at that moment. She was naked and vulnerable in a way that she and I had never known together. She was open to my clinical suggestions. She was open to the truth of her own life.

I immediately began investigating local inpatient programs. I also began exploring the new, more innovative "concierge treatment programs" that had recently been developed by Dr. Michael Scott, the former medical director of Sierra Tucson in Arizona. Dr. Scott's team offered individualized and specialized treatments in a desert setting. I knew this design would appeal to Penny's recovery style. She was interested, and this time the timing was right (Michael Scott, Personal Communication, 2010).

Penny moved quickly. She left home, arrived in the desert, and stayed nine days. She had a busy schedule of intensive psychoanalytic psychotherapy, adjunctive health treatments, pharmacological adjustments, somatic massages, and specialized trauma treatments. She felt contained and protected, nurtured and supported. She was able to trust and be open, to let go of mothering and her home life, and to rest and recover from the trauma of the previous month.

Penny also connected to some of the pain she had covered up with opiates and benzodiazepines. The treatment team suggested that she lengthen her stay and continue her work. She felt she had to return to her family. Her hopes were high and fears were great. She was heartened by Dr. Scott's words, "You responded."

Decompensation on the Return Home

Penny's fledgling gains quickly dissipated in the face of the harsh realities of her everyday life. Her children missed her, her home needed her, and her husband wished for a better life for himself and his family and a more fulfilling marriage. Penny was unable to keep up with herself, much less respond to her family. She tried to hang on. She tried to stay with what she had learned. She could not. Penny withdrew—from herself, her life, and me. She decompensated rather quickly. She took to her room with desperation and resignation.

I went into reverie. I clearly saw her incapacity. Penny needed more immediate care, and she and Roger needed my authoritative direction. I imagined they would both rebuff, and also welcome, any suggestions. I explored and found an inpatient residential facility for women. It felt like the right venue at the right time.

I had a serious conversation with Penny and Roger on the phone that night. "We all saw that you thrived and responded to your treatment. Unfortunately, your home, with all its demands and expectations, is not allowing this thriving to continue. It's trampling what was started and bringing you both so much pain and fear. I know that it is difficult and scary to leave your children. I also don't think that you are going to get the help that you need unless you remove yourself from your environment for an extended period of time. I think I have found a place that will work for you."

I had been in reverie about Penny's treatment in general and was more convinced about the dominance of her psychic retreat. "Your desire to be alone in your recovery does not feel right anymore. There is a missing piece, and it involves people. I firmly believe it's time to learn about being with others in ways that you have never experienced, and in ways that you have always wanted to avoid. It's the right time to begin to share with fellow sufferers the truth of your pain and the struggles of your recovery. Individualized treatment is no longer a responsible ally. The isolation is destructive."

Penny froze up and dug in her retreated heels. I felt her contempt and disdain. "I'm not going to go to a house and sleep in a strange bed and live with a group of strange women. I am not going to eat with them, go to the bathroom near them, or shower around them. I'm not going to do it. It does not feel right. While I know my life is not working and I need it, I'm not gonna do it. I'm not going to leave my house and my children—they need me. I can't do it. I will not hurt my children this way."

Penny was mad and felt cornered. She was cornered by her perversely promising mind. I listened as her husband chimed in, in an uncharacteristically firm manner, "Penny, I just ask you to be open, to listen to what Margy has to say about the next steps in treatment. You've done a great job learning how to be sober from pills. In my mind right now, your addiction is your isolation. We have to protect you from that drug. You take it like you took your Vicodin. You chip at isolation, like you chipped at Vicodin. Your chipping is stretching into longer and longer periods of using. You're a recluse in your own home. It's taking you and our family down. We have to face this. The children will be okay. They know that mommy is always sick, and can't get out of bed. They know something is wrong."

I valued Roger's incredible courage, insight, and wisdom. My sense of faith soars during moments like these. Penny's desire for individualized treatment had turned into a treatment perversion. It allowed too much room with no connection, too much space with no support. Her isolation became a hothouse for the workings of her retreated mind. We would soon see how much it kept her speechless and in pain, kept us stuck, and kept her recovery in a state of languish.

I hung up the phone with worry, wonder, exhaustion, and a tremendous sense of therapeutic satisfaction. I wondered how Penny would respond to my firm invitation to face the reality of her collapse, as well as the truth of what she needed for her recovery. I wondered if Roger would backpedal on his convictions. I wondered if they would gang up on me and form an alliance against health and progress. I was exhausted from all the work leading up to this moment. And, I was confident of my ability to hold a line and contain their anxiety and anger. I heard the voice of Ron Sager, psychoanalyst, in the background: "Trust your gut. Do what you think is right, and see what happens."

The next day, Penny and I talked on the phone. She was in bed and her voice was inaudible. She felt motionless. She told me she had been up all night thinking. She was scared and terrified. She paused often. I sensed that she was ready.

She courageously volunteered. "I feel like I am such a bad mother. I am overprotective and enmeshed with my girls. I have a hidden fear that I have no self, and that I have exposed this to my children. This is not the image I want to have as a mother.

"I'm all topsy-turvy. I am not in charge. I am doing a terrible job running the house. I'm incapacitated. I have no social life. I can't take care of myself physically. I don't cook; I don't clean. What do I do? Nothing. I'm starting to feel so worthless. It makes me think a month in this treatment place is not going to be enough. Maybe I need to go someplace for six months. I'm doing this for my children. I couldn't care less about myself. The only reason I'm going in this place is for them."

I sat, quiet and calm. For the first time during her year of sobriety, Penny was able to be with her incapacity and also share her human weakness with me. She was ready to face what was really happening in her life. She was asking for holding as well as help. For the first time, she wasn't telling me how her treatment should be done, but only asking that it happen. Unconsciously, she was ready to start living on another level (Grotstein, 2009).

During that next week, Penny and Roger told the girls, "Mommy is going to keep getting better in a place close to home." They also told them that it was going to be for a month. After sadness, tears, and wailing, they evidently accepted this reality with some level of relief. Two days later, the family visited the facility. The day before Penny entered, we had a family session at an equestrian facility. We brushed horses and picked hooves. We attended to the horses' well-being before we rode them. Equine Therapy provided a ritual of nurturance during such a difficult family time. Roger and the girls rode horses as Penny looked on with love and worried resignation.

Clearview Treatment Programs Exposes a Psychic Retreat

Penny joined a group of women in a small residential treatment home called Clearview Women's Center located in a coastal Los Angeles neighborhood.

Her fantasy treatment involved both work and pampering. Individual sessions, rest and time to herself, yoga, massage. She, like most who enter inpatient treatment, was not expecting or prepared for the intensity of interactions that occur among inpatient residents. A family atmosphere is designed to tap into infantile and childhood primitivity. The emotions that are evoked are very upsetting and confusing. Most residents are angry to be living in such a disturbing atmosphere and rebuff its utility. Most do not see that being present to these everyday experiences is part of the "work," and most start planning their exit.

Penny voiced her dissatisfaction with the age range and cruelty of some of her fellow residents on the first day. "How can I feel safe here? How can I open up? I will not share my life with these young, mean girls. We have nothing in common. I imagined I would be sharing with peers. That's what you told me would be happening." She was mad at me and the situation and afraid of the work. The first couple of days were very rocky; greater turbulence lasted eight days.

Penny rolled her eyes and said to me, "I don't think this place is a good fit for me. I don't think I can safely open up. I don't see how I could possibly do my work. You expect me to stay here? I don't think I can." I knew that she wanted me to acknowledge that, indeed, this was the wrong group of residents at the wrong time and that she was in the wrong treatment house.

I listened and felt differently. I had a strong clinical hunch that this was exactly the environment that would provoke historical anxieties and prompt use of Penny's psychic retreat. Without everyday demands and distractions, I sensed we would finally be able to view and articulate its complex operations, challenge its historical omnipotence, and encourage new opportunities for the expression of her truth and vulnerability. I had a sense that this environment would allow us to begin to create a shared language about her retreat's perverse protections. I was ready to wait my hunch through.

And eventually, this hunch turned into a conviction—this was exactly what Penny needed to experience, endure, and confront. She began living again in the unfathomable confusion and hostility of her traumatic early years in a violent, abusive, and neglectful home.

Regression, Retreat, and Courage

Penny's work was to make a home for herself. She gradually became a participant in her new family. She was able to be more present with the emotional violence in the house. She relived her past in the present.

The environment became more regressed. Penny allowed herself to experience confusion and terror. She desired retreat but fought to stay engaged. Little did Penny know that at these moments she was fighting against, not retreating from, all that had been wrong in her life.

Still, it took time. I watched her struggle with her rage as she reexperienced historical family trauma. She was furious at me for not providing "infantile" protection. I watched her "not leave."

Eventually, the regressed behavior in the household became too much. Not surprisingly, Penny returned to that retreated space in her mind that said, "Pull in and remain quiet." For the first time, she did not participate in groups and stayed in bed in her room. She stopped eating and told no one. She seemed distant and full of despair. I wasn't sure of what she was really thinking. She was going through the motions. Finally, she spoke and told me her biggest dread and fear: "I won't get what I need here. I'll leave and nothing will have changed. I will continue with my same pattern—trying to live, becoming overwhelmed, and then withdrawing in isolation." I listened intently, heard every word, and felt her terror. She seemed to understand that she alone had to feel these things through and make decisions about how she wanted to respond. She said with a faint yet fighting resignation, "For now, I am here. For now, I am staying here. For now, I am just going hour by hour. That's all I can do." I said, "I understand." I sensed her hold on to this lonely conviction as she never had before. I heard Ron Sager's words in my mind, "We are all fundamentally alone, yet not all of us really know what it feels like to be alone" (Personal Communication, 2010).

The next day, I got a call. The clinical director made a courageous treatment decision by referring a patient not suitable for this environment to another treatment facility. This decision restored this once-regressed house to more order. Penny felt that something that was wrong was now right. Faith lived again in her heart and also resided in the household. I celebrated with her, and also shared a measured response. "In the face of real uncertainty, you pushed through. You didn't stay retreated; you refused to hide. You didn't give into your fear. You kept fighting for your life. You kept trying to hold on to your voice. You fought for your future. You must have sensed that there was something in this experience that you needed, something in this experience that would provide an opening in your life."

Penny and I had a long discussion the next day. We caught up on our relationship. She told me that she was mad and confused by my behavior. She continued, "I figured you knew what you were doing, but I couldn't understand why you didn't support me, why you didn't acknowledge that this place was a mess." She continued, "The way we communicated in here was so different. I felt hurt and confused by your distance. This place was bad, everyone said it was bad, the staff said it was bad, and you said nothing. I wanted you to understand what I was living through and protect me."

I eventually replied, "Penny, you must have felt horrible. You must have felt abandoned and betrayed by me. That must have scared you so much." She agreed, nodded her head, and was silent. She continued, "Tell me what you were doing and thinking?"

I shared, "Penny, I was behind you. I listened intently to what you were experiencing each day. I knew this was an environment on the edge. I took in what you and your husband were thinking. I shared my concerns with the staff, and I trusted their judgments. They were in an ongoing intense evaluation process. I knew they would come to the right decision for every member of the house. I had faith in their years of experience.

"Since I believed that, I felt that these inpatient interactions and situations were exactly what was needed for your own growth and development. I sensed that you knew you couldn't continue isolating and retreating from reality and that you couldn't continue to deny the reality of your own feelings. I sensed that you didn't want to start withdrawing to your bedroom here, that you didn't want to retreat from your life. I saw you fight that old tendency. I felt your determination to be present to experiences that you have avoided your entire life. It was your time, and I was behind you, and it was your work to own and your work to do."

Penny said, "I get it." D. W. Winnicott does not assume that we all "live" a life. Penny had decided to live hers (Winnicott, cited in Bollas, 1989, p. 26).

Character and Characters of a Retreat

Adult patients often tap into their childhood imagination when they remember their early pains. They recall memories of how they coped. Many remember withdrawing as a way of feeling safe, a way of life. Eventually, some adults are able to put words to the imagery behind their long-term use of their retreated minds. This results in more vivid discussions about its prominence in everyday living operations.

Penny articulated her fantasy refuge during her inpatient stay. "During the last year, you used to ask me if I had an idea what my withdrawal into myself looked like. You used to ask me if I had some sense of what retreating felt like. I told you I didn't know because I couldn't access any ideas. The last couple of days, some images have developed and I wanted to tell you."

Penny held up her right hand, as if she were caressing something valuable, supporting something important. She continued, "When my hand goes up like that, I feel the need to turn and twist something, as if something needs to be screwed in place; it is as if I'm screwing in a lightbulb. My hands let me know that I am preparing to go to a place in my mind that says, 'Screw you' to everybody.

"This is how it starts. I feel disappointed from a conversation, let's say with my husband. Usually, it's when I try to convey to him that I am overwhelmed with being a mom, taking care of him, and taking care of the house. I feel unsure of myself and very shaky. It's hard to admit all this, so I'm not really that clear to him. I just hope he is able to get it. I want him to read between the lines, and hear me. Most often, he doesn't. I'm left hanging, and I start feeling let down, scared, and worried, then overwhelmed and lost. I don't know what to do, what the next step should be. I don't know how to handle feeling so insecure, so unsure of myself. It feels terrifying. I quickly look around to see if he notices. It looks like he doesn't see how frightened I am. It feels impossible to ask him for more, to ask him again. I suddenly feel like I can't take all these scary and confusing feelings for one more minute."

Penny continued with her fantasy. "That's when I reach for the lightbulb, and once the lightbulb is screwed in place, my mind says, 'That's it. I have to take charge here. My husband's not listening. He doesn't know what the real deal is, what I am going through; he doesn't have a clue how to help me navigate this lonely and horrific, crazy and chaotic place. He feels useless. I can't stand it, and I can't wait around anymore. I don't trust him or that he will understand what is really important to me. I don't trust that he will understand what I need to do now. I am alone, and I know it. Nobody can help me, not even Roger.'

"The lightbulb has voices behind it, and they start talking. They sound like confident and strong military commanders. They are determined to get me out of this jam. They are my fierce protectors and allies. They see what is going on; they see how alone I feel; they get that I tried to talk to my husband and that it didn't work. They assure me that I don't need to pursue a conversation with him anymore. They tell me that I've done enough asking for help, and now it's time to ignore all these silly feelings. They know I want to feel sure, strong, and confident.

"They tell me it's time to 'stand and deliver.' In this case, that means it's time to do my job and provide for my husband, children, and the house. They assure me that there is no reason to feel so confused, unsure, and scared. They remind me that my charm, talents, and ability to manipulate others will be enough to get the job done, that I will feel so much better if I just keep producing. They remind me that I always feel better after I do a great job for others and make everyone happy. I always get praise for the great job I do. This makes me think that I must be a good mom and wife and know what I'm doing. Life feels livable after I listened to the 'stand and deliver' commanders."

A lifetime of perverse problem solving was exposed, put into words, and shared in that conversation. After a sober year of so much stress, withdrawal, and confusion, we finally understood what we were up against. Characters of the mind that had sheltered vulnerability, prevented growth, and perpetuated pain were finally out in the open. Penny now had imagery that empowered her and that opened up choice in her life. It would not be easy.

As we talked, I sensed that Penny now held a thin thread connecting her recent pearls of triumph over those fierce commanders. She alone decided to get and stay sober, she alone decided to go to Arizona, and she alone decided to enter Clearview. She alone endured the bullying forces of her impatient household. She was a terrified inpatient, yet she was determined to finally stay present with her real experience. We replayed these pearl moments again and again.

Penny was also determined to listen harder for the commander's seductions, determined to have her truth drown out their propaganda. She felt she held a blueprint of her mind, and now finally a chance to navigate for herself. Below are examples of Penny's confrontations with her retreated mind.

Preparing for Discharge and a Home Pass

"The other day when I was in my room, I felt anxious. I started to think about when I would be discharged and have to return home. I got worried. I couldn't imagine how I was going to do it. I couldn't imagine how I could remain a patient in recovery and be a mother and a wife at the same time. I got very scared about this impossible task. That's when my right hand reached out for the lightbulb.

"The commanders heard me and offered some suggestions: 'This recovery pampering stuff is over. You've learned what you need; you've gotten enough. It's time to move on. It's time to take charge of your house, your children, your husband. It's time to do the task at hand, and do it well.'" Penny told me, "My protectors' words drowned out my fears and uncertainties. I started to feel confident, not scared. They helped me mobilize for the tasks after discharge. I felt ready to 'stand and deliver.'"

We continued to understand more about her retreated mind. Penny called me one day before a home pass. She talked about a fight with her husband, fears about reconnecting with her children after her treatment, the challenges of inpatient work, and the pressure she felt to be available for her girls during her upcoming pass. Her voice escalated; I felt her escaping from her body and retreating into her mind. I knew she was not listening to herself, paying attention to her fears, or open to our impact exchange. Penny's mind was occupied, and our connection felt distant. I knew it was her retreat pulling her into perverse and hostile protection.

The lightbulb screw seemed to be tightening around her. It promised reversal of pain, if only she would abandon herself and her true feelings. All she had to do was ignore her real concerns—how can I be a patient and a mother? How can I be true to my incapacity and, at the same time, be a capable mother for my girls?

The authorities continued their coaching, "You don't need to wrestle with any of that; you don't need to face those nasty dilemmas. You don't need to be scared; you certainly don't need to depend on your therapist. You don't need to talk about what's real. That's too humiliating—you can avoid this. All you need to do is turn a blind eye to your unsteady feelings about yourself, and your mothering. We will provide you with the energy and confidence you need to be the good, all-knowing mother you want to be. We know that you think this residential stay has dragged on long enough. We know that you want to 'stand and deliver' for your children. You don't need to be a patient anymore—you just need to be a mom. We will help you do it, and we will keep you company."

Embracing a Retreated Mind

I knew that the retreat's reign would remain unchecked as long as Penny dismissed her fears, remained a divided self. I waited for her in reverie. I sensed that she might be able to tolerate some vulnerability. We talked, and eventually she was able to open up: "I am feeling very shaky as a mom. I actually don't know how to be with my girls. I don't know how to be in my house or in my neighborhood. I think I need to shorten my home visit today. I'm terrified, and my husband is gone. I have to stop promising my children things I can't do and remember that I am still a patient."

I asked Penny what all this meant to her. What kind of things was she learning about herself? She warmly responded, "It's the way I abandon myself, and I see more clearly how insidiously and quickly my retreated mind goes into operation. I really get this 'stand and deliver' thing now. I am really beginning to understand how it came about as a child, and how it comes about today. There is an important moment that I can barely feel; my retreat seduces me in a nanosecond with such deviousness. I am in its grip before I know it. It starts with feeling scared and shaky, weak and ashamed, embarrassed and confused about being a patient, about being me right now. This is my real space—I'm a patient whose life stopped working in my own home. I stopped being able to be a woman with a body, a mom, and I stopped being able to be a wife. I needed to completely collapse and be in a place like this.

"All that is way too hard to keep acknowledging, way too humiliating to keep accepting. It's extremely painful to admit that so much of my life began when I entered Clearview. I feel so ashamed that I don't know what I'm doing, that I don't really know how to be a mother or a wife. It's hard to accept being a patient in recovery and also in inpatient treatment. It's hard to pay attention to all that and also be a mom. It's way too much, and it feels too impossible. That's when they come in. They grab that truthful and humiliating moment, and before I know it, they pull me away from these feelings and we are off and running. The real me is left behind, as I 'stand and deliver' and temporarily feel okay."

Penny continued, "It's frightening how fast all this works in my mind, how much of me passes me by. I'm beginning to really see how my mind has created these characters, these people, and how they have become my protectors. They saw how bad I felt when my mother ignored, mocked, or made fun of me when I was a child. They watched me look at her with hope and dread. They saw me get crushed. They convinced me that this humiliation and fear need never be felt again, if only I listened to their commandments. I see how they gave me false hope and false confidence. They have been in charge of me for years. I see how food, alcohol, and Vicodin took away the pain of living a 'stand and deliver' life.

"This is really a lot to see, but I am starting to get it. I get what these 'friends and allies' are really doing. I'm really glad we are talking about this this way.

It's very helpful. It's something I can use, and I will try to watch them operating in my mind today while I'm on my pass."

The pass went better than she thought. Such fine-grain articulation of the retreat's operations helped her navigate the afternoon. This work feels essential in early recovery treatment; it was essential that day. It defeated the retreat's operations, and it defeated their dominance. Penny listened to her own truth, not their propaganda. She shaved off activities, limited her time with her children, set limits with friends and family members, and returned to the facility early. She accepted her limitations and faced their sting. She was true to herself, not an image of herself promoted by her allies.

Gone were the demands of a house that overwhelmed her; a mothering style that excluded her; a martial relationship that intimidated her; a body that devoured her; and feeling states that suffocated her. Her decision to be in a residential facility gave her unencumbered room to tolerate experiencing and feeling more of her real self, and think important things through.

Penny finally got some space to listen to her mind, to begin to see how it really works and what it does with the pain of her reality. We paid attention to this very important early recovery task during her stay at Clearview. Penny began to understand and face the retreated aspects of her mind. She began acting on her own behalf, not on her "stand and deliver" commandments. Penny was starting to feel real, and also a little better.

We talked about a new space that was developing, a space between the imperatives of her retreated mind and the predictable collapse that follows after executing its brutal instructions. We began calling it the in-between space of Clearview. It was the space for her truth, her human weakness, and her vulnerability. Penny wanted to exist in this space; she wanted to befriend these neglected parts of herself, voice their existence, and do something with them. It was exciting and empowering, and also terrifying. She could return to the retreated space or enter the space in between. We had a language and some hope.

Sunday Afternoon Marital E-mails

Penny's inpatient stay opened up vision on her marriage. She was deeply saddened by what was missing. She reflected to herself, "All I want is my husband. I am so sad and worried about what has happened to us. I see now how far apart we are. The demands on each of us are brutal, and we drive ourselves to the brink. We finish the day angry and exhausted. We never talk. We both suspiciously pull in, watch the other, and keep our distance. It's really making me sad and scared. If we don't take care of this now, our marriage will end. I just know it. Once the girls leave home, we might see we have nothing between us. We better deal with this now. I want to work on this in here. I want to have lots of couples sessions. It feels like the most important thing. I need him and us—I really do."

It was Sunday, and Penny was in agony. She stayed alone in the treatment residence. She was terrified about her feelings about her husband, petrified of her perceptions, disgusted by her need. She stayed with her internal torture over a five-hour period. She did not retreat, or eat destructively, somaticize her emotions, zone out in sleep, or sit in blankness. She felt supported by the house's quiet environment. She was able to stay with her experience. She was existing in the in-between space of her truth.

After many hours, Penny sent an e-mail to me that read: "This is the crazy e-mail I sent Roger. I sent it out of sheer desperation."

> I can't imagine that you would know how gut wrenching it is for me to be here and still offer me no consolation. Nothing comes from you but your weariness at work and demands being made and me being one of the demands. Just another demand on you. What does it take to get your attention for a brief moment of tenderness? What do I have to do to earn that? I have spent hours here alone trapped wanting to hear some tiny bit of love from you. Even imagining very awful things that you feel about me or are planning for me.
>
> This is a harrowing experience and I feel powerless to ask for your love or attention least I unleash your wrath at me for creating stress for you during a busy, difficult time. I can't imagine disturbing you with my useless ridiculous feelings and needs. And yet I have taken a great risk in doing so.
>
> I have been suffering for days wanting to talk to you and wanting to hear something from you that I am not alone. That even though you are in inexhaustible demand that I am a priority. That you love me or think of me. I always say a little goes a long way. I feel awful asking you for anything and it turns to anger. I don't know what to say except it is horrible to feel so alone here and feel I have no voice. No right to ask for anything.
>
> I don't know what else to do. I have cried and imagined you taking the girls from me now that I am and have now been in an institution. I feel I am currently the vessel for all that is wrong with our lives. As you can see I am profoundly upset. I am sorry if this disturbs you. I truly have been wrestling with these feelings for many days now and could no longer contain it.

The characters of Penny's retreated mind had been campaigning for her loyalty all afternoon: "Your feelings are overblown and too intense. We understand them, but you don't need to talk to Roger about them; he won't get them. He is most likely going to think that you are silly, too sensitive, and accusatory. Furthermore, he won't have time for your feelings. He is busy, and it's not the kind of thing that he is interested in understanding. Maybe you should've married someone else. But you didn't, and you have children now. The best thing to do is to keep these feelings inside. We don't want you to face rejection, humiliation, and shame. There is no need for that. There is no need for you to expose yourself to him. That's not important in life. It doesn't get you anywhere. The important thing is that we understand your feelings and help you sort them out. We are here to keep you company. We will help you keep them quiet. Later on, we will figure out what you can do with them. Maybe we can help you 'stand and deliver'; that always seems to bring you a sense of pride about your abilities and strengths. We don't have to figure this out now. Just know we have something in mind that will help. We do know that your e-mail is useless, and you should not send it to Roger. For now, let's just stay here."

Penny fought these seductions and persuasions all afternoon. It was a bloody struggle and she barely made it. Exhaustingly and eventually, she clicked 'Send.' She was terrified of his response but strangely energized by her action. Her note to her husband was another triumph of allegiance to herself. She added another pearl to her thread.

It took Roger a couple of hours to respond. His e-mail reflected an openness and willingness. He was able to convey understanding, and hold her fragility.

> You are my first priority, honey. You and the girls. I'm sorry if I haven't made you feel that way. I know how awful and powerless it must feel . . . especially with Margy and I both out of the country, and me unreachable.
>
> I love you and I'm so so so sorry you're suffering. Everything I'm doing I'm doing for us and if I get the short term prioritization wrong . . . I'm doing the best I can, and it's so hard not being able to talk to you when I'm free . . . . But having to be free to talk to you when I'm not . . . If you can call tomorrow, please do so.
>
> I love you and I'm so sorry it's hard for you and you feel unloved and unheard. It just makes me sick to think about it. It's been very hard to be without you—I don't want to live a life without you; I just want you to be happier and feel better. I'm so sorry this is coinciding with this ridiculous Europe trip. We all love you and are trying so hard to keep it together to give you a break. It's out of deep respect and admiration for and trust in you. Call me tomorrow. I love you.

Penny felt so relieved by her husband's response. She held on to her pearl. "In the end, his response was not anywhere near as important to me as sending that e-mail. It was such a miserable afternoon. My feelings felt so wrong and bad, so unworthy to be shared. Yet, somewhere, I knew in my gut that the 'stand and deliver' commanders were not telling me the truth when they told me to ignore my feelings. They were trying so hard to convince me that my e-mail would backfire. But I couldn't go their way. I knew that I had to share all of me, if I wanted closeness with Roger."

Penny repeatedly recalled her Sunday afternoon agony. It felt important to remember the struggle. In the past, she had listened to the calls and comforts of the characters of her retreated mind. They repeatedly assured her that any risk with her husband would only humiliate and embarrass her. They stressed that it did not bring any kind of closeness, that it would only bring more trouble. She began to think otherwise. She retained a visceral memory of her choice that Sunday afternoon. She decided to aggressively challenge a lifelong marital pattern of avoidance and loneliness. She continued to risk, and continued to benefit from this risk. It is a loving, struggling, and viable marriage today.

Preparation for Departure

Penny's final days in treatment were looming. She had more home passes. For the first time, she began listening to herself while mothering, and voicing her true experiences to her husband. She remembered all the pearls on her thread. She knew that if she did not rebuff the 'stand and deliver' commanders, she would collapse around herself again. She understood the stakes and had determination. She said no or not now to her children's requests, and she asked her husband if they could talk. Her dreaded responses did not materialize; she developed some shaky confidence.

Still, she hit rough patches. She went away with her family on a weekend pass. They stayed in a hotel. Penny was overactive with her family, overresponsive to her children, overattentive to her husband. She also overate at dinner, overindulged in sweets after, and was up all night with a stomachache and worry. We talked, and she asked, "How did they get past me again? How is it that I could not listen to the part of me that said, 'This is all too much. I need to slow down; I need to take a break'? How is it that the 'stand and deliver' commanders won again? This is going to be so hard; this is going to take so long." Penny's initial response was disappointment, but she tried to embrace the concept of learning from experience. Reworking the dominance of retreated protectors takes years.

Discharge and First Days at Home After Clearview

The staff and I prepared for Penny's departure from five weeks of intensive inpatient treatment. There were couples sessions, family meetings, and increased individual therapy. The night before, she told me, "If I am truthful, like I am now, I know I have done a lot of work in here, and I also know that I'm not totally ready to leave. However, I can't see staying any longer. My family needs me, and I want to give my work here a try." She asked me what I thought, and I said, "I agree that a longer stay would help solidify your new responses to these difficult questions—should

I be truthful about my capacities or 'stand and deliver'? Should I express my fears to Roger or ignore them? Should I mother myself or mother my children? However, you seem to feel like you want to return home and practice what you've learned." Ron Sager's wisdom echoed again in our ears, "Trust your gut, do what you think is right, and see what happens."

Penny's children and her husband drove her home. She was excited and challenged, yet recalls feeling some "twinges of panic" as she drove away. She knew it was going to be very, very uncomfortable.

The first day went fairly well. Weeks of voicing her needs and wishes in a protected setting paid off. Her children showered her with excited requests; Penny said, "We'll see." She volunteered, "I'm going to be sleeping in one or two mornings during the week." She panicked if she felt a missed opportunity to connect with her husband on something important. She later requested more time to talk. Setting these limits also wore her down.

Understandably, Penny was back in the grip of her psychic retreat before she knew it. An accumulation of unhealthy choices throughout her second day at home resulted in despair. Penny recalled, "I got myself in some trouble here—I was willing to volunteer for the school for one hour, and the mother in charge convinced me to do half a day. I knew I could absolutely not handle that, but I felt I had no choice and could only do what she was asking.

"My children crowded in on a conversation with Roger. I didn't know how to say that 'Daddy and I are talking now.' I didn't think I could disappoint them and ask them to play in their room while I talked to Roger. I knew in my heart that I desperately needed to talk to him and get his support. I knew that it was the only thing that was important at that moment. I felt I had to put my children's needs ahead of mine.

"Later in the day, I needed to take a nap. I was utterly exhausted from so much stimulation. I didn't think it was fair to leave the girls after I had been gone for over a month. I knew that all I needed was a 45-minute nap but somehow didn't feel that I deserved it."

Her retreat was in full press. She had been seduced into abandoning her truth and encouraged to 'stand and deliver.' She capitulated without a thought. Her psychic retreat was crowding in around her. She was back in the fight of her life.

I felt a strong need to help Penny protect her inpatient gains. I was supportive but firm. "Here we are on day two. I think it's very important that I tell you how destructively familiar our conversation feels. Your retreat is once again at work, trying to convince you to ignore your truth and telling you to do more than you can really handle."

Penny was quiet and seemed a little overwhelmed. "I sensed I couldn't handle all these things, but I did the opposite to avoid embarrassment and shame. I'm mad at myself that this is happening again." She sighed, "Let's bring Roger in on this phone conversation. I hope he gets all this."

Roger listened to the events of the day, and he did get it. He spoke with clarity and conviction. He was not facile in retreat language, but he understood and embraced her fight to reject wishful thinking. He said with love, support, and certainty, "I want to help you tell everyone that things are different here now, that you are listening to your recovery—that you'll take that nap you need, that you'll come get me when you want to talk, that you'll let our kids know that they will have to wait, that you won't be volunteering to host multiple family events, that you won't be at the girls' school at the expense of recovery, and that you won't be staying in their room after singing time at night." Penny was listening. Roger grasped the imperative importance of overpowering her retreated mind's perverse manipulations. It was evident that he had learned many things himself while Penny was at Clearview.

I asked Penny how she was feeling about this conversation. She said, "It's a bit overwhelming, but it's extremely helpful. I am beginning to see that I do have choice, that I need to accept the truth of my limitations. Facing this is painful but real. Appearing to look and feel like a confident mother is a 'stand and deliver' lie. This is really going to be hard. I have to change the destructive instincts of a lifetime."

Penny continued, "The conversation has been hard, yet I feel some real energy coming back into my body. Roger really does seem to get all of this. He seems to understand my intense internal struggle with my retreating mind, and that feels so good. I thought this evening was a lost cause, and now it feels salvageable to me. Tomorrow feels scary, but I know that Roger and I can talk tonight."

First Months at Home

These were uneven times. Penny had real difficulty in accepting and holding on to the truth of her recovery life. It felt intolerable to be a recently discharged patient with so much need when she gazed in the eyes of her husband and children. Many times, however, she was able to make choices from her sober capacity. She set limits with her girls, carefully designed family outings and trips, was discerning with social engagements, and refused school and community projects. She came to therapy and tried hard to live from the "the in-between space of Clearview"—the space of her real capacity, not the space of stand and deliver.

Penny's early recovery days were now filled with transition moment questions—Can I handle what I'm about to do? Do I need to make real adjustments, or should I push through regardless? Many, many times her lightbulb screwed into place, she ignored her true self, pushed through anyway, and invariably had some kind of faltering. The commanders captured her more times than she wanted.

Toward the second month, Penny withdrew into her room, began some compulsive overeating and shopping, avoided in-person sessions, and cancelled a few sessions altogether. Her retreated mind was in charge again before we both knew it. This pattern was starting to repeat itself. It concerned both of us, and this time we were willing to use what we had learned about the operations of her mind.

We knew what we were up against and began talking. Many times, these conversations occurred in couples therapy. Roger was repeatedly in on Penny's struggles. He wanted to support her expressions of truth. They both liked their marital growth and new closeness, and they wanted to keep it going. Penny revealed to us one night, "This all happens so fast. My retreated mind is so circular and so sneaky. I know there is a part of me that doesn't know what I'm doing because I've been using drugs and alcohol all my life. I know my real self needs to be listened to. I know that and hate that. I think this recovery business should be over by now, and I should be into my life and taking care of my family. So I immediately drown out how frightened and ashamed I am—that at 49 years old, I still don't know how to take care of myself. I ignore my fears and take directions from the 'stand and deliver' commanders. It temporarily feels so much better, and then I am eating, not sleeping, completely overwhelmed, angry, and withdrawn. This is such a problem. I wish I had never started all this."

Roger so sweetly listened and replied, "Honey, this is what human beings do—we talk to each other about what we can handle, what we are really capable of. You never learned that as a child. I didn't either, in many ways. We are in our 40s and may be learning this late, but we are learning this with each other now. This is our life, our reality, and we both have to face it individually and together. Margy's right that we have to protect your recovery self. But it's going to be hard to figure all this out in the real world that you and I live in." Penny sent me an e-mail later saying that her husband's capacity for reflection, understanding, and support "blows my mind."

As this book goes to press, I am delighted to report that Roger began his own psychotherapy. He is regularly showing up, discovering and rediscovering himself. It took time for Roger to accept that he needed to be a patient too. It's going to make a difference.

As previously said, identifying and recovering from a retreating mind's trickery and thievery takes years. Penny relied on its protections during childhood to ease the unbearable pain of the violent rejection of her true being. Food, alcohol, and drugs provided years of reliable yet unsatisfactory relief. Sobriety exposed the landscape of her retreated mind and her inexperience with facing her true feelings and capacities. Early recovery work revealed new choices for Penny. She struggled, she felt, and she lived a previously unfelt and unlived life. She matured and experienced joy. Adam Phillips (2010) encourages each of us to create a life we feel like living.

Angela

Beside Herself

Angela's transition identity felt solid. She was not threatened by using. She showed up for therapy and seemed desirous of furthering her sober self-awareness (refresh your memory about Angela in Chapter 10, p. 188).

I opened the waiting room door. Angela was in motion with her body, her mind, and her mouth. She walked through the hallway, eager to tell me how she was doing. In my office, she pulled over the tissue box, got the trash can, and slouched on the couch. She had moved from a chair to the couch recently. It seemed to contain her agitation, and allow for more real expression. "You know, I was doing okay yesterday, but today things aren't so good." She looked worried; she seemed desperate to talk.

Angela continued, "I don't know, I mean, I had a good day a couple of days ago, and I was proud of myself. I walked the dog, I met a friend, I went to class, and then I was glad to come home. I had an okay night. I watched TV. It started when I woke up the next day. Even after 10 hours of sleep, I woke up feeling bad. I couldn't figure out what to do with myself. Hasn't this gone on long enough? All this therapy and I still can't figure things out. What's wrong with me?"

Angela went on to describe a day of lethargy and confusion, bewilderment and depression. She had no interest in doing anything; she was overwhelmed by her despair, disgusted by her lack of motivation. She was beside herself with herself (Eigen, 2004, pp. 8–10).

Rediscovering Time and Rediscovering People

Life's uneven pattern of a few good moments followed by some bad ones, a few bad days followed by some good ones had escaped her grasp. She was alarmed by the movements between good feelings and bad ones; she didn't know how to go with the back-and-forth. Overwhelming childhood trauma and later drug use prevented her from "being" with these experiences. Recognizing, accepting, and tolerating these daily rhythms requires hours of sober discovery. The recovering addict has to be willing to participate in these moments in time, not just pass over them. Learning about time's feel and flow is a necessary part of the work of recovery. I "held" Angela as she began to grapple with the reality of her lost experiences. An interest in what she could do with time slowly began to replace her dread of it.

Another important recovery task is helping the addict make sober sense of the place of people in his world. I began to notice that there were very few of them in Angela's life. She attended class, went to meetings, and occasionally talked to her family. There were no relationships of any meaning, no ongoing connections. We began exploring. Are relationships valuable to her? How does she feel about having people in her life? Would she prefer to be alone or in the company of others? Does she seek out the company of others? Does she feel that the company of others is interesting or comforting? What happens during and after spending time with people? What happens during and after spending time alone? What does all this mean?

Angela hadn't thought about this aspect of her being. Over a couple of sessions, she developed an interest in understanding more. "As a child and adolescent, I didn't want my friends to know how bad my house was. I didn't want them to hang around. If they did, they would see what goes on inside. I didn't want them to know that my mother was mean, that she screamed at me, beat me, and that our house was very scary. I didn't want anyone to know about my life—how I spent my afternoons looking out the window, waiting for her to come home, terrified about what she would do.

"I didn't understand all that was going on in my house. Sometimes I cried about it all in front of my mother; most of the time I just kept it inside. I knew the best thing to do was keep quiet, hide in my room, and let it pass. I also hid my life from my teachers, my friends, and their parents. I didn't think the other families lived like me. I didn't think they would approve. Something felt really wrong and very bad in my home."

Angela had little good to say about the people in her family. She brushed over a dad who left her for another family. "He didn't care; he left me behind and went on to create another life." She tersely shared, "I was dumped in my grandmother's lap at an early age. My mother went right back to work, and my grandmother raised me. My grandmother was mean, jealous, vindictive, and a gossip. I tuned her out most of the time. I still do." "My sister was the favorite and knew how to get all the attention. I just watched her—she got away with all kinds of lazy and bad behavior. She knew how to work things better than me." "My father's parents actually cared about me. I always liked to talk to them, but it was only for a short time. Then they were gone. My mother was violent with me."

"So," Angela said one day, "I kind of like the idea of people and want to be in a relationship with them. I also want to have a relationship with a man or maybe a woman. But as we talk more, I'm beginning to think I'm a loner. I watch people, and see people talking to each other. Much of the world seems in relationships; they look like a good idea, they seem important and good. It seems like something

I should want to do. I think doing it would make me feel normal. But I don't really get it. I don't think I ever have. I think that's why I'm a loner. I don't know, I don't get all this people stuff." Adam Phillips (1998) may shed light here: "We love people because they remind us of our earliest passions for our parents and ourselves" (p. 144). Angela continued, "Something is wrong with me. Why do I spend so much time alone? Other people don't seem to."

I encouraged her to befriend her loner being, not be edgy with it. "Let's keep talking." Angela began to notice things about her desire for people. She noticed that she didn't need people if she was having a good day; if she was having a bad day, she didn't want them around.

Putting Images to Work

As has been suggested, coping in early recovery often beckons reliance on a retreated state of mind. A clinician attentively hovers and listens for the addict's perceptions and responses to his pain.

It took some time to learn about Angela's current life of daily anguish—her hours and days of excruciating emotional distress. She sequestered herself in isolation. She zoned out in front of the TV or slept. She downplayed her painful existence. She excluded herself from herself, and I felt excluded as well. There was a growing distance between us; it felt familiar. Psychic retreats came to mind.

Angela had no desire to use drugs or alcohol to escape her pain. She also had no desire to reach out to others to talk about her distress, converse about her concerns, or hope for relief. It was an idea that never occurred to her. She spent all her time alone. I soon suspected that a psychic retreat was becoming her drug of choice, her ally during these depressing times.

We began talking about the retreating tendency of human beings, in general, and its widespread prevalence with addicts. She understood the concept and related to its use in her life. "Addicts need the escape of drugs. I know I did. Something feels bad, wrong, and off. I figured out what to do with this. My best feelings came after the first rush of heroin, the first jolt of cocaine. That first rush brought so much relief. I just went into a warm and peaceful oblivion. Then I was just out of it. That's where I wanted to be. That's how I lived, just dulled out day and night. I would stay there for hours and days. Drugs made sure I felt nothing."

Over time, we wondered together what she had done with her painful emotions prior to her drug use. Angela was intrigued by her mind's attempt to get rid of feelings of discomfort and dread. She reflected on her childhood days. She remembered terror and fear as a child. She cowered from her mom's violence. She worried in her room, wept in silence, exhausted herself, and eventually fell asleep. She talked to no one. What had she done with all the suffering?

We began talking about how a retreating mind establishes itself as a childhood friend. When the pain is too unbearable, there is a part of the psyche that quickly takes over. A retreating mind sends a clear, consistent, and seductive message. It assures the individual that the best responses to pain occur during withdrawal from the world. It convincingly encourages the avoidance of feeling, discourages vulnerability with others, and campaigns for solitary solutions for discomfort.

I gently brought it closer to home and suggested, "As a child, you seemed to be alone in all of your pain, and you were forced to figure things out by yourself. You tried to fathom your mother's cruelty, tried to protect yourself from her violence, and also your own fear. What do you think went on?" Angela was quiet, reflective. "I'm not sure. I just remember being alone, always alone. I cried until I fell asleep; I woke up hoping the pain would be gone. Staying alone in my room felt like the right thing to do. I was more comfortable alone; it felt better than being with people. I returned to my room again and again."

Angela was describing the physical exterior of a psychic retreat. I continued talking about its interior functions, and eventually said, "Many individuals have an image of their retreating mind, a story about its nature, the characters involved and the way it works. A retreat has a function and a feel, and it's different for everybody." She gestured for more. "Some say it's a force that sweeps one away from any pain, while others say it feels like a mafia gang of fierce protectors or a group of warm and friendly leprechauns. One person said, 'I ride in the *Charlie and the Chocolate Factory*'s great glass elevator.' Still others describe it as a table of statisticians filled with logic that fight feelings, a stage for resting when frightened in the presence of others, a lightbulb that screws into place, signaling that it's time to leave the rest of the world behind, a glass room that soothes and protects, or a swishing sound that holds one still during scary times. The moment unbearable feelings arise in the psyche, there seems to be an image or images that beckon entry into the shelter of a retreated mind. Some individuals seem to establish an ongoing relationship with this fantasy world."

I felt Angela's interest and asked if she had any sense of what her mind felt like when she was in pain as a child, and even now as a sober adult. She had been intently listening and now paused in reflection and with slight embarrassment. "It's kind of weird; but as I sit here, I can feel exactly what it is, what it looks like, and how it all works. It starts when I am alone, feeling sad and overwhelmed, when I feel like a nothing, like a blob, like I have no motivation, and that I'm really, really useless, unproductive, and bad. I feel like something is wrong with the way I'm doing things, that I'm worthless compared with everyone else."

Angela cautiously told me her story that afternoon. I listened with sensitivity and receptivity. "So I get all these feelings, and I don't know what to do. Then, I see this walkway in my mind. It's a path along a road. That's the beginning image." Angela motioned her hand, as if to say 'Enter this way.' "Something, someone beckons me to go on the road. I don't spend much time on it, and then I see an island. The island is only 8 feet by 8 feet. It's small, compact, composed of sand, and surrounded by water. The pathway leads to an island. It feels like a good and safe place." She continued, "Several residents live on the island and tell me that I need to stay here during this painful time. These people know that I feel really bad and that something is very wrong. They tell me that it's not smart to talk to anyone about how bad I feel, or tell them that I have no idea how to get out of this mess. These people are very firm, and I start to believe they have the right ideas, that they know how to help me."

Angela appeared more lively and coherent. She was describing a very familiar internal world, one she knew well and liked, respected, and trusted. The local residents continued their instructions. "In life, you are never to let on that you are in a bad and scary home, that you don't know what you are doing. Certainly, if you told your mother, she would laugh at you, maybe even hit you. It's not safe to tell her that you are confused about what is going on in the house, that you are very scared most of the time, and don't know what to do next. It's much better to keep it all with us, here on the island, and not tell her or show her that you are sad and upset."

Furthermore, the residents warned Angela never to tell her friends. "They will not understand, as nothing bad happens in their homes. Everything is good in their homes, and nothing is wrong. You will make a fool of yourself if you talk about how scared and worried you feel. The best way to get over all this is to listen to us. You just have to wait here on this island in silence. Maybe sleep, watch TV, color, read a book, play with dolls, or talk to your dog. The only thing that works in this situation is to stay here until the bad feelings are over. Stay on the island while in your room. It's the best solution; you will see. When enough time passes, eventually you will feel better. Once you feel a little better, and most of the pain is gone, you can leave the island. And after you leave the island, you can go visit your friends. Life will feel perfect then."

Angela concluded, "I think I learned that these local residents were friends, that they had my best interest at heart. When I listened to their instructions, eventually I felt okay, my home felt okay, and my friends thought I was okay. That's the way I took care of myself during all the violence in my household. I lived in fear every day. These island residents made me feel safe and not alone. They made sure I felt protected on the island. It was the only solution I had, and I kept following their instructions. Most of the time, I didn't even have to think about the island and its people; I just knew what to do."

Old Pain, New Pain, and Retreating

We talked about living the past in the present. Angela eventually paused and reflected, "Now that I think about it, the same kind of thing is going on right now. When I feel bad, I just sit in my apartment. I feel upset and confused, and then that mind thing starts happening again. In a flash, I see the path and the walkway. I know it leads to the island, and I know I need to get there and wait until time passes. I know that I will be okay there. Hours go by in my apartment, and I'm not really sure what is going on and what takes place. I kind of space out. Sometimes I watch TV. I sleep for a lot of hours, more than most people. I don't answer phone calls; I don't respond to e-mails. I eat junk food. I think I feel kind of lost. Days go by, and eventually the bad feelings leave me. I begin to feel things are good, even perfect. I start to clean up my apartment, and I take a shower. I begin to see a world out there. I begin to think that I can go out. I've waited long enough, so I know that I will be presentable."

Angela continued, "I get myself together and show up at school or at a meeting. I feel friendly and chipper, mostly because those horrible bad feelings have passed. It's a great sense of relief to feel better and to know that I am presentable to the world. I always hope that these good feelings will last. I never want them to go away. I try to keep them going for as long as I can.

"Sometimes then I do too much. I get excited about feeling good. I have lunch with people, try to take on a new project or activity, plan a trip to a conference. I lose steam and feel bad about myself, feel like I'm a loser, and the whole thing starts over again. I'm back on my island, waiting for the bad feelings to pass."

Grasping the mind's capacity to retreat is complex, and describing the images of this problem-solving phantasy is sometimes embarrassing. Challenging its sneaky and tricky operations takes much time. Angela continued, "I can really see that I'm doing the exact same thing that I did as a child. I feel frightened and scared, and sit alone, and wait. I wait alone, all alone, for hours and days."

Angela had a look on her face, as if to tell me, "This is hitting too close to home." I suspected it was. Talking about one's retreat feels destabilizing. For the first time, a very private, often wordless, way of dealing with pain and need is exposed and questioned; at the same time, a new response to pain tolerance is yet to be discovered. Is the retreater willing and able to continue this conversation? Can he trust the therapist as a co-journeyman during his search? Is the therapist willing to learn along the way?

Angela's Retreat

Angela started retreating in our therapeutic relationship. Her divorce attorneys demanded payment of a large sum of money for their services. She announced,

"I need to reduce our sessions from twice a week to once a week. It's a huge amount of money, and I need to conserve. I want to recoup this loss. It will just be for a while, I think." Something felt off.

I was suspicious for several reasons. Angela was living with agonies, and I had recently suggested more treatment, not less. She was a patient who usually welcomed clinical interventions, adopted treatment suggestions that made sense, and valued the consistency of hard work and growth. I suspected there was something powerful driving her decision to abandon her self-care patterns. I imagined our retreat discussion had something to do with this. I sensed it felt an overwhelming and overpowering conversation, an intrusion of her privacy. Too much exposure now needed too much retreat.

I gently probed, "I want to make sure I understand your thinking here." I paused. Angela continued, "I'm worried about the money. It's a big chunk of change. I am pulling back everywhere. Ultimately, I will be okay. It will just be a while here. I'll come back to twice a week." She looked sly as she changed her course, "And, you know, I want to see what I can do with all this pain myself. I think it would be good for me to figure that out alone. I don't want to be in therapy for the rest of my life."

The residents had her in their grip; she was cooperating with their instructions. We sat in silence.

I gently offered, "I understand your financial anxiety—it's a large sum; it's your money and your decision. I do think, however, there's something worth considering here. During a very painful and difficult time in your life, you are proposing less treatment and support, not more. We know that you are used to staying alone and trying to figure out things yourself. We both know it got you through miserable moments in your childhood. We also know it doesn't always help you in the long run."

I said this with a deep feeling of respect for Angela's urgent need to retreat. I was also clinically compelled to invite her to challenge this unhealthy alliance and allegiance. She listened, took it in, and said, "I'll think about what you said. It does make sense. But I think I want to be cautious with my finances. It's a real concern, you know." Her emotional life was a real concern too. She politely left the session.

Angela was suffering with need and was struggling with how to be dependent in our relationship. Could she tolerate the vulnerability of dependency? Would she allow me to provide containment for her agonies? Or would she need to circumvent these "humiliations" and shelter instead in the perverse protection of her retreat?

I imagined her allies shouting new instructions: "You've talked enough already. You told her too much about us and the way we work to protect you from pain.

You don't need to reveal anything more about your sadness or tell her that you don't understand how to handle it. Remember, it's all about being strong and tough.

"Your financial worries are real too. You do need to cut back on therapy. It makes sense. We know that. You are being responsible here. Margy doesn't get that. Don't get bullied by her. Do what you want to do. Don't let her intimidate you or push you around like your mother did. You have to stand up to her. Trust us. We have always steered you in the right direction, haven't we? After all, she's just a therapy junkie; she likes all this ridiculous talking, and remember, all she really wants is your business. She just wants to get more money out of you."

They probably continued, "Don't give in to her. If you do, you'll lose your way. This is critical here: No matter what she says, say no. It's time to assert yourself. You only need to meet once a week. You have a right to decide your own way. We know you feel like it will be a good thing. We are behind you."

Perverse Protection

The next session, Angela began, "At first, I was scared to bring this issue up, but as the session got closer, I was looking forward to standing up to you." She appeared flushed with anxiety but continued, "A couple of times in the past months, I've requested that we meet less often, and you have always responded that you don't think it's a good idea. I always went along with it because I respected you and your ideas. You're the professional; you have the experience. You always sounded helpful, yet I always felt bullied. I didn't say anything at these times, but now things feel different. I don't want to feel bullied. I hear what you say about more sessions. It does make sense on one level because I'm not feeling so good, but for now I just want to come in once a week. That's what I want to do. I want to see how I can figure things out by myself."

I went into reverie as I listened. Much was involved here. I was clinically convinced that Angela would benefit from more treatment. I was saddened by her decision to deprive herself of healthy dependency and care. She retreated in pain and panic. She had revealed too much to me and, in the process, dangerously loosened her grip on herself. Life outside a retreat feels like a treachery; life inside a retreat feels like a fidelity.

Angela came to our weekly sessions on time; she "reported" the torture she felt she had to endure. She was living in her retreat yet was still able to tolerate some connection between us. There was growth, even in our distance. Steiner (1993) reminds us that retreaters are often able to keep sufficient contact with reality while, at the same time, evading it (p. 12). I waited with respect, and I worried about her between sessions. I carefully worded an e-mail. "Have been wondering how things are going for you? I'm around."

Finding Herself

Angela fastened in and onto her protector's imperatives: "Your decision to come into treatment one time a week is just fine. We will take care of you. You don't need to pay attention to how bad you really feel, and you don't need to be worried. We will be with you at home. Remember, just wait on the island until things get perfect. Listen to us, and we will make sure that happens."

It was important for Angela to live with the sense that she was in charge of her suffering, to feel that I understood her need to retreat. It was just as important that she feel me waiting for her to return.

She frantically grasped for my gaze when I greeted her in the waiting room. She said, "After this much sobriety, I should be in a different place. One part of me is sad that I'm depressed and unmotivated. So many days this week I compulsively watched TV. I wanted to stop, but I couldn't. I can't jog, I can't walk the dog, I can't return my e-mails, or even listen to my phone messages. I go to my recovery groups, but don't feel like talking. I'm so upset. Another part of me doesn't care; another part of me is put off by how I am. I'm mad about all this, and I'm mad about the way I am and function. I should know better and do better by now. Damn all this."

Angela suffered greatly in between our weekly appointments. She lay on my office couch in exhaustion. She looked puffy and tired, preoccupied, worried, and frightened. She nervously described days of sleeping, nights of restlessness, not eating, and bingeing on junk food. She described spacing out too much and doing too little. She was pensive with pain, tragically twisted in her isolated mind, and overwhelmed with bad feelings.

Eventually one afternoon, she quietly offered, "I haven't been feeling well at all, and I'm beginning to look at the evidence. The evidence says that I've been doing poorly, even badly, since I reduced our number of sessions. My plan is not going so well. I am not better off. As a matter of fact, I am sinking deeper into depression. I'm beginning to see that I can't escape these facts. Yet there's another part of me that doesn't care about this evidence. I want to ignore it so I can stick with my decision to only see you once a week. I really don't want to give in. I don't want to feel bullied. I can figure this out alone. I want to stick to my plan."

Angela looked at me, sat quietly with herself for a few minutes, and cried for the first time in weeks. She said, with soft tears, "I really can't trust you, and I don't feel that I can listen to what you think is best for me." She looked at me with sad and pleading eyes. "This is crazy, though, really crazy. I'm not doing well, and I know it. Therapy is supposed to help me. That's why I am here. But I am so scared that if I give in, I'll feel like I didn't win, and I'll feel like I lost. This is all so hard." Angela was burdened by her needs and was now starting to feel conflicted about her retreated responses to them. She was questioning the island people's authority. What would she do? How could I support her terrifying ambivalence?

I listened in reverie, and eventually intervened, "How about trying this on, Angela? This all feels so very similar to your childhood. I imagine an afternoon when your mom beat you and after she was done, you slumped against the wall in hurt, terror, and disbelief. You were all alone and didn't know what to do, and there was no one you trusted to ask for help. You went upstairs, alone, to your room. So many times, you were stuck trying to figuring things out all by yourself. You were very determined, and I think you felt you were very good at taking care of yourself all by yourself.

"And I think you've been trying to do the same thing in the last weeks. To take care of yourself in the same way . . . all by yourself. I imagine you, in your apartment, just zoned out in pain, suffering and frozen. It doesn't seem like you have a sense that you can reach out and call me or anyone else and ask for help. It doesn't seem like you feel that is a useful idea at all. I sense your retreated mind is repeating the same childhood message, 'No matter how bad it feels, the only thing to do is just wait it out 'til it passes.'"

Angela was listening. We sat in silence for a while, and then I wondered aloud, "Do you want to wait it out or do something else?"

Venturing Out and Returning

Angela looked at me, and said, "I'm not sure, I'm really not sure, but I'll tell you something: Talking like this with you feels good." She lay back on the couch, looked momentarily content, and said, "You know, I feel like a little girl talking to my mom, and it's cool, really cool. We're just talking and nobody's mad, and we're just trying to figure things out. I like it." She was tearing up and smiling with a fullness. "I never got to do this, just talk about what's going on and try to figure out what's the best thing to do.

"This feels so different, so good." Angela was crying as she whispered, "I can't believe I'm about to say this, but as I sit here, I'm even thinking about changing my decision to wait another month until I start seeing you twice a week again. I'm even thinking that it's a smart thing to do, that it would help and that I need it, and that it might even feel good. I hate to admit I need help. I hate admitting that; I hate it. But that's what's going on." She stared off, and then sat up. "And, to tell you the truth, financially, I can do it. I can pull it off. I don't have to wait." Then she waffled, slyly grinned, and said, "But I've got to think about this because I don't want to be bullied. I need some time to see if this feels right."

I encouraged her to do just that. Angela's turtle head returned inside its shell as quickly as it had ventured out. She experienced moments of ecstasy in her relationship with me. She revealed as much as she could, felt as much as she could tolerate. She needed the protection of her retreat. She returned to her residence, and I waited outside.

Looking at an Old Solution, Considering New Ones

Angela returned to her retreat with a vengeance. Her incapacity was visible. She came in over the next couple of weeks, looking wrecked and feeling bad. I listened to her stories of immobility and despair. She wondered about medication adjustments. I responded, "I don't think pharmacology is the treatment needed here."

After much in-between session reverie, I offered, "I think this is about paying more attention to that evidence you discovered recently—those facts that pointed out that you felt worse when you pulled away from your therapy and our relationship, that things got more painful as you tried to figure things out on your own. Angela, I think this is all about figuring out how you want to face and work with your tendency to retreat when your pain feels unbearable, when withdrawing seems natural. I think this is about being willing to look at this old solution for what it is and what it really does.

"I know you wanted to save money, and I know that you hoped that you could push through all this pain on your own. I know you are trying to help yourself in ways that have always worked, but you recently said that it's not working, and I agree. I've witnessed and watched so much of your daily suffering. It's felt very destructive lately, destructive to your health, well-being, and recovery. I feel I need to help you out here, Angela, and help you get through something. I want to help you get unstuck from your old solutions to pain. I sense that you have been willing to think more about this lately and to look at your suffering and how you handle it. I want to put something out there.

"I believe you will feel more connected to yourself, and possibly feel better, if you and I talked more frequently. Our conversations might help you figure out something different to do with your pain. Let's consider meeting or touching base more often over the next two weeks. Let's see what making that contact will do; let's see how that connection will feel. Let's see how you respond and where you go with it." She looked slightly worried and gestured for more information—"How will that work?"

"Let's work it out together." And we did. Together we tentatively designed a treatment schedule geared toward more regular contact. It started with three days of scheduled 10- to 15-minute brief check-ins. Angela tolerated these connections. We gently probed the value of participating in a women's group. "I know you talked about the possibility of joining one of my biweekly women's groups. You said you wanted something more than the crosstalk of an AA meeting. You've said that you want to connect with some of the recovering addicts in the group, that you want conversations and more back-and-forth with these women. These are options to consider." Angela looked at me with interest and said, "These may be helpful; I'll consider them."

After six days of check-ins, Angela admitted with reluctance and reservation, "I think this is working. I think I feel slightly better." She seemed more comfortable in her skin, and she felt more comfortable to be around for the first time in weeks. She also decided to join one of my women's groups.

Resilience

Shortly after these changes and additions, Angela walked into my office with a feeling of reserved relief. She sat on the couch with dignity and a faint sense of hope. Angela was proud of our rhythms. She liked the way things happened between us. She felt respected and understood. She held on to her retreat until she discovered its shortcomings. She responded to some suggestions, but on her own terms. She walked away from her retreated allies when she was ready to tolerate some healthy dependency with me.

Our work was working. Angela's sobriety was intact, and her retreating ways had been identified. She tolerated their discovery and dared to reveal their precious operations. Over the next month, she was attracted to their promises, but let go of their hateful protections. She went inside those familiar walls, but often came out to try something new. She held on to them and then let go. She insisted on testing out her own ways and also owned any failures. She volunteered her true feelings and tolerated more real connection. Our relationship had endured a transformation, often too tender to talk about. She knew and I knew that she was opening herself to an unknown. She finally wanted a relationship with another human being to support her uncertainty and growth.

Angela was young and single, determined and ambitious, educated and smart. She was sober and had gained considerable self-awareness of her complex and debilitating responses to the pain in her life. She didn't want to retreat anymore; we worked on other responses to her pain. She cautiously flourished over a six-month period. We met weekly, and she joined my women's group. She cleaned her apartment; she got out in the world. She did better with her studies, and she talked more in recovery meetings. "I'm so relieved to not feel so bad. I can't even remember how horrible it felt."

Angela benefited from my knowledge, appreciation, and respect for John Steiner's original contributions on the mind's use of a psychic retreat to survive suffering.

I sensed its presence as I hovered around her early recovery responses to pain. Increasing distance between us and her persistent aloneness provided useful clues. I soon identified retreating as her drug of choice during this stage of recovery. Clinical finesse, respect for her choices, and patience seemed to contain her. She slowly developed a tolerance for her needs and a willingness to be vulnerable in our relationship. She cautiously began to feel some pleasures in relating to others. The world of people had finally opened up for Angela. Retreating would always feel alluring; however, she was willing to struggle for a healthier, more satisfying alternative.

CHAPTER SUMMARY AND REFLECTIONS

Summary

Early recovery explores the fit of the addict's environment and the state of his mind. This chapter asks the reader to consider a complex aspect of the mind that is camouflaged while under the influence and makes itself known during early recovery.

This chapter proposed that a clear understanding of the functions and facets of a psychic retreat, developed by psychoanalyst John Steiner, are needed to truly grasp the struggle and suffering of the patient during this stage.

Clinical cases suggested ways that the reader might begin to understand how a psychic retreat manifests itself in the mind of a recovering addict during this developmental stage. Therapeutic action moments suggest ways to identify a retreat's operations, connect with its functions, and encourage the patient to accept and understand these old solutions to suffering and vulnerability that prevent recovery and growth.

Reflections

Before leaving this chapter, make sure you:

- Know the primary and secondary tasks of the early recovery stage
- Have a solid understanding of the key theories and concepts presented
- Have examined their individual merit and critically analyzed and discussed your intuitive clinical responses to their application in therapeutic action moments in the clinical cases of this stage
- Have begun to design your own integrative treatment approach for this stage
- Are willing to read and reread this chapter

Chapter 12

The Integrative Treatment Model

The Ongoing Recovery Stage

Figure 12.1 The Ongoing Recovery Stage

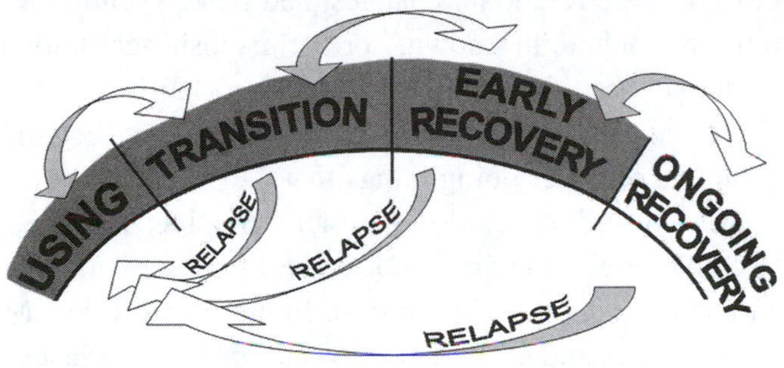

INTRODUCTION

Ongoing recovery is the last formal stage in addiction treatment. The migration of an identity is nearly complete. Sobriety or moderation seems secure on a conscious and unconscious level, wobbly legs are now sturdy, and a thinking mind feels better than a retreating mind. Adjustments and alterations in the environment feel familiar. The ongoing recovery addict holds memories of a tortured and destructive past, yet he lives with a tremendous amount of gratitude for the present. Living without the preoccupations of alcohol and other drugs (AOD) brings such freedom. Time's availability gives birth to new pockets of meaning. Family, friends, work, and new passions are nurtured and appreciated, long spared the ravages of drinking and drug episodes.

Many in this stage continue their ongoing involvement with, and loyalty to, Alcoholics Anonymous (AA). A special place in one's life is devoted to giving service, welcoming newcomers, and sponsoring deeper step work. Others continue in their psychotherapy or psychoanalysis with an ongoing commitment to explore the suffering underneath their addictions, as well as address new perplexities in living. In the process, addicts develop more psychological skills and deepen their experiential capacity. Years of sober living and allegiance to a recovery style finally bear a confidence. Addicts in this stage begin to imagine unknown futures and dream unimaginable possibilities.

A solidly sober identity is able to work through historical traumas that were held in abeyance during earlier stages of recovery. Unresolved historical issues surface while addressing career malaise, marital distance, or the raising of children. Deeper conflicts are exposed in relationships with employers and work colleagues as well as during the stresses of birth, illness, and death. Most are interested and willing to explore those parts of the past that still aggravate the present.

The working through of these conflicts brings emotional relief. What was repressed is released; some energy is now freed up and available to use. New ways of experiencing one's self encourage more risk taking, tolerance of more intense feeling states promotes relational changes, and new psychological capacities permit reflecting on "unthought known," or the dispositional knowledge of the true self that has not yet been thought (Bollas, 1989, p. 10).

Many in this stage of treatment begin to question what they thought they would never question and consider doing things that they thought they would never consider. Over time, the addict explores a more creative, flexible, and imaginative relationship with himself, one that is not as rigidly prescribed, planned, or premeditated. Psychotherapy conversations turn to future possibilities. Many are ready to experience new desires and execute new wishes during this last stage of treatment.

Ongoing recovery's primary tasks are twofold:

- **Listening** for the addict's idiomatic or unique expressions and **fostering the development** of his destiny or future
- **Incorporating clinical concepts** such as *the context of destiny, true self, idiom, village of living objects, ruthless usage, the context of fate* and *the false self*

Other tasks include:

- *Deepening* of psychodynamic or psychoanalytic therapy
- *Exploring* choices and meanings of intimacy, sexuality, and gender identity
- *Including* clinical concepts and treatment interventions from Chapters 9, 10, and 11

This chapter is divided into two sections. *Clinical Concepts* provides an overview of the British psychoanalyst Christopher Bollas's work on fate, destiny, and idiom development (refresh your memory about his theory in Chapter 7, p. 107). *Clinical Cases* demonstrates applications of these concepts in clinical cases.

Clinical Concepts is an attempt to imaginatively synopsize and integrate Bollas's exciting work into this last stage of recovery, as well as addiction treatment in general. Bollas provides treatment providers with clinical theories and interventions that exquisitely complement the addict's identity evolution during the ongoing recovery stage. His theories provide in-depth understanding of the addict's fated existence during his youth, using, and early recovery days, as well as his rediscovery of his destiny during this last stage of treatment. This overview includes two descriptions of developmental contexts of growth. The first is a favorable one, fostering the development of the child's sense of destiny. It describes a parental or caretaking environment that is delightfully devoted to the facilitation of a child's potential expressiveness and ultimately his sense of well-being in his own life. The second is an unfavorable one, resulting in the child's resignation to his discouraging world. It describes an environment filled with multiple parental or caretaking injunctions and commandments. These drown out the child's potential as well as his sense of his future. Many addicts feel fated in their early childhood and further fated in their addictions. Bollas (1989) encourages treatment providers to listen for the recovering addict's relationship to his sense of fate as well as his sober rediscovery of his sense of destiny (pp. 31–37).

Clinical Concepts also presents some of Mike Eigen's analytic elaborations. Eigen (1998) creatively furthers D. W. Winnicott's notions of the false self and the true self. These are very useful in capturing the nuanced false self-expressions of the fated child and, later, addicted adult. Eigen's work also reminds us to listen for the rediscovery of the true self during the ongoing recovery stage.

Clinical Cases focuses on the applications of these concepts in addiction treatment in therapeutic action moments in three clinical case studies. Alexandra, Rose, and James were solidly sober when I heard their idioms murmur for receptivity, encouragement, and containment. Their detailed histories poignantly portray their efforts to endure and survive fated childhoods, adolescence, and addicted adulthoods. Their ongoing recovery journeys reflect their courageous efforts to assertively promote their futures and their dreams.

Reading Guidelines

This chapter identifies a mix of theories and treatment concepts, therapeutic skills, and clinical caveats that are useful to understand and also apply during the addict's travels on ongoing recovery's terrain. This mix of concepts, skills, and caveats is for treatment providers to match with their own intuition, their own clinical style, and their patient's particular recovery path. Past and ongoing clinical cases put theory to practice in therapeutic action moments. A clinician prepared for ongoing recovery's primary and secondary tasks invites the addict to do the same. Study these ideas; make them useful in your own life, and also yours to use during recovery treatment; develop a tolerance for the unfamiliar; and go at your own pace as your mind struggles and then rests.

CLINICAL CONCEPTS

The Context of Destiny, True Self, Destiny, Idiom, Village of Living Objects, and Ruthless Usage

An infant marches forward into his destiny if he believes his true self, or inner essence, is seen and nourished by important people in his world. Bollas (1989), citing Winnicott, defines the infant's true self as his inherited potential that exists only in experiencing (pp. 8, 213). This experiencing is mercilessly dependent on the mother (or primary caretaker). The infant's inherited disposition needs her love and devotion as well as her interest and generosity. These encourage spontaneous expression of his being.

Ongoing contact with an attentive and intuitive mother enables him to have ongoing contact with his real essence. He feels safe to be, safe to explore, safe to share his unique approach to living. The infant's object world, then, is facilitating core self-expressiveness. The child flourishes and feels a delight in living (Bollas, 1989, p. 10).

If all goes well, the child, and then later adolescent, continues to experience his caretakers as regularly responsive to his true personality and its potential. This back-and-forth feels validating and brings forth more spontaneity. He continues to feel good, and a continuity of his being continues. The child discovers the rhythms of his own way. He experiences a sense of his unique personality progressing. He feels he is steering his own life. A destiny drive is born. Bollas (1989) refers to this as the urge within each person to articulate and elaborate his idiom through the selection and use of caretakers (objects) in his environment (pp. 8, 41, 211).

The idiom of a person refers to the unique nucleus of each individual (Bollas, 1989, p. 24). This specialness exists inside of each of us and expresses itself in dreams, personal myths, daydreams, and visions of the future (p. 35). This brand of uniqueness needs favorable environmental conditions to evolve and thrive. The child of his destiny innocently, unknowingly believes the world is there to support his defining essence. He freely moves forward, often engaged in a mission without words. He dreams; he skips steps (p. 197). He has a faith in the goodness of living. He is cautious but not afraid. His falterings are disappointing, but they feel only temporary. He moves on with what he wants to do. He knows it is right and good, for himself, others, and the world. He is an energized, grateful, and focused child (pp. 9–10).

The young idiomic resides within a village of living objects that have the potential to further his future (Bollas, 1989, p. 9). His keen eyes survey his surroundings. He senses what he needs, and he relies on others. He hopes his caretakers share his vision and steer him in the right direction. He looks for other people and things that will elaborate his creative strivings, provide the right conditions to evolve his idiom (p. 34). These may include coaches and teachers, preachers or therapists, mentors or advisers, as well as books, music, films, the Internet, sport, religion, and the like (p. 18). All of these help to establish a young personality that feels real and alive (p. 34).

Bollas (1989) identifies the essential ruthlessness of a child of his destiny (p. 42). The child feels free to assert his needs and aggressively express his wishes. He uses members of his living village for satisfaction and fulfillment of these. *This ruthless use of people and things is different than ruthlessly using them.* It is not harsh or selfish. Rather, it is a usage filled with confidence, purpose, focused determination, and gratitude (p. 30).

This young person feels free enough to be playfully punitive with important village friends. The latency child responds to his mother's confusing comments about a story he wants to publish: "You've got to be kidding. That's not the point. Mom, that's not what my story means at all. You don't even understand what I've written." His mother plays back, "Hey, hey! Are you calling me stupid? Now, now here. Stop that; show some respect. After all, I am your mother." The mother seems to place his "disrespect" in the context of her son's creative conviction—his belief in the rightness of his story. She understands and celebrates his ruthless aggression, and in doing so, she encourages continuation of the boldness of his dreams.

The ruthless young adult, filled with idiomatic urges, is besotted with his destiny. He seeks out the respected, questions the accomplished, and is not intimidated by power or fame. He recruits meaningful support and projects his future wishes onto others. These mentors are not offended by his boldness. They believe in the dreamer's belief in himself. They remember being supported for their dreaming; they want to return the favor. The young dreamer feels fortunate to be surrounded by such a supportive village. His style of appreciation reflects his confidence; his reciprocity is never overdone.

People of destiny are people we all know who are passionate about what they are doing in life and confident in how they relate to others. They ruthlessly choose schools and careers, mentors and advisers, friends and partners, cities and countries (Bollas, 1989, p. 42). They rely on their village to help them fulfill their dreams. They are not too selfish or too self-centered. They are very determined and aggressive. They are in touch with their true essence and unique destiny, and they seem to find their fortune. They usually achieve good things for self and others, if they stay true to their true sense of self.

The Context of Fate and False Self

If all does not go so well, an infant, child, and then later adolescent lives in a different kind of caretaking world. Spontaneous expressions of his true self are rejected or ignored. He does not feel safe to be, or safe to explore his essence and his world. Family moods and practices dictate an acceptable way of being instead (Bollas, 1989, p. 214). He feels compelled to adjust to this climate and does the best he can with the provisions provided. His true self adapts by going underground and also designs a self that is acceptable to the whispering or shouting in the walls of his household. His real voice feels fated to an anxious silence, and his life to endurance and survival.

Early on, he gets the sense that his natural responses and spontaneous expressions feel too much or too little, annoying or disgusting, pathetic or inadequate to others. He starts to feel that something is really wrong with his inner essence and core being (Eigen, 2009, pp. 77–79). He gets the sense that his caretakers convey an important message—"Life would be easier for us, and better for you, if you were different, if you would only adjust your ways of being." He feels tragically fated to adopt this message and comply with its orders.

The child, and then later adolescent, who is raised in this environment lives in a world of commandments. These are experienced as drastic demands dictated by his caretaker. These commands most often have nothing to do with his true self or inner essence. The child feels required to think a certain way, choose certain friends, attend certain schools, and dress in certain ways. These declarations feel topsy-turvy to his sense of self, but he feels fated to follow them anyway (Bollas, 1989, p. 45). A person who feels fated does not experience reality as conducive to the fulfillment of his idiom (p. 33). A sense of despair shadows his world. He loses all interest in the search for objects that will help his real personality progress. Profound sorrow fuels days of empty endurance. He feels fated to live a life that he is not really connected to. Without this connection, he is unable to steer for himself (p. 45).

A false sense of self develops, organized around the wishes, defenses, and dictates of others. A child feels terrible inside, but obedience to others ensures some kind of connection with the outside. A false self also needs a village of objects to thrive. Sadly, they are not "living" objects. They nurture a contorted sense of his true self that serves as the child's early guide and, more often than not, continues designing his life into adulthood (Bollas, 1989, p. 26). This false self-individual feels fated and despairingly moves forward. He knows no other way.

Mike Eigen (1998), in his book *The Psychoanalytic Mystic*, elaborates on our understanding of a false self. He describes an inauthentic expression of self that has two horns. One horn has a toughness to its edge; another horn is driven by a compulsion to please. It seems an individual's false self-expression can rely on one horn or a blend of both (p. 55).

A certain disposition develops a toughness to handle the horror of parental rejection. This toughness ensures everyday survival and brings a feeling of temporary triumph. This false self screams, "I can and I will!" (Eigen, 1998, p. 55). This sense of bravado persuades the true self to retreat in silence. It is seduced into protective submission. This shelter permits a way of functioning. Eigen reminds us that toughness can be counted on to maintain a sense of aliveness (p. 56). Careers are chosen, marriages are entered, and children are born from this deceptively determined, yet wayward, self-organization. These solutions bring moments of aliveness that can go on for years and decades. Sadly, they are based on self-fraudulence and conformity to social expectations.

The true self despairs its exile, and eventually the horn of toughness grows weary of its job. The individual lives with an empty heart and with frustration at the very core of his being (Bollas, 1989, p. 33). What has been accomplished in work and love can no longer be sustained. The fatigue cannot be avoided, and more often than not one's entire being fades out and goes under (Eigen, 1998, p. 57).

Another person's disposition develops a compliance as a way to respond to the pressures he feels to falsify his inner essence. Pleasing people and getting along with others ensure his everyday survival. The compliant individual discovers that being easy brings peace to his world. This false self screams, "I please and I placate." The compliant self finds safety and security in not being a burden, of any kind, to his caretaker. He learns to be loyal to others' wishes at the expense of his own. His school peers and friends, teachers, and co-workers take advantage of this willingness to cater. He marries to serve his partner. He parents to satisfy his child's every wish. His sense of sacrificial nobility muffles the intensity of his inner despair. Eventually, this compliant expression fatigues and fades out as well (Eigen, 1998, pp. 56–57).

The fated false self lives with a tension that feels excruciating and unreachable. The child doesn't know how to talk about his distress. His true self turns fatefully ill without a chance to express its inner essence. His idiom has no pulse, his destiny no course. Objects are picked that play along with the horns. Village residents are used with weary resignation, not assertive ruthlessness. He lives in a life of prolonged drudgery and loneliness.

Drugs and alcohol provide much comfort for the fated individual. He "ruthlessly" and repeatedly selects these as a reliable source of soothing and reprieve for his nameless dread (Bion, 1967, p. 116). The alcohol or drugs persuasively quiet his longing for true self expressions in his real life. They repeatedly reverse ongoing feelings of false self fraudulence. AOD seems the perfect complement to his painful, prescribed way of living without belief in the possibility of an alternative future. "I can live in this tough or compliant world if I'm protected by Vicodin or fortified with alcohol." A fated childhood, adolescence, and adulthood are now fated by addictive consumption.

Henry David Thoreau says that so many individuals in our culture live lives of quiet desperation (*Walden Pond*). They also live with addictions.

Implications for Treatment

Clinicians and the recovery treatment world are at a loss without a sense of Bollas's work, particularly in ongoing recovery. He provides a framework of infant and childhood development that is aligned with the development of an ongoing recovering identity. Eigen's elaborations on the true self and false self are both simpatico and complementary to Bollas's work.

In earlier stages of recovery, addicts need a treatment relationship that provides safety and direction, guidance and support. Saying no to years of using and staying sober are absolutely daunting. The work is grim and vigilant, the rebuilding arduous, the rewards slow. The solid identity of the ongoing recovery addict tentatively searches for object usage that allows inner essence expression, fosters idiomatic yearnings, and encourages destiny desires. Sober addicts respond to attentive hovering by important others, particularly ongoing recovery therapists. An available and trained ear hears a fragile essence yearning for a chance to express itself without fear of rejection or dismissal, commandments or dictates.

The therapist gently hovers around an individual who barely believes he has a life beyond his fated sense of duty, endurance, and survival. The ongoing recovery addict needs to believe that his wishes are worth expressing. Therapeutic hovering encourages their articulation. Footsteps of the true self are soon seen; voices of a future vision are faintly heard. Bollas (1989) urges therapists to consider being open to different usages based on the addict's expressions of these new dreams. "I feel one use of me is succeeded by another, in a movement of uses" (p. 111).

Later, Bollas articulates the therapist's task—the forces of destiny require an object world prepared for its use, and a child (/addict) can only elaborate his idiom through those objects provided for him by his parents (/therapists). The addict needs this receptive containment. It takes time for him to trust that his spontaneity is not impulsive, that his desires are not reckless. It takes time to learn that risking is not abandoning practicality. It takes even more time to know and trust the levity of living that begins to be felt in ongoing recovery.

The pace and rhythm of ongoing recovery treatment develop some buoyancy. A sober confidence yearns for fanciful exploration of dreams and fantasies. If listening occurs, the formerly fated child, later masquerading as an adult with the elixir's false protections, soon begins to explore an unimaginable life of his wishes. It requires the fortune of staying drug-free, as well as focused determination, and a long, steady road of very bewildering and difficult recovery work. It also requires some healthy assertion and aggression to get what you need, and certainly attempt to take what you want (Bollas, 1989, p. 31).

On to clinical cases, to see how this mix of treatment concepts, therapeutic skills, and clinical caveats has been applied in therapeutic action moments.

CLINICAL CASES

Alexandra

Early Fates, False Self, and Idiom Wishes

Alexandra was 52 years old when she began recovery for "my wine and champagne addiction." She was born and raised in Western Europe. Over five years of treatment, she told me of her fated childhood. She lived in an apartment with her parents and older sister until she was 3. Her true self wanted more time with her parents; she didn't know how to influence them with her wish. She felt betrayed and lost when the family grew bigger. "The family energy changed when we moved into a building with my extended family. Each family had their own apartment. Nothing was right after that. I have no happy memories of my childhood. I really didn't get to see my parents, and I don't think they ever got to know me."

Her father developed obsessions about "something." Alexandra remembers his preoccupations with the next-door neighbor turning to violence. She was four years old. She didn't understand what was happening, and she was scared of his anger. She remembers his bulging eyes. He had a "nervous breakdown" and was in a psychiatric institution for a year. When he returned home, "I never knew if he was going to explode. I lived in fear of his moods. I kept a tight lid on myself. My mother kept threatening him, 'I'm going to lock you up if you get crazy again.'"

Alexandra felt so unimportant to her parents. "They seemed to forget their job as mother and father to me. I felt like I didn't matter to them. It was a terrible feeling, and I didn't know what to do." She lived with a sense of badness. She longed for her mother's touch and her father's approval. She got neither.

Alexandra lived within the tragedy of a fated childhood. She lived with incomprehensible terrors that no one explained to her. She felt bad most of her childhood and was unable to influence her parents in any way. Her true self went into hiding when she realized that she could not talk about her worries or express her wishes. Her physical self hid behind a table in the dark hallway of her home most of the time. "I hoped they would find me—they never even looked." Her true essence was never connected to; her idiomatic desires were buried.

Alexandra's early false self showed signs of toughness. She was raised with two boy cousins. Her aunt, uncle, and father favored them. Alexandra felt hurt; she began to feel unimportant because she wasn't a boy. Her "I can and I will" false self went to work. She believed there might be some relief in fighting her gender. She tried to emulate her cousins. She wore little boy pants, and she hoped that her father would find her important. "I couldn't find my place in my family, so I thought if I acted and dressed like a boy, my father would notice me."

Children like Alexandra cannot make sense of the pain that comes from living in such an inhospitable climate, one that is unwelcoming to their unique existence. They are scared to express themselves and can't articulate their needs. They go underground instead. Even in early infancy and childhood, they design a scheme, a false self guide. This fabricated expression of self brings hope, and its presentation seems to get a more favorable response from their environment. Their little being feels temporarily buoyed. They feel they have discovered their answer to living: "Try on and out different things, see if they work, and just get through."

By the first grade, Alexandra remembers, "I was already a work of art." She lived with a sense of disgrace through elementary and middle school. She didn't know what to do, how to be, and whom to talk to. She couldn't pay attention in class; she was always distracted. She was never confident among her peers and never prepared with her homework. Alexandra was ridiculed by the nuns often, and she suffered many nosebleeds at their hands. She was always forced to sit in the back row of the classroom. She felt marked and labeled, humiliated and disgraced. "I was in a class with kids born to be good, and I was born to be bad." She began organizing strikes against the nuns and stealing her classmates' snacks. She acted like a bad girl; her tough self pulled her through again.

Alexandra remembers a wonderful day in the third grade. A substitute teacher arrived in class. The assignment was to write a composition about a bird. Alexandra loved writing this essay. She felt so free. The words flowed. It was easy to express her story. Her substitute teacher evidently loved her story as well. She called her up to the front of the class and asked her to sit in the first row. The teacher read her composition aloud in front of the entire classroom. Alexandra remembers, "I couldn't believe that she was real, that she saw me and liked what I wrote. She called me to the front of the class because I was an exemplary girl, not a horrific girl. That was the only time I felt special. It was the only time I felt like I mattered and that I was a good girl. I hold on to that feeling. It is an anchor of sorts. I go back to it when I want to feel joy, even today. I just remember that feeling she gave me about myself, and I know that I have the capacity to feel good and happy."

Self-Medicating a Fated Life

Alexandra prepared to enter high school with the nuns' guidance, "Your daughter is a bright girl, and she has a good mind. However, we can't get anything out of her; she doesn't apply herself." She recalls, "From that point on, I knew that no one was going to help me out. I knew at that moment that my life was all about escaping."

Life became about finding a safe spot. "I defined a safe spot as impulsively moving from one experience to another." Alexandra found a boyfriend, later a girlfriend, and eventually boyfriends and girlfriends. She traveled throughout Europe in high school. She began dabbling in drugs and became more deeply involved with them. There was no joy or purpose; she was fated to her fate. Her tough false self drove her to the edge. She put herself in harm's way, but never took herself to the point of no return.

College was a drug haze. Alexandra ingested lots of pills. Her favorites were downers. She liked drugs that got her "a little high and a little drowsy." She found some pills from Mexico. They were called "Mandras, I think." They were white pills in green wrappers. She took 10 to 12 a day. She was unable to finish college at this time; she did drugs instead. She found heroin and other opiates and became a heroin addict and dealer. She traveled around the world and survived by prostituting and stealing. She had sex with both sexes and relationally dabbled with both as well. She never went home.

A Village of Helpers and Drinkers, and Detox

Alexandra recalls cleanup times throughout those years. These saved her life. She remembers, "Someone always seemed to always take an interest in me." This village of objects provided an apartment and supplied her with methadone. She got a break and was able to breathe, only to return again to her world of destructive safety. She got a kidney infection and had a temperature of 104 degrees. Her friend said, "I'm going to take you to the hospital; you're going to die." Alexandra responded that she did not care. She was in her 20s, and dying did not bother her at all.

Eventually, she found another village of women who wanted to do more than help her through detox. They nursed her to health, helped her get through her college studies, and encouraged her developing love of all things intellectual. She thrived with their support; she managed to start and finish her PhD. These women, one after another, became her family. She liked them a lot. "But they all drank."

While Alexandra never understood drinking, she took it up anyway. She stomached wine with water, while they drank scotch. She pondered alcohol's lack of mystery. She thought the substance stupid; she felt it lacked enchantment. "After all, liquor is sold on every street corner. There is no plot or intrigue to alcohol."

Nonetheless, she was finished with heroin but not finished with her pain. "Addiction, whatever drug you choose, is there to cover up a sense of unworthiness and a life without love." She struggled with both and began a decade-long affair with alcohol. She drank most nights and cultivated an appreciation for alcohol's mediocrity. Champagne bubbles provided a euphoria she remembered, and passing out gave her a blankness she knew. Both mimicked a heroin high. They provided a disconnect she craved. It didn't take much alcohol to take her there. She was hooked on a substitute.

By now, Alexandra was living in southern California. She was a professor, alone, and had her own home. She had dogs she loved and women who became girlfriends. She drank alcohol every night, until one close friend visited and said, "I hate to see you do this to yourself. You are treating yourself so badly. Here is a brochure for a treatment facility that you may want to check out; you may be able to get some help there." Alexandra said that her friend's words coincided with a growing sense inside her that "this is it; it's over now." My name was on the brochure. She called me, and we began our treatment relationship. At 52, she was ready to confront her fated existence.

Alexandra's tough self had a plan. She did not want to go through the pain of her heroin and nicotine withdrawals. She discovered the alcohol detox program of the medical intuitive Rhonda Lenair. She scheduled a weekend session. She went, received her treatments, and lost her cravings and desire for alcohol. The visit was six years ago, and she hasn't had a drop since. In a field where little is proven, all becomes potentially useful. This method was most helpful to Alexandra's recovery.

While her craving was removed, her identity needed evolution. We worked through each of the stages of recovery. Alexandra was numb and detached during the first year, but she showed up religiously. She didn't suffer with threats of relapse; she took up an interest in herself instead. She visited her retreated mind often enough, but she chose not to dwell there.

Eventually, Alexandra wanted to talk about what had happened. She wondered aloud about her family life and childhood wounds. She reconsidered her primary relationship as well as her choice of profession. She became more intrigued by her body's aches and pains and pondered her lonely nature. She explored her sexuality. She traveled back and forth to Europe. She never wanted to drink, and she never did. "That persona is gone." She was sober, busy, and still agitated with herself when her father died. It affected her deeply and altered her life.

Alexandra returned to the United States in a state of deep depression. She was in excruciating pain, yet she refused medication. We struggled together for weeks. The pain was painful to abide by. She cried, she slept, and she wept and writhed in torture. She endlessly reviewed the last days of her father's life, and she collapsed in exhaustion at the end of her day.

Footsteps of the True Self

During this time, Alexandra also repeatedly referred to the ongoing fatigue of being a professor. "Same classes, same meetings, same students, same bureaucracy. I mean, it saved my life after heroin, but I feel so stuck and tired now. I am bored with teaching and bored with academia. I always imagined I would be at the university forever—right now, I can't stomach that possibility. I'm not sure what to do, but this is on my mind a lot now." Alexandra was in ongoing recovery. I started to attentively hover as she repeatedly articulated frustrations and disappointments with her fated choice of a career path. I faintly heard her opening up to a new sense of possibilities. We talked about the twisted path of her career history. We talked about her dissatisfactions. We talked about her real interests.

Alexandra was asked to write a review of a book. She recalled her third-grade substitute teacher and her love of writing. She reconnected to an old essence and her writing flowed. She brought pages to her therapy sessions and wanted to discuss them together. She was intrigued by aspects of a psychoanalytic theory we had touched upon in previous sessions. She wanted to include it in the review. "It feels creative, a stretch. It's something different, and I want to try it out. I want to shake up the way people are thinking." She asked for my help, "If I tell you my ideas, would you be able to help me include this theory in my book review?"

Alexandra's sober identity was migrating through ongoing recovery, and her idiomatic desires were now free to blossom. Her creative assertion was flourishing. Indeed, she was writing the essay again, with the same ease. She was alive in the third grade, and she was sitting in the front row. I felt her spontaneity and enthusiasm; I felt Alexandra's sense of destiny come alive. I became a leading player in her village of objects. She ruthlessly used me during our sessions in many different ways. Bollas (1989) reminds us to be alert and accepting and responsive to these requests. I was an idea collaborator, a theory integrator, a story sounding board, an editor, and a mentor. I was delighted to be used in the furtherance of her future dreams.

Alexandra's review was published and well received. She felt destined to continue. Over four months and right before my weekly eyes, she wrote an entire screenplay. She lived in passionate devotion to her writing 24 hours a day. She completed professional and practical duties and returned with lust to her writing every night. She was excited by her creativity and time flew by in its rapture. She lived with a sense of belonging and significance that she had never felt before. She was not manic; rather, her true self was finally free, her idiomatic urges alive. I witnessed the birth of her destiny.

We played together with her fantasies; we played together for months (Bollas, 1989, p. 74). "This is my heart's work, and this is my chance." She called them "puffy dreams": dreams she had always kept in a drawer, dreams that she never dared to look at. One of her puffy dreams was now released and floating, and Alexandra was writing again. She was flying with future possibilities.

Alexandra was also fortunate to deeply desire sobriety; her recovery identity felt very solid. She said, "I am on the right track for the first time in my life." Her illusions had potential; her omnipotence had a soul. She was determined to write and comfortable with assertion. She attended industry workshops and symposiums on weeknights and weekends. She inhaled new learnings and incorporated them into her script. A once-shy professor was now bold with her new mission. She approached a presenter if she liked the workshop. If she got an ear, she was ready to deliver her story, as well as a written packet of her material. Initial responses were promising. She was buoyed but, not surprisingly, often disappointed. It's a tough business to crack, yet even today she remains undaunted, consistently recruiting new members into her object village and persistently pursuing her dream. She believes in herself, and they believe in her belief. I wouldn't be surprised if her puffy dream became a real dream.

Living Her Life

Alexandra now believed that her life had an evolution that made sense. "I have been building and building, and things are becoming clearer and clearer. Destruction allowed me to survive. There were so many close calls. I'm amazed I didn't die. I am alive now and feel real." Her ongoing recovery countenance felt so different; she oozed desire.

Her sexuality went through some transformations as well. She was clear that she wanted some kind of relationship; she was not particular about the gender. "The person has to be interested in their life and passionate about living it." Alexandra was open to this relational possibility, but her puffy dream was her priority.

"I've experienced so much in my life, and now I feel like I am that 8-year-old girl in the third grade. I have that same feeling, that feeling that I am good and I can write. I want this feeling to stay, not remain fleeting. I took a big, dark detour in my life, and on that detour I saw many things. My life is about experiencing again, but not the kind of experiences I had while in high school, college, or traveling. My safe spots are no longer destructive. I don't look back now; I just look to the future."

Once again, I experienced the celebratory aspects of treatment during ongoing recovery. There is joy in facilitating a patient's reconnection to his true essence, his real being. There is joy in watching previously fated individuals open their eyes to self-experiences they never knew existed. It is joyous to see them plant themselves in future dreams and move with faith to make them happen. It is joyous to see the birth of an idiom that was buried in a tragic existence. It is joyous to see destiny's daring nature soar in a once-deadly addicted heroin addict. It is joyous to see hope reside in Alexandra's heart.

Rose

An Adult with a Fated Childhood

Rose is 45. She is 22 years sober. She is a very active member of Alcoholics Anonymous, attending three meetings a week, and is a sponsor and is sponsored. She has worked through the 12 steps of AA several times. She is also a believer in psychotherapy. I have worked with Rose over a 15-year period. She seeks help during a relational crisis, works hard, and leaves. She returns regularly. More recently, she decided to stay.

Rose's family life was disturbing. Her parents divorced when she was a young child. She was raised in the suburbs of New York by a critical and unforgiving drunken mother and a loving, drunken stepfather. She had several brothers.

Rose's recollection of her childhood is akin to an alcoholic brownout; she remembers only sketchy details. "I remember my grandmother and grandfather's house. It was consistent and loving. They tucked me in tight at night. I had a feeling that all was okay and that my needs were attended to. Things felt good in that house—I had some room to be me. It was fun. I think they liked me." Her grandparents nurtured her true sense of self. Both of her fathers did as well. She loved her ongoing connections with these members of her village of living objects.

Rose cherished her stepdad, even though he drank often and died of cirrhosis of the liver. "He didn't have a 'personality change.' I can live with that." He was kind and consistent; she enjoyed spending time with him. Rose's biological dad was in and out of her childhood. She loved him, but he was preoccupied with drinking as well. He drank daily, stocked the house and garage with wine and alcohol, and traveled with a "traveler" (portable alcohol) during his daily commute home. Since his personality did not change either, his preoccupation with alcohol did not preoccupy her. She loved him and sometimes longed for more, but she felt she couldn't ask and told herself, "It's okay with what I have."

Rose was terrified of her mother and more terrified of her mother's drinking. She described an all-day drunk who started a little before noon, passed out on and off throughout the day, and escalated into violence in the evening. The environment felt "so bad on so many levels."

Rose felt pressured by unfair and unrelenting commandments and demands in her childhood. Every day she was left a chore note—"Mow the lawn, clean the house, cook the dinner, take care of your brothers, and do your homework." Every evening, there was a chore inspection. She can still hear her mother's harsh words through a drunken stupor: "This is not done correctly. You failed your inspection once again. Start from the beginning and repeat this task." Rose was panicked and lived frozen in fear most of the time. She always struggled for breath and developed asthma and allergies. She lived terrified in unprotected emotional space, and in a house that had no locks on the doors or windows. She was unable to sleep at night. She lay awake, preparing for her mother's violent entry into her bedroom. She was dragged from her bed and forced to listen to drunken rants. She felt trapped by her mother, and also developed a tenacity to defy her existence. Rose developed a tough horn to counter this violent treatment of her true essence.

Fated Responses, and Searching for Living Objects

Rose couldn't concentrate in school. She felt, "I must be stupid." She spoke back to her teachers and was unable to finish her homework. By the fifth grade, she was smoking pot and drinking daily with the other kids in the fields. Most of them were "richer than me. I never felt like I fit in, with my matted hair and disheveled dress. The other girls teased me, and the boys didn't like me." She continued, "The only thing that was good was Mrs. Bredlau. She had a reading contest, and I found out that I loved to read books."

Rose felt out of place in her private high school. She was uncomfortable socially and unprepared academically. The girls teased her to tears, and she was always behind in class. Her family life was no better. Her stepfather died suddenly, and no one "helped me understand." She was panicked about losing this parent, friend, and ally. She remembers saying to herself, "Things are really going to get much worse from now on."

Rose's mother's chore list grew longer, and her drinking got worse. "We finally figured out that when she was asleep, she was drunk. We let her sleep and avoided evening inspections. That was a great discovery." Her mother was also intrusive: "She wanted to know everything: who I was talking to, what I was doing at school, and if I was interested in boys. She badgered me with questions. She was drunk, and she was mean. I kept my distance."

"The rich kids had plenty of access to cocaine. Things started to get worse; I was driving drunk, and I was doing lots of drugs." Rose felt desperate. She fantasized that living in a tough neighborhood in New York City would be easier than living at home. She ran away to Harlem in New York City. This got her mother's attention. She was sent to therapy and was quickly pulled out when "I started talking too much about my drunk mother and our home life."

A great thing happened to Rose in high school: She met Peter. He was a good kid from a good family—not too much money and not too much drinking. Rose loved hanging around his house and talking to him every day. He cared about her and listened to what she had to say. He did some drugs but would not get too high; he drank but not too much. They would laugh and have a good time at parties. Peter would always drive her home. Decades later, she fondly recalls, "Peter gave me so much solace during a horrible time in my life. I always felt so safe around him. I could just be me, and it was okay for him. I will always remember him."

A letter she wrote to him in 2010 expresses similar feelings. She wrote from her heart, and he never wrote back. She said she was okay with that.

> Dear Peter,
>
> I have been thinking of you. When I go through big changes, I think back on my teenage and college years and how much you supported me. I still have a deep sense of regret for not being able to get help and stop drinking sooner. I know it was a long time ago, but I still think about all the pain I caused you.
>
> I just wanted to say hello. It would be great to hear how you are doing, but I understand that you might not be comfortable writing back.
>
> In September, I will have 22 years in AA. I am so glad to have a community of others who don't drink and who have found other ways to have fun. I have a lot to be thankful for, but still regret my inability to do a better job in our relationship. I hope you are well and happy.
>
> Always,
> Rose

More History in Her Village of Mixed Objects

Peter and Rose ended up in the same college. She studied hard during the week and partied on weekends. Her drinking got worse; she regularly drank to oblivion. Peter invited Rose to join him in graduate school. She was more interested in drinking and she declined.

Rose had lots of time and lots of space without Peter. She continued her drinking and blacked out on a regular basis. She was hitting her low point with alcohol, her bottom, without Peter's protection. She worked in a restaurant, lived with "a crazy guy who shot up drugs all day," and traveled with *lower companions*; this is an Alcoholics Anonymous term to describe "friends" who bring out the worst, not the best. Rose was living the worst.

Rose was raised in a mixed emotional climate. Her true sense of self felt crushed by some people, yet found support from others. Her mother's violent love affair with alcohol dominated the household. Rose lived in fear and was fated to vigilance. She did chores to perfection and stayed out of her mother's way. Her life was dedicated to circumventing her drunken wrath. She hardened with a toughness; her compliance and obedience were for self-protection, not a desire to please.

Rose screamed, "I can and I will beat this woman." She shut down her heart to her mother, and her mind to learning; became reckless; and used drugs and alcohol at an early age.

All was not lost with Rose, though. She kept her eyes open as she roamed the neighborhood. She watched people, observed families, talked to safe adults, and listened to her friends' stories. She found a village of objects, peopled with people who mattered. Mrs. Bredlau paid attention to her true being, and Rose responded. Her spirit soared with passion about reading, and she soon won every contest. She felt good, liked, and valued. "Mrs. Bredlau believed in me, and I believed in her. I felt important, and my love of reading felt important. I always looked forward to her reading contest, and I couldn't wait to win. I knew I was the best and I felt like I could do anything around Mrs. Bredlau."

This teacher clearly facilitated the evolution of Rose's inner essence and idiomatic desires. Rose felt an excitement she had never felt at home. She imagined success with each reading contest. She had determination and drive, and she felt focused and proud. She experienced the joy and pleasure we feel when our world supports our inner essence and furthers our destiny drive.

Rose's true self was also nurtured by Peter. Her tough false self evaporated around him. She was able to laugh and play, and enjoy his love and protection. She felt free to explore her sexuality with him; she desired his presence. She felt safe to be dependent; she counted on him to help her figure out her young life. She watched his family; she asked a lot of questions. She wasn't embarrassed about her chaotic and drunken home. She shed tears of sorrow, not tears of shame or humiliation. She finally got a chance to feel real in a life that had felt so unreal for so many years.

Rose's idiomatic urges flourished. She got a chance to experience a sense of possibilities; she got a chance to feel that her life might have a future. She discovered some of her talents with Mrs. Bredlau, and she developed a young confidence about intimacy with Peter. Both of these relationships provided an important reprieve from her fated existence. While she remained stunted and frightened inside her home, her weary but also ruthless true self flourished within these relationships. Her true essence grew during these times. These hours and days of aliveness would serve her well in the future.

Thinking About Drinking

Rose's drinking got worse in her 20s. She imbibed every day. She couldn't imagine not. She partied with lower companions, who later became sober higher companions. One of her girlfriends "would not back off." Patty "got in my face all the time and forced me to look at my drinking. I was annoyed at this but also loved her for it. I couldn't believe someone would stick with me and not back down." Patty was the higher companion who got her thinking about what she was doing with her life.

Rose kept on drinking, though, and found her way to acupuncture. Jay was also a therapist. He was another person in a village of objects who responded to her essence, and she responded back. She and Jay talked about her childhood, her pain, and her future. She liked talking to him, and she asked him, "Do you think I'm an alcoholic?" She can't remember his response; she was only glad that she felt safe enough to pose the question. She kept talking to Jay and thinking about her drinking.

Rose started to find support groups. She went to Al-Anon meetings for the families of alcoholics. She liked them. She was perturbed by her eating and disturbed by her body. She went to Overeaters Anonymous meetings for bulimics and anorexics. She liked the people and felt kinship and community. She was looking for a home in many new houses.

Rose's higher companion friends tricked her about an upcoming trip. She thought she was attending a work conference—it turned out to be an AA convention. Rose vividly remembers standing outside the convention hall and saying to herself, "Finally, finally, I can admit what's going on." Her dogged friend, Patty, responded to the expression on Rose's face: "Finally, you get it." That was Rose's transition moment forward. She became an active member of AA and she remains active, committed, and very involved to this day.

Rose reunited with her biological father, who had also stopped drinking. They talked sobriety struggles and shared stories; she cherished their closeness. It was a dream relationship come true; it went on for eight years. She was devastated when he suddenly died: "It was the worst thing that I have ever been through in my life." She thinks that the loss of her dad instigated the end of her five-year marriage. His absence reminded her of the emptiness she experienced with her husband.

Rose recommitted to a strong recovery program during her grief but felt she needed professional help. She began therapy with me at this time. She mourned her father. She struggled to make her marriage work, and then she let it go. She felt a professional success and a relational failure. She worked during her short periods of therapy. She would come and go, but she always returned.

Deeper Therapy

Rose called me years later—"I need to come in about my mother; she's affecting my work." She felt despairingly fated in this relationship.

They now lived on different coasts. She felt obligated to call her on birthdays and continued to visit her on holidays. Rose was repeatedly criticized during these drunken days and nights. She waffled between sadness and despair, edgy irritation and angry outbursts. Rose tried and tried over many years. She was frustrated at the core, "She sucked the life out of me."

Rose managed to compartmentalize her physical contact with her mom, but she was unable to rebuff the long-lasting emotional impact. It repeatedly manifested itself in her relationships with controlling female bosses or never satisfied and angry male co-workers. Her employment pattern was consistent—find appealing work; provide a very valuable contribution; become embroiled in a conflict with a boss or co-worker, usually a woman; and abruptly leave or be asked to leave.

This pattern haunted her for years. Rose was ready to face this conflict, not repeat it. She lived a confident life without alcohol. She was available for the deeper work of ongoing recovery.

The Past in the Present and the Present Filled with the Past

Rose was a director of benefit relations in a large corporation. She worked hard, was counted on, and produced. She soldiered on and was loyal. She had no joy at work—it was all duty, all obligation, all the time. She was fated to endurance and tragically disconnected from her true essence or idiom.

Rose was approaching a reckoning with her past that would open up unimaginable possibilities for her future. She was still unaware of a flame within that would ignite a search for more meaning and fulfillment (Eigen, 2009, p. 1).

Rose was once again embroiled in a tense and problematic work situation. Her department relied on a close working relationship with the information technology support staff. She needed their cooperation to deliver a product and satisfy her sense of accomplishment. She was frustrated with Dr. Black, the female director of this department, who required endless documents and made irrational requests. Dr. Black was also "sullen, bitchy, unpredictable, and mean. I really feel that she was out to get me. She never listened and showed me no respect. She seemed to mock me with disdain. I really felt she wanted me fired." Rose bit her tongue and held her breath. She had sleepless nights, and her asthma flared up. She didn't want to blow up; she didn't want another problem at work. She said to me, "I don't want this to happen again. Let's get deeper here."

We began talking about the eerie sense of familiarity she felt in the presence of Dr. Black. Dr. Black's outbursts reminded her of her mother's nightly drunken chore inspections. She felt the same frozen terror. She felt like the little girl who could not speak up and defend the quality of her chores. She felt silent and enraged once again. This time, she didn't want to remain voiceless, and she didn't want to leave or lose her job.

During this same time period, she was at her rope's end with her mother's hostile, dismissive, disrespectful, and drunken calls. Her mother demanded that she return for the holidays. She attempted to intimidate Rose and would sulk until she agreed to travel across the country. Rose felt silenced and felt compelled to obey. She suffered with sleepless nights and worry-filled days.

Rose's experiences with Dr. Black felt similar to the ones that she had endured for her entire lifetime with her mother. Her experiences with her mother were ones she was repeating with Dr. Black. She felt trapped in two bad situations.

Crisis and Breakthrough

Rose was in ongoing recovery with a sober identity that was not easily threatened. She was ready to work at the source. She decided to directly address her mother. She no longer wanted to act out this overtired pattern in the workplace.

Rose's sessions were tearful and breathless postmortems of her phone conversations with her mother. She called me one day after a particularly disturbing phone call. Her mother was drunk at noon and began ranting nonsense stories. Rose dutifully listened and cringed with agony inside. She felt just like that little girl trapped on the bed, forced to listen to an inebriated, cruel, and unloving mom. She felt the same fear and had the same loathing. Her mother managed to ask, "How are you doing?" She felt numb and barely remembers saying these words: "Mom, I'm having a hard time. I came back into therapy, and I'm working on childhood issues. It's painful to remember what went on in our house. It was bad, day and night; and it's painful to listen to you now. I know you're drinking, and I sense you're drunk. It's still as scary as it was when I was a child. I need some time away from you, Mom. I'll call you when I'm ready."

Rose's mother seemed to register her truthfulness and took her seriously. She said, "Okay," and hung up the phone. They have not talked since. Rose was agitated and relieved when she ended our phone conversation that day, "I think she really heard me this time." As time passed, she developed more confidence in her decision and began relating to her co-workers with a conviction that she had never known before.

A large meeting with Rose's department and Dr. Black's was scheduled for a Monday morning. Her true self called me over the weekend in a panic. It was unusual for her to reach out. She normally felt she had to handle everything by herself. We had a good conversation. She felt bolstered by the support.

The meeting began; differences of opinion engendered conflict. Rose felt terrified as Dr. Black "bullied, lied, tried to intimidate me, and humiliated me in public. I froze and then suddenly felt a surge of strength, a sense of conviction and power. My voice was calm. I told her that I would not be talked to in this way, and if she wanted to resolve these issues, we needed to do it in a different way." She continued, "We've gotten hot together before, and I don't want to do that now. We can figure this out. I want to, Dr. Black; this is too hard on both of us."

Rose looked around the room, and no one looked upset or mad. Rather, they all seemed as calm as she felt. They were listening. Dr. Black seemed calm too as she began a discussion of their different views on the problem. Her tone was different. Rose sat in shock and delight. This had never happened before. Previous conflicts with female bosses had resulted in heated deadlocks that ended in Rose's terminating her employment or being terminated.

Rose bathed in joy with her emotional evolution. She never imagined she could stand up to these two frightening and intimidating women or dreamed that they would listen and respect her wishes. She felt a freedom that she had never experienced. "Could my days of vigilance be over?" She felt a new confidence and was "looser" at work. She felt less anxious and had more room to think. She soon surprised herself with her dreaming.

An Idiom's Wish

Coincidentally, the corporation restructured and layoffs were announced. Eventually, Rose's department was given pink slips. Rose began her old pattern of worry. She fretted and feared the shape of her future. She began scouring the human resources field and networked for opportunities. She bore in and bore down. She was grim with a sense of her fate.

During one session, Rose revisited an idea briefly explored over the years. She had always passionately and joyfully talked about her love of recovery, her work with her sponsees, and her gratitude toward all those persons that had supported her throughout her 22 years of sobriety. A friend once commented, "You have sobriety in your heart, but not the professional qualifications. Did you ever think about going back to school?" That felt a ridiculous suggestion and an impossible possibility.

Rose now revisited this idea and was open to its reality. She expressed herself in ways that I had never experienced. Her overpractical mind seemed almost unhinged as she screamed, "Oh my golly, instead of looking for another job in a field I hate and with people who hate it too, I'm going to start talking to more people about how I could work in the recovery field. What do you think?" she asked with timid delight.

Rose dreamed out loud, "I wonder if I could ever work in a field that I love. I wonder if I could financially survive doing work that feels useful for humanity. I would love to spend my days supporting people's efforts to become sober. I know so much about drunks and drunken days, the lies and embarrassments, the shame and utter terror. You know, I know what it feels like. I know the pain that brings it on, the trap you fall into, and the lies that keep it going. I also know about the hope on the other side."

Rose was experiencing an unbridled enthusiasm she had never allowed herself to know. She wished for a work life she had never allowed herself to imagine. William Blake encourages each of us to do the same: "If the fool would persist in his folly, he would become wise." Such wisdom, Adam Phillips (1998) suggests, is based on the fact that imagination creates reality, and as desire is a part of imagination, the world we desire is more real than the world we passively accept (p. xviii).

Rose was more excited than I had ever seen her. Her eyes danced: "Could life be lived in the direction of my interests?" She was touching a level of experience that made her dizzy. For the first time, she sent me an e-mail:

> Hi Margy,
>
> I did not want our session to end today. I came back feeling so excited. I felt so full of feeling that I thought I was going crazy. I don't think I am. I'm grateful for all your help.
>
> —Rose

A Destiny Is Born

Rose's fever of possibilities continued. Her village of objects suddenly expanded. She explored an alcohol counselor certificate program and master's programs in clinical psychology and social work. She talked to everyone, sent more e-mails to me, and requested additional sessions. She was using me for her future.

Rose sat down one day and looked tense. I wondered why. She said, "I am frustrated. I want to go back to school, and I don't see how I can. I keep thinking and thinking, and I just can't imagine how I could go to school and work at the same time. I just couldn't do it. I'm afraid to spend my savings. I wouldn't be able to sleep if I did that. I mean, I think I have enough, but I couldn't do that."

Rose motioned her hand up and down in frustration. She looked as if she was throwing a temper tantrum. "I want to be able to figure out what I am doing here. I can't tolerate not figuring this out. I'm so frustrated, so frustrated."

It had been difficult to sit across from Rose that day. I registered her impact, and it felt brittle with confusion. She felt as if she was feeling one thing and trying to express something else. I sat in reverie as I listened. "I'm trying to figure out where you are today, what's really going on inside." She quickly responded, "I don't know." I continued, "I feel like there may be something under that temper tantrum, something about how hard it is to be figuring out this next part of your life all alone." Rose responded, "Yeah, I do want somebody to help me with all of this. It would feel good, really good. I always do it all by myself, you know; no husband to talk to or help me out financially. Yeah, I want help."

Rose then became quiet, relaxed her shoulders, and sat very still for minutes. She looked down and started to cry. "I know what I'm really feeling now. It's about my real dad. I wish he were here." She began sobbing. "He would be behind me, he would help me, and he would say, 'Just go do it. Just do what is important to you. You only live once, my little Rose.' He would tell me not to worry, that it would all work out in the long run. He might even give me some money to go to graduate school." We sat together in silence for minutes.

"I didn't know all of this was inside of me. I thought I was just frustrated. Thanks." Rose left the session and called within five hours. Her message began, "I normally don't call you, but I wanted to tell you about something that feels really big and different. The most amazing thing happened to me, and I would love to talk to you."

I was able to return Rose's call quickly. She blurted out, "I don't know what is going on. I had to call you. I feel like I'm losing it. I've never felt this before, and I need you to tell me if I'm going crazy. I think I might be manic. I've never felt so excited." She continued, "You know what? I just decided I'm going to go to school, and I know I can do it. I can figure it out financially. I can work around my job. It hit me this afternoon that this is what I want to do. I'm tired of these boring bureaucratic jobs that I do so very well and feel so miserable doing. I feel exhausted, depleted, and sleepless, and I don't even like what I do. I can do this, and I am going to. I want to go to school, to learn more about an area of work that I love. I want to pursue what I want. I've never felt like this before. I feel crazy with joy."

An Ongoing Rebirth and Ongoing Joy

Rose's abstinence and diligent recovery work paid off. Her sober confidence allowed for a deeper exploration of old patterns. Her true self responded to intimidations that had always silenced her. She freed herself from a fated relationship pattern with her mom and asserted her freedom of expression with her colleagues at work. Her determination and commitment to the ongoing recovery stage facilitated the appearance of her true essence and the birth of her idiomatic desires. Her "enduring" false self receded as she dared to listen to her imagination and her dreams. For the first time, she believed that a passion and devotion could turn into a profession. She envisioned days of meaning while earning a living. Her false self had always said, "I can't." Her true self now imagined and screamed, "I want, and I will." She felt on the right track for the first time in her life. Bollas (1989) links this with the connection to one's idiom.

AA had supported her through years of recovery. She worked and reworked steps; she dutifully sponsored her newcomers. She was a good girl; she always completed the chore list of others. Today she wanted to write her own. "I love AA and always will, and I'm glad I came to therapy. I didn't get this kind of support from my AA world. AA stresses being grateful, and you can stay with that too long. Therapy has been so helpful over the years—that's why I want to go back to school. I'm so excited that I figured out what I want to do."

Rose believed in designing her future, and she was elated with its possibilities. Over the next months, she reassembled her village of objects. She called professional friends in recovery, searched for contacts, applied to schools, and looked for jobs in the field. She felt she was in charge and could create her own life path. She felt ruthless with desire. She was determined and aggressive, shocked by her tolerance for risk, and solidly sober, and she had some good fortune. She was streaming in destiny.

Rose was accepted into graduate school and began preparing for entry. There was a lightness in her step and a smile in her eyes. Her fated life of childhood destruction, survival, and endurance was over. Psychoanalytic listening had been receptive to her essence and had fostered the birth of her true self. Again, D. W. Winnicott cautions us, "Don't assume that we all live a life" (in Bollas, 1998, p. 26). At 45, Rose was destined for an aliveness in living that she never knew existed.

James

It's Never Too Late

James's years of heavy drinking ended at age 52. His wife, Sarah, finally called the paramedics after his four days of solitary drinking and restless sleeping in a bedroom in the basement of their Ojai, California home. Sarah checked on him, fed him soup, and watched over him. On the fifth day, she could not wake him. She feared he was in a coma and near death. She called members of his family. They said to call an ambulance right away. His blood alcohol content (BAC) was near .500, indicating coma conditions and possible death. Sarah found several empty vodka bottles in his closet as the paramedics drove away.

For the first time ever, James had no concern or calculation about how his solitary drinking episode would be managed, interpreted, reinterpreted, or end. He went into that room after years of being the only breadwinner for the family, and after being the caretaker for Sarah during her diagnosis and treatment of stage four cancer. He went in there amid a Christmas visit from Sarah's Midwest family. He went in there after he finished a big project for his law firm. He went in there after life-threatening complications from her latest chemotherapy treatment. He went in there without a cover-up or a care. He easily could have died.

James was a classic example of the psychological dependency, not yet physical profile (see Chapter 4, p. 48). He was psychologically dependent on alcohol and did everything he could to stave off physical dependency. He lived a life of compulsive obligations, superior performance, and heavy daily drinking. He "died" during his evening blackouts and was "resurrected" each morning when he opened his eyes. His "rising" convinced him that he was ahead of this game and beating its odds (Szasz, cited in Levin, 2001, p. 213). James went to the gym at 4 o'clock every morning. He worked through his hangover and worked all day. He poured his first drink in the car on the way home. He was long past socializing in a bar; he was unimpressed with their weak drinks. He was not interested in conversation. It interfered with his focus—to drink to a state of numbing oblivion. His was the classic example of the perversion of social drinking into solitary excess (Rotskoff, 2002, p. 74). He drank alone every night while Sarah slept alone upstairs. Only the occasional drunken outburst disrupted their "stable existence." A life and a marriage were crumbling beside this deal with the devil.

Two Admissions, Two Discharges

The paramedics took James to a local emergency room. He was stabilized and his BAC dropped to .200. He was admitted to Vista Del Mar, the detox and dual diagnosis treatment facility located in Ventura, California. James's first five days in Vista were a blur. He was given Librium for detox, was medically observed, and was allowed to sleep. He ate his meals in bed. His privileges were restricted owing to severe dehydration, malnutrition, high blood pressure, and muscle weakness. He attended some groups and attempted some exercise. His exhaustion, confusion, and disorientation kept him on bed rest until the day before his discharge. In hindsight, it was a premature discharge.

James returned home and attended an AA meeting with Sarah. She noticed his anxiety, agitation, and weakness. He had trouble speaking and stumbled while walking. She asked him how he was doing, and he assured her, "I'm doing just fine. It's good to be out of the hospital. I really want to do this. You can go to bed now."

Within five minutes, he was at the local market and had bought two bottles of vodka. He drank them quickly; agitation set in. He walked out in the rain with a tarp. He was beside himself. He ended up in the backyard doghouse. He cried and gashed his forehead. He proceeded to run around the neighborhood in the rain and eventually returned home. When he walked in, Sarah was in a panic. She had been pacing and sadly proclaimed, "Oh my god, you're drunk again." James headed to the couch, sat in defeat and despair, and said he wanted to die. Sarah called the paramedics and once again, he returned to the emergency room. After BAC stabilization, he was transported to a locked unit in Vista Del Mar. James decided to end his drinking days while he was being searched for contraband. His transition moment was stark, clean, and forward moving. He stepped into his transition identity. He never turned back.

Devotion to Recovery

The next day, James was removed from the locked unit and began a week of detox and treatment. He attended and participated in groups at Vista Del Mar, and he followed every recommendation without protest. He went on Campral, the neurotransmitter brain rebalancer, and began taking an antidepressant. He enrolled in an Intensive Outpatient Program (IOP) that included group meetings four nights a week. He attended AA meetings and felt protected by his strong recovery structure. He went back to work. We began intensive psychotherapy.

James's near death propelled him into recovery. The years of discounting the existence, significance, and impact of his alcoholism were quickly obliterated. James possessed an eyes-wide-open approach to all aspects of his fragile transition stage. He was hungry with interest. He read and studied. I got the sense that his recovery identity was "nailed in place." His impact was expansive to feel, and he was a joy to work with.

James's early days of transition were filled with wonder and terror, excitement and dread, fragility and determination, grace and chutzpah, quietude and community. He dove into each path in front of him. He questioned but not too much. He felt for the first time in years. He counted on others for assistance in ways he had never done before. It was a bewildering experience that James was not too bewildered by. Without the booze, he could tolerate the dizziness of this newfound freedom (Kierkegaard, 1849, in Levin, 2001, p. 4).

James engaged in AA recovery tasks with easy intensity. He got a sponsor, attended a rigorous study group, read *The Big Book* of Alcoholics Anonymous, and searched for spirituality. He worked harder than ever, ran longer than ever, and walked miles and miles alone.

James was also in the most pleasant of hallucinatory states—how could this be that he was not drinking? That is all he had known—hard work, arduous exercise, caring for his wife, and always drinking. He felt he was living in an altered state. No matter how surreal he felt, he was gently and vigorously compelled to move forward.

James talked to his wife, and in those early days, they tenderly agreed that things "are different but better. There's less screaming, less worry, but it's strange." They didn't seem to know what to do with each other. James suggested couples therapy; Sarah said it was too much work. They kept a polite distance. Sarah was consumed with her illness and glad he was not drinking. James instead felt worried. Life felt new; many old decisions felt outdated. Could his marriage make it? He was advised by AA elders not to think too hard about too many things. "The work of recovery is the focus; all else will fall into place."

It was a strange time for James, like no other time in his life. He felt so relieved to be free of the burdens of constant escape. He reflected so often on the wasted moments, hours, and days of dreaming of drinking, drinking, and then hiding his hangover. He was comforted by the community of AA. He felt among people who understood his furtive affair, an affair that knew no thought, only repetition and superficial relief. There was no cherishing, only ravaging. Addiction is a violent scavenger that consumes one's life.

Recovery with Ongoing Intensity

James had a solid recovering identity and moved quickly through transition and early recovery. He engaged in a level of therapeutic work that takes place in ongoing recovery. He investigated his life with a vengeance. "I've wasted enough time." James began to think his marriage was based on a Faustian deal—Sarah fed on James's financial provisions and James fed on his drinks. They both settled for this comfort and protection. They had interest in neither themselves nor their marriage. The death instinct predominated over the life instinct.

James reflected on the meaning of his marriage in therapy. Over time, he became confident that it needed to end. Sarah did not quarrel. They did not want to disrupt their lifestyle. They decided to divorce and remain in the same household. They were tense but polite. It was a distant and resigned household when Sarah suddenly died. James felt both despair and relief. Grief took its time. He wrestled with the loss of his marriage and the loss of his wife.

James lived a fated life until he was 52. He began his recovery in an emergency room while the medical staff attempted to lower a BAC of .471. He had a one-day relapse after his first discharge. His recovering identity moved continuously forward, as he reflected on his past.

James's Fated History

James was raised within a Protestant ethic. He had one sister and one brother. He was the middle child. There was some wealth, including a meticulously decorated winter home and a well-appointed summer home. There were maids and drivers, country clubs and private schools. There was emotional deprivation from a seemingly well-meaning, yet psychologically limited, demanding mother and a well-meaning, yet emotionally limited father. There were discipline and order, clear expectations, and family loyalty. "To whom much is given, much is required" was the childhood refrain in the household. There was plenty of attention to the children's lives and activities; there was little regard for their internal world. Intentions were good; lack of emotional capacity was incapacitating.

Mike Eigen (1996) says it best: "The usual story of emotional poverty in a luxurious setting" (p. 3). All was perfect on the surface—children and parents were well mannered, attractive, and fit. There was much anxiety below the surface. The parents did not "live" their marriage. The children were polite but distant. There was little family intimacy.

James seemed to feel the emotional vacancy more than the others. He was athletically gifted and temperamentally blessed with an infectious enthusiasm. He was popular with his peers and performed well enough. His gifts and social graces belied his loneliness and anxiety, which apparently began at birth. He was a colicky baby, sucked his thumb into his teens, slept poorly, worried often, and took to diary writing as soon as he could write.

James's childhood entries were filled with worries about doctor's visits and potential illnesses, anxieties about his parents' relationship and their possible death, and his everyday fears. His adolescent writings explored female bodies and sexual desire. He fell in love with Paula in high school and wanted her to become his exclusive girlfriend. Parental expectations clashed with his; he was ordered to date other girls if he wanted to continue with Paula. This was devastating news to James, and it felt so unfair. He was innocent and in love and could not fathom this cruel parental commandment.

Years of blind obedience had taken its toll—James had reached his limit. He wanted to fulfill his adolescent desires. He politely pleaded with his mother to no avail. He looked for comfort among his siblings, but they saw him as a troublemaker. He felt a terror he did not understand and sensed a lonely journey ahead. James rebelled against years of commandments and demands, orders and expectations, loneliness and alienation. He started to distance himself from his siblings; he gave up on addressing conflict within his family and began sneaking around to see Paula. Unfortunately, this began a fated course of living for James that would last for decades.

Escapes from Fates

James's true self was unable to flourish in childhood. His parents seemed to foreclose on its expression and elaboration. While considerable skills were encouraged and reinforced for future survival, what was missing was more important. James lost out on the development of his true self; he lost experience with the back-and-forth between mother and child. His world did not facilitate the elaboration of his idiom. He put his destiny in his diary instead. Still, much was provided, and he was able to carve out a youth, despite the immovable weight he carried within his body.

There were costs. James began drinking and smoking pot. He was always able to keep up with his schoolwork, yet he never excelled. He graduated high school and college, and he eventually applied to law school. He graduated from a mediocre school and flunked the bar exam twice before passing. He serially dated, never getting close to anyone. James was cobbling a life together but without a core sense of self. He was unhappy and didn't know why; and there was no passion or joy. Drinking got him through. He knew something was wrong, but his "independence" from other people prevented him from understanding why. James was the psychic retreater who counted on a group of leprechauns for company and support throughout his life (see James's letter in Chapter 11, p. 209). He tried therapy, but alcohol worked better. He muddled through relationships with women and migrated from law firm to law firm. He drank to blackout every night. He attended family events, his despair masked by breeding, manners, and an anxious enthusiasm.

More Fated Decisions

James panicked in his mid-30s and married Sarah, a woman without education or ambition. She was kind and undemanding; it momentarily felt safe, some emotional space with room and possibilities. The opposite occurred. Within two months of his marriage, he was diagnosed in an emergency room with ketoasidosis, a diabetic coma. His parents asked Sarah if it was due to drinking; at first, she said no.

James stopped drinking for seven years, and his despair grew worse. He realized he had married on impulse. He resigned himself to the mismatch. A fated life does not expect to find pleasure and joy in intimacy.

James felt trapped by the commandments of his vows; he did not feel trapped by his ambition. He derived all meaning from his professional advancements. He excelled in his profession and developed a solid reputation. He rediscovered his childhood passion of rock climbing. He and his wife carved out separate existences. They told themselves, "We are independent people who let each other be. We are not like other couples that have to do everything together." These words masked an alienated union. Life already felt bewildering when Sarah was diagnosed with lung cancer.

The commandments once again drastically commanded, and James assumed an extensive caretaking role. It provided a climate of affection between the two of them.

They united around her cancer, and James took up drinking again. Years drifted by in the agony of her sickness, and their alienation increased. His drinking got worse; her cancer worsened. He was now fated to drink over his fated life. Sarah allowed it "because you work so hard. You're intense in everything you do, including drinking. I'll take the good with the bad." He kept the extent of his drinking from his family. Social drinking deteriorated into solitary excess filled with daily blackouts. It was at this time that he ended up in the emergency room.

Ongoing Usages

James entered the ongoing recovery stage with determination. His identity migration was smooth, fast, and productive. His sobriety was solidly in place. He mourned a marriage. He revenged against the dictates of his childhood. He eventually grieved for both. The years of halfhearted wandering and wondering and endless amounts of destruction had come to an end. The fated life that led to a fated solution was over.

James's five days of solitary drinking could have killed him. He was lucky. He got to fade away and come alive again. His true sense of self was finally free to evolve. He developed a more spontaneous expression, he felt lighter, and his friends and family said he looked younger. He was filled with an energy and desire he had never known.

Our therapy had lighter moments as well. Bollas (1989) reminds treatment providers to be watchful of the patient's object use of them (pp. 34–32). He suggests that it changes over the course of one's analysis; it certainly changes during a recovering addict's identity migration through the four stages of recovery. By ongoing recovery, I sensed my best usage would be to provide a calm, constant, and loving atmosphere that would facilitate the evolution of James's emerging true self. Mike Eigen suggests this promotes the development of faith (1989, p. 32).

I listened for the slightest articulation of idiom urges expressed in James's dreams, daydreams, personal myths, and visions of the future. Dreams, Bollas (1989) reminds us, are where futures are hatched; they constitute a fictional forerunner of reality (p. 47). James dared to start living ever so slightly ahead of what seemed practical or possible; he imagined swimming while still only crawling (p. 35).

Lending myself to James this way led him to believe more and more in his own true potential, connect to his idiom, and begin to find a taste for his destiny. Therapy that was once treacherously dire and ever vigilant to day-to-day recovery tasks now became more affectively playful. James presented dreams about his future. He wanted me to mull them over, to play with his play. There was joy in celebrating his decision to really live his life.

Destiny's Passions

James's fated existence had driven him into a productive yet dreary work style. The passion he lacked, he reclaimed now. He saw more opportunities and participated in designing his own path. His legal skills became sharper, his analytic thinking more critical, and his capacity to engage with others more spontaneous. He created a job description for himself that included duties he enjoyed and that would also advance his career and benefit his law firm.

James also reinvented himself as a more daring rock climber. He trained harder, practiced technique, and challenged his capacity. He reunited with fellow college climbers. They went on treks together and reminisced about old times and dreamed about new ones. They decided to produce a photo book that chronicled rock-climbing adventurers around the United States. They believed in their dream, worked hard on its development, and boldly sought contacts through their village of objects. Their book was on the shelves of Patagonia, a well-regarded international sports store, within a year.

Slowly, James ventured into the world of dating. He felt fated with fear and inability during transition and early recovery. By ongoing recovery, he began to believe in future possibilities. Several people set him up on blind dates, and he joined several online dating sites. He was tentative and cautious. His lack of experience shamed and overwhelmed him. He was terrified to be vulnerable; he had avoided this experience most of his life. We repeatedly spoke about these emotions in our sessions together. James dated some old girlfriends, revisited lost loves, and kept on searching. His destiny was on the move, yet he still lived with some residual sense of fate and despair in the areas of closeness and intimacy. His wounds were deep, the damage complex. He may always have some hesitancy in this area. Ed Khantzian offers wise simplicity: "Some of us are better than others in relationships" (Khantzian and Albanese, 2008, p. 17).

James was finally living his life and living in the world of vibrant objects (Bollas, 1989 p. 26). His ongoing recovery work was both painful and joyous. He finally and fully embraced the pathos of his sorrowful childhood. He also ruthlessly searched for more in ways that felt both foreign and fanciful. He used me with anger, aggression, hesitancy, and tenderness. He grew in unfathomable ways. It was not too late, and James knew it.

CHAPTER SUMMARY AND REFLECTIONS

Summary

Ongoing recovery is the last formal stage in addiction treatment and this is the last chapter of this book. The migration of a recovering identity is nearly complete.

Many addicts in this stage of treatment begin to question what they thought they would never question, consider doing things that they thought they would never consider. Psychotherapy conversations turn to future possibilities. This chapter provided readers with clinical theories and interventions that exquisitely complement the addict's identity evolution during this stage. Psychoanalyst Christopher Bollas's work on fate, destiny, and idiom development was introduced. Mike Eigen, psychoanalyst, elaborated on D. W. Winnicott's notions of the true self and false self, and these were also explored. Three encouraging and joyful case studies suggested uses of these concepts during this last stage of treatment.

Reflections

Before leaving this chapter, make sure you:

- Know the primary and secondary tasks of the ongoing recovery stage
- Have a solid understanding of the key theories and concepts presented
- Have examined their individual merit and critically analyzed and discussed your intuitive clinical responses to their application in therapeutic action moments in the clinical cases of this stage
- Have begun to design your own integrative treatment approach for this stage
- Are willing to read and reread this chapter, and all the treatment chapters

Epilogue

Hopefully, *Perspectives on Addiction* has provided you with a reflective grasp on a complex body of knowledge, as well as an appreciation of what we know and don't know about addiction and its treatment. In addition, I hope you have found a desire to explore your own need to escape and expand consciousness; a curiosity about societal influences, scientific discoveries, and diagnostic developments; an excitement and passion for the inclusion of psychoanalytic theory in addiction treatment; an imagination for your own creative contributions to the field; and a yearning for continual learning.

References

Alcoholics Anonymous World Services, Inc. (1981). *Twelve Steps and Twelve Traditions*.

Alcoholics Anonymous World Services, Inc. (2001). *Alcoholics anonymous: The big book* (4th ed.). New York.

American Psychiatric Association. (2000). *Diagnostic and statistical manual of mental disorders* (Rev. 4th ed.). Washington, DC: Author.

American Society of Addiction Medicine. www.asam.org

Baker, H., & Baker, M. (1987). Heinz Kohuts' self psychology: An overview. *American Journal of Psychiatry, 144*, 1–9.

Barrows, S., & Room, R. (Eds.). (1991). *Drinking behavior and belief in modern history*. Berkeley: University of California Press.

Beck, A. T. (1979). *Cognitive therapy and the emotional disorders*. Madison, CT: International Universities Press.

Beck, A. T., Wright, F. D., Newman, C. F., & Liese, B. S. (1993). *Cognitive therapy of substance abuse*. New York: Guilford Press.

Berlin, I. (1953). *The hedgehog and the fox*. New York: Simon & Schuster.

Bersani, L., & Phillips, A. (2008). *Intimacies*. Chicago: University of Chicago Press.

Bion, W. R. (1967). *Second thoughts*. London: Karnac.

Bion, W. R. (1992). *Cogitations*. London: Karnac.

Bloch, H. A. (1949). Alcohol and American recreational life. *American Scholar, 18*(1), 54–66.

Bollas, C. (1989). *Forces of destiny: Psychoanalysis and human idiom*. London: Free Association Books.

Bollas, C. (2007). *The Freudian moment*. London: Karnac.

Bourne, E. (2000). *The anxiety and phobia workbook*. Oakland, CA: New Harbinger Publications.

Breacher, E. M., & The Editors of Consumer Reports (1972). *Licit and illicit drugs*. Boston: Little, Brown.

Brower, K. J., Blow, F. C., & Beresford, T. P. (1989). Treatment implications of chemical dependency models: An integrative approach. *Journal of Substance Abuse Treatment, 6*(3), 147–157.

Brown, S. (1985). *Treating the alcoholic: A developmental model of recovery*. New York: John Wiley & Sons.

Brown, S. (1988). *Treating adult children of alcoholics: A developmental perspective*. New York: John Wiley & Sons.

Brown, S. (2004). *A place called self: Women, sobriety & radical transformation*. Center City, MN: Hazelden.

Brown, S. (Ed.), & Yalon, I. D. (General Ed.). (1995). *Treating alcoholism*. San Francisco: Jossey-Bass.

Cameron, D. (1995). *Liberating solutions to alcohol problems*. Northvale, NJ: Jason Aronson.

Cantor, C. (1996). *Phantom illness: Shattering the myth of hypochondria*. Boston: Houghton Mifflin.

Caper, R. (1999). *A mind of one's own: A Kleinian view of self and object*. London: Routledge.

Chessick, R. (1992). *What constitutes the patient in psychotherapy*. London: Jason Aronson.

Clark, R. P. (2010). *The glamour of grammar: A guide to the magic and mystery of practical English*. New York: Little, Brown.

Costello, R. B. (Ed.). (1997). *Random House Webster's college dictionary* (2nd ed.). New York: Random House.

Denzin, N. (1987). *The alcoholic self.* Newbury Park: Sage.

Director, L. (2005). Encounters with omnipotence in the psychoanalysis of substance users. *Psychoanalytic Dialogues, 15*(4), 567–587.

Dodes, L. (2002). *The heart of addiction*. New York: HarperCollins.

Doweiko, H. E. (2009). *Concepts of chemical dependency* (7th ed.). Belmont, CA: Brooks/Cole.

Earleywine, M. (2002). *Understanding marijuana: A new look at the scientific evidence*. Oxford: Oxford University Press.

Efran, J. S., Lukens, M. D., & Lukens, R. J. (1990). *Language structure and change*. New York: W. W. Norton.

Eigen, M. (1986). *Psychotic core*. Northvale, NJ: Jason Aronson.

Eigen, M. (1996). *Psychic deadness*. Northvale, NJ: Jason Aronson.

Eigen, M. (1998). *The psychoanalytic mystic*. London: Free Association Books.

Eigen, M. (1999). *Toxic nourishment*. London: Karnac.

Eigen, M. (2001). *Ecstasy*. Middletown, CT: Wesleyan University Press.

Eigen, M. (2002). *Rage*. Middletown, CT: Wesleyan University Press.

Eigen, M. (2004). *The sensitive self.* Middletown, CT: Wesleyan University Press.

Eigen, M. (2004). *The electrified tightrope* (Adam Phillips, Ed.). London: Karnac.

Eigen, M. (2006). *Lust*. Middletown, CT: Wesleyan University Press.

Eigen, M. (2007). *Feeling matters*. London: Karnac.

Eigen, M. (2009). *Flames from the unconscious*. London: Karnac.

Eigen, M. (2010). *Eigen in Seoul: Volume one, madness and murder*. London: Karnac.

Eigen, M., & Govrin, A. (2007). *Conversations with Michael Eigen*. London: Karnac.

Emerson, H. (1932). *Alcohol and man.* Norwood, MA: Norwood Press Linotype, Inc.

Epstein, M. (1995). *Thoughts without a thinker: Psychotherapy from a Buddhist perspective*. New York: Basic Books.

Erickson, C. K. (2007). *The science of addiction from neurobiology to treatment*. New York: W. W. Norton.

Fetting, M. (2009a). Presidential reverie: An invitation to become a country of thinkers. *California Society for Clinical Social Work, 38*(7), 1–7.

Fetting, M. (2009b). Let's make it through transition: A time of fits and starts. *California Society for Clinical Social Work, 38*(10), 3.

Fetting, M. (2011). An interview with Ed Khantzian.

Fetting, M. (2011). An interview with Stephanie Brown.

Fields, R. (2010). *Drugs in perspective* (7th ed.). New York: McGraw-Hill.

Fletcher, A. (2001). *Sober for good*. New York: Houghton Mifflin.

Flores, P. J. (2001). Addiction as an attachment disorder: Implications for group therapy. *International Journal of Group Psychotherapy, 51*(1), 64.

Frank, J. D. (1963). *Persuasion and healing: A comparative study of psychotherapy*. New York: Schocken Books.

Franklin, J. (1987). *Molecules of the mind*. New York: Del Publishing.

Garner, D. M., & Garfinkel, P. E. (Eds.). (1985). *Handbook of psychotherapy for anorexia nervosa and bulimia*. New York: Guilford Press.

Gregson, D., & Efran, J. (2002). *The Tao of sobriety: Helping you to recover from alcohol and drug addiction*. New York: Thomas Dunne Books.

Gold, M. S., & Brandt, J. F. (2005). Handbook of clinical alcoholism treatment. *The American Journal of Psychiatry, 162*(5), 1038–1039.

Gorski, T. T., & Miller, M. (1986). *Staying sober: A guide for relapse prevention*. Thorofare, NJ: Independence Press.

Gottman, J., Schwartz Gottman, J., & DeClaire, J. (2007). *Ten lessons to transform your marriage: America's love lab experts share their strategies for strengthening your relationship*. New York: Random House.

Gottman, J. (1995). *Why marriages succeed or fail*. New York: Simon & Schuster.

Grinberg, L., Sor, D., & de Bianchedi, E. T. (1977). *Introduction to the work of Bion*. Lanham, MD: Jason Aronson.

Grotstein J. S. (2009). *"...But at the same time and on another level...": Psychoanalytic theory and technique in the Kleinian/Bionian mode*. (Vol. 1) London: Karnac.

Grotstein, J. S. (2009). *"...But at the same time and on another level...": Clinical applications in the Kleinian/Bionian mode*. (Vol. 2) London: Karnac.

Guralnik, D. B., & Friend, J. H. (Eds.). (1968). *Webster's new world dictionary of the American language* (college ed.). Cleveland: World Publishing Co.

Hanson, D. J. (1995). *Preventing alcohol abuse: Alcohol, culture, and control*. Westport, CT: Praeger.

Hanson, G. R., Venturelli, P. J., & Fleckenstein, A. E. (2009). *Drugs and society* (10th ed.). Sudbury, MA: Jones and Bartlett.

Horvath, A. T., & Velten, E. (2000). Smart recovery: Addiction recovery support from a cognitive-behavioral perspective. *Journal of Rational-Emotive & Cognitive-Behavior Therapy, 18*(3), 181–191.

Humphreys, K. (2003). A research-based analysis of the moderation management controversy. *Alcohol and Drug Abuse, 54*(5), 621–622.

Hyman, S. E. (1995). A man with alcoholism and HIV Infection. *Journal of the American Medical Association, 274*(10), 837–843.

Inaba, D. S., & Cohen, W. E. (2007). *Uppers, downers, all arounders* (6th ed.). Medford, OR: CNS Publications.

Institute of Medicine. http://www.ion.edu/About-IOM.aspx

Jaggar, M., & Richards K. (1966). *Mother's little helper. On Aftermath* [Record]. *London: London Records*. Los Angeles: RCA Studios.

Jellinek, E. M. (1960). *The disease concept of alcoholism*. New Haven, CT: Hillhouse Press.

Johnson, J. L. (2004). *Fundamentals of substance abuse practice*. Belmont, CA: Thomson Brooks/Coler.

Khantzian, E. J. (1985). The self-medication hypothesis of addictive disorders: Focus on heroin and cocaine dependence. *American Journal of Psychiatry, 142*(11), 1259–1264.

Khantzian, E. J. (1999). *Treating addiction as a human process*. Northvale, NJ: Jason Aronson.

Khantzian, E. J. (2011). *Reflections on treating addictive disorders—A psychodynamic perspective*. Unpublished manuscript.

Khantzian, E. J., & Albanese, M. J. (2008). *Understanding addiction as self medication*. Lanham, MD: Rowman & Littlefield.

Knapp, C. (1997). *Drinking: A love story*. New York: Dell.

Knapp, C. (2003). *Appetites: Why women want*. New York: Counterpoint.

Kosok, A. (2006). The moderation management programme in 2004. What type of drinker seeks controlled drinking? *International Journal of Drug Policy, 17*(2006), 295–303.

Kuhn, C., Swartzwelder, S., & Wilson, W. (2008). *Buzzed: The straight facts about the most used and abused drugs from alcohol to ecstasy* (3rd ed.). New York: W. W. Norton.

Lasater, L. (1988). *Recovery from compulsive behavior: How to transcend your troubled family*. Deerfield Beach, FL: Health Communications.

Lenair Healing Center. www.lenair.com

Levin, J. (2001). *Therapeutic strategies for treating addiction*. Northvale, NJ: Jason Aronson.

Loose, R. (2002). *The subject of addiction: Psychoanalysis and the administration of enjoyment*. London: Karnac.

Marlatt, G. A. (1996). Come as you are. *Addictive Behaviors, 21*(6), 779–788.

Marlatt, G. A. (Ed.). (1998). *Pragmatic strategies for managing high-risk behaviors*. New York: Guilford Press.

Marlatt, G. A., & Gordon, J. R. (Eds.). (1985). *Relapse prevention*. New York: Guilford Press.

Martin, S. C. (2006). From temperance to alcoholism in America. *Reviews in American History, 34*(2), 231–237.

McGoldrick, M., Giordano, J., & Garcia-Preto, N. (Eds.). (2005). *Ethnicity & family therapy* (3rd ed.). New York: Guilford Press.

Miller, W. R., & Rollnick, S. (2002). *Motivational interviewing: Preparing people for change* (2nd ed.). New York: Guilford Press.

Milkman, H. B., & Sunderwirth, S. G. (2009). *Craving for ecstasy and natural highs*. Los Angeles: Sage.

Mitrani, J. (2001). *Ordinary people and extra ordinary protections: A post-Kleinian approach to the treatment of primitive mental states*. London: Routledge.

Moderation Management. http://www.moderation.org/whatisMM.shtml

Molino, A. (Ed.). (1998). *Freely associated: Encounter in psychoanalysis with Christopher Bollas, Joyce McDougall, Michael Eigen, Adam Phillips, Nina Coltart*. London: Free Association Books.

Nakken, C. (1996). *The addictive personality*. Center City, MN: Hazelden Foundation.

Obholzer, A., & Roberts, V. Z. (Eds.). (1994). *The unconscious at work: Individual and organizational stress in the human services*. London: Routledge.

Ogden, T. H. (2005). *The art of psychoanalysis*. London: Routledge.

Ogden, T. H. (2009). *Rediscovering psychoanalysis: Thinking and dreaming, learning and forgetting*. London: Routledge.

Peele, S., & Brodsky, A. (1991). *The truth about addiction and recovery*. New York: Simon & Schuster.

Pelled, E. (2007). Learning from experience: Bion's concept of reverie and Buddhist meditation: A comparative study. *International Journal of Psychoanalysis, 88*(6), 1507–1526.

Perez Foster, R. M., Moskowitz, M., & Javier, R. A. (Eds.). (1986). *Reaching across boundaries of culture and class*. Northvale, NJ: Jason Aronson.

Phillips, A. (1994). *On flirtation*. Cambridge, MA: Harvard University Press.

Phillips, A. (1996). *Monogamy*. New York: Vintage Books.

Phillips, A. (1998). *The beast in the nursery*. New York: Vintage Books.

Phillips, A. (2001). *Promises, promises*. New York: Basic Books.

Phillips, A. (2005). *Going sane*. New York: HarperCollins.

Phillips, A. (2006). *Side effects*. New York: HarperCollins.

Phillips, A. (2010). *On balance*. New York: Farrar, Straus & Giroux.

Phillips, A., & Taylor, B. (2009). *On kindness*. New York: Farrar, Straus & Giroux.

Prochaska, J. O., DiClemente, C. C., & Norcross, J. C. (1993). In search of how people change: Applications to addictive behaviors. *Journal of Addictions Nursing, 5*(1), 2–16.

Quinodoz, J. M. (1993). *The taming of solitude: Separation anxiety in psychoanalysis*. New York: Routledge.

Quinodoz, J. M. (2008). *Listening to Hanna Segal: Her contribution to psychoanalysis*. London: Routledge.

Ratey, J. J., & Johnson, C. (1997). *The shadow syndromes*. New York: Pantheon Books.

Rilke, R. M. (1993). *Letters to a young poet*. New York: W. W. Norton & Company.

Rinsley, D. (1988). The dipsas revisited: Comments on addiction and personality. *Journal of Substance Abuse Treatment, 5*, 1–7.

Rosenberg, C. E. (2006, Summer). Contested boundaries; Psychiatry, disease, and diagnosis. *Perspectives in Biology and Medicine, 49*(3), 407–424.

Rotskoff, L. (2002). *Love on the rocks: Men, women, and alcohol in post–World War II America*. Chapel Hill: University of North Carolina Press.

Ruden, R. (1997). *The craving brain*. HarperCollins.

Ruiz, P., Strain, E. C., & Langrod, J. G. (2007). *The substance abuse handbook*. Philadelphia: Lippincott Williams & Wilkins.

Schaeff, A. W. (1987). *When society becomes an addict*. San Francisco: Harper & Row.

Schlaadt, R. G., & Shannon, P. T. (1994). *Drugs: Use misuse and abuse*. Englewood Cliffs, NJ: Prentice-Hall.

Schuckit, M. A. (2010). *Drug and alcohol abuse: A clinical guide to diagnosis and treatment* (6th ed.). New York: Springer.

Seinfeld, J. (1991). *The empty core: An object relations approach to psychotherapy of the schizoid personality.* Northvale, NJ: Aronson.

Severns, J. R. (2004). A sociohistorical view of addiction and alcoholism. *Janus Head, 7*(1), 149–166.

Shaffer, H. J. (1987). The epistemology of "addictive disease": The Lincoln-Douglas debate. *Journal of Substance Abuse Treatment, 4*, 103–113.

Shaffer, H. J. (1999, Fall). On the nature and meaning of addiction. *National Forum, 79*(4), 9–14.

Shaffer, H. J., LaPlante, D. A., LaBrie, R. A., Kidman, R. C., Donato, A. N., & Stanton, M. V. (2004). Toward a syndrome model of addiction: Multiple expressions, common etiology. *Harvard Review of Psychiatry, 12*, 367–374.

Siegel, R. K. (2005). *In intoxication: Life in pursuit of artificial paradise*. Rochester, VT: Park Street Press.

Soanes, C., & Stevenson, A. (Eds.). (2009). *Concise Oxford English dictionary* (11th ed.). Oxford: Oxford University Press.

Steiner, J. (1993). *Psychic retreats*. London: Routledge.

Steiner, J. (2011). *Seeing and being seen: Emerging from a psychic retreat.* London: Routledge.

Steinglass, P., Bennett, L. A., Wolin, S. J., & Reiss, D. (1987). *The alcoholic family.* New York: Basic Books.

Stolorow, R. D. (2007). *Trauma and human existence.* New York: Taylor & Francis Group.

Stolorow, R. D. (2009). Identity and resurrective ideology in an age of trauma. *Psychoanalytic Psychology, 26*, 206–209.

Street Drugs. (2005). *A drug identification guide*. Long Lake, MN: Publishers Group.

Szasz, T. S. (1972). Bad habits are not diseases: A refutation of the claim that alcoholism is a disease. *Lancet, 2*, 83–84.

Szasz, T. (1988). A plea for the cessation of the longest war of the 20th century—The war on drugs. *The Humanistic Psychologist, 16*(2), 314–322.

Tatarsky, A. (Ed.). (2002). *Harm reduction psychotherapy: New treatment for drug* and *alcohol problems*. Northvale, NJ: Jason Aronson.

Thombs, D. L. (2006). *Introduction to addictive behaviors* (3rd ed.). New York: Guilford Press.

Traynor v. Turnage, 485 U.S. 535 (1988).

Ulman, R. B., & Paul, H. (2006). *The self psychology of addiction and its treatment.* New York: Routledge.

USC School of Social Work incoming Class Profile. (2010). Los Angeles: Office of Admission.

Vaillant, G. E. (1983). *The natural history of alcoholism: Causes, patterns, and paths to recovery.* Cambridge, MA: Harvard University Press.

Van, Wormer, K. & Davis, D. R. (2008). *Addiction treatment: A strengths perspective* (2nd ed.). Belmont, CA: Thomson Brooks/Cole.

Walant, K. (1995). *Creating the capacity for attachment.* Northvale, NJ: Jason Aronson.

Weegmann, M. (2006). Edward Khantzian interview. *Journal of Groups in Addiction and Recovery, 1*(2), 15–32.

Weil, A. (2004). *From chocolate to morphine*. New York: Houghton Mifflin.

White, M. (1995). *Re-authoring lives: Interviews* and *essays*. Adelaide, South Australia, Australia: Dulwhich Centre Publications.

White, W. L. (2010). On science and service: An interview with Tom McLellan. *Counselor, 11*(4), 24–35.

White, W. L. (2011). *Unraveling the mystery of personal and family recovery: An interview with Stephanie Brown, PhD.* Retrieved from http://www.williamwhitepapers.com/pr/2011 Dr. Stephanie Brown.pdf

White, W. L., Boyle, M., & Loveland, D. (2002). Alcoholism/Addiction as a chronic disease: From rhetoric to clinical reality. *Alcoholism Treatment Quarterly, 20*(3/4), 107–130.

Wilson, H. T. (Ed.). (2010). *Drugs, society, and behavior 09/10. (24th ed.).* Boston: McGraw-Hill.

Winnicott, D. W. (1958). The capacity to be alone. *International Journal of Psycho-Analysis, 39,* 416–420.

Winnicott, D. W. (1960). Ego distortion in terms of true and false self. In *The maturational processes and the facilitating environment* (pp. 140–152). New York: International Universities Press, 1965.

Wolburg, J. M. (2005). How responsible are "responsible" drinking campaigns for preventing alcohol abuse? *The Journal of Consumer Marketing, 22*(4/5), 176–177.

Wurmser, L. (1978). *The hidden dimension: Psychodynamics in compulsive drug use*. Northvale, NJ: Jason Aronson.

Wyatt, R. C., & Yalom, V. (2007). *An interview with Stephanie Brown, PhD.* Retrieved from http://www.psychotherapy.net/interview/stephanie-brown

Yalom, I. D. (2002). *The gift of therapy*. New York: HarperCollins.

Z. Phillip, A. (1991). *Skeptic's guide to the twelve steps: What to do when you don't believe.* New York: HarperCollins.

Zoja, L. (2000). *Drugs, addiction and initiation: The modern search for ritual*. Boston: Sigo Press.

Glossary

Addiction of Exclusion: Addiction that results from self-medicating for the feelings of alienation and helplessness that come from being marginalized from participation in contemporary culture.

Addiction of Inclusion: Addiction that results from self-medicating for the pressures and stresses that come from of trying to "fit in" or "succeed" in our contemporary culture.

Addictive Context: The societal institutions, laws, and policies and the political, cultural, and economic forces that shape the patterns of our daily existence and also contribute to widespread addiction.

Ambivalence: The addict's true response to his relationship with AOD. He loves it and hates it.

Analytic Hovering: A psychoanalytic technique. Freud recommends that the therapist or the analyst listen to her patients with a hovering and suspended attention, and rely on her unconscious to do the rest.

AOD: Alcohol and other drugs.

Archetypal Need: A universal human need that must be satisfied through healthy cultural rituals and experiences or the human being searches for its satisfaction in unhealthy ways.

Authoritative Versus Authoritarian Hint: An authoritative hint gives the addict room to make something of his own of it, and also gives him space to dream up something from it. An authoritarian hint is more like an order.

Authority: The sense of ownership that patients and addicts have about the direction of their own lives and what they think is the best course of treatment for them.

Blind Eye: Noticing something but not registering its real impact.

Context of Destiny: An ongoing relationship with an attentive and intuitive caretaker that allows the child to have ongoing contact with his real essence.

Context of Fate: An ongoing relationship with an inattentive caretaker. The child does not feel safe to be or safe to explore his essence and thus feels compelled to adjust to a prescribed climate of commandments.

Counseling: A form of psychotherapy that is supportive, clarifying, and encouraging. Counseling usually does not involve the in-depth working through of early trauma.

Countertransference: The analyst's or therapist's transference to the analysand, or patient. This includes the analyst's realistic reaction to the reality of the patient's life, to her own life as it may become affected by the patient, and the analyst's reaction to the transference.

Death/Rebirth Moments: When an individual says no (death) to a part of his life he has outgrown and says yes (rebirth) to an unknown future. Often experienced in developmental rites of passage.

Destiny: The urge within each person to articulate and elaborate his own idiom through the selection and use of caretakers (objects) in his environment.

Detotalization of Identity: When a therapist demonstrates interest in more than just the patient's problem, thus reducing his overidentification with his pathology.

Discounting: When an addict discounts the existence, significance, and impact of a problem as well as the ability to do anything at all to address it.

DSM-IV-TR: Current edition of *Diagnostic and Statistical Manual of Mental Disorders,* which provides uniform terminology and diagnostic categories.

DSM-V: Updated edition of DSM-IV-TR (scheduled for publication in 2013), which includes changes in the conceptualization of dependence and abuse and proposes new diagnostic categories with new criteria.

False Self: A sense of self that develops around the wishes, defenses, and dictates of others and that cannot experience life or feel real.

Families in Transition: The work of families during the transition stage of recovery.

Fantasy: A daydream.

Fated: Can be described as the feeling the child has when his spontaneous self-expressions are rejected and he feels forced to adapt to others' commandments of living.

Four Stages of Recovery: Developmental stages of recovery in Stephanie Brown's model and in the Integrative Model of Treatment: the drinking and using stage, the transition stage, the early recovery stage, and the ongoing recovery stage.

Grand Way Theory: Repeatedly losing control of AOD in a grand way; generally calls for abstinence.

Holding Environment: Created when the mother allows an infant's true self to develop. A therapist provides a similar space, and gives the true self another chance to emerge.

Hovering and Hinting Rather than Possessing and Ordering: An analytic intervention style that encourages listening and suggesting from the unconscious rather than consciously coercing and controlling.

Identity Reconstruction: The essence of recovery; the developmental evolution of a using, transition, early, and ongoing recovering identity.

Idiom: The unique nucleus of each individual.

Integrative Model of Treatment: A stage-driven model of treatment that incorporates the work of addiction specialists and includes an analytic attitude and a psychoanalytic theoretical perspective.

Interests of Transition: The rediscovery of the addict's interest in himself, long lost to the necessities of survival through addictive behaviors.

Interventions During Transition: Active interventions to save a life or reflective interventions to encourage thinking.

Loss of Initiation Rituals in Contemporary Culture: Results in the individual's perverted search for death/rebirth moments in addictive, gang, or terrorist rituals.

Multi-Focused Models of Treatment: When chemical dependency is conceptualized as originating from multiple causal sources. Recovery addresses these.

Natural History: The rhythm and course of one's distinct using relationship with AOD, and the rhythm and course of one's distinct path of recovery.

Pause Factor: A using-phase intervention that encourages addicts and alcoholics to pause and reflect on their own self-reported consequences of destructive AOD use before a drinking/drugging experience.

Phantasy: An unconscious element of the evolving structure of the mind.

Primary Tasks of Each Stage of Recovery: The work required for the migration of the addict's identity through four stages of recovery, including the treatment provider's work as she guides the addict through these stages.

Profiles/Clinical Descriptors of Addiction: Progressive continuum of categories of substance use, misuse, and addictive disorders.

Psychic Retreats: An area of the mind where reality does not have to be faced, where fantasy and omnipotence can exist unchecked, and where growth and development are sacrificed.

Psychoanalysis: A form of psychiatric treatment that uses the analysand's (patient's) transference to the analyst (therapist) as the primary source for working through deep conflicts.

Psychoanalytic Attitude: When an analyst or therapist receives the patient's (the addict's) infantile and unmetabolized feelings and projections and, as far as possible, refrains from reacting to them, with the result being that, eventually, the addict (patient) is able to take these feelings and projections back and integrate them into his own thinking and emotional mind.

Psychodynamic Therapy: A form of psychotherapy that considers the influence of historical traumas on one's current life, and can be supportive, be educational, or involve deeper explorations of traumas.

Receptivity: An attitude of listening without penetrating or intruding.

Registering Impacts: Allowing the experiences of events and other personalities to wash over and through one.

Relational Home: A secure relationship that provides a safe context for the reworking of early trauma. A therapist provides a relational home for recovery work during all four stages of addiction treatment.

Resurrective Ideology: Used here to describe the mythical world of addiction that offers false promises and temporary empowerment.

Reverie: Dreaming or imagining the patient/addict's (or child's) world.

Ruthless Usage: When a child of his destiny feels free to assert his needs and aggressively express his wishes. He uses members of his village of living objects for satisfaction and fulfillment of these needs and wishes.

Self-Medication Theories: Theories that emphasize and identify the psychological suffering driving the need for destructive use of AOD. Addicts self-medicate because they are unable to self-care.

Single-Focused Models of Treatment: When chemical dependency is conceptualized as originating from one causal source. Recovery addresses this.

Therapeutic Action Moments: When treatment theories and psychoanalytic concepts are practically applied to the struggles of each stage.

Totalization of Identity: When a patient or addict's view of himself is overdetermined by his addiction or substance use disorder.

Transference: A libidinal phenomenon. The analysand, or patient, ascribes unsatisfied libidinal impulses from infancy and childhood to the analyst or therapist. Love for the analyst provides the necessary extra force to induce the ego to give up its resistances, undo the repressions, and adopt a fresh solution to its ancient problems.

Transition Moment: A question for the addict: "Will my identity grow forward into my recovery, will I languish and lose some vigor, or will I move backward into destruction?" The addict meets this moment in those first hours of recovery and is challenged by its reappearance throughout this stage of recovery.

Transition Moments Revisited: Growth questions that reappear throughout all stages of recovery.

Transition's Identity Reconstruction: The deconstruction of a using identity and the construction of a recovering identity.

Transition's Time: A sober relationship with time.

Trauma: A sudden, unexpected event that severely interrupts one's sense of a continuity of being.

True Self: Inherited potential that exists only in experiencing. The true self is able to experience life and feels real.

Village of Living Objects: People and things that will foster the elaboration of the child's creative strivings and provide the right conditions to evolve his idiom.

Index

Note: In page references, f indicates figures and t indicates tables.

Author Bio

Margaret Fetting, PhD, attended Rosemont College and received her baccalaureate degree from George Washington University and her master's and doctorate from the University of Pennsylvania. Her doctoral dissertation was on an application of dialectical theory, family systems theory, and social systems theory to the interorganizational conflict in a child advocacy system. Fetting has been teaching about substance dependence and abuse in southern California for 22 years. She has been primarily affiliated with the School of Social Work at the University of Southern California. She has also taught in the Sociology Department at USC, the University of California Los Angeles, Antioch University in Los Angeles and Santa Barbara, and California State University at Channel Islands and San Marcos.

In addition, Fetting has created and designed hundreds of workshops on substance dependence and abuse throughout the state of California. She has taught these courses for licensing boards, hospitals, social service organizations, school districts, and continuing education sponsors. In 2002, she was hired by Mike Garrett, the former USC athletic director, to work with the 18 men's and women's athletic teams in the area of substance dependence and abuse.

Fetting has been in clinical private practice for over 20 years. She specializes in the treatment of addiction for individuals, couples, and families. She is affiliated with Clearview Treatment Programs, a nationally respected and multileveled treatment facility in southern California.

Fetting currently writes on addiction as well as on the application of psychoanalytic thinking to contemporary culture. She is interested in writing a book on the lives of women who decide not to have children.